Linux Recipes for Oracle DBAs

Darl Kuhn, Charles Kim, Bernard Lopuz

⟨IOUG⟩
Independent oracle users group

Apress®

Linux Recipes for Oracle DBAs

Copyright © 2009 by Darl Kuhn, Charles Kim, Bernard Lopuz

ISBN-13 (pbk): 978-1-4302-1575-2

ISBN-13 (electronic): 978-1-4302-1576-9

Printed and bound in the United States of America 9 8 7 6 5 4 3 2 1

Trademarked names may appear in this book. Rather than use a trademark symbol with every occurrence of a trademarked name, we use the names only in an editorial fashion and to the benefit of the trademark owner, with no intention of infringement of the trademark.

Lead Editor: Jonathan Gennick
Technical Reviewers: Bernard Lopuz, Charles Kim
Editorial Board: Clay Andres, Steve Anglin, Mark Beckner, Ewan Buckingham, Tony Campbell,
    Gary Cornell, Jonathan Gennick, Michelle Lowman, Matthew Moodie, Jeffrey Pepper, Frank Pohlmann,
    Ben Renow-Clarke, Dominic Shakeshaft, Matt Wade, Tom Welsh
Project Manager: Kylie Johnston
Copy Editor: Kim Wimpsett
Associate Production Director: Kari Brooks-Copony
Production Editor: Elizabeth Berry
Compositor: Susan Glinert Stevens
Proofreader: Nancy Sixsmith
Indexer: Carol Burbo
Artist: April Milne
Cover Designer: Kurt Krames
Manufacturing Director: Tom Debolski

Distributed to the book trade worldwide by Springer-Verlag New York, Inc., 233 Spring Street, 6th Floor, New York, NY 10013. Phone 1-800-SPRINGER, fax 201-348-4505, e-mail orders-ny@springer-sbm.com, or visit http://www.springeronline.com.

For information on translations, please contact Apress directly at 2855 Telegraph Avenue, Suite 600, Berkeley, CA 94705. Phone 510-549-5930, fax 510-549-5939, e-mail info@apress.com, or visit http://www.apress.com.

Apress and friends of ED books may be purchased in bulk for academic, corporate, or promotional use. eBook versions and licenses are also available for most titles. For more information, reference our Special Bulk Sales–eBook Licensing web page at http://www.apress.com/info/bulksales.

The source code for this book is available to readers at http://www.apress.com.

To Heidi, Brandi, and Lisa, who put up with the long hours. Also to Paul and Deni, for teaching me the value of hard work.
—Darl Kuhn

I dedicate this book to my precious wife, Melissa, and our three boys, Isaiah, Jeremiah, and Noah, for their support during the project and sacrifice of precious family time. Thank you for your unceasing prayers and encouragement.
—Charles Kim

To my wife, Leizle, and daughters, Juliet and Carol.
—Bernard Lopuz

independent oracle users group

About IOUG Press

IOUG Press is a joint effort by the **Independent Oracle Users Group (the IOUG)** and **Apress** to deliver some of the highest-quality content possible on Oracle Database and related topics. The IOUG is the world's leading, independent organization for professional users of Oracle products. Apress is a leading, independent technical publisher known for developing high-quality, no-fluff content for serious technology professionals. The IOUG and Apress have joined forces in IOUG Press to provide the best content and publishing opportunities to working professionals who use Oracle products.

Our shared goals include:

- Developing content with excellence
- Helping working professionals to succeed
- Providing authoring and reviewing opportunities
- Networking and raising the profiles of authors and readers

To learn more about Apress, visit our website at **www.apress.com**. Follow the link for IOUG Press to see the great content that is now available on a wide range of topics that matter to those in Oracle's technology sphere.

Visit **www.ioug.org** to learn more about the Independent Oracle Users Group and its mission. Consider joining if you haven't already. Review the many benefits at www.ioug.org/join. Become a member. Get involved with peers. Boost your career.

www.ioug.org/join

Apress®

Contents at a Glance

Contents

▌CHAPTER 6   Archiving and Compressing Files 127

■CHAPTER 7   Shell Scripting 147

■CHAPTER 8   Analyzing Server Performance 183

About the Authors

DARL KUHN is currently a DBA with Sun Microsystems. He has coauthored two other books: *RMAN Recipes for Oracle Database 11g: A Problem-Solution Approach (Apress, 2007)* and *Oracle RMAN Pocket Reference (O'Reilly, 2001)*. He also teaches advanced database courses at Regis University and performs volunteer database administration work for the Rocky Mountain Oracle Users Group. He has a graduate degree from Colorado State University and currently lives near Spanish Peaks, Colorado, with his wife, Heidi, and daughters, Brandi and Lisa.

CHARLES KIM serves as the practice manager of database technologies at Novara Solutions. He has more than 18 years of IT experience and has worked with Oracle since 1991. Charles is an Oracle ACE, coauthor of *Oracle Database 11g New Features for DBAs and Developers* (Apress, 2007), and author of the "Maximum Availability Architecture" case study at Oracle's web site (http://www.oracle.com/technology/deploy/availability/htdocs/FNF_CaseStudy.html); he has certifications in Oracle, Red Hat Linux, and Microsoft. Prior to Novara Solutions, Charles functioned as the chief Oracle database engineering counsel for Fidelity National Information Services and worked at companies such as GMAC Mortgage, Oracle Corporation, and i2 Technologies.

Charles has presented advanced topics for IOUG and Oracle OpenWorld on such topics as RAC/ASM and 24/7 high availability considerations. Charles also blogs regularly at http://blog.dbaexpert.com and provides technical solutions to Oracle DBAs and developers.

BERNARD LOPUZ is currently a senior technical support analyst at Oracle Corporation. In the early years of his IT career before he became an Oracle database administrator, he was a programmer developing Unisys Linc and Oracle applications, as well as interactive voice response (IVR) applications such as telephone banking voice-processing applications. He has wide experience using Red Hat AS and Oracle Enterprise Linux (OEL). Bernard was the technical reviewer of *RMAN Recipes for Oracle Database 11g: A Problem-Solution Approach* (Apress, 2007) and is an Oracle Certified Professional (OCP). He is pursuing a master's degree in computer information technology at Regis University in Denver, Colorado, and has a bachelor's degree in computer engineering from the Mapúa Institute of Technology in Manila, Philippines. Bernard lives in Ottawa, Canada, with his wife, Leizle, and daughters, Juliet and Carol.

Acknowledgments

Special thanks go to Jonathan Gennick. He skillfully guided and directed every aspect of this book, from its inception to print. This book would not have been possible without him.

We're thankful to Kylie Johnston for being an effective and enthusiastic project manager. We also want to acknowledge the contributions of production editor Elizabeth Berry, the meticulous work of our copy editor Kim Wimpsett, and the entire production and marketing team at Apress for all the effort they put into producing the final book.

Darl Kuhn, Charles Kim, and Bernard Lopuz

A huge thanks goes to Heidi Kuhn who taught me that the short hills build overconfidence; it's the long uphill rides that give character to your lungs, and with effort, today's long hills become tomorrow's short ones. Also, it has been a special pleasure to work with my two coauthors, Charles Kim and Bernard Lopuz, who are both excellent Oracle DBAs and Linux experts.

Thanks to the system administrators who answer my "dumb DBA" questions: Mike Tanaka, Will Thornburg, Khanh Truong, Dona Smith, and Mike O'Neill.

Thanks to John "Chief" Lilly and Dave Wood for providing a challenging work environment. Thanks also to the talented "A" team: Todd Wichers, Joey Canlas, Jeff Shoup, Steve Buckmelter, Casey Costley, John Goggin, Randy Carver, Pascal Ledru, Kevin O'Grady, Peter Schow, Brett Guy, Eric Wendelin, Zack Tillotson, and Jessa Rothenberg. Thanks also to the operations team Kier Gombart, Laurie Bourgeois, Scott Elvington, Jen Simsick, Jeff Markland, Simon Ip, and Joe Foote.

Thanks to Dave Jennings and Kevin Quinlivan for my first DBA job. A huge thanks to Barbara Lewis for having me on her IT team. Also thanks to the numerous DBAs who I've learned from: Sujit Pattanaik, Doug Davis (and his scripts), Shawn Heisdorffer, Janet Bacon, Kevin Bayer, Sam Falkner, Mehran Sowdaey, Gaurav Mehta, Inder Ganesan, Sue Wagner, Ken Roberts, Tim Gorman, Pete Mullineaux, Abid Malik, Margaret Carson, Roger Murphy, Dan Fink, Roy Backstrom, Guido Handley, Tim Colbert, Nehru Kaja, Jon Nordby, John Liu, Lou Ferrante, Bill Padfield, Glenn Balanoff, Brad Blake, Mike Nims, Mark James, Sam Conn, Dan Likarish, Ravi Narayanaswamy, Dave Hathway, Kevin Hoyt, Abdul Ebadi, Trent Sherman, Sandra Montijo, Jim Secor, Sean Best, Krish Hariharan, Theresa Haisley, Stephan Haisley, Patrick Gates, Geoff Strebel, Chris Blais, Sherry Glass, Sloan Stricker, Jan Toom, Frank Bommarito, Maureen Frazzini, Ken Toney, Bob Suehrstedt, Tom Wheltle, Debbie Earman, Greg Roberts, Gabor Gyurovszky, Gary Smith, Michael Del Toro, Mark Lutze, Mark Blair, Dave Bourque, Kevin Powers, James Jackson, Greg Oehmen, and Kathi Gregarek and the CCI team.

Thanks also to supportive colleagues: Tae Kim, Steve Roughton, Ambereen Pasha, Thom Chumley, Jeff Sherard, Lori Isom, Kristi Jackson, Karolyn Vowles, Brad Vowles, Arvin Kuhn, Mohan Koneru, Liz Brill O'Neill, Darcy O'Connor, Kye Bae, Dinesh Neelay, Philippe Nave, Peggy King, John King, and Jim Stark.

Also thanks to previous coauthors who have added encouragement and sage advice: Sam Alapati, Arup Nanda, and Scott Schulze.

Darl Kuhn

I would like to extend my appreciation to Nitin Vengurlekar, a RAC Pack engineer at Oracle Corporation and a member of the technical staff. Nitin is the coauthor of the best-selling *Oracle Automatic Storage Management* book. Nitin's review of the ASM chapter proved invaluable, provided great insight, and enhanced the overall quality of the chapter.

I would also like to thank a colleague and fellow respected RAC database administrator in the Oracle community, Tom Roach, for reviewing the RAC chapter. Thank you for the valuable time and recommendations.

Charles Kim

Any time I accomplish something, I am always reminded of the words of Dr. José P. Rizal, Philippine national hero: "He who does not know how to look back at where he came from will never get to his destination." I feel it is appropriate that I acknowledge the people who have shared a wonderful 40 years with me and one way or another have greatly influenced who I am today.

First and foremost, I am deeply grateful to our God the Almighty for a beautiful life; for a lovely and faithful wife, Leizle; and for blessing us with two daughters, Juliet and Carol, who are the source of my inspiration. Also, a million thanks to my parents, Jeremias and Salud Lopuz, and Leizle's parents, Virgilio and Felisa Alinas, for their unconditional love and understanding. Without them, my wife and I would never have been in this world. Many thanks also to the enormous support and encouragement of my immediate families, namely, Willy and Flor, Hermie and Raquel, Jay, and Joey, as well as my sister-in-law, Liviliza, and her husband, Frank. Even though they are miles away, they remain always close to my heart.

I would like to thank my (past and present) managers at Oracle Corporation, namely, Mike Craig, Brent Chin, Sue Alsbury, Sharon Yourth, Martin Ingram, Maggie Wells, Sam Riley, Khaled Kassis, Chris Warticki, Katherine Mason, Ana Cristina Nickolayeva, Cathy Scully, John Donlin, Amin Abbas, and Christine Mok. I am also indebted to my mentors at Oracle Support, namely, Matt Arrocha, Matt Hart, Demetre Vlachos, Rodica Mihaila, Bill Loi, and Wes Root, as well as the following (past and present) Oracle engineers/analysts, namely, Fred Wong, Michael Chang, Jason Hsu, Chris Bryczkowski, Sylvia Gaw, Sabrina Hutchison, Sebastian Zinkiewicz, Sam Perciasepe, Harry Joseph, Marc Savereux, Andrew Duffus, Christina Lee-Yow, Marianne de Melo, Julie Dagostino, Anwar Naim, Cindy Johnson, Andrew Soutar, Renu Tikku, Gord Leach, Andy Socha, Yoly Young, Cliff Sowa, Daniel Mateos, Linda Boldt, Michelle Harris, Reem Munakash, Samer Salem, Anca Stevens, Ray Ming, Alysa Leeve, Peter Trent, Patti Trainor, Mark Batchelder, Luz Rodriguez, My-Le Rutledge, Joe Krismer, Frank Sanchez, Robert Kohon, Brian Judd, Susan Wagner, Jose Perez, Kevin Cook, Ken Janiec, Vinson Nichols, Scott Jesse, Derek Callaghan, David Vespa, and Sharmila Kamath. You guys are one of the reasons why Oracle rocks!

For my first job in Canada, I am immensely indebted to Nortak Software under the tutelage of Norio Takemura, Mike Oneil, Gus Rodriguez, and Michael Davidson. Also, I owe a lot to Fred Gallagher, president of TKM Communications, for the opportunity to sharpen my Oracle DBA skills. At TKM, I miss the company of Francois, Rodger Archer, Steve Henderson, Saywack, and Alan Ip.

I also would like to acknowledge my former co-workers at National Steel Corporation, namely, Antonio Besas, Richard Aranas, Robert Ham, Audie Battad, Malou Esmores, Gerry Cruzabra, Jenny Lacar, Rey Orbe, Elmer Gopo, Laureano Pabello, Casilda Sabolboro, Cesar Mozar, Dr. William Torres, Cesar Canlas, Donna Lim, Brenda Gallegos, Robert Caballes, Faith Longakit, Leah Zerna, Eva and Nereus Babiera, Joselito Asibal, Roy Jakosalem, Susan Fortinez, Raul Mercado, Norman Tito Lluisma, Rey Bautista, Joselito Angeles, Abraham Torcende, Alan Lagua, Rex Michael and Mary Leah Hisona, Rey Dalagan, Edgar Moso, Ellen Membreve, Baby Dy, and Daisy Bama. Our learning experience employing Unisys and Oracle technologies has certainly put many of us in different corners of the globe.

My escapades during high school are still fresh in my mind even though I am about to celebrate my silver jubilee next year. For the memorable years I spent at La Salle Academy, I am thankful to my teachers and schoolmates, namely, Mif Obach, Bro. Andrew Jacobson, Martha Giltendez, Mila Manatad, Atty. Rolly Marapao, Johnny Fetalvero, Ricky Jaro, Nico Nabua, Genevieve Cabildo, Lee Quijano, Clifford Tamula, Bong Saroca, Kim Obach-Monterroyo, Ralph Obach, Orwell Obach, Leila Simbajon, Dr. Tonton Eltanal-Pascual, Angeli Echiverri, Mariter Alejo, Mark Siangco, Gina May Adeva, Eric Regala, Eric Capitan, Eric Siao, Eric Sobremisana, Manny Cabili, Bernard Pacaa, Vinci Casas, and Dr. Celina Torres. Likewise, I love to reminisce about my five years at Mapúa Institute of Technology and my college buddies, namely, Medel Macatula, Arnol Magtibay, and Tyrone Florendo.

To my classmates, the staff, and the professors at Regis University, led by my advisor, Daniel Likarish; professors Sam Conn and Donald Archer; and practicum leader, Rossie Trujillo—thank you for your support while I aspire to complete my master's degree in computer information technology.

I am proud to mention the football fanatics in Iligan, led by our football guru Consor Manreza, as well as my teammates, namely, Carlos Buenavista, Jr., Rolly dela Cruz, Monico dela Cruz, Jr., Mateo Oliveros, Nene Arat, and Gifford Balucan. I hope someday we can play football together again.

By the time you read this book, my family and I will have already moved to Canada's capital city. I am delighted to return to Ottawa and see my friends, including Jun and Flor Barbon, Askhan and Desiree Zandi, Mark and Ethel Bergado, Rohnny and Wilma Bayona, Manfred and Jane Cantal, Cesar and Malou Ong, Raffy and Maribel Caday, Al and Lucille Sasedor, Gerry and Myrna Panes, Celso and Vicky Salvatierra, Rey and Edna Noynay, Mac and Ivy Manning, Oni Alday, Alex and Bambeth Fortinez, Melvin and Lolit Milan, Rene and Marilyn Flores, Joey and Joyce Bunagan, and Manny and Jenny Villanueva. Thanks for your outpouring of support and for welcoming us back.

After nine years in Toronto, my family and I have mixed emotions as we depart our friends, Leo Arthur and Marivic Padilla, Gerard and Maricon Nisce, Christian and Cristine Manuel, Roy and Marivic Llanes, Tito and Estrelita Bravo, Gil and Carmencita Caluen, Ervin and Emma Aspiras, Josenilo and Aida dela Cruz, Romy and Lina Yuayan, Jun and Alma Casilang, Benjie and Divine Tabucan, Jimmy and Jette Carillo, Juanito Jumao-as, Dinah Lil Alcoseba, Oliver and Dolly Valera, Ruth Garcia, and Fr. Randy Hendriks.

I also would like to express my profound thanks for the support and prayers of my extended families and friends: Nathan and Araceli Javier, Albert and Honeylet de Pedro, Jojo and Janice Jandayran, Roger and Fina Hidalgo, Tony Obed, Baby Abunda, Ismael Gabriel, Vilma Fortunado, Flor and Lydia Bajo, Deborah Steele, and Dino Awil. I am also grateful for the generosity of the Espenido family, namely, Tiburcio, Visitacion, Merck, Ruperto, Fidel, Flora,

Lilia and Aurie; I would never forget the summer vacations at their Quezon City residence. I also appreciate the care provided by Dr. Gary Mok, who makes sure I am alive and kicking.

I am fortunate to have worked with an excellent team, particularly Darl Kuhn and Charles Kim; I have the utmost respect and admiration for their broad IT skillsets and and thank them for generously sharing their ideas. Special thank you to Darl for inviting and trusting me as technical reviewer and coauthor of this book. I also salute the amazing people behind this book: the vision and guidance of Jonathan Gennick, the incredible project management of Kylie Johnston, the careful copy editing of Kim Wimpsett, and the impressive production work led by Elizabeth Berry, as well as the rest of the magnificent Apress team. Also, thanks to Sam Alapati for his encouraging words and pushing me to be an author. Last but not the least, my sincerest thanks to you, our dear readers; I hope you enjoy reading this book. ☺

Bernard Lopuz

Introduction

Successful organizations utilize data to gain insights about their operations to make better decisions and discover new growth opportunities. Gathering and storing data and extracting business intelligence are critical for success in today's competitive environment. Server technologies and database software are used in combination to transform information assets into profitable actions.

The databases that house important business data require a stable and effective operating platform. The Linux operating system continues to build momentum as a cost-effective and reliable database server. Year after year, more companies report success stories of migrating from expensive hardware to commodity servers running a flavor of the Linux operating system such as Red Hat, SUSE, or Oracle Enterprise Linux. More and more Fortune 1000 companies are embracing Linux as part of their enterprise solution to address today's dynamic business requirements. Linux has repeatedly proven itself to be a viable operating system for mission-critical applications and databases.

As a database administrator, it's inevitable that you will shoulder the responsibility of implementing and maintaining corporate databases on Linux boxes. Your job depends on your ability to work seamlessly with the server hosting your databases. The more you understand about the operating system and tools, the better you'll be able to perform. The best DBAs are the ones who know how to use which operating system features in which situations.

This book provides you with task-oriented, ready-made solutions for Oracle DBAs in a Linux environment. We cover Linux topics from the DBA's perspective of utilizing the operating system. You don't have to read the book cover to cover. Rather, each recipe is a how-to guide for a particular problem. This format allows you to focus on a Linux/Oracle topic and its corresponding solution.

Audience

This book is for database administrators who work in Linux/Unix environments. We focus on command-line tools and techniques for working with the operating system from a DBA's viewpoint. If you're a DBA who wants to operate expertly with Linux technology, then this book is for you. Whether you are new or experienced, you'll find solutions for the gamut of tasks that DBAs perform on Linux servers.

Book Structure

Each recipe title acts as pointer to the *problem* at hand. Each recipe contains a to-the-point *solution* and a detailed explanation of *how it works*. The first few chapters are introductory topics for database administrators working in Linux/Unix environments. These first chapters provide the foundation for the more complex topics covered later in the book. Subsequent chapters cover advanced technical topics. These chapters build on the foundation material and allow you to expertly leverage the Linux operating system.

Conventions

The following typographical conventions are used in this book:

- $ is used to denote Linux commands that can be run by the owner of the Oracle binaries (usually named oracle).

- # is used to denote Linux commands that should be run as the root user.

- *Italic* is used to highlight a new concept or word.

- Monospaced font is used for code examples, utility names, file names, and directory paths.

- UPPERCASE indicates view names, column names, and column values.

- **Constant width bold** is used to highlight the statements being discussed.

Downloading Linux and Oracle

Whether you have a powerful Linux server or an old Pentium III box, you can use the following web sites to download the Oracle Enterprise Linux (OEL) operating system and Oracle relational database management system (RDBMS) software:

- Download OEL from the E-Delivery web site: http://edelivery.oracle.com/linux. This web site has instructions on how to download and install Oracle Enterprise Linux and Oracle VM products.

- Obtain the RDBMS and documentation at Oracle Technology Network: http://otn.oracle.com. From this web site, you can obtain the latest versions of Oracle for the various supported operating systems and hardware platforms.

Comments

We value your input. We'd like to know what you like about the book and what you don't like about it. You can send us comments via email to feedback@apress.com. When providing feedback, please make sure you include the title of the book in your note to us.

We've tried to make this book as error free as possible. However, mistakes happen. If you find any type of an error in this book, whether it be a typo or an erroneous command, please let us know about it. Please e-mail the problem to support@apress.com. Your information will be validated and posted on the errata page to be used in subsequent editions of the book. The corrigendum can be viewed on the book's web page at http://www.apress.com.

Contacting Us

You can contact us directly at the following e-mail addresses:

Darl Kuhn: darl.kuhn@gmail.com

Charles Kim: charles@dbaexpert.com

Bernard Lopuz: bernard.lopuz@hotmail.com

In addition, Charles Kim maintains a web site and a blog at http://www.dbaexpert.com and http://blog.dbaexpert.com, respectively. Bernard's web site is at http://www.geocities.com/bslopuz/.

CHAPTER 1

■ ■ ■

Getting Started

Linux continues to gain market share as a reliable 24/7 mission-critical enterprise server platform. A rapidly increasing number of employers are specifically seeking database administrators (DBAs) with Linux expertise. In fact, as a database administrator, it's inevitable that you'll someday find yourself using Linux servers to store your data. You will be responsible for ensuring that your database is working symbiotically with the underlying Linux operating system. Managers will look to you to guarantee that corporate databases are competently implemented and maintained.

DBAs are crucial members of every information technology team (well, that's our unabashed and biased opinion). Database administrators are responsible for mission-critical tasks such as the following:

- Installing software and creating databases

- Providing a highly scalable and well-behaving database environment

- Monitoring and maintaining company databases

- Ensuring that your corporate data is backed up, secured, and protected

- Troubleshooting system performance and availability issues

- Being the holistic source of database engineering information

DBAs must possess a combination of database and operating system (OS) expertise. It's a fact that you (the DBA) cannot architect, implement, and maintain a large, high-transaction database environment without being intimately familiar with the underlying operating system. In many situations, the OS is your only conduit to the database. Therefore, it's imperative that you *must* be particularly knowledgeable of the operating system to competently perform your database administration duties.

When first building a database, DBAs have to be able to specify solid, reliable, and scalable system configurations. Furthermore, DBAs often find themselves as the cog between system administrators, (damn) users, network administrators, managers, and corporate executives. If you're working (after the fact) on a poorly designed system, you have to possess the tools to diagnose and resolve bottlenecks in the entire stack of technology. Regardless of the source of the <fill in the blank> issues, team members often look to the seasoned database administrator to resolve systemic performance and availability concerns. We know this to be true because we live it every day (including nights and weekends).

The information in this book will enable you to function as an expert DBA in performing key responsibilities. We provide direct answers to specific problems regarding Oracle database technology and the Linux operating system. The recipes in this first chapter assume you know nothing about Linux and cover situations that you'll be presented with when first connecting to a server and using operating system commands. If you are already fairly experienced with the Linux operating system, then you may want to skip this chapter.

In this chapter, we start by walking you through some of the most common methods for logging on to a Linux server. We then cover the basics of running Linux commands and detail how to use the built-in help and online documentation. We finish the chapter by showing techniques for correcting command-line mistakes and resetting your terminal screen.

■**Note** You might be wondering, what is the difference between Linux and Unix? On the surface, Linux and Unix are mostly (83.1 percent) identical in commands and syntax. However, as a DBA, you must understand the nuances of the Linux kernel and how it impacts the database. These important concepts are explained in later chapters in this book.

1-1. Connecting Securely to a Remote Server

Problem

You want to securely connect over the network to your remote Linux database server.

Solution

This solution shows how to download and use the PuTTY application to initiate secure remote connections over the network:

1. To get started, first open your favorite Internet search engine, and search for the string *PuTTY download*. You should see information on your screen similar to Figure 1-1.

PuTTY Download Page
So if you want to browse **PuTTY's** revision history, you could **download** that, local Subversion client at it. Click here to **download** the ...
www.chiark.greenend.org.uk/~sgtatham/**putty/download**.html - 18k - Cached - Similar pages - Note this

PuTTY: a free telnet/ssh client
Download PuTTY! Subscribe to the **PuTTY**-announce mailing list to Feedback and bug reporting: contact address and guidelines. ...
www.chiark.greenend.org.uk/~sgtatham/**putty**/ - 4k - Cached - Similar

Figure 1-1. *Internet page with link to PuTTY download*

2. Click the link to the PuTTY download site. In this example, that link is titled "PuTTY Download Page." On the PuTTY download site, you'll find links that will allow you to download the PuTTY application. You can download just the putty.exe file or all utilities available via the putty.zip file.

3. After you have downloaded the desired files, navigate on your personal computer to the directory where you downloaded the PuTTY utility. You should see a screen similar to Figure 1-2. Double-click the PuTTY icon to start the connection utility.

Figure 1-2. *PuTTY application icon*

4. Figure 1-3 shows a partial screen shot of what you are presented with next. From this screen you can enter the hostname or IP address and connection port of the remote server to which you want to connect. Enter the connection details of your Linux database server, and click the Open button to initiate a remote connection. If you are not sure about the connection information, then contact your system administrator for details. `

Figure 1-3. *PuTTY connection details*

5. Once you have connected to your database server, you should see the screen shown in Figure 1-4. Enter your username and password (contact your system administrator if you don't know your username and password). From here you can run Linux shell commands to perform tasks on your database server.

Figure 1-4. *Linux server logon screen*

How It Works

PuTTY is a free open source utility that allows you to create a secure shell (SSH) connection to your remote database server. This utility is popular because it's a free, easy-to-use application that allows you to connect securely over the network to remote Linux database servers. This tool allows you to store your server preferences and connection information, which eliminates the need to retype lengthy hostnames or IP addresses.

Note Other utilities also allow you to initiate remote connections via a secure shell. For example, the Cygwin/X application is a popular Windows-based implementation of the X Window System. This Cygwin/X utility allows you to run X applications on your Windows desktop and start remote secure shell connections to your database server.

You can also use PuTTY to connect via proxy servers and SSH tunneling. Examples of doing this are explained briefly in the next sections.

Connecting via a Proxy Server

Many companies require all their Internet connections to pass through a proxy server for security and performance reasons. To use PuTTY to connect via a proxy server, open the PuTTY Configuration dialog box, and click the Proxy node under the Connection category, as shown in Figure 1-5.

Select HTTP for the proxy type, and provide the hostname or IP address of the proxy server, as well as the corresponding port number. Save the changes of your PuTTY configuration for future use.

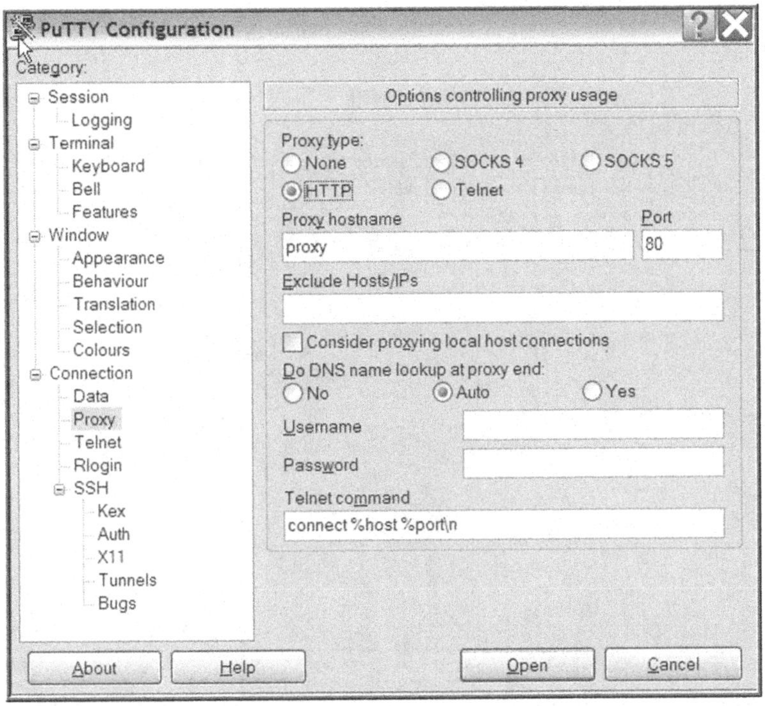

Figure 1-5. *PuTTY—proxy server configuration*

Connecting via SSH Tunneling

You can also use PuTTY to tunnel (also called *port forwarding*) to a remote server. To use tunneling, open the PuTTY Configuration dialog box, as shown in previously in Figure 1-3, and then choose the SSH as the connection type. Next, provide the hostname or IP address of the designated SSH server, as well as the SSH port number (the default is 22). Afterward, click the Connection node, then the SSH node, and finally the Tunnels node, as shown in Figure 1-6.

In the "Source port" field under the "Add new forwarded port" section, provide the port number you will connect to at your Windows client. In the Destination field, provide the hostname or IP address of the Linux database server, as well as the port number. Save the changes of your PuTTY configuration for future use.

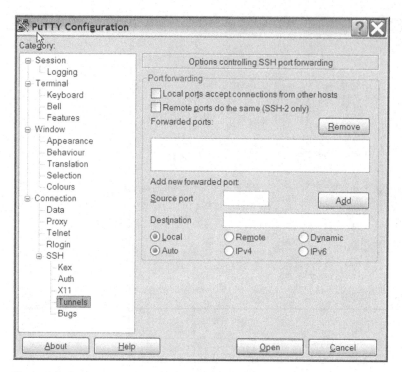

Figure 1-6. *PuTTY—SSH tunneling configuration*

1-2. Logging On Remotely via the Command Line

Problem

Your system administrator has just provided you with a username and password to your database server. You now want to log on to a Linux server via a command-line utility such as telnet or ssh.

Solution

This example assumes you can access a terminal from which you can initiate an ssh command. Depending on your environment, your "terminal" could be a PuTTY session (see recipe 1-1) on your home PC or workstation. Ask your system administrator for help if you're not sure how to start a terminal session (this can vary quite a bit depending on your working environment).

In this next line of code, the username is oracle, and the hostname is rmoug1:

```
$ ssh -l oracle rmoug1
```

If ssh successfully locates the database server, you should be prompted for a password (the prompt may vary depending on the version of the operating system):

```
oracle@rmoug1's password:
```

For security purposes, your password will not be displayed as you type it. After typing your password, hit the Enter or Return key to complete the logon process.

Tip If you think you have made a mistake while entering your password, press Ctrl+U to erase all invisible text from the password line. This technique will save you time and prevent many accidental failed logins. Alternatively, you can try to use the Backspace key or the Delete key to erase any text you've entered.

How It Works

By default, most SSH servers listen on the TCP port 22. If your system administrator has set up the server to listen on a different port, then you will have to explicitly specify it with the -p (port) option. This example connects as the oracle user to the rmoug1 server on port 71:

```
$ ssh -p 71 -l oracle rmoug1
```

After entering a valid username and password, your system may display information such as the last time you logged on, from what machine you initiated the connection, whether your account has unread mail, and so on. Additionally, if your system administrator has entered any text within the /etc/motd file (message of the day), then that information will also be displayed. The following text is a typical login message:

```
Last login: Tue Dec 25 15:31:31 2007 from 63-227-41-191.hlrn.qwest.net
```

After your username and password have been successfully authenticated by the Linux server, you should see a $ (dollar sign) prompt:

```
$
```

The $ character signifies you are at the shell command-line prompt. The $ character is the default command-line prompt for most Linux/Unix systems. All command-line examples in this book will show the $ prompt. You don't have to type the $ prompt as part of any of the example commands in this book.

Your system administrator may have configured your account to display a different prompt (other than the $ character). See recipe 2-6 for changing your command-line prompt from something other than the default.

Note If you are logged as the root (sometimes called superuser) account, the default command-line prompt is the # character.

Some servers accept remote connections from telnet clients. For security reasons, we recommend you do not use telnet to initiate a logon to a server over the network. The telnet utility does not use encryption and is vulnerable to hackers snooping on the network. Whenever possible, you should use the secure ssh tool for remote connections. However, you may occasionally have to use telnet because ssh isn't available. The following example uses telnet to log on to a remote server over the network:

```
$ telnet -l oracle dbsrver
```

1-3. Logging Off the Server

Problem

You want to log off the server.

Solution

Three methods for logging out of the database server are covered in this solution:

- Pressing Ctrl+D
- Typing exit
- Typing logout

The quickest way to log off is to press Ctrl+D. This will immediately log you off your server. In this next example, the keys Ctrl and D are pressed at the same time:

```
$ Ctrl+D
```

You should now see a message like this:

```
Connection to <your server> closed.
```

You can also type the exit command to log off your database server:

```
$ exit
```

You should now see a message like this:

```
Connection to <your server> closed.
```

You can also type the logout command to log off the system:

```
$ logout
```

You should now see a message like this:

```
Connection to <your server> closed.
```

How It Works

If you have started a subshell within an existing shell session, then the logout techniques described in the "Solution" section will exit you from only the innermost shell. For example, say you have logged on to your Linux server and then issued the following command:

```
$ bash
```

You now have started a subshell. If you want to exit the subshell, use one of the techniques described in the "Solution" section:

```
$ exit
```

Similarly, if you have issued an su command to switch to another user, then when exiting from that session, you will be returned to the shell from which you initiated the su command.

It's a good security practice to log out of your operating system session if you plan on being away from your terminal. As a DBA, you'll typically find yourself logged on to the server as the user who owns the database binaries (usually the oracle operating system account). The oracle account is like a database superuser account.

The database operating system account can do potentially damaging operations like drop databases, remove database files, and so on. Logging out ensures that your database operating system account isn't compromised.

■**Tip** Set the TMOUT variable to limit the amount of idle time a session can have before it is automatically logged off. This parameter can be set globally in the /etc/bashrc file. See recipe 2-5 for automatically setting variables when logging on to a server.

1-4. Running a Command

Problem

You're new to Linux, and you want to run a shell command from the operating system prompt.

Solution

Linux commands are run from the command line by typing them and pressing the Enter or Return key. This example uses the df (disk-free) command to display the amount of unused disk space on the database server:

```
$ df
```

By default, the output of the commands is displayed on your screen (standard output). After running the df command, you should see some output similar to this:

```
Filesystem          1K-blocks     Used Available Use% Mounted on
/dev/sda2          236141180   7026468 217119380   4% /
/dev/sda1             101086      9448     86419  10% /boot
none                 1037452         0   1037452   0% /dev/shm
```

How It Works

When you log on to a Linux or Unix box, you are by default placed at the command line. The command line is where you type shell commands to accomplish a given DBA task. The default command-line prompt for most systems is the $ character.

You can modify the default behavior of a command by running it with one or more *options* (sometimes called *flags* or *switches*). This next example shows using the ls (list) command with the -a option to display all files:

```
$ ls -a
```

Commands may also take *arguments*. Arguments typically designate a file or text that the command should use. When running a command, arguments are usually placed after the options. This next example uses the df (disk-free) command with the -h (human-readable) option and uses the argument of /dev/sda2 (which is a directory):

```
$ df -f /dev/sda2
```

This book does not detail the use of various graphical user interfaces (GUIs) or browser user interfaces (BUIs). These tools are great for situations when you don't know the actual command. As useful as these graphical tools are, we strongly recommend you explore using Linux commands from the command-line prompt. As a DBA, you will encounter situations where the GUI/BUI tool doesn't do everything you need in order to accomplish a task. For some problems, you will need access to the command line to debug and troubleshoot issues. Many complicated or custom DBA tasks require that you be proficient with command-line programming techniques (see Chapter 7 for more information on shell scripting).

If you don't know the appropriate shell commands and their features, then you'll potentially waste a lot of time trying to solve a problem when it could have easily been resolved had you known which tools and options were available.

GOLDEN HAMMER RULE

The Golden Hammer Rule can be stated as "When the only tool you have is a hammer, everything looks like a nail." What does that mean? When people find a tool that solves a problem, they have a natural tendency to use that tool again and again to solve other problems. This might be because once you're familiar with a given tool or technique, you'll continue to use it because it's available, you've had training with the tool, and you've developed a skill set.

Nothing is wrong with that approach per se. However, if you want to be a more marketable DBA, then you should expand your horizons from time to time by learning new skills and investigating up-to-date methods for solving problems. In today's ever-changing technology environment, the DBA with the most current skills is often the one who survives the longest.

It's getting harder and harder to find database environments that don't use Linux. As a DBA, you should take the initiative to learn about Linux and how this technology is used by companies around the world to provide cost-effective information technology solutions. In today's world, Linux is an operating system that every DBA needs to be familiar with.

1-5. Getting Help

Problem

You want to find more information about how to use a shell command.

Solution

One extremely nice feature of Linux is that there are several options for quickly obtaining more information regarding shell commands. Listed next are command-line help features that are readily available on most Linux systems:

man: Read the online manual for a command.

whatis: View a brief description of a command.

which or whereis: Find a tool.

--version: Display the version.

--help: Show help.

apropos: Display manual page documentation.

info: List extensive documentation.

Tab key: Show available commands.

Each of the help methods in the previous list will be described in the following subsections.

Reading Manual Pages

The man (manual) page for a command displays online documentation for almost every shell command. The following command displays information about man:

```
$ man man
```

Here's a partial listing of the output:

```
NAME       man - format and display the on-line manual pages
SYNOPSIS   man [-acdfFhkKtwW] [--path] [-m system] [-p string] [-C config_file]
     [-M pathlist] [-P pager] [-S section_list] [section] name ...
```

The man command uses a screen pager—usually the less command—to display the help page. The less utility will display a : (colon) prompt at the bottom-left corner of the screen. You can use the spacebar to go to the next page and the up and down arrows to scroll through the documentation line by line. Table 1-1 lists the less command options available to you while viewing man pages. Press the Q key to exit the man utility.

Table 1-1. *The less Command Options Available While Viewing man Pages*

Keystroke	Action
J, E, or down arrow	Move down one line.
K, Y, or up arrow	Move up one line.
Up arrow	Move up one line.
Down arrow	Move down one line.
/<string>	Search for <string>.
N	Repeat the previous search forward.
Shift+N	Repeat the previous search backward.
H	Display help page.
F, spacebar, or Page Down	Move down one page.
B or Page Up	Move up one page.
Q	Exit man page.

The man pages are usually divided into ten sections. The man command will display the first man page match it finds for a specified command. The following list shows the section number and type of commands documented in each section:

1. User commands

2. System calls

3. Subroutines (library functions)

4. Devices

5. File formats

6. Games

7. Miscellaneous

8. System administration

9. Local

10. New

Sometimes a Linux utility will be documented in more than one man section. To view all man documentation available for a tool, use the -f option (this is equivalent to running the whatis command). This example views all man pages available with the cd command:

```
$ man -f cd
```

From the output, you can see that cd is documented in two different man sections:

```
cd                      (1p)  - change the working directory
cd [builtins]           (1)   - bash built-in commands, see bash(1)
```

Sometimes DBAs are confused when they type man cd and are presented with the Bash shell's built-in documentation. To view the man documentation specific to the cd utility, then specify the 1p page:

```
$ man 1p cd
```

To scroll through all man sections associated with a command, use the -a option. When in this mode, press the Q key to advance to the next man section of information.

CAPTURING MAN PAGES IN A TEXT FILE

Sometimes it's helpful to capture the output of a man command in a file that can be used later to search and scroll through with a text editor. The following command writes the output of the man page for the find command to a file named find.txt:

```
$ man find >find.txt
```

However, if you inspect the output of the find.txt file, you'll notice that it contains unreadable characters that are produced from the man page output. Run the following command to clean up the output of the man page:

```
$ man find | col -b >find.txt
```

The previous command takes the output from the man command and sends it to the col -b (postprocessing filter) command. This filtering command will remove the unreadable backspace characters from the man page output and make it human-readable.

Viewing a Brief Description of a Command

If you're new to Linux (or if you're old to Linux and have forgotten the material), use the aptly named whatis command to answer the question, "what is" a command's basic information? The whatis command lists the first line of text from the man (manual) page. This next example shows how to use the whatis command to find more information about the pwd command:

```
$ whatis pwd
pwd                     (1)  - print name of current/working directory
pwd [builtins]          (1)  - bash built-in commands, see bash(1)
```

The number (enclosed by parentheses) specifies the section of the man page where you can find the command. When you see multiple lines listed by whatis, this indicates the command is documented in more than one location in the man pages. The output also indicates there is a built-in Bash version of the command (see recipe 2-15 for more details about built-in commands).

Another interesting use of the whatis command is to view a one-line description of commands in the /bin directory. This example uses whatis with ls, xargs, and less to view, one page at a time, the descriptions of all commands in the /bin directory:

```
$ cd /bin
$ ls | xargs whatis | less
```

The previous line of code will first list the files in the /bin directory; then, the output of that is piped to the xargs command. The xargs command will take the output of ls and send it to the whatis utility. The less command will display the output one page at a time. To exit from the documentation (displayed by less), press the Q key (to quit).

Note The whatis command is identical to the man -f command.

Locating a Command

Use which or whereis to locate the executable binary file of a command. This next line of code locates the binary man executable file:

```
$ which man
/usr/bin/man
```

The output indicates that man is located in the /usr/bin directory. The whereis command locates the binary file, source, and manuals for a particular utility. The following example displays the location of the echo command and its corresponding man documentation files:

```
$ whereis echo
echo: /bin/echo /usr/share/man/man1/echo.1.gz /usr/share/man/man1p/echo.1p.gz
```

Getting the Version

Sometimes it's useful to see the version of a command. This next example uses the --version option to display the version of the who command:

```
$ who --version
who (coreutils) 5.2.1
```

Showing Help

Use the --help option to quickly display basic information about a tool's usage and its syntax. This next example demonstrates how to get help for the df command:

```
$ df --help
```

Here's a partial listing of the output:

```
Usage: df [OPTION]... [FILE]...
Show information about the filesystem on which each FILE resides,
or all filesystems by default. Mandatory arguments to long options are mandatory
for short options too.
  -a, --all              include filesystems having 0 blocks
  -B, --block-size=SIZE use SIZE-byte blocks
  -h, --human-readable  print sizes in human readable format (e.g., 1K 234M 2G)
```

Depending on the version of the operating system, all Linux operating system commands may not have a --help option. If this is the case, you'll have to use one of the other documentation sources listed in this recipe.

Finding Manual Page Documentation

If you can remember only partially the name of the utility you seek, then use the apropos command to find more documentation. The apropos command is similar to whatis except that it searches for any string that matches your input. For example, the following example searches the whatis database for the string find:

```
$ apropos find
```

Here's a partial snippet of the output:

```
find                (1)  - search for files in a directory hierarchy
find                (1p) - find files
find2perl           (1)  - translate find command lines to Perl code
findchip            (8)  - checks the FIR chipset
findfs              (8)  - Find a filesystem by label or UUID
```

The previous output shows you that many different types of find commands are available. Use the man command (previously discussed in this recipe) to view more information about a particular find command. The number in the second column (in the parentheses) lists which section of the man page the documentation is contained in.

■**Note** The apropos command is equivalent to man -k.

Listing Extensive Documentation

The info utility often contains extensive documentation on many Linux commands. To view all documents available, type info with no parameters, as shown here:

```
$ info
```

Figure 1-7 shows the info introduction screen.

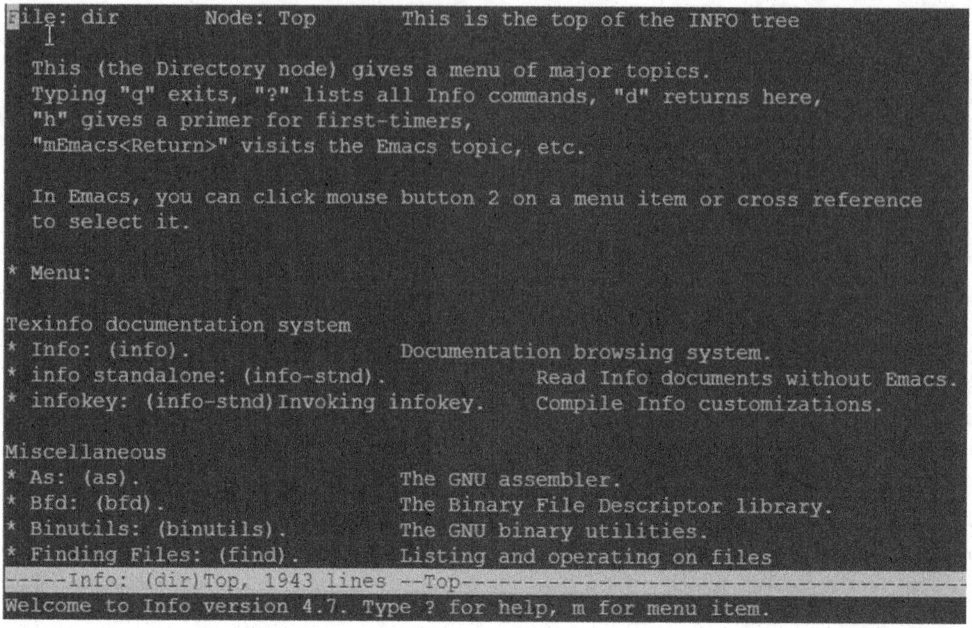

```
File: dir          Node: Top        This is the top of the INFO tree

  This (the Directory node) gives a menu of major topics.
  Typing "q" exits, "?" lists all Info commands, "d" returns here,
  "h" gives a primer for first-timers,
  "mEmacs<Return>" visits the Emacs topic, etc.

  In Emacs, you can click mouse button 2 on a menu item or cross reference
  to select it.


* Menu:

Texinfo documentation system
* Info: (info).                    Documentation browsing system.
* info standalone: (info-stnd).              Read Info documents without Emacs.
* infokey: (info-stnd)Invoking infokey.    Compile Info customizations.

Miscellaneous
* As: (as).                        The GNU assembler.
* Bfd: (bfd).                      The Binary File Descriptor library.
* Binutils: (binutils).            The GNU binary utilities.
* Finding Files: (find).           Listing and operating on files
-----Info: (dir)Top, 1943 lines --Top--------------------------------------
Welcome to Info version 4.7. Type ? for help, m for menu item.
```

Figure 1-7. *The info command introduction screen*

Once within the utility, use the N key to go to the next section. The P key will take you to a previous section. Any line that starts with an asterisk (*) is a link to other sections (nodes) in the document. To go to a linked document, navigate to the line containing the asterisk and press the Enter or Return key. Press the Q key to exit the info page. Table 1-2 lists some of the commonly used navigational info commands.

Table 1-2. *Commonly Used Navigation Keystrokes Within the info Utility*

Keystroke	Action
N	Move to the next section.
P	Move to the previous section.
Return	Move to a linked document.
Q	Exit.
?	List all commands.
D	Return to introduction page.
H	Go to the tutorial.

You can also view information regarding specific commands. This next example starts the info utility to display help for the cpio command:

```
$ info cpio
```

To view a tutorial on info, type the following:

```
$ info info
```

Showing Available Commands

You can use the Tab key to show all executable files that start with a certain string. For example, if you want to view all commands that start with the string ls, then type ls and hit the Tab key twice (with no space between the ls command and pressing the Tab key):

```
$ ls<Tab><Tab>
ls          lsb_release   lsnrctl      lspgpot
lsattr      lshal         lsnrctl0     lss16toppm
```

You should hear a bell sound (sometimes called a *beep*) after you press the first Tab. After pressing the second Tab, the Bash shell will attempt to find all commands that start with ls that are located in any directories contained in the PATH variable.

This feature of automatically looking for files is known as *command completion*. See recipe 2-2 for more details on command completion.

How It Works

The "Solution" section of this recipe contains some of the most useful information you'll need to elevate your Linux skills. You should take some time to familiarize yourself with all the helpful techniques described in this recipe.

You'll find that Linux has extensive utilities for easily viewing command documentation. Using these built-in help features allows you to quickly find basic syntax and usage of a given shell command. We suggest you become particularly familiar with man and info. You'll use these informational tools on a regular basis.

1-6. Correcting Command-Line Mistakes

Problem

You're a typical DBA, and you often mistype things on the command line. You wonder whether there are command-line tools to correct your typing mistakes.

Solution

Press Ctrl+_ at the same time to undo what you just typed at the command line. Notice that you'll have to use the Shift key to get the underscore (_) character. If you type a long command string, then pressing Ctrl+_ will erase everything to the left of the prompt. If you have backspaced over a command, pressing Ctrl+_ will undo what you have backspaced over.

How It Works

Other keystrokes are also available to help you undo what you just typed. For example, you can use Ctrl+T to transpose two characters just to the left of the prompt (ensure there is no space between the command characters and Ctrl+T). This next bit of code will use Ctrl+T to transpose the last two characters of the letters pdw:

```
$ pdw Ctrl+T
```

You should now see the following:

```
$ pwd
```

Table 1-3 summarizes the commands available to you to correct typing mistakes at the command line.

1-7. Clearing the Screen

Table 1-3. *Command-Line Keystrokes to Correct Typing Errors*

Keystroke	Action
Ctrl+_	Undo what was just typed in.
Ctrl+U	Clear out everything to the left of the prompt.
Ctrl+T	Transpose two characters that are immediately to the left of the prompt.
Alt+T	Transpose two words that are to the left of the prompt.

Problem

Your screen has become cluttered with command output. You want to clear the screen of any previously displayed text or command output.

Solution

Either use the clear command or press Ctrl+L to clear your terminal screen. The clear command works in most Linux/Unix shells, and it does what you would expect—it clears the screen. Simply type the command as shown with no options or arguments:

```
$ clear
```

Another method for clearing the screen (on some Linux systems) is to press Ctrl+L:

```
$ Ctrl+L
```

One nice feature about Ctrl+L is that you can enter this command while typing other commands on the command line. Pressing Ctrl+L will clear the screen and retain any current commands you have entered on the command line. For example, say you are in the middle of typing a find command; you can enter Ctrl+L as shown here:

```
$ find . -name *.sql Ctrl+L
```

When you press Ctrl+L, it will clear the screen and place the command you are currently typing at the top of the screen. In this example, the find command appears at the top of the screen:

```
$ find . -name *.sql
```

How It Works

The clear command removes all output visible on your screen. This command retrieves environment information from the terminal database to determine how to clear the screen. To see more information on the terminal database, use the man terminfo command.

The Ctrl+L keystroke works with the Bash shell, and it may work with other shells depending on your version of the operating system. Unlike the clear command, Ctrl+L will retain whatever command you are currently typing and display that at the top of the cleared-out screen.

1-8. Resetting the Screen

Problem

Your screen has become cluttered with strange, unreadable characters. The clear and Ctrl+L commands don't seem to have any effect.

Solution

Try to use the reset command to restore the screen to a sane state:

```
$ reset
```

If the reset command doesn't work, then try the stty sane command:

```
$ stty sane
```

If that doesn't work, try exiting your terminal session and restarting it. That's not the ideal solution, but sometimes that's the only thing that will work.

How It Works

Sometimes your screen can become cluttered with unreadable characters. This might happen if you accidentally use the cat command to display the contents of a binary file. Use either the reset or stty sane command to restore your screen to a normal state.

The reset command is actually a symbolic link (see recipe 5-33 for more details on links) to the tset (terminal initialization) command. View the manual pages for tset for more details on this utility. The reset command is particularly useful for clearing your screen when a program abnormally aborts and leaves the terminal in unusual state.

The stty (set terminal type) command displays or changes terminal characteristics. If you type stty without any options, it will display the settings that are different from those set by issuing the stty sane command

CHAPTER 2

■ ■ ■

Working in the Shell

Every Linux system includes at least one command-line interpreter that enables you to interact with the operating system. This interpreter is known as a *shell*. This is an appropriate moniker because the shell's purpose is to act as a layer that shields you from having to know the internal workings of the operating system. The shell allows you to perform complex tasks using simple commands.

If you're a DBA, you should become familiar with running shell commands from the command line (operating system prompt). Yes, you can perform many DBA tasks through various graphical user interfaces (GUIs) or browser user interfaces (BUIs). However, regardless of the robustness of the GUI or BUI, you will still be required to use the command line to perform tasks that the graphical user interface can't handle. For example, you may find yourself in a stressful database restore and recovery situation in which you have access only to a terminal to run the appropriate commands. In this scenario, your job depends on you being able to work from the command line to diagnose possible media failures and then perform the appropriate database restore and recovery operations.

Many command-line interpreters ship with your Linux server, such as the Bourne Again (Bash) shell, Korn shell, C shell, and so on. The Bash shell is usually the default command-line interpreter on Linux systems. Therefore, the focus of this chapter (and book, for that matter) centers on how to perform DBA tasks using the Bash shell. We strongly encourage you to use the Bash shell for your default command-line interpreter. This is because the Bash shell incorporates most of the useful features of other available shells and provides additional functionality.

Where appropriate, we'll also juxtapose key features of the Bash shell with both the Korn shell and the C shell. DBAs in Unix environments tend to use the Korn shell, so it's important to understand how various Korn shell features compare with the equivalent Bash shell commands. The C shell is also worthy to note because it is always installed, regardless of the Linux or Unix operating system version, whereas the Bash shell and Korn shell may not be universally available (especially on older systems).

When you log on to your Linux database server, you are "in" a shell. This means you can enter commands that the shell will interpret and run for you. The most common default shell prompt in Linux is the $ character (the dollar sign). For this reason, most of examples in this book denote the shell command line with the $ character. The # character (the hash) will be used for the prompt to denote operations that need to be performed as the root user. Figure 2-1 shows a typical screen where you type commands.

Figure 2-1. *Typical shell prompt ready to accept command input*

In this chapter, we cover Linux topics such as obtaining information about your shell environment and customizing it. The solutions will enable you to work efficiently at the command line on database servers. The command line is where you will perform most of your database administrator activities.

A typical DBA spends several hours per day furiously typing commands at the shell prompt. Therefore, the shell is a tool that all DBAs must thoroughly understand. The solutions in this chapter will form the building blocks for the more complex DBA tasks covered in the rest of this book.

2-1. Running Previously Entered Commands

Problem

You find yourself spending a lot of time retyping commands you've previously entered. You want to view, edit, and rerun shell commands that were recently executed.

Solution

One timesaving feature of the Bash shell is that it has several methods for editing and rerunning previously executed commands. This bulleted list highlights several options available for manipulating previously typed commands:

- Scrolling with the up and down arrow keys

- Using Ctrl+P and Ctrl+N

- Listing command history

- Searching in reverse

- Setting the command editor

Each of these techniques is described briefly in the following sections.

Scrolling with the Up and Down Arrow Keys

Use the up arrow to scroll up through your recent command history. As you scroll through previously run commands, you can rerun a desired command by pressing the Enter or Return key.

If you want to edit a command, use the Backspace key to erase characters, or use the left arrow to navigate to the desired location in the command text. After you have scrolled up through the command stack, use the down arrow to scroll back down through previously viewed commands.

■**Note** If you're familiar with Windows, scrolling through the command stack is similar to the DOSKEY utility.

Pressing Ctrl+P and Ctrl+N

The Ctrl+P keystroke (pressing the Ctrl and P keys at the same time) will display your previously entered command. If you have pressed Ctrl+P several times, you can scroll back down the command stack by pressing Ctrl+N (pressing the Ctrl and N keys at the same time).

Listing Command History

Use the history command to display commands that have been previously entered by the user:

```
$ history
```

Depending on how many commands have previously been executed, you may see a lengthy stack. You can limit the output to the last *n* number of commands by providing a number with the command. For example, the following lists the last five commands that have been run:

```
$ history 5
```

Here is some sample output:

```
273  cd -
274  grep -i ora alert.log
275  ssh -Y -l oracle 65.217.177.98
276  pwd
277  history 5
```

To run a previously listed command in the output, use an exclamation point (!, sometimes called the *bang*) followed by the history number. In this example, to run the pwd command on line 276, use ! as follows:

```
$ ! 276
```

To run the last command you ran, use !!, as shown here:

```
$ !!
```

Searching in Reverse

Press Ctrl+R (press the Ctrl and R keys at the same time), and you'll be presented with the Bash shell reverse search utility:

```
$ (reverse-i-search)`':
```

From the reverse-i-search prompt, as you type each letter, the tool automatically searches through previously run commands that have similar text to the string you entered. As soon as you're presented with the desired command match, you can rerun the command by pressing the Enter or Return key. To view all commands that match a string, press Ctrl+R repeatedly. To exit from the reverse search, press Ctrl+C.

Setting the Command Editor

You can use the set -o command to make your command-line editor be either vi or emacs. This example sets the command-line editor to be vi:

```
$ set -o vi
```

Now when you press Esc+K (press the Esc key and K key at the same time), you are placed in a mode where you can use vi commands to search through the stack of previously entered commands.

For example, if you want to scroll up the command stack, you can use the K key, and similarly, you can scroll down using the J key. When in this mode, you can use the slash (/) key and then type a string to be searched for in the entire command stack.

■**Tip** Before you attempt to use the command editor feature, ensure that you are thoroughly familiar with either the vi or emacs editor (see Chapter 4 for details on using vi).

A short example will illustrate the power of this feature. In this example, say you know you ran the ls -altr command about an hour ago. You want to run it again but this time without the r (reverse sort) option. To enter the command stack, press Esc+K:

```
$ Esc+K
```

You should now see the last command you executed. To search the command stack for the ls command, type /ls and then hit Enter or Return:

```
$ /ls
```

The most recently executed ls command should appear at the prompt:

```
$ ls -altr
```

To remove the r option, use the right arrow key to place the prompt over the r on the screen, and press X to remove the r from the end of the command. After you've edited the command, press the Enter or Return key to have it executed.

How It Works

Your *command history* is a stored sequential list of all the commands you have previously entered. You can use any of the techniques described in the "Solution" section of this recipe to view and manipulate previously entered commands.

The Bash shell command history is stored in your home directory in a file named .bash_history. If your current working directory is your home directory, then you can view the contents of this file with a utility such as cat. The following example uses the cd command to navigate to the home directory and then displays the contents of the .bash_history file with the cat command:

```
$ cd
$ cat .bash_history
```

The number of entries stored in the .bash_history file is determined by the HISTSIZE operating system variable. You can verify the history size using the echo utility. On this system, the command history size is 1000:

```
$ echo $HISTSIZE
10000
```

Usually system administrators will set the HISTSIZE variable in the /etc/profile file (which is automatically executed whenever a user logs on to a server). You can override the system's default value for command history by setting the HISTSIZE variable in a special startup file (see recipe 2-5 for details).

The easiest way to view the Bash shell command history is to use the up and down arrows to find the command of interest and the left and right arrows and/or the Backspace key to modify the command. Other shells typically do not allow the use of the up and down arrows. Table 2-1 lists common shells and what types of command history manipulation each tool supports.

Table 2-1. *Command History Options Available in Each Shell*

Shell	Up/Down Arrows	Reverse Search	Ctrl+P and Ctrl+N	set -o	Command History
Bash	Yes	Yes	Yes	Yes	Yes
Korn	No	No	No	Yes	Yes
C	No	No	No	No	Yes

2-2. Automatically Completing Long Commands

Problem

You get tired of typing long commands. You wonder whether there is some way the Bash shell can automatically fill in the text for long command strings.

Solution

The Tab key can be used for command completion. For example, say there are two files in the current directory named initRMOUGDB.ora and initBRDSTN.ora:

```
$ ls
initBRDSTN.ora initRMOUGDB.ora
```

In this example, you want to edit the initRMOUGDB.ora file with the vi utility. All you have to type is enough to make the file name unique within a directory and then press the Tab key (ensure that there is no space between the text and the Tab key):

```
$ vi initR<Tab>
```

Since there are no other files in the current directory that begin with the string initR, the Bash shell will automatically fill in the text initRMOUGDB.ora:

```
$ vi initRMOUGDB.ora
```

Now you can press the Enter or Return key to edit this file. One thing to note is that you can use this technique on any program, directory, command, or file. For example, if you need to change directories to a subdirectory named products and there are no other directories beneath your current working directory that start with the letter p, you can type cd p and then hit the Tab key. Your prompt will then show the following:

```
$ cd products/
```

You can now press the Enter or Return key to execute the cd products command.

How It Works

A timesaving feature of the Bash shell is *command completion*. This feature allows you to only partially type a program, command, file, or directory and then hit the Tab key, and the shell will attempt to complete the rest of the text.

If the Bash shell can't uniquely identify a program, command, file, or directory, then it will beep after you press Tab. In this situation, if you press Tab again, the shell will display all the possible programs, commands, files, or directories that match what string was partially typed.

For example, command completion can be used to show all executable files that start with a certain string. If you want to view all commands that start with the string di, then type di and hit the Tab key twice:

```
$ di<Tab><Tab>
diff        diff-jars   dir         dirname     disable     disown
diff3       dig         dircolors   dirs        disol
```

You should hear a bell (sometimes called a *beep*) sound after you enter the first Tab. The Bash shell will search for commands that start with the string di that are located in any directories contained within the PATH variable.

2-3. Viewing Environment Variables

Problem

You want to view the current settings of your environment variables.

Solution

You can use any of the following Linux commands to display operating system variables:

- printenv

- env

- set

- export

- echo

To display all variables set in your environment, then use any of the following commands (without any options): printenv, env, set, or export. The next bit of code uses the printenv command to show all environment variables:

```
$ printenv
```

Here's a partial listing of the output:

```
HOSTNAME=rmg.rmg.org
TERM=cygwin
SHELL=/bin/bash
HISTSIZE=1000
SSH_TTY=/dev/pts/0
USER=oracle
```

If you know the name of the variable you want to display, you can display it directly with the echo command. To display the contents of an operating system variable, you must preface it with a $ (dollar sign) character. This example uses the echo command to display the contents of the USER variable:

```
$ echo $USER
oracle
```

You can also use the printenv command to display environment variables. The following example uses printenv to show the current setting of the USER variable:

```
$ printenv USER
oracle
```

How It Works

Most DBAs work with multiple database servers. Every time you log on to a server, certain operating system variables are automatically set for you. Table 2-2 lists several environment variables you should know. Use any of the commands described in the "Solution" section of this recipe to view variables in your environment.

Sometimes you may not know the exact name of the variable. In situations like this, use the grep command to filter the output. This next example uses the set command and sends the output to the grep command for filtering any variables related to secure shell (SSH):

```
$ set | grep ORA
```

Table 2-2. *Commonly Used Environment Variables*

Variable	Description
PATH	Contains a list of directories in which the shell will look to find the executable commands. This variable is usually set by a shell startup script.
USER or LOGNAME	Contains the user account you used to log in to the server. This is automatically set for you when you log on.
HOME	Holds the home directory for a user. This is set for you when you log on.
~	Holds the home directory for a user. The tilde character is a shorthand way to reference your home directory. This is set for you when you log on.
PWD	Contains the location of the current working directory. This is set whenever you use cd to navigate to a new directory.
SHELL	Contains the name of your login shell.
EDITOR	Holds the name of the default editor used with some utilities (such as cron).
PS1	Contains the values used for displaying the command prompt.
SHLVL	Keeps track of how many subshell levels deep your current shell is.
DISPLAY	Is used by X applications to determine the display server used for input and output.

Here's some typical output from the previous command:

```
ORACLE_BASE=/oracle
ORACLE_HOME=/oracle/product/10.2
ORACLE_SID=RMDB1
PS1='[\h:\u:${ORACLE_SID}]$ '
```

■**Tip** For details on all variables set by the Bash shell in your environment, inspect the output of the man bash command. Search the man page for *shell variables*.

2-4. Displaying the Current Shell

Problem

You want to verify which shell you are currently using.

Solution

One quick way to display your shell is to echo the SHELL variable. You must specify a $ in front of the variable to display its contents:

```
$ echo $SHELL
```

In this example, the Bash shell is in use:

```
/bin/bash
```

How It Works

You may occasionally find yourself logged on to a box and wonder why certain Bash shell commands aren't working. In shops that have a large number of Linux and Unix servers, there may not be a consistent shell standard. In environments like this, first verify the current setting of your shell.

You can also use the $0 variable to show your current working shell. The $0 variable holds the name of the shell or script that is currently running. In this example, the Bash shell is the current shell:

```
$ echo $0
-bash
```

Another method for viewing the current shell is by running the ps command without any options:

```
$ ps
```

The first line of the output will show which shell you are currently using. You should see output similar to this:

```
PID TTY          TIME CMD
9088 pts/1    00:00:00 bash
9137 pts/1    00:00:00 ps
```

2-5. Automatically Setting Shell Variables

Problem

You want to automatically set various database variables whenever you log on to your database server.

Solution

Place shell variables that you want automatically set (when you log on) in the .bash_profile file in your home directory. In the next example, the ORACLE_SID variable is set to BRDSTN. The following text is placed in the .bash_profile file:

```
export ORACLE_SID=BRDSTN
```

Now if you log off and log back on, you can verify that this variable has been set by echoing it:

```
$ echo $ORACLE_SID
BRDSTN
```

If you don't want to log off and back on, then run the file manually using the . (dot) command. This command executes the lines contained within a file. The following example runs the .bash_profile file:

```
$ . $HOME/.bash_profile
```

The . instructs the shell to *source* the script. Sourcing tells the shell process that you are currently logged on to inherit any variables set with an export command in an executed script. If you don't use the . notation, then the variables set within the script are visible only within the context of the subshell that is spawned when the script is executed.

Note In the Bash shell, the source command is equivalent to the . (dot) command.

How It Works

When using the Bash shell, several special startup files can potentially be executed for you when first logging on to your database server:

- /etc/profile

- ~/.bash_profile

- ~/.bash_login

- ~/.profile

Note Depending on the version of the Linux operating system, there may be different startup files in use. Run the ls -altr in command in your home directory to view all files available.

The /etc/profile file is maintained by your system administrator, and you need root privileges to modify it. This file sets systemwide variables common to all users logging on to the system. Here is a snippet of some typical entries in the /etc/profile file:

```
# No core files by default
ulimit -S -c 0 > /dev/null 2>&1
# Set OS variables
USER="`id -un`"
LOGNAME=$USER
MAIL="/var/spool/mail/$USER"
HOSTNAME=`/bin/hostname`
HISTSIZE=1000
```

After running the /etc/profile file, the Bash shell will next search for the following files and run only the first file it locates (in the following order): ~/.bash_profile, ~/.bash_login, ~/.profile.

Here are some typical entries in the oracle user's ~/.bash_profile file:

```
# User specific environment and startup programs
PATH=$PATH:$HOME/bin
# Source the oracle OS variables for BRDSTN database
. /var/opt/oracle/oraset BRDSTN
```

You should be aware of two additional important startup type files:

- ~/.bashrc

- ~/.bash_logout

If you start a nonlogin Bash shell by typing bash at the command line, then the ~/.bashrc file will automatically be executed for you. DBAs will place commands in ~/.bashrc to ensure that database-related operating system commands are consistently set regardless of whether they are using a login shell or a nonlogin shell. A common technique to address this is to place the following code in the ~/.bash_profile file:

```
# Run .bashrc if it exists
if [ -f ~/.bashrc ]; then
        . ~/.bashrc
fi
```

When first logging on to a Linux server, the previous bit of code checks to see whether the ~/.bashrc file exists and, if so, then runs it. This method ensures that aliases and functions are defined in a consistent manner regardless of whether it's a login or nonlogin shell.

The ~/.bash_logout file is appropriately named and is executed when you issue the exit command. Typically you might see the clear command executed in the ~/.bash_logout file to clear text off the terminal when logging out.

2-6. Customizing the Command Prompt

Problem

You work with several database servers. You typically have several terminal screens open simultaneously on your screen. To avoid confusion, you would like the hostname and username to be displayed in the command prompt.

Solution

The special operating system variable PS1 holds the text string of what appears in the command prompt. This example changes the PS1 variable to hold the hostname and username:

```
$ PS1='[\h:\u]$ '
```

The \h and \u are special Bash variables that hold the hostname and username, respectively. After setting PS1 in this example, the prompt now shows the following:

```
[rmougprd1:oracle] $
```

The string rmougprd1 is the hostname, and oracle is the current operating system user.

How It Works

Setting your command prompt to something informational can be invaluable for DBAs who work with multiple servers and operating system accounts. Table 2-3 lists many of the Bash shell backslash-escaped special variables that you can use to customize your command prompt.

■**Tip** You can also view all variables available in your environment by issuing a man bash command. Search for *PROMPTING* in the man page.

You will most likely want to have your command prompt automatically set for you when you log on to a database server. To do this, place the command that sets the PS1 prompt in a special startup file (see recipe 2-5 for more details on how to do this).

Table 2-3. *Bash Shell Backslash-Escaped Variables Used for Customizing Command Prompt*

Variable	Description
\a	ASCII bell character.
\d	Date in "weekday month date" format (for example, Thu Aug 21).
\e	ASCII escape character.
\h	Hostname.
\j	Number of jobs managed by shell.
\l	Base name of shell's terminal device.
\n	Newline.
\r	Carriage return.
\s	Name of shell.
\t	Time in 24-hour HH:MM:SS format.
\T	Time in 12-hour HH:MM:SS format.
\@	Time in 12-hour a.m./p.m. format.
\A	Time in 24-hour HH:MM format.
\u	Current username.
\v	Version of Bash shell.
\V	Release of Bash shell.
\w	Current working directory.
\W	Base name of current working directory.
\!	History number of command.
\$	If effective UID is 0, then display #. Otherwise, display $.

You can combine the characters in Table 2-3 with other regular characters or variables. For example, if you want your prompt to always display the current hostname and database SID, then place the following bit of code in your `.bashrc` file:

```
PS1='[\h:${ORACLE_SID}]$ '
```

The previous line of code ensures that every time you log on to the server or start a new Bash shell, your prompt will automatically be set to contain the current value of ORACLE_SID. Additionally, if you change the value of ORACLE_SID, your prompt will automatically reflect the new setting. This can be an invaluable tool to eliminate confusion for DBAs who operate on Linux servers that run multiple databases on one physical server.

2-7. Creating a Command Shortcut

Problem

You find yourself frequently retyping long sets of commands and want to somehow create a shortcut to the lengthy commands.

Solution

There are two very common methods for creating shortcuts to other commands: aliases and functions. These two techniques are described in the following sections.

Using an Alias

Suppose you find yourself often navigating to a database background process logging destination to view log files. You would have to type something similar to this:

```
$ cd /oracle/BRDSTN/admin/bdump
```

You can use the `alias` command to create a shortcut to accomplish the same task. This example creates an alias named bd that will change directories to a background location that is dependent on the value of the ORACLE_SID variable:

```
$ alias bd='cd /oracle/$ORACLE_SID/admin/bdump'
```

Now you can type bd, which will do the same thing as changing your current working directory to the Oracle background dump directory.

Using a Function

You can also use a function to create command shortcuts. We provide only a brief example of how to use a function in this recipe; for full details on using functions, see Chapter 7.

The following line of code creates a simple function named bd:

```
$ function bd { cd /oracle/${ORACLE_SID}/admin/bdump; }
```

You can now type bd at the command line to change your working directory to the Oracle background dump directory.

How It Works

An *alias* is a simple mechanism for creating a short piece of text that will execute other shell commands. To show all aliases that have been defined, use the alias command with no arguments:

```
$ alias
```

Listed next are some common examples of alias definitions that DBAs use:

```
alias l.='ls -d .*'
alias ll='ls -l'
alias lsd='ls -altr | grep ^d'
alias bd='cd $ORACLE_BASE/$ORACLE_SID/admin/bdump'
alias ud='cd $ORACLE_BASE/$ORACLE_SID/admin/udump'
alias sqlp='sqlplus "/ as sysdba"'
alias shutdb='echo "shutdown immediate;" | sqlp'
alias startdb='echo "startup;" | sqlp'
alias valert='view $ORACLE_BASE/admin/$ORACLE_SID/bdump/alert_$ORACLE_SID.log'
```

You may have to modify some of the previous alias definitions depending on your implementation of Oracle's Optimal Flexible Architecture (OFA) standard. This is especially true if you're using Oracle Database 11g, because the OFA standards changed in regard to the location of the alert.log file.

If you want to remove an alias definition from your current environment, then use the unalias command. The following example removes the alias for lsd:

```
$ unalias lsd
```

Using aliases is a common way to create command shortcuts. However, we recommend using functions over aliases. Functions are more powerful because of features such as the ability to operate on parameters passed in on the command line. Functions are described in much more detail in Chapter 7.

DBAs commonly establish aliases and functions by setting them in the $HOME/.bashrc file. For example, here we create a file named dba_fncs and place in it the following lines of code:

```
#-----------------------------------------
# cd to bdump
  function bd {
    cd /oracle/${ORACLE_SID}/admin/bdump
  } # bd
#-----------------------------------------
# View Oracle Database 11g alert.log file
function valert2 {
view $ORACLE_BASE/diag/rdbms/$(echo $ORACLE_SID|\
tr A-Z a-z)/$ORACLE_SID/trace/alert_$ORACLE_SID.log
} # valert2
#-----------------------------------------
```

A common practice is to create a bin directory beneath the oracle account's home directory and place the dba_fncs file in HOME/bin. The dba_fncs file is sourced as follows:

```
.  $HOME/bin/dba_fcns
```

Now every time you log on, the functions in the dba_fncs file are sourced and available for you to use as command shortcuts.

If you ever wonder whether a shortcut is an alias or a function, use the type command to verify a command's origin. This example verifies that bd is a function:

```
$ type bd
bdump is a function
bdump ()
{
    cd /oracle/${ORACLE_SID}/admin/bdump
}
```

2-8. Providing Input to Commands

Problem

You want a shell command to receive its input from a file or another process instead of commands typed from the keyboard.

Solution

In Linux you can instruct a command to receive its input from a file with the < character. This technique is known as *redirection*. In this example, we use the mail command to send a log file named output.log to an e-mail account of heera.chaya@yahoo.com:

```
$ mail heera.chaya@yahoo.com <output.log
```

You can also use the output of one command as the input to another command. This technique is known as *pipelining.* The pipe (|) character instructs a process to receive its input from the output of another process. In this example, we use the output of the cat command as the input to the mail command:

```
$ cat output.log | mail heera.chaya@yahoo.com
```

This technique of piping the output from one command to another is an extremely powerful tool. DBAs use this method to chain commands together to perform complex tasks. We provide many examples of this approach throughout the book.

How It Works

In Linux there are three data streams associated with a process:

- Standard input (also called *standard in* or *stdin*)

- Standard output (also called *standard out* or *stdout*)

- Standard error (also called *stderr*)

Figure 2-2 displays the three data streams associated with each Linux process. Starting on the left side of the figure, standard input is the data provided to the Linux process. This is usually data entered by you from the keyboard. As demonstrated in the "Solution" section of this recipe, standard input can also come from a file or as the output of another process.

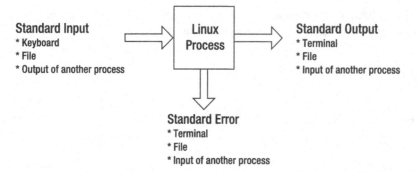

Figure 2-2. *The process input and output data streams*

Shell programs often generate output data. By default, standard output data is directed to the terminal. Standard output can also be redirected to a file or another Linux process. Recipe 2-9 demonstrates how to redirect standard output to a file or another process.

Sometimes shell programs generate error messages. By default, standard error messages are displayed to your terminal. Like standard output, standard error messages can be redirected to a file or another process.

The Linux process doesn't care where its input comes from or where the output is delivered. This means you can string together combinations of commands that feed output from one command to be used as the input to another command. This piping of command output to another command's input is a very powerful and flexible feature of the shell. Table 2-4 summarizes the ways in which standard input, output, and errors can be redirected using the Bash shell.

Table 2-4. *Command Input and Output Redirection Operators*

Operation	Bash Shell Redirection Syntax
Read standard input from a file.	`command <file`
Read standard input until end of marker.	`command <<end of marker`
Write standard output to a file.	`command >file`
Append standard output to end of file.	`command >>file`
Write standard output and standard error to separate files.	`command >file 2>file2`
Write standard output and standard error to the same file.	`command >file 2>&1`
Write standard output and standard error to the same file.	`command &> file`
Append standard output and standard error to the end of a file.	`command >>file 2>&1`
Send (pipe) standard output of first command to input of second command.	`command	command2`
Send (pipe) standard output and standard error to input of second command.	`command 2>&1	command2`

Some additional explanation is required for interpreting the second column of Table 2-4. Notice that the < and << characters are used to redirect standard input. The > and >> characters are used to redirect standard output. Also notice that the characters > and >> are shorthand for 1> and 1>>. Likewise, < and << are shorthand for 1< and 1<<.

The 2> and 2>> characters are used to redirect standard error. Also note that the syntax 2>&1 means to redirect the standard error stream to the same location as standard output. In the Bash shell, you can also use the syntax &> to send both standard error and standard output to the same file.

The &0, &1, and &2 characters are used to represent the files used for standard input, standard output, and standard error, respectively. Put another way, the &0, &1, and &2 characters are synonyms for the /dev/stdin, /dev/stdout, and /dev/stderr files, respectively. To illustrate this point, this example uses the file /dev/stdout to redirect standard error to the same location as standard output:

```
$ cat initBRDSTN.ora 1>myfile.txt 2>/dev/stdout
```

The previous command is equivalent to the following:

```
$ cat initBRDSTN.ora 1>myfile.txt 2>&1
```

The previous command directs the standard output 1> to be sent to myfile.txt. If any errors are encountered when issuing the command (for example, if file initBRDSTN.ora doesn't exist), the standard error stream >2 is sent to the same location as standard out (which is myfile.txt).

2-9. Redirecting Command Output

Problem

You want to save the output of a command to a file.

Solution

By default, the output from a command will be displayed on your terminal. The > character is used to redirect the output of a command to a specified file. The > character is synonymous with 1>. For example, the following command will take the output of the cat command and place it in a file named output.txt:

```
$ cat init.ora >output.txt
```

If the init.ora file doesn't exist, then you'll receive an error message such as this:

```
cat: init.ora: No such file or directory
```

How It Works

You should know about some other interesting features of redirecting command output. For example, you can also instruct the shell command to redirect any errors that are encountered when running a script to a separate file. The 2> characters specify where errors should be written. Just as > means redirect output to a file, 2> means redirect error messages to a file. This example redirects standard output to the file output.txt and sends any error messages encountered to errors.txt:

```
$ cat init.ora >output.txt 2>errors.txt
```

You can also use a shorthand notation to send both standard output and error messages to the same file:

```
$ cat init.ora >output.txt 2>&1
```

The 2>&1 notation instructs the shell to send output stream number 2 (error output) to the same place as output stream number 1 (standard output). You'll find it useful to use this notation when running scripts such as database-monitoring jobs.

If for any reason you don't want to overwrite the output file, then use the >> syntax. The >> syntax instructs the shell to append any messages to the end of an existing file:

```
$ cat init.ora >>output.txt 2>&1
```

2-10. Sending Output to Nowhere

Problem

You want to run a command, but you don't want the output to be shown or saved anywhere.

Solution

If you do not want text to appear on your screen or to be saved in a physical file, then you can send it to the proverbial "bit bucket" (the /dev/null device). The following example uses the dd command to read a file one block at a time without writing the output to a file:

```
$ time dd if=/ora01/BRDSTN/user_data01.dbf of=/dev/null
```

The previous command is useful for troubleshooting disk I/O issues without the overhead of physically creating a file. If you divide the datafile size by the total time the command took to run, this will give you the disk I/O rate. You can compare that value with V$BACKUP_ASYNC_IO.EFFECTIVE_BYTES_PER_SECOND to help you determine whether RMAN has a potential I/O problem.

How It Works

The /dev/null file is a special file known as the *null device*. It also called *slash dev slash null* or the *bit bucket*. It contains nothing, and any output you send to this special file will never be seen again.

The null device is useful in situations where you don't want to see all the error messages generated by a command. For example, the following find command will generate error messages for directories that it can't read.

```
$ cd /
$ find . -name "alert*.log"
```

Here is a partial snippet of the output:

```
find: cannot read dir ./var/fm/fmd/xprt: Permission denied
find: cannot read dir ./var/fm/fmd/rsrc: Permission denied
find: cannot read dir ./var/fm/fmd/ckpt: Permission denied
```

To eliminate those error messages, send the error output to the null device:

```
$ find . -name "alert*.log" 2>/dev/null
```

If you know you're going to be running a program or command that generates output you don't need, then you can redirect the output to the /dev/null file. This file can also be used to quickly reduce a large file to 0 bytes without deleting the original file (see recipe 5-31 for details).

CHECKING FOR DATAFILE CORRUPTION

In the old days, before there were tools like dbverify and Oracle Recovery Manager (RMAN), DBAs needed a method to detect corrupt blocks in datafiles. To accomplish this, DBAs would use the export utility. As the export utility runs, it will write information on detected corrupt blocks to the database alert.log file.

If the DBA wanted only to check for block corruption without saving the output of the export to a file, the output can be sent to the /dev/null file, as shown here:

```
$ exp user/pass full=y file=/dev/null
```

Thus, the DBA could detect database corruption without actually having to create a potentially large export file. Having said that, you should not rely on this approach for detecting database corruption because it has several known limitations like not being able to detect corruption in blocks above a table's high water mark (see Oracle's MetaLink Note 214369.1 for details). You should instead use dbverify or RMAN to detect for bad blocks in Oracle database datafiles.

2-11. Displaying and Capturing Command Output

Problem

You want to see the output of a command on your screen, and additionally you want to store the output in a file.

Solution

If you want to capture only the output associated with the execution of a specific operating system command, then you can use the tee command. The tee command enables the writing of any output generated by a command to both the screen and a designated file.

The following example runs the ls command to list all files in a directory. It also saves that output to a file that can later be viewed to determine the names and sizes of files on a particular date:

```
$ ls -altr /ora01/BRDSTN | tee /home/oracle/log/oct15_df.log
```

Here is some sample output of what is displayed to the screen and recorded in the log file:

```
-rw-r-----  1 oracle oinstall  52429312 Oct 15 08:00 redo03a.log
-rw-r-----  1 oracle oinstall 838868992 Oct 15 08:25 undotbs01.dbf
-rw-r-----  1 oracle oinstall 524296192 Oct 15 08:30 system01.dbf
-rw-r-----  1 oracle oinstall  15056896 Oct 15 08:37 control01.ctl
```

How It Works

The tee command is useful when you want to interactively see the output of a command displayed on the screen and also require that the display be logged to a file that can be inspected later for debugging or troubleshooting activities.

■**Tip** The tee command is similar to a plumbing t-splitter pipe in that it allows one input stream to be bifurcated into two output pipes.

2-12. Recording All Shell Command Output

Problem

You're performing a database upgrade, and you need to run several SQL scripts. You want to record the output of everything printed to your screen to a log file.

Solution

The script command enables the recording of all output printed to your screen to also be written to an operating system file. This example writes all output to a file named upgrade.log:

```
$ script upgrade.log
Script started, file is upgrade.log
```

From this point on, all output printed to your terminal is also recorded in the script upgrade.log. To end the script logging session, press Ctrl+D or type exit. You should see this message similar to this:

```
Script done, file is upgrade.log
```

How It Works

The script command is invaluable when you need to capture all output being printed to the terminal. This command will store all output in an operating system file that can later be used to verify what tasks were performed and whether the operations succeeded or failed.

If you don't specify a file name when using script, a default file with the name of typescript will be created. If you need to append to an already existing file, use script with the -a option, as shown here:

```
$ script -a upgrade.log
```

This enables the capturing of all output from all scripts that are being run. This can be extremely useful when you have a mix of operating system commands and database commands and want to capture the output of every operation.

DBAs use the `script` command in situations where the person who developed upgrade scripts (DBA #1) is passing the scripts to a different team member (DBA #2) to have those scripts executed in another database environment. In this scenario, DBA #2 will start a `script` job, run the upgrade scripts, end the `script` logging, and send the generated log file to DBA #1 for verification purposes.

2-13. Changing the Login Shell

Problem

Your system administrator has set your operating system account to use the Bash shell, and you want to change it to the Korn shell.

Solution

Use the `chsh` (change shell) command to change the default login shell. You can specify the desired login shell directly with the -s option. In this example, I'll change the default shell for the `oracle` user to the Korn shell:

```
$ chsh -s /usr/bin/ksh
Changing shell for oracle.
Password:
```

After successfully entering the password, a message "shell changed" will be displayed. If you don't specify a shell with the -s option, then you will be prompted for a password and then a shell:

```
$ chsh
Changing shell for oracle.
Password:
```

Enter the password for your operating system account. You should now see the following text:

```
New shell [/usr/bash]:
```

To change your shell to the Korn shell, enter the following text:

```
/usr/bin/ksh
```

And you should see a message confirming that your shell has been changed:

```
Shell changed.
```

How It Works

Most Linux operating system accounts are created with the Bash shell as the default. In most circumstances, the Bash shell is the preferred shell. However, if you're migrating to Linux from another Unix operating system, you may have a preexisting affinity to a non-Bash shell.

The valid shells available on your server are stored in the /etc/shells file. You can use the chsh -l command or use the cat command to view the contents of the /etc/shells file. This next example uses the cat command to display the available shells:

```
$ cat /etc/shells
/bin/sh
/bin/bash
/sbin/nologin
/bin/ash
/bin/bsh
/bin/ksh
/usr/bin/ksh
/usr/bin/pdksh
/bin/tcsh
/bin/csh
```

We recommend that you use the Bash shell on Linux systems. The Bash shell is very robust and incorporates most of the useful features from the Bourne shell, Korn shell, and C shell. Table 2-5 describes the various shells available in Linux environments.

Table 2-5. *Descriptions of Some of the More Popular Linux Shells Available*

Shell	Description
bsh or sh	The original Bourne Unix shell written by Steve Bourne.
bash	The Bourne Again shell is considered to be one of the most robust shells and is used extensively on Linux systems.
ash	The Almquist shell has a smaller footprint as the Bash shell and is useful on systems where disk space is limited.
ksh	The Korn shell is popular among DBAs on many varieties of Unix.
pdksh	This is a public domain implementation of the Korn shell.
tcsh	The TENEX C shell is an enhanced version of the C shell.
csh	The C shell is like the C programming language and is popular on many older variants of Unix.

You can verify what your default login shell has been set to by viewing the contents of the /etc/passwd file. For example, to view the default shell for the oracle user, use the cat and grep commands:

```
$ cat /etc/passwd | grep -i oracle
oracle:x:500:500::/home/oracle:/usr/bin/ksh
```

Note You do not need any special privileges or the assistance of your system administrator to use the chsh command.

2-14. Modifying Command Path Search

Problem

You need your shell to automatically find executable programs that are not currently in a directory that is included in your PATH variable. You want to add directories to your PATH variable.

Solution

You can manually add a directory to your PATH variable by using the export command. The following example appends the /oracle/product/11.0 directory to the current contents of the PATH variable:

```
$ export PATH=$PATH:/oracle/product/11.0
```

In the previous line of code, the PATH variable is defined to be the current contents of PATH plus the directory of /oracle/product/11.0. You separate directories in the PATH variable with a colon (:).

If you want to have a directory added to your PATH variable every time you log on to your database server, then place the export command in a special startup file (see recipe 2-5 for details).

How It Works

The export command allows you to define variables that will be available to subsequently executed commands. You can add directories to the PATH variable by exporting it. To verify the contents of your PATH variable, you can use the echo command:

```
$ echo $PATH
```

Occasionally you might encounter an Oracle RMAN issue when the directory /usr/X11R6/bin appears in the PATH variable before the ORACLE_HOME/bin directory. Here, attempt to start rman:

```
$ rman target /
rman: can't open target
```

You received this error because there is an rman executable in the /usr/X11R6/bin directory that has nothing to do with the Oracle rman backup and recovery utility. In this scenario, you'll have to modify your PATH variable to ensure that ORACLE_HOME/bin comes before /usr/X11R6/bin:

```
$ export PATH=$ORACLE_HOME/bin:$PATH
```

The other alternative is to rename the rman executable in /usr/X11R6/bin to something like rman.X11.

Tip See Oracle's MetaLink Note 101050.1 for issues regarding your PATH variable and the rman executable.

CURRENT WORKING DIRECTORY AND PATH

To set your path to include the current working directory, simply do this:

```
$ export PATH=$PATH:.
```

Security experts recommend against having the current working directory referenced near the beginning of your PATH variable. This is because a malicious person could place a program in a directory that does bad things to your system. For example, somebody could place a script named ls in a user's home directory and have commands within the ls script delete files recursively. If the bad ls script is referenced before the ls command in /bin or /usr/bin, then the results could be ugly.

2-15. Viewing Built-in Commands

Problem

You wonder whether you're running a built-in version of a shell command or whether you're using the binary program located in the /bin directory.

Solution

Use the help command to view all built-in commands. For example, if you type help with no arguments, then all built-in commands will be displayed:

```
$ help
```

Here is a partial listing of the output:

```
alias [-p] [name[=value] ... ]
bind [-lpvsPVS] [-m keymap] [-f fi
builtin [shell-builtin [arg Figure
.]]
case WORD in [PATTERN [| PATTERN].
command [-pVv] command [arg ...]
complete [-abcdefgjksuv] [-pr] [-o
declare [-afFirtx] [-p] [name[=val
disown [-h] [-ar] [jobspec ...]
```

You can also use the type command to determine whether a program is built in. Use the -a option of type to print all locations in the PATH variable that include a command (including all aliases and functions). The following example shows that there is a built-in pwd command and also a pwd program in the /bin directory:

```
$ type -a pwd
pwd is a shell builtin
pwd is /bin/pwd
```

■ **Note** You might wonder why Linux provides both a built-in command and a program for pwd. This is because some shells may not have a built-in command for pwd, so a Linux program is explicitly provided in the /bin or /usr/bin directory.

How It Works

Some commands are built in to the Bash shell. *Built-in* simply means that the shell contains its own version of the command. Therefore, if you run a built-in command such as pwd, the Bash shell will run its version of the pwd command rather than the executable program located in the /bin or /usr/bin directory. If you want to explicitly run the pwd command in the /bin directory, then specify the complete path and file name. This example shows how to run the pwd program located in the /bin directory:

```
$ /bin/pwd
```

In some situations, it's important to know whether a command is built in to the shell or not. Built-in commands execute faster than their counterparts in the /bin or /usr/bin directory. This is because there is no overhead of looking in directories for the command and then loading the command into memory for execution.

Additionally, there are code portability issues to consider. Built-in commands typically have the same behavior from one Linux vendor to another, whereas the commands in the /bin and /usr/bin directories may behave differently between different ports of Linux (especially older versions).

Built-in commands do not start a separate process (sometimes called *forked, child*, or *spawned*) when they are executed. This is a requirement of some commands such as cd. This is because a child process cannot modify its parent process. If cd were executed as a child process, it would not be able to modify the current working directory of the parent process and therefore wouldn't be of much use. For this reason, the Bash shell contains its own executable code for the cd command. Table 2-6 describes some of the more commonly used Bash built-in commands.

Table 2-6. *Commonly Used Bash Built-in Commands*

Bash Built-in Command	Description
cd	Changes directories
echo	Displays strings and the contents of variables
help	Displays help on Bash built-in commands
history	Shows recently run commands
pwd	Prints the current working directory
ulimit	Sets and displays various system resource limits imposed on the shell

You can instruct the Bash shell to explicitly run a built-in command with the builtin command. Sometimes this is useful when porting scripts between different versions of Linux.

The `builtin` command will run the built-in version of the command even if there is an alias declared for it. This example runs the `pwd` built-in command:

```
$ builtin pwd
```

Likewise, you can explicitly instruct Bash to run the Linux program version of a command, even if there is a built-in command or alias defined with the same name. This example runs the program version of the `pwd` command that is located in the `/bin` directory:

```
$ command pwd
```

You can also use the `enable` command to enable or disable the use of a built-in command. This example uses `enable -n` to disable the `pwd` built-in command:

```
$ enable -n pwd
$ type pwd
pwd is /bin/pwd
```

This example reenables the `pwd` command:

```
$ enable pwd
$ type pwd
pwd is a shell builtin
```

■Tip You can also use the `man bash` command to view all built-in commands. When viewing the `bash` man page, search for *shell built-in commands*.

2-16. Setting the Backspace Key

Problem

You've entered in a command incorrectly, and you want to backspace over previously entered characters so that you can correct them. When you attempt to use the Backspace key, instead of it deleting previously entered characters, it shows the ^?characters.

Solution

Use the `stty` command to set your Backspace key to delete characters properly. The following bit of code sets the Backspace key to delete characters:

```
$ stty erase Ctrl+Backspace
```

In the previous command, ensure that you press the Ctrl key and Backspace key at the same time. This may vary depending on your Linux system; for example, the following is an alternative way of setting the Backspace key:

```
$ stty erase <Backspace>
```

In the previous line of code, don't type the word Backspace; rather, you need to press the Backspace key.

How It Works

When working with older versions of Linux or Unix, you may find yourself logged on to a server and the Backspace key doesn't work. In situations like these, you'll have to manually set the Backspace key to function correctly. If you want the Backspace key to be automatically set every time you log on to the server, then place the stty command in a special startup file (see recipe 2-5 for details).

■**Note** On some older Linux or Unix systems, you may need to use the stty erase ^H command or the stty erase ^? command to set the Backspace key.

2-17. Typing a Long Command in Multiple Lines

Problem

You want to type a long command, but it doesn't fit nicely on one line.

Solution

Use the backslash (\) character followed by pressing the Enter or Return key to extend a line of code to the next line. The following example shows how to break a long rman connection command over several lines:

```
$ /usr/oracle/product/10.2.0/db_1/bin/rman \
> target / \
> catalog rman/rman@db11g_bllnx1 \
> cmdfile=/home/oracle/scripts/rmancheck.rmn \
> msglog=/home/oracle/rmanlog/rmancheck01.log append
```

You could have typed the previous command on one line. In situations where you have a limited terminal width, though, you may want to consider breaking a command up into multiple lines.

How It Works

Sometimes it's desirable to extend a command across multiple lines for readability reasons. When you type \ followed by the Enter or Return key, the next line will be preceded by the > character. This indicates the command has been extended to the next line. Both the backslash and the new line marker will be ignored when using this technique.

It doesn't matter at what position within the command you use the backslash. You can break a command over as many lines as necessary.

CHAPTER 3

■ ■ ■

Managing Processes and Users

Diagnosing and resolving availability and performance issues are a key part of every database administrator's job. When troubleshooting problems, DBAs often start by identifying what processes are currently running and identifying details about users logged on to the server. It's critical you know how to extract process and user activity from the Linux operating system.

When working with operating system users and processes, some tasks require root privileges. For example, when installing database software on a Linux server, one of the first steps is to create an operating system user and group. These tasks require root privileges. Depending on your environment, you may not have a system administrator (SA) to perform these operations. In this scenario, you'll have to log on to the server with root privileges and perform these tasks yourself. Even if you do have a system administrator, you'll need to adequately document and communicate to your SA the database setup tasks that require root privileges. Therefore, it's important you know which database tasks require root privileges and the commands to execute them.

This chapter starts by showing commands that get information about processes and users. It then progresses to examples of how to access the root account. The chapter ends with common database installation tasks that require root privileges, such as adding users and groups.

3-1. Listing Processes

Problem

You want to view processes currently running on the database server.

Solution

To view process information, use the ps (process status) utility. If you type the ps command without any parameters, you'll see all processes that have been started by the user you're currently logged on as:

```
$ ps
  PID TTY          TIME CMD
24975 pts/5        0:00 ps
15127 pts/5        0:00 bash
```

If you want to view all processes running on a box, then use the -e and -f options to show every process in a full output format. If many processes are running on a box, it's useful to pipe the output of ps to grep and restrict the search for a particular user or process name. In this example, ps and grep are used to show any processes that contain the string smon:

```
$ ps -ef | grep -i smon
oracle  2950    1   0   May 04 ?         12:12 ora_smon_CHAYA
oracle  2952    1   0   May 04 ?         12:08 ora_smon_HEERA
```

The previous output shows that each Oracle system monitor (SMON) background process was started on May 4 and that each has consumed a little more than 12 hours of CPU time. The second column contains the process ID.

How It Works

Every time you run a Linux command, a process is automatically created for you. Each process is assigned a unique number called a *process identifier* (PID). DBAs use the ps utility for a couple of important reasons:

- Checking on background processes

- Identifying hung or runaway processes that need to be killed

When there are database connectivity issues, the ps command is useful for quickly identifying whether a required database background processes is running. To list all processes for a specific user, use the -u (user) option, and specify a username. This example lists all processes running under the oracle user with a full listing of the output:

```
$ ps -fu oracle
```

Here's a snippet of the output:

```
UID       PID PPID C STIME TTY       TIME CMD
oracle   7884    1 0 Apr15 ?      00:00:00 ora_pmon_RMDB1
oracle   7886    1 0 Apr15 ?      00:00:00 ora_pspo_RMDB1
oracle   7888    1 0 Apr15 ?      00:00:00 ora_mman_RMDB1
```

Similarly, if you know the process ID, you can view any associated processes by using the -p option with a PID. This example lists the full output of processes associated with the PID of 7884:

```
$ ps -fp 7884
```

3-2. Terminating Processes

Problem

You're running a database backup job, and you think the process is hung. You want to kill the process.

Solution

The PID can be used as input to the kill utility to terminate a process. In this next example, ps is used to show the PID of a backup job that seems to be hung and needs to be terminated:

```
$ ps -ef | grep rman | grep -v grep
oracle   22827 22793  0 14:42 pts/2    00:00:00 rman target /
```

The PID is 22827 in this example. To kill that process, issue a kill command, as shown here:

```
$ kill -9 22827
```

The -9 option sends a kill signal to the process, which will cause it to terminate.

■**Note** To list all types of kill signals available, use the kill -l command.

Oftentimes you will have more than one process running with the same name. For example, in this scenario two rman processes are running on the database server:

```
$ ps -ef | grep rman | grep -v grep
oracle   14626 14574  0 11:20 pts/4    00:00:01 rman target /
oracle   14717 14685  0 11:20 pts/5    00:00:01 rman target /
```

When you have multiple processes with the same name, how do you uniquely identify a session? In these scenarios, use the tty command to print the session's terminal information. In this next example, we temporarily exit the rman utility and run tty to identify the session's terminal:

```
RMAN> host;
tty
/dev/pts/5
```

You can now type exit to return to the rman prompt. The tty information in the previous example is /dev/pts/5. You can now tell from the prior ps output that this session has the process ID of 14717.

How It Works

Sometimes it's necessary to use the kill command to terminate unresponsive user and database processes. To run the kill command, you either need to own the process or have root privileges. Be careful when using the kill command. If you accidentally nuke the wrong process, you could cause inadvertent downtime for your database application.

Sometimes in an Oracle environment you'll find yourself in situations where you need to kill a hung SQL process. To accomplish this, you need to first identify the PID by querying the data dictionary as shown here:

```
SELECT s.username "ORACLE USER"
      ,p.pid       "PROC PID"
      ,s.process   "SESS PID"
      ,s.osuser    "OS User"
      ,s.terminal  "Terminal"
      ,s.machine   "Machine"
      ,s.sid       "SESS ID"
      ,s.serial#   "SESS Serial#"
FROM v$process p
    ,v$session s
WHERE p.addr = s.paddr
/
```

Here is some sample output from the previous query:

ORACLE USER	PROC PID	SESS PID	OS User	Terminal	Machine	SESS ID	SESS Serial#
SYS	19	9478	oracle	pts/5	shrek2	1076	1304
HEERA	20	9515	oracle	pts/7	shrek2	1077	1649
HEERA	21	17239	oracle	pts/1	cns-dba	1073	440

The user's session process identifier (SESS PID) in the output maps to the operating system PID. There are two HEERA sessions in the previous output. To uniquely identify one session, while connected via a HEERA session, from the SQL*Plus prompt issue the ! SQL command to run the tty operating system command:

```
SQL> !tty
/dev/pts/7
```

To kill the SQL*Plus process being run by the HEERA schema identified by the previous command, issue the following from the operating system as the oracle user on the server that is running the SQL process:

```
$ kill -9 9515
```

You won't see any output from the kill command. It unceremoniously removes the specified process. However, the SQL*Plus session that gets killed should show output similar to this:

```
SQL> killed
```

You can also kill a SQL session with the SQL*Plus alter system kill session command by using the session ID and serial number. As a DBA, the following command will kill the SQL session that has the session ID of 1073 and the serial number of 440:

```
SQL> alter system kill session '1073,440';
```

Another useful operating system utility available for killing processes is killall. This tool allows you to stop all processes running a certain command. This can be a useful alternative to the kill command, which requires that you specify the PID you want to terminate. This can be most useful in a situation where you have a program that has malfunctioned and is spawning multiple processes. In this scenario, it may be difficult to track down all the specific PIDs in a timely manner.

The syntax for running killall is as follows:

```
$ killall [options] program_name
```

When used with no options, then all occurrences of the specified program name will be terminated. This next example terminates all instances of sqlplus running:

```
$ killall sqlplus
```

Use the -i option to be prompted with the process name and PID for confirmation before terminating the process. This allows you to selectively halt instances of a program:

```
$ killall -i sqlplus
Kill sqlplus(32402) ? (y/n)
```

■**Note** The killall program will never commit suicide. In other words, if you run a killall killall command, it will cease other instances of killall on the system but not the currently running process.

3-3. Listing the Users Logged On

Problem

You are experiencing performance problems with your database server. To help diagnose the issues, you first want to view all users currently logged on to the box.

Solution

Use the who command to display the users logged on to a box:

```
$ who
```

The output consists of four columns: users logged on, their terminal name, the time they logged on, and from where they logged on. Here's a typical listing of the who command:

```
ptownshend    pts/1        Jun 15 14:17 (vpn-229-150-36-51.com)
rdaltrey      pts/2        Aug 10 22:11 (122.120.44.181)
jentwistle    pts/3        Aug 16 03:14 (111.155.23.114)
kmoon         pts/4        Sep  4 01:23 (10.6.77.121)
kjones        pts/6        Dec  4 06:66 (101.120.23.171)
```

You can also use the who command with the am i option to display your current user information:

```
$ who am i
oracle    pts/2         Aug  4 15:30 (vpn-109-150-32-93.brdstn.com)
```

■**Tip** You can also use whoami or the id -un to display information about your current user. Contrast this with the who am i command, which always shows which user you initially used to log on to a server. For example, if you su to a different user, whoami displays your current user status, whereas who am i shows which user you originally logged on to the server as.

How It Works

The who command is important for listing a snapshot of users logged on to the server. An alternative to the who command is the w utility. This shortly named (but powerful) tool is an extension to the who command. Its output is like a combination of the listings from the who, uptime, and ps -a commands. This example uses the w command to eavesdrop on who is logged on to the system and what they are doing:

```
$ w
17:59:54 up 9 days,  5:37,  4 users,  load average: 0.00, 0.00, 0.00
USER      TTY      FROM              LOGIN@   IDLE   JCPU   PCPU WHAT
enehcd    pts/1    vpn-128-156-33-6  12:32    5:46   0.12s  0.12s -bash
evork     pts/2    vpn-129-156-33-6  15:22    34:14  0.01s  0.01s -chmod
aznoga    pts/3    vpn-129-156-32-6  17:22    55:24  0.03s  0.01s -sleep
wroot     pts/4    vpn-129-150-150-  17:48    0.00s  0.02s  0.00s w
```

The first line of the w output is similar to that produced by the uptime command; it shows current time, how long the system has been up, number of users, and system load averages. After the header line, it displays users logged on, from where and what time, how long they've been idle, current job CPU (JCPU), foreground process CPU (PCPU), and what command the user is running.

To specifically look at one user, specify the process name as an option. The following command looks at all oracle accounts logged on to the server:

```
$ w oracle
```

The following output indicates that there are two active oracle users on the box:

```
14:14:58 up 130 days, 21:52,  2 users,  load average: 0.00, 0.00, 0.00
USER      TTY      FROM              LOGIN@   IDLE   JCPU   PCPU WHAT
oracle    pts/1    63-231-82-100.hl  13:10    0.00s  0.03s  0.00s w oracle
oracle    pts/2    63-231-82-100.hl  14:14    6.00s  0.01s  0.01s -bash
```

If user has logged on twice to a server (like in the previous output), you can use the tty command to identify a session. While logged on to one of the oracle sessions, here is the tty command and its output:

```
$ tty
/dev/pts/1
```

You can also use the `finger` command to display information about users logged on to a server. If you don't provide the `finger` command with a username, then it will display all users on a system:

```
$ finger
Login       Name      Tty      Idle  Login Time   Office     Office Phone
oracle                pts/0          Jun 20 13:29 (br-ea-fw-nat.surg.com)
oracle                pts/1       2  Jun 20 13:29 (br-ea-fw-nat.surg.com)
```

The `pinky` command is a lightweight version of the `finger` command. If no users are specified, then all users logged on will be displayed:

```
$ pinky
Login       Name      TTY      Idle  When         Where
oracle                pts/0          Jun 20 13:29 br-ea-fw-nat.surg.com
oracle                pts/1    00:03 Jun 20 13:29 br-ea-fw-nat.surg.com
```

3-4. Listing the Last Logon Time of a User

Problem

You think that somebody may have hacked into the database operating system account. You want to see when the last time the `oracle` account was logged on to the Linux database server.

Solution

Use the `last` command to determine the last login time of a user. This next bit of code determines when the last time the `oracle` account logged on to the database server:

```
$ last oracle
oracle    pts/1      63-227-41-191.hl Fri Dec 21 17:18    still logged in
oracle    pts/1      63-227-41-191.hl Mon Dec 17 15:55 - 17:53  (01:58)
oracle    pts/1      63-227-41-191.hl Mon Dec 17 11:55 - 13:33  (01:38)
oracle    pts/1      63-227-41-191.hl Mon Dec 17 08:28 - 10:45  (02:17)
oracle    pts/0      63-227-41-191.hl Sat Dec 15 20:59 - 22:00  (01:00)
oracle    pts/0      63-227-41-191.hl Sat Dec 15 20:43 - 20:59  (00:15)
```

The output indicates that the `oracle` user is currently logged on and has logged on several times in the month of December.

How It Works

If you use the `last` command without any arguments, then it displays the last logon time of all users. You can pipe the output of `last` to the `less` command to display one page at a time:

```
$ last | less
```

You can also limit the output of `last` by piping its output to the `head` command. The following will display the last ten users logged on:

```
$ last | head
```

■**Tip** The `last` command retrieves its information from the `/var/log/wtmp` file. This file records all logons and logouts on the server.

Another useful command in regard to last logons is the `lastb` utility. This useful command displays a list of recent bad logon attempts. When first using `lastb`, you might see the following output:

```
lastb: /var/log/btmp: No such file or directory
Perhaps this file was removed by the operator to prevent logging lastb info.
```

The previous message means that the `/var/log/btmp` file needs to be created. You can enable `lastb` by running the following commands as root:

```
# touch /var/log/btmp
# chown --reference=/var/log/wtmp /var/log/btmp
# chmod --reference=/var/log/wtmp /var/log/btmp
```

3-5. Limiting the Number of User Processes

Problem

For security purposes, your database installation instructions indicate that you need to limit the number of processes that can be started by the database operating system account. By limiting the number of processes a user can start, you can ensure that no single user can consume inordinate amounts of resources on the server.

Solution

As the root user, add an entry in the `/etc/security/limits.conf` file that restricts the number of concurrently running processes for an operating system account. The following lines of code (in the `limits.conf` file) establishes a soft limit of 2047 and imposes a hard limit of 16,384 processes for the `oracle` operating system user:

```
oracle          soft    nproc           2047
oracle          hard    nproc           16384
```

A soft limit will enforce that at most 2,047 processes can be running simultaneously by the `oracle` operating system user. The `oracle` user can manually override the soft limit (with the `ulimit` command) and increase the limit on the number of processes up to 16,384 processes. Only the root user can modify the hard limit to be higher.

■**Tip** See Chapter 9 for full details on configuring `oracle` shell limits.

How It Works

If you're feeling brave, you can test the maximum number of processes allowed by running this function:

```
: () { :|:& };:
```

The previous bit of code creates a function called : that recursively calls itself and puts its processes in the background. Be warned that you can lock up your system if you don't properly have process limits in place. This type of program is known as a *fork bomb*. It's appropriately named because it continuously creates (forks) new processes on the system. Because the program starts itself in the background, it cannot be stopped by pressing Ctrl+C.

3-6. Viewing How Long the Server Has Been Running

Problem

You want to view how long the server has been running.

Solution

Use the uptime command to determine how long your database server has been running:

```
$ uptime
08:37:00 up 33 days, 16:14,  1 user,  load average: 0.00, 0.00, 0.00
```

From the output, this Linux server has been up for a little more than 33 days.

How It Works

Sometimes when resolving database availability issues, it's helpful to know when the server was last rebooted. That's because (not surprisingly) there's a direct correlation between the server being down and the database being unavailable. Viewing the server uptime can help determine whether the database was unavailable because of a system reboot.

Interestingly, the output of uptime is identical to the first line of the w command. The next example shows running the w command and the corresponding output:

```
$ w
 08:37:01 up 33 days, 16:14,  1 user,  load average: 0.00, 0.00, 0.00
USER     TTY      FROM            LOGIN@   IDLE   JCPU   PCPU WHAT
oracle   pts/0    63-227-41-191.hl 07:11    0.00s  0.06s  0.00s w
```

In the first line of the output, 08:37:01 is the current time on the server. Also displayed in the first line are load averages for the past 1, 5, and 15 minutes.

3-7. Viewing How Long a Process Has Been Running

Problem

You wonder how long the Oracle database background processes have been running.

Solution

Use the ps -ef command to determine how long a process has been running. This next line of code uses ps with the egrep command to find out when the Oracle system monitor process was started:

```
$ ps -ef | egrep 'smon|UID' | egrep -v egrep
UID         PID  PPID  C STIME TTY          TIME CMD
oracle     8843     1  0 Oct31 ?        00:02:33 ora_smon_RMDB1
```

In the previous command, the process status output is filtered by egrep to list any lines that contain either smon or UID. When you filter also for the UID string, this displays the header of the ps command. In the output, the SMON process was started on October 31 and has consumed 2 hours and 33 minutes of CPU on the database server.

How It Works

Sometimes when troubleshooting database problems, it's useful to know when your database was last started. For example, you may have had an unexpected server reboot, which caused the databases to stop and restart. You can verify the time your database process was started by using the ps command.

The following is another slight variation of how DBAs use the process status command:

```
$ ps -ef | grep smon | grep -v grep
oracle     8843     1  0 Oct31 ?        00:02:33 ora_smon_RMDB1
```

The previous command will limit the output to just the specific process that you're interested in observing. The grep -v grep code strips out any lines containing the string grep from the output.

3-8. Displaying Your Username

Problem

You want to display your operating system username.

Solution

Use the id command to display the operating system account you're current logged on as:

```
$ id
```

Listed next is a sample of output. By default, both the user and group information are displayed:

```
uid=56689(oracle) gid=500(oinstall) groups=500(oinstall),501(dba)
```

■**Tip** Use the groups command if you just want to display the groups of your current operating system account.

How It Works

An effective DBA has to be good at multitasking. You'll find yourself logged on to multiple boxes in a myriad of development, test, and production environments. It's easy to lose your bearings, and when you do, you'll then want to identify the operating system account you're currently using. You can instinctively fulfill this need with the id command.

You can also use the who command with the am i option to display the user who you used to log on to the box:

```
$ who am i
oracle    pts/2         Aug  4 15:30 (vpn-109-150-32-93.brdstn.com)
```

You can also use whoami or id -un to display information about your current user, whereas the who am i command shows information about the user you used to originally log on to the box. For example, if you initially log on to a box as oracle and then switch to the root user, the whoami command will display root, whereas the who am i command will display oracle:

```
# who am i
oracle    pts/2         Jun 20 14:20 (br-ea-fw-nat.surg.com)
# whoami
root
```

3-9. Changing Your Password

Problem

You have just been handed a new database server and want to change your password to something more secure than changeme.

Solution

Use the passwd command to change your password. Log on to the user account you want to change the password for and type passwd with no options:

```
$ passwd
```

After you type the passwd command, you will be prompted to type the current password and then to enter the new password twice:

```
Changing password for user oracle.
Changing password for oracle
(current) UNIX password:
New UNIX password:
Retype new UNIX password:
passwd: all authentication tokens updated successfully.
```

How It Works

As a DBA, you'll have to manage the passwords for various operating system accounts on the database servers that you log on to. Use the passwd command to ensure that your database operating system user is secure and available for your use.

If you have access to the root user, you can change passwords for other users. This example changes the password for the oracle operating system user:

```
# passwd oracle
```

You will then be prompted to type a new password for the oracle operating system user:

```
Changing password for user oracle.
New UNIX password:
Retype new UNIX password:
passwd: all authentication tokens updated successfully.
```

To set up additional password security, use the chage program. This utility can be used to set the maximum amount of time that a password is valid. This next example is run as the root user specifies that the oracle user will have to change its password after 60 days:

```
# chage -M 60 oracle
```

To verify the changes to the oracle user, use the -l option:

```
# chage -l oracle
Minimum:          0
Maximum:          90
Warning:          7
Inactive:        -1
Last Change:              Sep 30, 2007
Password Expires:         Dec 29, 2007
Password Inactive:        Never
Account Expires:          Never
```

The chage utility is part of the Shadow Password Suite. This suite includes programs such as chfn, chpasswd, chsh, dpasswd, expiry, faillog, and so on. You can add this group of programs to your system to provide extra security. These utilities allow you to encrypt user passwords in the /etc/shadow file. This shadow file is readable only with root privileges.

3-10. Becoming the System Privileged (root) User

Problem

You're installing Oracle on a database server. You don't have a system administrator. You need to become root (sometimes referred to as the *superuser*) so that you can add new operating system groups and user accounts.

Solution

You have to access to the root user password for this recipe to work. Use the su - command to switch to the root account. The - (hyphen) option specifies that the target user's login shell will be invoked (runs all login scripts of the target user):

```
$ su - root
```

You should now see a prompt similar to this:

```
Password:
```

After a successful logon, your shell prompt will change to the # character (on most Linux systems) indicating you are now logged on as root:

```
#
```

You can now perform such tasks as adding the groups and users required for the database installation. To exit from the root user, type the following:

```
# exit
```

Note You can also press Ctrl+D to exit a shell login.

How It Works

Some database installation tasks require root privileges. Sometimes there isn't an SA available to perform these tasks, or your system administrator might be comfortable with temporarily providing you access with the root account. However, competent system administrators rarely give out the root password to DBAs (or any non-SA users, for that matter). There are several problems with providing carte blanche superuser access:

- It's hard to trace who did what on the system

- Security is better administered by granting privileges on an "as-needed" basis and not through wide-open system access.

If several people have direct access to the root password and one of them logs on to the system and accidentally removes critical files, it's hard to tell who did the damaging deed. For this reason, SAs do not usually provide direct root access. Rather, they provide auditable and/or limited access to root privileges through the sudo command (see recipe 3-11 for details).

3-11. Running Commands As the root User

Problem

You want to access to commands that can be run only by root, but your security-conscious system administrator won't give you the root password.

Solution

Have your system administrator insert the appropriate entries in the /etc/sudoers file to grant access to restricted commands. You can be granted complete root access or can be granted access to only specified commands.

As the root user, use the visudo command to add an entry to the /etc/sudoers file. The visudo command ensures that the /etc/sudoers file is edited in a secure fashion. When using visudo, the sudoers file is locked to disallow multiple users from simultaneously editing the file. The visudo command will also perform a syntax check on any edits to the /etc/sudoers file and will save only correct entries.

For example, your SA can provide root access to the oracle account by adding the following line to the /etc/sudoers file:

```
oracle ALL=(ALL) ALL
```

The oracle account can use sudo to execute commands (that would otherwise be required to run as the root user). For example, the groupadd command can now be run by oracle as follows:

```
$ sudo /usr/sbin/groupadd dba
```

The first time you run sudo, you will be prompted for your password (not the root password). For a short period of time (by default, five minutes), you will be able to run sudo without being prompted for your password again.

You can also specify that only certain commands can be run with root privileges. For example, if your system administrator wanted to limit the oracle account to the commands that add groups and users, then the /etc/sudoers entry would be as follows:

```
oracle ALL=/usr/sbin/groupadd,/usr/sbin/useradd
```

This method allows your SA to limit access to specific commands that require root privileges. You can view the commands you are allowed to run as sudo with the following command:

```
$ sudo -l
```

The following output shows that this server has been configured to allow the oracle account to run the following commands:

```
User oracle may run the following commands on this host:
    (root) /usr/sbin/groupadd
    (root) /usr/sbin/useradd
```

How It Works

The sudo command allows a command to be executed as the root user. The sudo permissions are maintained in the /etc/sudoers file by the system administrator.

One compelling reason for using sudo is that it allows your SA to grant superuser access without having to give out the root password. This allows system administrators to temporarily grant root access to consultants who may have short-term assignments and require root access. SAs can also quickly revoke root access by deleting the appropriate entry from the /etc/sudoers file without affecting other users.

Another advantage of using sudo is that it provides an audit trail. An entry is written to a system log file in the /var/log directory whenever a sudo command is issued. Additionally, you can specify a log file for sudo activity by placing the following line in the /etc/sudoers file:

```
Defaults logfile=/var/log/sudolog
```

After successfully adding the previous line to the /etc/sudoers file, all commands run as sudo will be logged on to /var/log/sudolog.

3-12. Adding a Group

Problem

You're performing a database installation and need to add an operating system group.

Solution

Use the groupadd command to add operating system groups. Typical Oracle installations require that you add two groups named oinstall and dba. If you have root access, you can run the groupadd command as shown here:

```
# groupadd oinstall
# groupadd dba
```

If you don't have access to a root account, then you'll need to get your system administrator to run the commands in this recipe. Sometimes SAs are amenable to granting root access via the sudo command (see recipe 3-11 for details).

If you have a company requirement that a group be set up with the same group ID on different servers, then use the -g option. This example explicitly sets the group ID to 505:

```
# groupadd -g 505 dba
```

Sometimes it's desirable to consistently create groups with the same group ID across multiple servers. For example, in Network File System (NFS) environments, you might encounter permission problems unless the group is set up with the same group ID across multiple servers.

How It Works

Sometimes as a DBA you will be required to perform system administration tasks such as adding (or deleting) users and adding (or deleting) groups. This is because in some environments, you may not have an SA available. Or you might be installing database software on your home Linux box (and you are the system administrator). Regardless of the situation, you should be familiar with these types of tasks so that you're able to build and maintain your database server.

You can verify that the group was added successfully by inspecting the contents of the /etc/group file. Here are the entries created in the /etc/group file after running the commands in the "Solution" section of this recipe:

```
oinstall:x:500:
dba:x:501:
```

If for any reason you need to remove a group, then use the groupdel command (see recipe 3-13 for details). If you need to modify a group, use the groupmod command.

■**Tip** If you have access to an X Window terminal, you may want to investigate using the system-config-users utility. This is a graphical tool that allows you to add and delete users and groups.

3-13. Removing a Group

Problem

You want to clean up a database server and remove an old dba operating system group.

Solution

Use the groupdel command to remove operating system groups. This command requires root access. The following command will delete the dba group:

```
# groupdel dba
```

If you don't have access to a root account, then you'll need to get your system administrator to run the commands in this recipe. Sometimes SAs are willing to granting root access via the sudo command (see recipe 3-11 for details).

How It Works

You will not be prompted on whether you really want to delete a group, so make certain you really want to delete a group before using the groupdel command. You can view the /etc/group file to verify that the group has been deleted.

■**Note** You cannot remove a group that is a user's primary group. You must first modify or delete the users who have the group to be deleted (so that the group isn't the primary group of any user on the system).

3-14. Adding a User

Problem

You're doing a database installation and need to create an operating system user.

Solution

Use the useradd command to add operating system users. This command requires root access. The following command will create an operating system account named oracle, with the primary group being oinstall and the dba group specified as a supplementary group:

```
# useradd -g oinstall -G dba oracle
```

If you don't have access to a root account, then you'll need to get your system administrator to run the commands in this recipe. Sometimes SAs are agreeable to granting root access via the sudo command (see recipe 3-11 for details).

If you have a company requirement that a user be set up with the same user ID across multiple servers, use the -u option. This example explicitly sets the user ID to 500:

```
# useradd -u 500 -g oinstall -G dba
```

Sometimes it's desirable to consistently create a user with the same user ID on different servers. For example, in Network File System (NFS) environments, you might encounter permission problems unless the user is set up with the same user ID on all servers.

How It Works

Sometimes as a DBA you will have to perform system administration type tasks such as adding (or deleting) users and adding (or deleting) groups. In some environments, you may not have an SA available. Or you might be installing database software on your home Linux box. Regardless of the situation, you should be familiar with these types of tasks so that you're better able to build and maintain your database server.

You can verify user account information by viewing the /etc/passwd file. Here is what you can expect to see after running the useradd command in the "Solution" section of this recipe:

```
oracle:x:500:500::/home/oracle:/bin/bash
```

When creating a new user, the /etc/skel directory contains the files and directories that are automatically created for a new users added to the server with the useradd command. Typical files included are .bashrc, .bash_profile, and .bash_logout. The location of the /etc/skel file can be changed by modifying the value of SKEL in the /etc/default/useradd file.

The userdel command can be used to delete a user (see recipe 3-15 for details). Use the usermod command to modify existing accounts.

■**Tip** If you have access to an X Window terminal, you may want to investigate using the system-config-users utility. This is a graphical tool that allows you to add and delete users and groups.

3-15. Removing a User

Problem

You want to clean up a server and remove an old oracle operating system account.

Solution

Use the userdel command to remove an operating system account. You need root privileges to run the userdel command. This example removes the oracle user from the server:

```
# userdel oracle
```

If you don't have access to a root account, then you'll need to get your system administrator to run the commands in this recipe. Sometimes SAs are open to granting root access via the sudo command (see recipe 3-11 for details).

How It Works

You will not be prompted on whether you really want to delete a user, so make certain you absolutely want to remove a user before using the userdel command. You can view the /etc/passwd file to verify that the user has been deleted (by the absence of the user).

You can also instruct the userdel -r command to remove the user's home directory and any files in that location. This example removes the oracle account and its home directory:

```
$ userdel oracle -r
```

Before you use this command, make sure the user doesn't need any of the files in the user's home directory tree ever again. You can use a command like tar to do a quick backup of the files in a user's home directory (see Chapter 6 for details).

CHAPTER 4

■ ■ ■

Creating and Editing Files

If you want to survive in a Linux environment, then you must be adept with at least one command-line text editor. DBAs use text editors on a daily basis to manipulate database initialization files, create scripts to automate tasks, modify operating system scheduler jobs, and so on. In a Linux shop, you won't be able to do a good job as a database administrator unless you're proficient with a text editor.

Dozens of text editors are available. To that end, there have been entire books written on text editors available in Linux/Unix environments. The three most common command-line text editors in use are vi, Vim, and emacs. This chapter focuses on the vi text editor (pronounced "vee-eye" or sometimes "vie"). We chose to concentrate on this editor for the following reasons:

- The vi editor is universally available on all Linux/Unix systems.

- DBAs tend to use vi more than any other editor.

- You can't consider yourself a true Linux geek unless you know vi.

The goal of this chapter is to give you enough information to efficiently use the vi editor. We don't cover every facet of vi; rather, we focus on the features that you'll find yourself using most often to perform daily editing tasks. When you first use vi, you may soon wonder why anybody would use such a confusing text-editing tool. To neophytes, many aspects of vi will initially seem counterintuitive. Not to worry, with some explanation, examples, and hands-on practice, you'll learn how to use this editing tool to efficiently create and manipulate text files. This chapter contains more than enough material to get you started with vi. The problems described are the most commonly encountered editing tasks.

If you are new to vi, we strongly encourage you to not just read the solutions in this chapter but actually to start up a vi session and practice entering the commands shown in the examples. It's like riding a bicycle, and you can't learn how to ride until you physically get on the bike and attempt to go forward. It's the same with vi. You can't just read about how to use this tool; you have to type commands before the learning takes place.

■**Note** All the solutions and examples in this chapter also work nearly identically with the Vim editor. The vi-improved (Vim) editor provides many enhancements to vi.

4-1. Creating a File

Problem

You need to create a text file.

Solution

To create a file named foo.txt, run the vi utility from the command line, as shown here:

```
$ vi foo.txt
```

You should now see a blank screen with several tilde (~) graphemes displayed in the far-left column of the screen. Within a file being edited by vi, the ~ character indicates a line that has no text on it. Depending on your version of vi, you may see the name of your file in the bottom-left corner:

```
"foo.txt" [New file]
```

To enter text, first type i. You can now enter text into the file. To save your changes and exit from vi, first press the Esc key, and then type :wq for write and quit:

```
:wq
```

You should now be back at the operating system command prompt. You can verify that the new file has been created with the ls command:

```
$ ls foo.txt
foo.txt
```

Note See recipe 4-2 to learn how to move your cursor around within a file.

How It Works

The most common way to start vi is by providing it with a file name to operate on:

```
$ vi <filename>
```

Several options are available when first invoking vi. Table 4-1 lists some of the more commonly used command-line choices.

Once you've started a vi session, it's critical to understand that there are two distinct operating modes:

- Command mode

- Insert mode

Table 4-1. *Some Helpful* vi *Command-Line Startup Options*

Option	Action
vi	Starts editing session in memory.
vi <file>	Starts session and opens the specified file.
vi <file>*	Opens first file that matches the wildcard pattern. Use :n to navigate to the next matched file.
view <file>	Opens file in read-only mode.
vi -R <file>	Opens file in read-only mode.
vi -r <file>	Recovers file and recent edits after abnormal abort from editing session (like a system crash).
vi +n <file>	Opens file at specified line number n.
vi + <file>	Opens file at the last line.
vi +/<pattern> <file>	Opens file at first occurrence of specified string pattern.

The vi editor behaves very differently dependent on its mode. When you first enter vi, you are by default in *command* mode. In this mode, you can enter commands that control the behavior of vi. For example, you can issue commands to do the following:

- Save a file.

- Enter insert mode.

- Exit vi.

When in command mode, everything you enter is interpreted as a command by vi. You cannot enter text into your file while in command mode. You must place vi in *insert* mode before you can start entering text. Table 4-2 lists several methods of placing vi in insert mode. Keep in mind that these commands are case sensitive. For example, the A command comprises pressing the Shift and A keys simultaneously.

Table 4-2. *Common Techniques to Enter* vi *Insert Mode*

Enter Insert Command	Action
i	Insert text in front of the cursor.
a	Insert text after the cursor.
I	Insert text at the beginning of the line.
A	Insert text at the end of the line.
o	Insert text below the current line.
O	Insert text above the current line.

The easiest way to change from command mode to insert mode is to press i on the keyboard. This allows you to begin entering text at the place on the screen where your cursor is currently located. When in vi insert mode, you can perform two activities:

- Enter text.

- Exit from insert mode.

While in insert mode, you should see text at the bottom of your screen indicating that you are in the correct mode (this may vary depending on your version of vi):

```
-- INSERT --
```

You can now enter any desired text into the file. Everything you type will be interpreted by vi as text that you want entered into the file.

To exit from insert mode (and back to command mode), press the Esc key. There's nothing wrong with pressing Esc multiple times (other than wasting energy). If you are already in command mode and press the Esc key, you may hear a bell or a beep.

You can exit from vi (back to the operating system prompt) once you are in command mode. To save the file and exit, type :wq (write quit):

```
:wq
```

If you've made changes to a file and want to exit without saving, then type :q!, as shown here:

```
:q!
```

Table 4-3 details some of the more common exit methods. Keep in mind that you have to be in command mode before you can type a vi exit command. If you don't know what mode you're in, press the Esc key to ensure you're in command mode. Notice that these commands are case sensitive. For example, the ZZ command is executed by simultaneously pressing the Shift key and the Z key twice.

Table 4-3. *Useful vi Exit Commands*

Exit Command	Action
:wq	Save and exit.
ZZ	Save and exit.
:x	Save and exit.
:w	Save the current edits without exiting.
:w!	Override file protections and save.
:q	Exit the file.
:q!	Exit without saving.
:n	Edit next file.
:e!	Return to previously saved version.

4-2. Maneuvering Within a File

Problem

You want to navigate efficiently within a text file while editing with vi.

Solution

The most intuitive way to move around is by using the up/down/right/left arrows. These keys will work whether you are in command mode or insert mode. However, you may encounter some keyboards on which the up/down/left/right arrows don't work. In those cases, you'll have to use the J, K, H, and L keys to move you down, up, left, and right respectively. You must be in command mode to navigate with these keys. If you're in insert mode and try to use these keys, you'll get a bunch of jjj kkkkk hhh llll letters on your screen.

Using these keys may seem cumbersome at first. However, you'll notice after some time that you can navigate quickly using these keys because you don't have to move your fingers from their natural typing positions.

How It Works

You can use a myriad of commands for moving around in a text file. Some of these commands may seem confusing. However, with a little practice, the navigational commands will soon become second nature to you. Keep in mind that the vi editor was designed to allow you to perform most tasks without having to move your hands from the standard keyboard position.

Table 4-4 contains commonly used commands to navigate within vi. Remember that you must be in command mode for these keystrokes to work. Notice that these commands are case sensitive. For example, to navigate to the top of the page, use the 1G command, which is comprised of first pressing the 1 key and then simultaneously pressing the Shift and G keys.

Table 4-4. *Common Navigation Commands*

Command	Action
j (or down arrow)	Move down a line.
k (or up arrow)	Move up a line.
h (or left arrow)	Move one character left.
l (or right arrow)	Move one character right.
Ctrl+f (or Page Down)	Scroll down one screen.
Ctrl+b (or Page Up)	Scroll up one screen.
1G	Go to first line in file.
G	Go to last line in file.
nG	Go to n line number.
H	Go to top of screen.
L	Go to bottom of screen.

Table 4-4. *Common Navigation Commands (Continued)*

Command	Action
w	Move one word forward.
b	Move one word backward.
0	Go to start of line.
$	Go to end of line.

4-3. Copying and Pasting

Problem

You want to copy and paste text from one section of the file to another.

Solution

Use the yy command to yank (copy) lines of text. Use the p command to put (paste) lines of text elsewhere in the file. As with all vi commands, ensure that you are in command mode (press the Esc key) before using a command. The following example copies five lines of text from the current line that the cursor is on and four lines below the current line (for a total of five lines):

5yy

You should see an informational line at the bottom of the screen indicating success (or not) of placing the copied lines in the copy buffer:

5 lines yanked

To paste the lines that have been copied, use the p command. To put the lines beneath the current line your cursor is on, ensure you are in command mode, and issue the p command:

p

You should see an information line at the bottom that indicates the lines were pasted below the line your cursor is on:

5 more lines

How It Works

Copying and pasting are two of the most common tasks when editing a file. Sometimes you may want to cut and paste. This task is similar to the copying and pasting example in the "Solution" section of this recipe. Instead of using the yy command, use the dd (delete) command. For example, to cut five lines of text (inclusive with the line your cursor is currently on), issue the dd command:

5dd

You should see a message at the bottom of the screen indicating that the lines have been cut (deleted):

```
5 fewer lines
```

Those lines are now in the buffer and can be pasted anywhere in the file. Navigate to the line you want to place the previously cut lines after, and press the p command:

```
p
```

You should see an informational line at the bottom that indicates the lines were pasted after the line your cursor is on:

```
5 more lines
```

There are many commands for cutting and pasting text. Table 4-5 describes the copying, cutting, and pasting commands. Notice that these commands are case sensitive. For example, use the X command to delete one character to the left of the cursor, which means pressing the Shift and X keys simultaneously.

Table 4-5. *Common Options for Copying, Deleting, and Pasting Text*

Option	Action
yy	Yank (copy) the current line.
nyy	Yank (copy) n number of lines.
p	Put yanked line(s) below the cursor.
P	Put yanked line(s) above the cursor.
x	Delete the character that the cursor is on.
X	Delete the character to the left of the cursor.
dw	Delete the word the cursor is currently on.
dd	Delete current line of text.
ndd	Delete n lines of text
D	Delete to the end of the current line.

4-4. Manipulating Text

Problem

You wonder whether there are some commands to modify the current text you're working on, such as changing a character from lowercase to uppercase.

Solution

Use the ~ (tilde) command to change the case of a character. For example, say you have a string in a file with the text of oracle and you want to change it to Oracle. Place your cursor over the o character. Hit the Esc key to ensure that you're in command mode. Type the ~ character (which requires you to press the Shift key and the ~ key at the same time). You should see the case of the character change from o to 0.

How It Works

Several commands are available for manipulating text. Table 4-6 lists common options used to change text. Notice that these commands are case sensitive. For example, the C command is executed by pressing the Shift and C keys simultaneously.

Table 4-6. *Common Options for Changing Text*

Option	Action
r	Replace the character that the curser is on with the next character you type.
~	Change the case of a character.
cc	Delete the current line and insert text.
C	Delete to the end of the line and insert text.
c$	Delete to the end of the line and insert text.
cw	Delete to the end of the word and insert text.
R	Type over the characters in the current line.
s	Delete the current character and insert text.
S	Delete the current line and insert text.

4-5. Searching for and Replacing Text

Problem

You want to search for all occurrences of a string and replace it with another string.

Solution

If you want to search only for a string, then use the / command. The following example searches for the string ora01 in the file:

/ora01

To search for the next occurrence of the string, use the n (next) command:

n

To search backward for a previous occurrence of the string, use the N command:

N

If you want to search for text and replace it, then use the s option to search for text, and replace it with an alternate string. The following example searches for the string ora01 and replaces it with ora02 everywhere in the file:

```
:%s/ora001/ora02/g
```

All occurrences of ora01 should now be displayed as ora02.

How It Works

Searching for strings is one of the most common tasks you'll perform while editing database initialization files. Table 4-7 lists some of the more common options for searching for text.

Table 4-7. *Common Options for Text Searching*

Option	Action
/<pattern>	Search forward for a string.
?<pattern>	Search backward for a string.
n	Repeat the search forward.
N	Repeat the search backward.
f<character>	Search forward for a character in the current line.
F<character>	Search backward for a character in the current line.

4-6. Inserting One File into Another

Problem

While within vi, you want to copy in another file that exists in the current working directory.

Solution

Use the :r command to read in a file. This has the effect of copying in a file and pasting it starting at the current cursor location. This next example reads a file named tnsnames.ora into the current file:

```
:r tnsnames.ora
```

The previous example assumes that the tnsnames.ora file is in your current working directory. If the file you want to bring in is not in your current working directory, then you'll need to specify a path name. This example reads in a file from a directory that is not the current working directory:

```
:r /oracle/product/11.1/network/admin/tnsnames.ora
```

If you have an operating system variable that contains a path, you can use that directly. This example copies in a file contained in a path specified by a variable:

```
:r $TNS_ADMIN/tnsnames.ora
```

How It Works

You'll often find the need to insert the content of a file into the current file you're editing. Doing so is a quick and easy way to add text to your current file that you know is stored correctly in a separate file.

You have a few other interesting ways to read in files. The next example copies in a file and places it at the beginning of the current file:

```
:0r tnsnames.ora
```

The following bit of code reads in the file at the end of the current file:

```
:$r tnsnames.ora
```

4-7. Joining Lines

Problem

You have one line of text just after the current line you are editing. You want to join the text after the current line to the end of the current line.

Solution

First ensure you are in command mode by pressing the Esc key. Next place your cursor on the first line that you want to join with the line after it. Then type the J (capital J) command to join the end of the current line to the start of the line after it.

An example will help illustrate this concept. Say you have these two sentences in a file:

```
select table_name
from dba_tables;
```

If you want to join the first line to the second line, place your cursor anywhere on the first line, and type the following:

```
J
```

You should now see both lines joined together:

```
select table_name from dba_tables;
```

How It Works

You'll use the J command often to join two lines of code together in a text file. You can also join any number of consecutive lines. For example, say you have the following three lines in a file:

```
select
username
from dba_users;
```

You want the three lines to be joined together on one line. First place your cursor anywhere on the first line, and then while in command mode type the following:

```
3J
```

You should now see the three lines joined together, as shown here:

```
select username from dba_users;
```

4-8. Running Operating System Commands

Problem

While editing text within vi, you want to run an operating system command.

Solution

First make sure you are in command mode by entering the Esc key. Use the : ! command to run operating system commands. For example, the following bit of code runs the operating system date command without exiting vi:

```
:!date
```

Here is the output for this example:

```
Sat Feb 10 14:22:45 MST 2008
~
Hit ENTER or type command to continue
```

Press the Enter or Return key to place you back into vi command mode. To read the output of date directly into the file you're editing, use this syntax:

```
:r !date
```

How It Works

Running operating system commands from within vi saves you the hassle of having to exit the utility, run the OS command, and then reenter the utility. DBAs commonly use this technique to perform tasks such as listing files in a directory, printing the date, or copying files.

The following example runs the ls (list) command from within vi to view files in the current working directory:

```
:!ls
```

Once the file of interest is identified, then you can read it in with the : r syntax. This example reads the script1.sql file into the file currently being edited:

```
:r script1.sql
```

If you want to temporarily place yourself at the shell prompt and run several operating system commands, then type your favorite shell with the : ! syntax. The following example enters the Bash shell:

```
:!bash
```

To return to vi, use the exit command to log out of the shell. At this point, you need to hit the Enter or Return key to return to vi command mode:

```
Hit ENTER or type command to continue
```

4-9. Repeating a Command

Problem

You find yourself typing commands over and over again. You wonder whether there is a way to repeat the previously entered command.

Solution

Use the . (period) command to repeat the previously entered command. For example, suppose you delete a large section of code but only want to delete ten lines at time. To achieve this, first ensure you're in command mode (by pressing the Esc key), and then enter the following:

```
10dd
```

To repeat the previous command, type a period:

```
.
```

You should see another ten lines deleted. This technique allows you to quickly repeat the previously run command.

How It Works

You can use the . command to repeat any previously typed command. You'll use the repeat command feature quite often. It will save you a great deal of time and typing. If you find yourself often retyping lengthy commands, consider creating a shortcut to the keystrokes (see recipe 4-13 for details).

4-10. Undoing a Command

Problem

You want to undo the last command you typed.

Solution

To undo the last command or text typed, use the u command. Make sure you are in command mode, and type u, as shown here:

```
u
```

You should see the effects of the command that was typed in previously to the u command being undone.

How It Works

The u command is handy for undoing the previous command. If you want to undo all commands entered on one line, use the U command. The U command operates only on the last line you changed. Your cursor must be on the last line you changed for this command to work.

If you want to undo changes since the last time you saved the file, type the following:

```
:e!
```

Sometimes the previous command is handy if you want to undo all edits to a file and start over. This is quicker than exiting the file with the :q! (quit without saving) command and reopening the file.

■**Note** The behavior of u and U may slightly vary depending on your version of vi. For example, with vim, you can use the u command to undo several previous edits.

4-11. Displaying Line Numbers

Problem

You want to display line numbers in your text file.

Solution

Use the set number command. The following command will change the screen to display the line number on the left side of each row:

```
:set number
```

You should now see line numbers on the left side of the screen. The following is a snippet from the init.ora file with the set number option enabled:

```
1 db_name=RMDB1
2 db_block_size=8192
3 compatible=10.2.0.1.0
4 pga_aggregate_target=200M
5 workarea_size_policy=AUTO
6 sga_max_size=400M
7 sga_target=400M
8 processes=200
```

How It Works

Sometimes when you're dealing with files, it's nice to see a line number to assist with debugging. Use the set number and set nonumber commands to toggle the number display.

Tip Press Ctrl+G (the Ctrl and G keys pressed simultaneously) to display the current line number.

4-12. Automatically Configuring Settings

Problem

You want to configure vi to start up with certain settings. For example, you'd like to have vi always start up in the mode of displaying line numbers.

Solution

If you want to customize vi to automatically show line numbers, then create a file named .exrc in your home directory, and place the desired settings within it. The following example creates a file named .exrc in the home directory:

```
$ vi $HOME/.exrc
```

Enter the following text in the .exrc file:

```
set number
```

From now on, every time you start vi, the .exrc file will be read, and the settings within it will be reflected in the files being edited.

How It Works

Setting the line numbers to automatically appear is just one aspect that you can configure in the .exrc file. To view all settable attributes in your environment, issue the following command within vi:

```
:set all
```

Here is a very small snippet of the output:

```
--- Options ---
ambiwidth=single     joinspaces          softtabstop=0
noautoindent         keywordprg=man -s   startofline
noautoread           nolazyredraw        swapfile
noautowrite          lines=30            swapsync=fsync
noautowriteall       nolist              switchbuf=
background=light      listchars=eol:$     tabstop=8
```

Notice that options that expect a value contain an = sign in the output. To view the current setting of a feature, use set and the option name. This example displays the term setting:

```
:set term
term=cygwin
```

To view which options are different from the defaults, use the set command with no options:

```
:set
```

■**Tip** You can also put shortcuts for commands in your .exrc file. Recipe 4-13 describes how to create command shortcuts (also referred to as *command maps*).

4-13. Creating Shortcuts for Commands

Problem

You find yourself using a certain command over and over again. You wonder whether there's a way to create a shortcut for the command.

Solution

Use the map command to create a shortcut for a sequence of keystrokes. One set of keystrokes that is typed often is xp. This command will transpose two characters (it performs a delete and then a put). This example creates a macro for the xp command:

```
:map t xp
```

You can now use the t command to perform the same function as the xp command.

How It Works

Mapping commands is a useful way of creating shortcuts for frequently used sequences of keystrokes. If you want mappings defined for each vi session, then place the mappings in your .exrc file (see recipe 4-12 for details).

To view all defined mappings, type :map without any arguments:

```
:map
```

To disable a mapping, use the :unmap command. The following example disables the t mapping:

```
:unmap t
```

4-14. Setting the Default Editor

Problem

You're editing the cron table on a new database server. The default editor used for cron is emacs. You want to set your default editor to be vi.

Solution

Use the `export` command to set the default editor. The following example sets the default editor to the `vi` utility:

```
$ export EDITOR=vi
```

How It Works

Some utilities like `cron` inspect the operating system `EDITOR` variable to determine which editor to use. Some older systems may use the `VISUAL` variable as well. The following lines can be placed in your `HOME/.bashrc` startup file to ensure that the editor is automatically set when logging in:

```
export EDITOR=vi
export VISUAL=$EDITOR
```

We recommend that you set both the `EDITOR` and `VISUAL` variables because some utilities (like SQL*Plus) will reference one or the other.

SETTING THE SQL*PLUS DEFAULT TEXT EDITOR

In Oracle you can specify the default text editor used by SQL*Plus by defining its `_EDITOR` variable. This example sets the default editor to be used by a SQL*PLUS session:

```
SQL> define _EDITOR=vi
```

The `_EDITOR` variable can be defined in the `glogin.sql` server profile or the `login.sql` user profile. The `glogin.sql` file is located in the `ORACLE_HOME/sqlplus/admin` directory. In Linux, the `login.sql` is executed if it exists in a directory contained within the `SQLPATH` variable. If the `SQLPATH` variable hasn't been defined, then SQL*Plus will look for `login.sql` in the current working directory from which SQL*Plus was invoked.

If the `_EDITOR` variable is not set, then the operating system `EDITOR` variable will be used to set the SQL*Plus editor. If the `EDITOR` variable is not set, then the `VISUAL` variable setting will be used. If neither the `EDITOR` nor `VISUAL` variable is set, then the `ed` editor will be used as the default.

CHAPTER 5

■■■

Managing Files and Directories

An intricate part of every Oracle DBA's job involves dealing with files and directories. Therefore, database administrators must be experts with manipulating files. Your job requires skills such as implementing database security, performing backups and recovery, monitoring, and troubleshooting performance issues. These critical tasks are all dependent on a command-line knowledge of managing files. Expert DBAs must know how to administer files and navigate within the filesystem.

The basic building block of a Linux system is a *file*. A file is a container for information stored on disk. You access a file by its *file name*. We use the terms *file* and *file name* synonymously in this book. File names can be up to 256 characters long and can contain regular letters, numbers, and the ., _, and - characters.

A *directory* is like a folder; its purpose is to provide a logical container that facilitates working with groups of files. Every Linux system has a root directory indicated by a forward slash (/); think of the forward slash as a tree falling forward from left to right. This is the topmost directory on every Linux server. The / directory is like an upside-down tree where the trunk is the root directory and the branches of the tree are subdirectories. Figure 5-1 shows some of the more common subdirectory structures used on a Linux database server.

Be aware that Figure 5-1 shows only a fraction of the directories typically created. The main point of the diagram is to give you an idea of the treelike directory structure that is used for a Linux database server. Because of the complexity of the directory structures, database administrators must be fluent with command-line directory navigation and file manipulation.

This chapter shows common problems and solutions you'll encounter when working with files and directories. It starts with the basics such as viewing directory structures and then progresses to more complicated topics such as finding certain types of files.

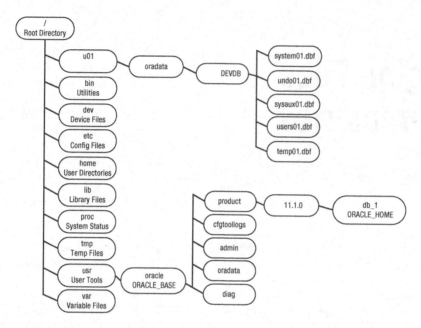

Figure 5-1. *Some common directories used on a Linux database server*

5-1. Showing the Current Working Directory

Problem

You want to view the current directory path.

Solution

Use the pwd (print working directory) command to display the full path name of your current working directory:

```
$ pwd
/home/oracle
```

From the previous output, /home/oracle is the current working directory.

■ **Note** If you're a Windows user, the Linux pwd command is similar to the DOS cd command when issued with no options. The DOS cd command without any options will simply print the current working directory.

How It Works

In Linux, the directory you are working in is defined to be your *current working directory*. The pwd command isn't very complicated; it simply prints the current working directory. As simple as it is, you'll find yourself using it all the time. DBAs constantly use this command to verify that they are in the correct directory. Before you manipulate directories or files, it's wise to verify that you are where you think you should be.

The pwd command has two interesting options: -L and -P. The -L option prints the logical path and is the default. The -L option always prints the value of the operating system PWD variable. For example, the following two commands always display the same directory:

```
$ echo $PWD
/home/oracle
$ pwd
/home/oracle
```

The -P option prints the actual physical path. These options are useful if you're working on systems that have directories that have been navigated to via a symbolic link (see recipe 5-33 for a discussion on soft links). The -L option will print the directory name as defined by the symbolic link. The -P option will display the directory as defined by the actual physical path.

An example will help illustrate the value of knowing when to use the -P option. On a database server, we have a symbolic link defined to be oradev that exists under the root directory. Here is an example of the long listing of the symbolic link:

```
$ ls -altr /oradev
lrwxrwxrwx  1 root root 9 Apr 15 19:49  oradev -> /oradisk2
```

First you navigate to the directory via the symbolic link and issue a pwd command with the -L option:

```
$ cd /oradev
$ pwd -L
/oradev
```

Now without changing directories, you use the pwd command with the -P option:

```
$ pwd -P
/oradisk2
```

If you work in environments that use symbolic links, then it's important to understand the difference between the -L and -P options of the pwd command.

5-2. Changing Directories

Problem

You want to change your current working directory to a different location.

Solution

Use the cd (change directory) command to navigate within the filesystem. The basic syntax for this command is as follows:

```
cd <directory>
```

This example changes the current working directory to /oracle/product/10.2:

```
$ cd /oracle/product/10.2
```

It's usually a good idea to use the pwd command to verify that the cd command worked as expected:

```
$ pwd
/oracle/product/10.2
```

You can also navigate to a directory path that is stored in an operating system variable. The next set of commands displays the contents of the TNS_ADMIN variable and then navigates to that directory:

```
$ echo $TNS_ADMIN
/oracle/product/10.2/network/admin
$ cd $TNS_ADMIN
$ pwd
/oracle/product/10.2/network/admin
```

If you attempt to navigate to a directory doesn't exist, then you'll receive an error similar to this:

```
No such file or directory
```

Also, for any directories that you own, you must minimally have execute permission on the directory before you can navigate to it. For example, listed next are the permissions for a scripts directory that oracle owns:

```
$ ls -ld scripts
d---rwxrwx  2 oracle oinstall 4096 Jul 30 19:26 scripts
```

You receive this error when attempting to navigate to the scripts directory:

```
$ cd scripts
-bash: cd: scripts: Permission denied
```

If you modify the directory to include the owner execute permission, you can now navigate to it successfully:

```
$ chmod 100 scripts
$ cd scripts
```

How It Works

The cd command is a powerful utility that you'll use often in your DBA life. The following sections contain techniques to make you more effective when using this command.

Navigating HOME

If you don't supply a directory to the cd command, then by default the directory will be changed to the value in the variable of HOME. The next example demonstrates this concept by viewing the current directory and then by displaying the value of HOME and using cd to navigate to that directory:

```
$ pwd
/oracle/product/10.2
```

Next, display the contents of the HOME variable:

```
$ echo $HOME
/home/oracle
```

Now change directories to the value contained in HOME by not supplying a directory name to the cd command:

```
$ cd
$ pwd
/home/oracle
```

In the Bash and Korn shells, the tilde (~) character is a synonym for the value contained in the HOME operating system variable. The following two lines of code will also change your directory to the HOME directory:

```
$ cd ~
$ cd $HOME
```

Navigating to the Parent Directory

The .. (two periods) directory entry contains the value of the parent directory of the current working directory. If you want to change your directory to the parent directory, then use the following syntax:

```
$ cd ..
```

You can navigate up as many parent directories as there are in a given path by separating the .. strings with a forward slash character. For example, to navigate up three directories up, use this command syntax:

```
$ cd ../../..
```

You can also use the .. directory entry to navigate up a directory tree and then down to a different subdirectory. In the following example, the current working directory is /home/oracle/scripts, and the cd command is used to navigate to /home/oracle/bin:

```
$ pwd
/home/oracle/scripts
$ cd ../bin
$ pwd
/home/oracle/bin
```

Navigating to a Subdirectory

To navigate to a subdirectory, specify the directory name without a forward slash in front of it. This example first prints the current working directory, then navigates to the admin subdirectory, and finally verifies success with the pwd command:

```
$ pwd
/home/oracle
$ cd admin
$ pwd
/home/oracle/admin
```

Using Wildcards

You can also use the wildcard asterisk (*) character with the cd command to navigate to other directories. In this next example, the current working directory is /oracle, and the product subdirectory is the target directory:

```
$ cd p*
$ pwd
/oracle/product
```

When navigating to a subdirectory, you must specify enough of the directory to make its name unique to any other subdirectories beneath the current working directory. If multiple directories match a wildcard string, depending on your version of Linux, you may or may not get the desired directory navigation. Always verify your current working directory with the pwd command.

You can also use the Tab key to complete keystroke sequences. For example, if you have only one subdirectory that starts with the letter p, you can cd to it as follows:

```
$ cd p<Tab>
```

In this example, there is only one subdirectory beneath the current working directory that starts with a p, so you now see the following on the terminal:

```
$ cd product/
```

Now you can press the Enter or Return key to complete the command. This is a feature of the Bash shell and is known as *tab completion* (see recipe 2-2 for more details).

Navigating to the Previous Directory

The hyphen (-) character is commonly used to navigate to the previous working directory. In the next example, the current working directory is /oracle01, and the previous working directory is /oracle02. To navigate to /oracle02, provide - to the cd command, as shown here:

```
$ cd -
```

The OLDPWD variable contains the location of the previous directory. To navigate to the most recently visited directory, you can change directories, as shown here:

```
$ cd $OLDPWD
```

5-3. Creating a Directory

Problem

You desire to store your SQL scripts in a special directory. To do this, you first need to create a directory.

Solution

Use the mkdir (make directory) command to create a new directory. This example creates the directory named scripts underneath the /home/oracle directory:

```
$ cd /home/oracle
$ mkdir scripts
```

Now use the cd and pwd commands to verify that the directory exists:

```
$ cd scripts
$ pwd
/home/oracle/scripts
```

When navigating to another directory, if the directory doesn't exist, then you'll receive an error message similar to this:

```
No such file or directory
```

How It Works

Before you create a directory, you must have write permission on the parent directory in order to create a subdirectory. If you attempt to create a directory and don't have write permission on either the user or group level, you'll receive an error. This example attempts to create a directory named oradump under the / directory:

```
$ mkdir /oradump
mkdir: cannot create directory `/oradump': Permission denied
```

The permissions on the / directory show that only the root user has write permissions (and is therefore the only user who can create a directory under /):

```
$ ls -altrd /
drwxr-xr-x  29 root root 4096 Apr 15 19:49 /
```

If you don't have root access, then you'll need to work with your system administrator to create any desired directories under the / directory. See recipe 3-11 for examples of obtaining access to root privileges.

Sometimes you'll find it convenient to create several directories in a path with one command. This example uses the -p (parent) option to create the directory backups and any parent directories that don't already exist in the path:

```
$ mkdir -p /oradump/db/dev/backups
```

The previous directory creation technique is extremely handy when you need to create long complex directory structures and you don't want to create them one directory at a time.

5-4. Viewing a List of Directories

Problem

You want to just list the directories and not other files in your current working location.

Solution

Use the `ls -l` command in combination with grep to list only directories. The following example lists directories beneath the current working directory:

```
$ ls -l | grep '^d'
```

The previous command instructs `ls` to print a long listing of files and then pipe the output to grep, which looks for files that begin with the d character. The caret (^) character is a regular expression that tells the grep command to match the d character at the beginning of the string.

How It Works

DBAs will typically create an alias or a function to facilitate typing the command shown in the "Solution" section of this recipe. This command creates an alias named lsd that can be used to list directories:

```
$ alias lsd="ls -l | grep '^d'"
```

After the alias is created, you simply type lsd, and it will run the `ls` and grep commands. See recipe 2-7 for details on creating aliases and functions.

Another way to view directories is to use `ls -p` and grep for the forward slash character. The next example uses `ls -p`, which instructs Linux to append a / on the end of every directory. The output of `ls -p` is piped to grep, which searches for the / character:

```
$ ls -p | grep /
```

Sometimes when trying to locate a directory, it's convenient to use a wildcard character. For example, say you want to determine all directories and files that are in the ORACLE_HOME directory that begin with the b character. To determine this, you attempt to issue this command:

```
$ ls $ORACLE_HOME/b*
```

The output of this command may not be what you expect. If a wildcard matches a directory name, the entire contents of the directory (not the directory name) will be listed. In this example, the output contains all the files listed in the ORACLE_HOME/bin directory; here's a short snippet of the output:

```
adapters          emutil          lxegen          oraxml
agentok.sh        emwd            lxinst          oraxsl
agtctl            emwd.pl         makerootca.sh   osdbagrp
```

To avoid this behavior, use `ls -d` to list directories and not their contents. The following command lists all directories that begin with the letter b that are beneath ORACLE_HOME:

```
$ ls -d $ORACLE_HOME/b*
/oracle/product/11.0/bin
```

5-5. Removing a Directory

Problem

You want to remove a directory and all files that exist beneath that directory.

Solution

Use the rmdir command to remove a directory. This command can be used only to remove directories that don't contain other files. In this example, the rmdir command is used to remove a directory named scripts that exists beneath the current working directory:

```
$ rmdir scripts
```

If the directory isn't empty, you'll see an error similar to this:

```
rmdir: scripts: Directory not empty
```

If you want to remove directories that contain files, then use the rm -r (remove recursively) command. In practice, the rm -r command is used much more than the rmdir command. The following example removes the directory scripts plus any files and subdirectories that exist beneath the scripts directory:

```
$ rm -r scripts
```

How It Works

If the rm -r command encounters any files that don't have write permission enabled, a message like this will be displayed:

```
rm: remove write-protected regular file '<file name>'?
```

If you want to remove the file, type y (for yes). If many files are write-protected (such as in oracle-owned directories), then typing y over and over again can get tedious.

You can instruct rm to remove write-protected files without being prompted with the -f (force) option. This example removes all files beneath the subdirectory scripts without prompting for protected files:

```
$ rm -rf scripts
```

Sometimes when you're removing old database installations, it's convenient to use the rm -rf command. This will wipe out entire directory trees without asking for confirmation when deleting write-protected files. Make sure you know exactly what you're removing before running this command.

■**Caution** Use the rm -rf command judiciously. This command will recursively remove every file and directory beneath the specified directory without prompting you for confirmation.

5-6. Listing Files

Problem

You want to see what files exist in a directory.

Solution

Use the ls (list) command to list the files (and directories) in a specified directory. This next line of code uses the ls command without any options to list the files in the current working directory:

```
$ ls
```

Here is a partial listing of the output:

```
alert.log          gcc-3.4.6-3.1.x86_64.rpm  ora01    ss.bsh
anaconda-ks.cfg    install.log               ora02    test
```

How It Works

The ls command without any options is not very useful and will display only a limited amount of file information. One of the more useful ways to use ls is to list all the files, protections, ownership, sizes, and modification times, all sorted from most recently created to last. This is achieved with the -altr options:

```
$ ls -altr
```

Here is a partial listing of the output:

```
-rwxr-x---   1 oracle oinstall   92 Oct 17  2007 dbaFunk.bash
-rw-r--r--   1 oracle oinstall  142 Jan  1 18:43 kill.sql
-rw-r--r--   1 oracle oinstall   22 Mar 16 15:54 freesp.sql
drwx------  20 oracle oinstall 4096 May  3 10:43 ..
drwxr-xr-x   2 oracle oinstall 4096 May  3 11:02 log
lrwxrwxrwx   1 oracle oinstall   22 May  3 11:10 oraset -> /var/opt/oracle/oraset
drwxr-xr-x   3 oracle oinstall 4096 May  3 11:10 .
```

The -a (all) option specifies that all files should be listed, including hidden files. The -l (long listing) option displays permissions, ownership, size, and modification time. The -t (time) option will cause the output to be sorted by time (newest first). To have the latest file modified listed at the bottom, use the -r (reverse) option. Table 5-1 shows how to interpret the long listing of the first line of the previous output.

Table 5-1. *Interpreting Long Listing Output*

Type and Permissions	Number of Links	Owner	Group	Size in Bytes	Modification Date	File Name
-rwxr-x--	1	oracle	oinstall	92	Oct 17 2007	dbaFunk.bash

The first column of Table 5-1 has ten characters. The first character displays the file type. Characters 2 through 10 display the file permissions. The characters r, w, and x indicate read, write, and execute privileges, respectively. A hyphen (-) indicates the absence of a privilege. The following output summarizes the first-column character positions and meanings of the long listing of a file:

```
File Type            User Perms   Group Perms   Other Perms
Column 1             2   3   4    5   6   7     8   9   10
-, d, l, s, c, b     r   w   x    r   w   x     r   w   x
```

In the first character of the first column of output, the hyphen indicates that it is a regular file. Similarly, if the first character is a d, then it's a directory. If the first character is an l, then it's a symbolic link. Table 5-2 lists the different file types on Linux systems.

Table 5-2. *Long Listing First Character File Type Meanings*

File Type Character	Meaning
-	Regular file
d	Directory
l	Symbolic link
s	Socket
c	Character device file
b	Block device file

The ls command may vary slightly between versions of Linux. This command typically has more than 50 different options. Use the man ls command to view all features available on your system.

USING ECHO TO DISPLAY FILES

Interestingly, you can also use the echo command to list files. For example, you can use this command to list files in the current working directory:

```
$ echo *
```

The echo command is a built-in command (see recipe 2-15 for details on built-in commands). This means that if for some reason the filesystem that contains the ls executable is unavailable (perhaps because of corruption), you can still use the echo command to list files.

5-7. Creating a File Quickly

Problem

You're setting up Oracle RMAN backups. You want to quickly create a file so that you can test whether the `oracle` user has the correct permissions to write to a newly created directory.

Solution

Use the `touch` command to quickly create a file. This example uses `touch` to create a file named `test.txt`:

```
$ touch test.txt
```

Now use the `ls` command to verify that the file exists:

```
$ ls -al
-rw-r--r--  1 oracle oinstall 0 Dec 28 15:15 test.txt
```

From the output, the file is created and has nothing in it (indicated by a 0-byte size).

Note See Chapter 4 for details on how to edit a text file.

How It Works

Sometimes you'll find yourself in a situation where you just need to create a file to test being able to write to a backup location or check the functionality of some aspect of a shell program. You can use the `touch` command for this purpose. If the file you are touching already exists, then the `touch` command will update the file's last-modified date.

If you `touch` a file that already exists, then its access time and modification time will be set to the current system time (this includes a date component). If you want to modify only the access time, use the `-a` option of `touch`. Similarly, the `-m` option will update only the modification time. Use the `--help` option to display all options available with `touch` on your version of Linux.

There are many techniques for quickly creating a file. For example, you can also quickly create a file using the following `cat` command:

```
$ cat /dev/null> test.txt
```

Be careful when running the previous command; if the file already exists, concatenating `/dev/null` to a file will erase anything contained within the file.

5-8. Changing File Permissions

Problem

You want to change the permission on a file so that there is no public-level access.

Solution

Use the chmod command to alter a file's permissions. This example changes the permission of the scrub.bash file to 750:

```
$ chmod 750 scrub.bash
```

A quick check with the ls command shows that the permissions are set correctly:

```
$ ls -altr scrub.bash
-rwxr-x--- 1 oracle oinstall 0 May  3 10:43 scrub.bash
```

The previous output indicates that the owner has read, write, and execute permissions; the group has read and execute; and the rest of the world has no permissions (see recipe 5-6 for a discussion on file permissions listed by the ls command).

■**Note** You must have root access or be the owner of the file or directory before you can change its permissions.

How It Works

DBAs often use the chmod command to change the permissions of files and directories. It's important that you know how to fluently use this command. Correct file access is critical for database security. In many circumstances, you will not want to grant any public access to files that contain passwords or other sensitive information.

You can change a file's permissions either using the numerical format (like 750) or using letters. When using the numerical format, the first number maps to the owner, the second number to the group, and the third number to all other users on the system. The permissions of 750 are translated to indicate read, write, and execute for the owner; read and execute for the group; and no permissions for other users. Inspect Table 5-3 for the translations of the numeric permissions.

Table 5-3. *Meanings of Numeric Permissions*

Numerical Digit	Permissions	Octal Number	Letter Format
0	No permissions	000	---
1	Execute only	001	--x
2	Write only	010	-w-
3	Write and execute	011	-wx
4	Read-only	100	r--
5	Read and execute	101	r-x
6	Read and write	110	rw-
7	Read, write, and execute	111	rwx

You can also change a file's permissions by using letters. Sometimes this is more intuitive to new Linux users. When using letters, keep in mind that the o permission doesn't designate "owner"; rather, it specifies "other." Table 5-4 lists the meanings of to whom the permissions are applied.

Table 5-4. *To Whom the Permissions Are Applied*

Who Letter	Meaning
u	User (owner)
g	Group
o	Other (all others on the system)
a	All (user, group, and other)

This next example makes the file executable by the user (owner), group, and other:

```
$ chmod ugo+x mvcheck.bsh
```

The next line of code takes away write and execute permissions from the group (g) and all others (o) for all files that end with the extension of .bsh:

```
$ chmod go-wx *.bsh
```

You can use three operands to apply permissions: +, -, and =. The plus (+) character adds permissions, and the minus (-) character takes away privileges. The equal (=) sign operand assigns the specified permissions and removes any not listed. For example, the following two lines are equivalent:

```
$ chmod 760 mvcheck.bsh
$ chmod u=rwx,g=rw,o= mvcheck.bsh
```

A quick listing of the file verifies the permissions are set as expected:

```
$ ls -altr mvcheck.bsh
-rwxrw----  1 oracle oinstall 0 May  8 07:58   mvcheck.bsh
```

You can also recursively change permissions of files in a directory and its subdirectories. Sometimes this is desired when installing software. The following bit of code recursively changes the permissions for all files in the current directory and any files in subdirectories to 711 (owner read, write, execute; group execute; other execute):

```
$ chmod -R 711 *.*
```

You can also use the chmod utility to change the permissions of files to match the settings on an existing file. This example changes all files ending with the extension of .bsh in the current directory to have the same permissions as the master.bsh file:

```
$ chmod --reference=master.bsh *.bsh
```

Default permissions are assigned to a file upon creation based on the umask setting. The file creation mask determines which permissions are excluded from a file. To view the current setting of your file creation mask, issue umask with no options:

```
$ umask
0022
```

You can also view the character version of the umask settings by using the -S option:

```
$ umask -S
u=rwx,g=rx,o=rx
```

When you create a regular text file, the permissions are set to the value of 0666 minus the umask setting. If the umask setting is 0022, then the permissions of the file are set to 0644, or -rw-r--r--.

Another concept related to the chmod command is the setuid permission (sometimes referred to as *suid*). Inspect the permissions of the oracle binary file:

```
$ cd $ORACLE_HOME/bin
$ ls -l oracle
-rwsr-s--x  1 oracle  dba      126812248 Jun 12 15:24 oracle
```

Notice that the owner and group executable setting is an s (and not an x). This indicates that the setuid permission bit has been set. This means that when somebody runs the program, they run it with the permissions of the owner of the file and not the permissions of the process running the file. This allows a user to run the oracle binary file as if it had the permissions of the oracle user. Therefore, server processes can execute the oracle binary file as if they were the owner (usually the oracle operating system user) to read and write to database files.

To set the setuid permission, you must specify a preceding fourth digit to the numeric permissions when changing file permissions with chmod. If you want to enable the setuid permission on both the user and group level, then use a preceding 6, as shown here:

```
$ chmod 6751 $ORACLE_HOME/bin/oracle
$ ls -l oracle
-rwsr-sr-x  1 oracle  dba      118965728 Jun 16  2006 oracle
```

If you want to enable the setuid permission only at the owner level, then use a preceding 4, as shown here:

```
$ chmod 4751 $ORACLE_HOME/bin/oracle
$ ls -l oracle
-rwsr-x--x  1 oracle  dba      118965728 Jun 16  2006 oracle
```

As a DBA, it's important to be aware of the setuid permission because depending on the release of Oracle, you may have to troubleshoot file permission issues. For example, see MetaLink Note 271598.1 for issues related to Enterprise Manager Grid Control and setuid dependences. Additionally, you can run into Oracle accessibility issues when there are non-oracle users on the same server as the database software. In these situations, it's important to understand how the setuid permission affects file access.

THE STICKY BIT

Do a long listing of the /tmp directory, and inspect the permissions:

```
$ ls -altrd /tmp
drwxrwxrwt  4 root root 4096 May 10 17:24 /tmp
```

At first glance, it looks like all users have all permissions on files in the /tmp directory. However, notice that the "other" permissions are set to rwt. The last permission character is a t; this indicates that the sticky bit has been enabled on that directory. When the sticky bit is enabled, only the file owner can delete a file within that directory. The sticky bit is set with the following syntax:

```
chmod +t <shared directory>
```

   or

```
chmod 3775 <shared directory>
```

Setting the sticky bit enables the sharing of files in a directory among many different users but prevents a user from deleting a file that they don't own (within the directory that has the sticky bit enabled).

5-9. Changing File Ownership and Group Membership

Problem

You need to change a file's file ownership and group membership so that it is owned by the oracle operating system user and its group is dba.

Solution

You need root privileges to change the owner of a file. Use the chown (change owner) command to change a file's owner and its group. This first example changes the owner on the /var/opt/oracle directory to oracle and its group to dba:

```
# chown oracle:dba /var/opt/oracle
```

The file listing now shows the directory owner is the oracle user and the group it belongs to is dba:

```
$ ls -altrd /var/opt/oracle
drwxr-xr-x  2 oracle dba 4096 Dec 28 10:31 /var/opt/oracle
```

If you want to change only the group permissions of a file, then use the chgrp command. You must be the file owner or have root privileges to change the group of a file. This example recursively changes (in the current directory and all subdirectories) the group to dba for all files with the extension of .sql:

```
$ chgrp -R dba *.sql
```

How It Works

When setting up or maintaining database servers, sometimes it's required to change the ownership on a file or directory. The following lines show the chown syntax for changing various combinations of the owner and/or group:

```
chown user file
chown user:group file
chown :group file
```

If you have root access, then you can directly change file ownership yourself. If you don't have root privileges, sometimes system administrators will grant you access to commands that require the root privilege through the sudo utility (see recipe 3-11 for details).

You can also change the ownership or the group of a file based on the settings of an existing file. This next line of code recursively changes the ownership and group of all files in a directory tree based on the ownership and group of the current working directory:

```
$ chown -R --reference . *
```

5-10. Viewing the Contents of a Text File

Problem

You want to view the contents of a text file, but you don't want to open the file with an editor (like vi) because you are afraid you might accidentally modify the file.

Solution

Use either the view, less, or more command to only view (and not modify) a file's contents. The view command will open a file using either the vi or vim editor in read-only mode. When you open a file in read-only mode, you are prevented from saving the file with the vi editor :wq (write and then quit) command. The following example views the init_BRDSTN.ora file:

```
$ view init_BRDSTN.ora
```

The view command is the same as running the vi -R command or the vim -R command (see Chapter 4 for more details about vi). To exit the view utility, enter the command of :q. We should point out that when viewing a file, you can force a write when exiting with the :wq! command.

If you want to display the contents of a file one page at a time, then use a paging utility such as more or less. This example uses less to view the init_BRDSTN.ora file:

```
$ less init_BRDSTN.ora
```

The less utility will display a : (colon) prompt at the bottom-left corner of the screen. You can use the spacebar to go to the next page and the up and down arrows to scroll through the documentation line by line. Enter q to exit less.

This next example uses the more command to page through the file:

```
$ more init_BRDSTN.ora
```

Like the less utility, use the spacebar to display the next page and q to exit more.

How It Works

The more and less utilities are referred to as *pagers* because they display information on the screen one page at a time. These utilities have similar features, and one could argue that they are . . . more or less the same. For the way that DBAs use these utilities, that's mostly true. For hardcore Linux users, the less utility is a bit more robust than more. Use the man less and man more commands to view all options available with these utilities.

When using either more or less, you can use vi commands to navigate within the displayed output. For example, if you want to search for a string, you can enter a forward slash and a string to search for text within the more or less output. This example searches for the string sga_max_size within the output of less:

```
$ less init_BRDSTN.ora
/sga_max_size
```

We should point out that you can also use the cat command to quickly display the contents of a file to your standard output (usually your screen). This example dumps the output of the init_BRDSTN.ora file to the screen:

```
$ cat init_BRDSTN.ora
```

Using cat to display the contents of files works fine when you have small files. However, if the file is large, then you'll just see a large amount of text streaming by too fast to make any sense. It's almost always better to use view, less, or more (rather than cat) to view a file's contents. These commands allow you to quickly inspect a file's contents without risking accidental modifications.

5-11. Viewing Nonprinting Characters in a File

Problem

You're trying to load text strings from a file into the database with a utility such as SQL*Loader, but the data appears to be corrupted after it is inserted into the target table. You want to view any control characters that may be embedded into the file.

Solution

Use the cat -v command to view nonprinting and control characters. This example displays nonprinting and control characters in the data.ctl file:

```
$ cat -v data.ctl
```

■**Note** The cat -v command will not display linefeed or Tab characters.

How It Works

Sometimes when dealing with data being loaded into the database from text files, you might find your SQL queries don't behave as expected. For example, you might search for a string, and yet the SQL query doesn't return the expected data. This might be because of nonprinting characters being inserted into the database. Use the cat -v command as described in this recipe to troubleshoot these kinds of data issues.

To illustrate the viewing of nonprinting characters, you spool the following output from a SQL*Plus session:

```
SQL> spool out.txt
SQL> select chr(7) || 'ring the bell' from dual;
SQL> exit;
```

Here you use cat to display the contents of the file out.txt:

```
$ cat out.txt
```

```
SQL> select chr(7) || 'ring the bell' from dual;
CHR(7)||'RINGT
--------------
ring the bell

SQL> exit;
```

Notice the ^G ASCII ring bell or beep control character in the last line of the output when you use the -v option:

```
$ cat -v out.txt
```

```
SQL>  select chr(7) || 'ring the bell' from dual;
CHR(7)||'RINGT
--------------
^Gring the bell

SQL> exit;
```

5-12. Viewing Hidden Files

Problem

You want to view the names of hidden configuration files and/or hidden directories in your home directory.

Solution

Use the ls command with the -a (all) option. This next bit of code lists all files using a long listing format and sorted in the reverse order in which they were modified:

```
$ ls -altr $HOME
```

Here is a sample of part of the output:

```
drwxr-xr-x  3 root    root      4096 Sep 29 13:30 ..
-rw-r--r--  1 oracle oinstall  124 Sep 29 13:30 .bashrc
-rw-r--r--  1 oracle oinstall   24 Sep 29 13:30 .bash_logout
-rw-r--r--  1 oracle oinstall  223 Sep 29 13:53 .bash_profile
drwxr-xr-x  2 oracle oinstall 4096 Oct  2 17:55 db
drwxr-xr-x  2 oracle oinstall 4096 Oct 15 08:33 scripts
drwx------  2 oracle oinstall 4096 Oct 15 08:34 .ssh
-rw-------  1 oracle oinstall 6076 Oct 15 13:19 .bash_history
-rw-------  1 oracle oinstall 5662 Oct 15 13:41 .viminfo
drwx------  5 oracle oinstall 4096 Oct 15 13:55 .
```

Any of the files in the previous listing that begin with a . (dot or period) are classified as hidden files. When using the Bash shell, common hidden files in your home directory are .bash_profile, .bashrc, .bash_logout, and .bash_history (see recipe 2-5 for uses of these files).

How It Works

The only difference between a hidden file and a nonhidden file is that the hidden file begins with a . (dot or period) character. There isn't anything secretive or secure about hidden files. Hidden files are usually well-known files with distinct purposes (such as storing environment configuration commands).

You may not want to muddle the output of an ls command with every file in a directory. The default behavior of the ls command is not to list hidden files. The -a option specifically tells the ls command to list all files, including hidden files. If you want to list all files except the . and .. files, then use the -A option:

```
$ ls -A
```

■**Note** The . file is a special file that refers to the current working directory. The .. file refers to the parent directory of the current working directory.

5-13. Determining File Type

Problem

You want to display whether a file is a directory or a regular file.

Solution

Use the ls command with the -F option to display the file name and file type. This example lists file names and file types within the current working directory:

```
$ ls -F
```

Here is a partial listing of some sample output:

```
alert.log         gcc-3.4.6-3.1.x86_64.rpm  ora01/    ss.bsh*
anaconda-ks.cfg   install.log               ora02/    test/
```

The ls -F command will append to the file name a special character to indicate the file type. In the previous output, the file names appended with / are directories, and the file name appended with * is an executable file.

Tip Another method of determining file type is to use the ls --color command. This will colorize the file depending on its type.

You can also use the file command to display characteristics of a file. This command will display whether the file is an ASCII file, a tar file, or a details executable file. For example, one way that DBAs use the type command is to tell whether the oracle binary file is 32-bit or 64-bit. The following shows that the oracle binary file on this Linux server is 32-bit:

```
$ file $ORACLE_HOME/bin/oracle
/oracle/product/10.2/bin/oracle: setuid setgid ELF 32-bit LSB executable, Intel
80386, version 1 (SYSV), for GNU/Linux 2.2.5, dynamically linked (uses shared libs),
not stripped
```

How It Works

You can display an indicator for a file by using the -F option of the ls command. Table 5-5 describes the different file name type indicators. File type indicators allow you to filter the output and look for a certain file type. For example, to list all directories, search the output of the ls -F command for the / character:

```
$ ls -F | grep /
```

DBAs often encapsulate strings of commands like this within aliases or functions. This allows you to create shortcuts to long commands (see recipe 2-7 for details).

Table 5-5. *File Type Indicator Characters and Meanings*

Indicator Character	Description
/	The file is a directory.
*	The file is an executable.
=	The file is a socket (a special file used in process to process communication).
@	The file is a symbolic link (see recipe 5-33 for more details).
|	The file is a named pipe (a special file used in process to process communication).

■**Tip** Use the `type` command to determine the characteristics of a Linux command file. This will show whether the command is a Linux utility, a built-in command, an alias, or a function.

The `stat` command is another useful command for displaying file characteristics. This command prints in human-readable format the contents of an inode. An *inode* (pronounced "eye-node") is a Linux data structure that stores information about the file. The next example displays the inode information for the `oracle` binary file:

```
$ stat $ORACLE_HOME/bin/oracle
```

Here is the corresponding output:

```
 File: `/oracle/product/10.2/bin/oracle'
 Size: 93300099        Blocks: 182424     IO Block: 4096    regular file
Device: 802h/2050d     Inode: 23281668    Links: 1
Access: (6751/-rwsr-s--x) Uid: (  500/  oracle)   Gid: (  500/oinstall)
Access: 2008-05-03 12:01:06.000000000 -0600
Modify: 2007-10-02 17:36:16.000000000 -0600
Change: 2007-10-02 17:52:21.000000000 -0600
```

Some of the previous output you can obtain from the `ls` command. However, notice that the `stat` output also contains information such as the number of blocks allocated; the inode device type; and the last time a file was accessed, the last time a file was modified, or when its status was changed.

5-14. Finding Differences Between Files

Problem

You have two databases that were supposed to be set up identically. You want to see any differences in the initialization files.

Solution

Use the `diff` (difference) command to identify differences in files. The general syntax for this command is as follows:

```
$ diff <file1> <file2>
```

This example uses `diff` to view the differences between two files named `initDEV1.ora` and `initDEV2.ora`:

```
$ diff initDEV1.ora initDEV2.ora
```

Here is some sample output showing the differences in the files:

```
6,7c6,7
< sga_max_size=400M
< sga_target=400M
---
> sga_max_size=600M
> sga_target=600M
20a21
> # star_transformation_enabled=true
```

How It Works

The key to understanding the output from diff is that it is providing you with instructions on how to make file1 look like file2. The output tells you how to append, change, and delete lines. These instructions are signified by an a, c, or d in the output.

Lines preceded by < are from file1. Lines preceded by > are from file2. The line numbers to the left of an a, c, or d apply to file1. The line numbers to the right of an a, c, or d apply to file2.

From the previous output in this recipe's solution, the first line, 6,7c6,7, is translated to mean change lines 6 and 7 in file1 to lines 6 and 7 in file2. The The second to last line of the output is 20a21. That means after line 20 in file1, append line 21 from file2.

The output of diff is known as a *difference report*. This difference report can be used in conjunction with the patch command to make file1 look like file2. Before you can use the patch command, you first have to save the difference report output in a file. The following example stores the difference output in a file named init.diff:

```
$ diff initDEV1.ora initDEV2.ora > init.diff
```

To convert initDEV1.ora to initDEV2.ora, use the patch command with the difference report output:

```
$ patch initDEV1.ora init.diff
```

You can also use the sdiff (side-by-side) utility to display file differences. The sdiff output is usually easier to interpret than the diff command because differences are juxtaposed visually in the output. The following example uses sdiff to display the differences between two files:

```
$ sdiff initDEV1.ora initDEV2.ora
```

Here is a snippet of the side-by-side differences:

```
sga_max_size=400M                    |  sga_max_size=600M
sga_target=400M                      |  sga_target=600M
                                     >#star_transformation_enabled=true
```

■**Tip** Use the diff3 utility to compare the differences between three files.

5-15. Comparing Contents of Directories

Problem

You want to ensure that two different directories have identical contents in terms of the number of files, the file names, and the file contents.

Solution

You can use the `diff` command to display any differences in two directories in terms of file names and file contents. This example compares the files in the `/ora01/upgrade` directory with the files in the `/cvsroot/prod_scripts` directory:

```
$ diff /cvsroot/prod_scripts /ora01/upgrade
```

If there are no differences, then you won't see any output. If there's a file that exists in one directory but not the other directory, then you'll see a message similar to this:

```
Only in /ora01/upgrade: tab.sql
```

If there are differences in any files in each directory, then you'll see a message similar to this:

```
22c22
< # cd to udump
---
> # cd to udump directory.
```

See recipe 5-14 for details on interpreting the output of the `diff` utility.

How It Works

Occasionally you may need to compare the contents of directories when maintaining database environments. In these situations, use the `diff` command to compare the contents of one directory with another.

If you want to recursively look in subdirectories and compare files with the same name, you can use the `-r` option. This example recursively searches through subdirectories and reports any differences in files that have the same name:

```
diff -r /cvsroot/prod_scripts /ora01/upgrade
```

You can also use the long listing of the recursive option to achieve the same result:

```
diff --recursive /cvsroot/prod_scripts /ora01/upgrade
```

5-16. Copying Files

Problem

You want to make a copy of a file before you modify it.

Solution

Use the cp (copy) command to replicate a file. The following example uses the cp command to make a backup of the listener.ora file:

```
$ cp listener.ora listener.old.ora
```

You can verify that the copy worked with the ls command:

```
$ ls listener*.ora
listener.old.ora listener.ora
```

How It Works

DBAs often need to create copies of files. For example, the cp utility provides a method to create backups of files or quickly replicate directories. The cp command has this basic syntax:

```
cp [options] source_file target_file
```

Be careful when copying files. If the target file exists prior to issuing the copy command, it will be overwritten with the contents of the source file. If you'd like to be warned before overwriting an existing file, then use the -i (interactive) option. In this example, there already exists a file named init.old.ora:

```
$ cp -i init.ora init.old.ora
cp: overwrite `init.old.ora'?
```

Now you can answer y or n (for yes or no, respectively) depending on whether you want the target file overwritten with the source. Many DBAs create a shortcut command for cp that maps to cp -i (see recipe 2-7 for details on how to create shortcuts). This helps prevent you from accidentally overwriting previously existing files.

You can also copy files directly into an existing directory structure using this syntax:

```
cp [options] source_file(s) directory
```

If the destination is a directory, the cp command will copy the file (or files) into the directory. The directory will not be overwritten. The next example copies all files in the current working directory with the extension .sql to the scripts directory:

```
$ cp *.sql scripts
```

When you copy a file, the original timestamp and file permissions may differ between the original file and the file newly created by the copy command. Sometimes it's desirable to preserve the original attributes of the source file. For example, you may want to make a copy of a file but for troubleshooting purposes want to still be able to view the original timestamp and ownership. If you want to preserve the original timestamp, ownership, and file permissions, use the -p (preserve) option:

```
$ cp -p listener.ora listener.old.ora
```

You can also use the cp utility to create the directory structure associated with the source file by using the --parents option. For this command to work, the destination must be a directory.

This example creates a network/admin/log directory and copies any files ending with the extension of .ora to a directory beneath the destination ~/backup directory:

```
$ cp --parents network/admin/*.ora ~/backup
```

Any files with the extension of .ora in the source directory should now exist in the ~/backup/network/admin destination directory.

5-17. Copying Directories

Problem

You want to copy all files and subdirectories beneath a directory to a new location.

Solution

Use the cp command with the -r option to recursively copy all files in a directory and subdirectories. This example copies all files in the /orahome/scripts directory tree to the /orahome/backups directory:

```
$ cp -r  /orahome/scripts /orahome/backups
```

The /orahome/backups directory now should have an identical copy of the files and subdirectories in the /orahome/scripts source directory. Be aware that if the /orahome/backups directory already exists before you issue the cp command, it will be overwritten with the source of the copy. If you want to be prompted before you issue the cp command, use the -i (interactive) option.

How It Works

Sometimes DBAs need to synchronize directories between disparate servers. You might need to do this if you are remotely installing software or if you just want to ensure you have a backup of files copied to a remote box.

You can accomplish this task in a couple of ways. If you need to securely copy files, use the scp (secure copy) command.

The basic syntax for scp is as follows:

```
scp [options] sourcefile[...] destinationfile
```

The source and destination files can be directories. The destination file in the prior syntax line can take one of the following general forms:

```
file
host:file
user@host:file
```

Use the -r and -p options of the scp command to recursively copy and preserve the file modification time, access time, and mode. This example recursively copies the scripts directory from the local box to a remote box named rmougdev2 as the oracle user:

```
$ scp -rp scripts oracle@rmougdev2:/home/oracle/scripts
```

If you just want to copy a file to a remote server and have it placed in the remote user's HOME directory, specify a . for the destination file location. To illustrate this concept, here we copy a file named initRMUG.ora to the remote rmougdev2 box and place the file in the oracle user's HOME directory.

```
$ scp initRMUG.ora oracle@rmougdev2:.
```

Another powerful utility used to synchronize directories is the rsync command. The basic syntax for rsync is as follows:

```
rsync [options] sourcefiles destinationfile
```

If the source and destination are on the same server, then ordinary file and directory names can be used. If the source and destination files are on remote servers, then they take the following general form:

```
user@host:port/filename
```

The rsync utility has an extensive set of options for copying directory trees. Use the -r and -a options to recursively copy a directory tree and preserve permissions and ownership. This example recursively copies the contents of the contents of the local scripts directory to the remote rmougdev2 server:

```
$ rsync -ra --progress scripts rmougdev2:/home/oracle/scripts
```

The --progress option will interactively show the work that the rsync command is performing. By default, the rsync tool will transfer only the differences that it finds between the source and destination. This makes it a very fast and efficient method to synchronize a local directory tree with a remote server directory.

5-18. Moving Files and Directories

Problem

You want to rename or relocate a file.

Solution

Use the mv (move) command to relocate a file or rename it. This example renames a file from initdw.ora to a new name of initDWDB.ora:

```
$ mv initdw.ora initDWDB.ora
```

You can also use the mv command to relocate a file to a different directory. This next bit of code moves a file from the current working directory to its parent directory:

```
$ mv scrub.sql ..
```

Quite often you'll encounter the need to move a file from the current working directory to a subdirectory. This example moves a file from the current working directory to a subdirectory named scripts:

```
$ mv scrub.sql scripts
```

In the previous line of code, if the `scripts` subdirectory didn't exist, then you would end up renaming the `scrub.sql` file to a file named `scripts`. In other words, the destination subdirectory must exist before you issue the `mv` command (otherwise you'll end up renaming the file).

It's also possible to relocate directories. The following example moves the `scripts` directory to the `sqlscripts` directory:

```
$ mv scripts sqlscripts
```

In the previous line of code, if the `sqlscripts` directory already exists, then the `scripts` directory is created as a subdirectory beneath the `sqlscripts` directory. This might seem a little confusing if you're not expecting this behavior. One way to think of this is that the `mv` command does not overwrite directories if they already exist.

How It Works

The `mv` command is used to relocate or rename a file or a directory. The `mv` utility uses the following syntax:

```
mv [options] source(s) target
```

Be aware that the `mv` command will unceremoniously overwrite a file if it already exists. For example, say you have the following two files in a directory:

```
$ ls
initdw.ora init.ora
```

If you move `initdw.ora` to the name of `init.ora`, it will overwrite the contents of the `init.ora` file without prompting you. To protect yourself against accidentally overwriting files, use the `-i` (interactive) option:

```
$ mv -i initdw.ora init.ora
mv: overwrite `init.ora'?
```

You can now enter a y or a n to indicate a yes or no answer, respectively. You can easily implement the `mv` command as `mv -i` via a function or an alias to protect yourself against erroneously overwriting files (see recipe 2-7 for details on command shortcuts). Table 5-6 describes the various results of the `mv` operation depending on the status of the source and target.

Table 5-6. *Results of Moving File(s) and Directories*

Source	Target	Outcome
File	File doesn't exist.	Source file is renamed to target.
File	File exists.	Source file overwrites target.
File(s)	Directory exists.	Source file(s) moved to target directory.
Directory	Directory doesn't exist.	Source directory renamed to target.
Directory	Directory exists.	Source directory created as a subdirectory beneath target directory.

5-19. Renaming a File or Directory

Problem

You want to change the name of a file or directory.

Solution

In Linux, you have to use the mv (move) command to rename a file. For example, the following line of code renames a file from credb1.sql to credatabase.sql:

```
$ mv credb1.sql credatabase.sql
```

You can also rename a directory. The following renames a directory from dev to test:

```
$ mv dev test
```

Be aware that when renaming directories, if you attempt to rename a directory to the name of an existing directory, a new directory will be created as a subdirectory beneath the already existing directory. See Table 5-6 for details on the behavior of the mv command.

How It Works

Linux also has a rename command that can be used to change the name of files. The rename utility has the following syntax:

```
rename oldname newname files
```

This has a big advantage over the mv command in that it allows you to rename several files at once. For example, here is how you would rename all files in a directory that end with the extension of .trc to the new extension of .trace:

```
$ rename .trc .trace *.trc
```

You can also use rename to change the name of just one file. Here we rename the file initDEV.ora to initTEST.ora:

```
$ rename initDEV.ora initTEST.ora initDEV.ora
```

We recommend that you compare the uses of rename command described in this recipe to the application of the mv utility described in recipe 5-18.

5-20. Removing a File

Problem

You want to remove a file from disk.

Solution

First use the ls command to identify the files you want to remove. In this example, we display any files with the extension of .trc:

```
$ ls -altr *.trc
```

After visually verifying the files you want to remove, then use the rm command to permanently delete files:

```
$ rm *.trc
```

How It Works

Be very careful using the rm command. Once the files have been removed, the only way to get them back is from a backup (if there is one). DBAs can get themselves in a lot of trouble by accidentally removing files. DBAs typically are logged on to a server as the oracle operating system user. This special user is usually the owner of all the critical database files. This means this user can remove database files, even if they are currently in use.

Because the rm command doesn't prompt you for confirmation, we recommend you always use the ls command to verify which files will be removed.

If you want confirmation before removing a file, use the -i option:

```
$ rm -i *.trc
```

You will now be prompted for confirmation before each file is deleted:

```
rm: remove regular file `rmdb1_j001_11186.trc'?
```

Type y to have the file removed or n if you want to keep the file. This method takes longer but provides you with some reassurance that you're deleting the correct files.

Another technique for preventing the accidental deletion of the wrong files is to use the !$ variable. The !$ character contains the last string entered on the command line. For example, to use !$ to remove files, first use the ls command to list the files targeted for deletion:

```
$ ls *.trc
```

Now the value *.trc is stored in the !$ parameter. This allows you to use rm to remove the files listed by the previous ls command:

```
$ rm !$
```

If you're ever unsure of the contents of the !$ variable, use the echo command to display its contents:

```
$ echo !$
```

5-21. Removing Protected Files Without Being Prompted

Problem

You want to remove all the files associated with an old installation of the database. However, when you issue the rm (remove) command, you are presented with this prompt:

```
rm: remove write-protected regular empty file
```

You wonder whether you can run the rm command without being prompted.

Solution

There are two techniques for removing write-protected files: `rm -f` and yes. This next example uses `rm -rf` (remove, recursive, force) to recursively remove all files beneath a directory without being prompted:

```
$ rm -rf /oracle/product/8.0
```

The next example uses the yes command to recursively remove all files beneath a directory without being prompted:

```
$ yes | rm -r /oracle/product/8.0
```

If you type the yes command without any options, the subsequent output will be a repeating y on your screen until you press Ctrl+C. You can pipe the output of the yes command to another command that is expecting a y or n as input for it to proceed.

How It Works

Be very careful when using the removal methods described in the "Solution" section of this recipe. These techniques allow you to easily remove entire directories and subdirectories with one command. Use these techniques only when you're absolutely sure you don't need a directory's contents. Consider using tar or cpio to recursively back up a directory tree before you delete it (see Chapter 6 for details)

5-22. Removing Oddly Named Files

Problem

Somehow a file was created with the odd name of -f and apparently cannot be removed with the rm (remove) command. You wonder how you can remove it using the rm command.

Solution

First use the ls command to view the oddly named file:

```
$ ls
-f
```

You next attempt to remove the file with the rm command:

```
$ rm -f
```

However, the rm command thinks -f is an argument to the command and does nothing with the -f file. To remove the file, specify the current path with the file name, as shown here:

```
rm ./-f
```

How It Works

Files with odd names are sometimes created by accident. Sometimes you can type a command with the wrong syntax and end up with a file with an undesirable name. For example, the following will create a file name of -f:

```
$ ls > "-f"
```

Now when you list the contents of the directory, you'll see a file named -f:

```
$ ls
-f
```

Worse yet, you might have a malicious user on your system who creates a file like this:

```
$ ls > "-r home"
```

Be *extremely* careful in this situation. If you attempt to remove the file without specifying a path, the command will look like this:

```
$ rm -r home
```

If you happen to have a directory named home in the current directory, then that command will remove the home directory. To remove the file, use the current path ./, as shown here:

```
$ rm "./-r home"
```

In the previous command, you need to enclose the path and file name in quotes because there is a space in the file name. Without quotes, the rm command will attempt to remove a file named ./-r and another file named home.

5-23. Finding Files

Problem

You want to locate a certain file on the database server.

Solution

Use the find command to search for a file. The most basic way to search for a file is to instruct find to look for a file recursively in the current working directory and any of its subdirectories. The following command looks in the current directory and any subdirectories for any file that begins with the string alert and ends with the extension of .log:

```
$ find . -name "alert*.log"
```

Here's some sample output indicating the location of the found file relative to the current working directory:

```
./RMDB1/admin/bdump/alert_RMDB1.log
```

How It Works

It's well worth the effort to spend some time getting to know the find command. This command will allow you to easily search for files from the command line. Because this utility is used in so many different ways, we decided to include individual recipes to document these tasks. The next several recipes of this chapter show examples of how DBAs use the find command.

If your operating system account doesn't have correct access permissions on a directory or file, then find will display an error message. This example changes directories to the / directory and issues a find command:

```
$ cd /
$ find . -name "alert*.log"
```

Here is a partial listing of output indicating that there is not access to certain directories:

```
find: ./proc/11686/task/11686/fd: Permission denied
find: ./proc/11688/task/11688/fd: Permission denied
find: ./proc/15638/task/15638/fd: Permission denied
```

To eliminate those error messages, send the error output to the null device:

```
$ find . -name "alert*.log" 2>/dev/null
```

5-24. Finding Strings in Files

Problem

You want to search for a string in a text file that could be located somewhere beneath a given directory path.

Solution

Use a combination of the find, xargs, exec, and grep commands to search for a string that exists in a file in a directory tree. The first example uses find to locate all SQL files beneath a directory and pipes the output to xargs, which executes the grep command to search for a string of create table:

```
$ find . -name "*.sql" | xargs grep -i "create table"
```

You can also use the find command with exec, grep, and print to search for strings within files. The following command searches for the string error in any files ending with the extension of .trc. This command will search the current working directory and all its subdirectories:

```
$ find . -name "*.trc" -exec grep -i "error" '{}' \; -print
```

In the previous line of code, the find command finds all files in a directory tree with the extension of *.trc. The output is passed to the -exec '{}' command, which feeds each file found to the grep -i command. The \; marks the end of the -exec command, and -print displays any files found.

How It Works

The example in the "Solution" section of this recipe will display a line for every string that it finds that matches in the file. If you want to display only the first occurrence of the string in the file, then use the -q option. This example displays only one line per file that the string is in:

```
$ find . -name "*.trc" -exec grep -qi "error" '{}' \; -print
```

■**Note** On some systems, the -q option may not be available. For example, the similar functionality would be implemented with the -l option. Use man grep to display all options available on your server.

Sometimes you want to search for the incidence of two or more strings in a file. Use grep with the -e option to accomplish this. This command searches for the strings of error or ora-:

```
$ find . -name "*.trc" -exec grep -ie "error" -e "ora-" '{}' \; -print
```

Occasionally you might run into the need to look in a binary file for a certain string. You might have a system core file or a database file that you want to inspect. Use the strings command to search a binary file for printable text. This example uses the strings command and pipes the output to more to view the contents of a system core file:

```
$ strings core | more
```

If you want to search for a specific string, then pipe the output of strings to the grep command. This example searches the users01.dbf file for the string of denver:

```
$ strings users01.dbf | grep -i Denver
```

This next example peeks inside the system01.dbf datafile for undo segment information:

```
$ strings system01.dbf | grep _SYSSMU | cut -d $ -f 1 | sort -u
```

Here is a partial listing of the output:

```
_SYSSMU1
_SYSSMU1
_SYSSMU10
_SYSSMU2
_SYSSMU2
_SYSSMU3
_SYSSMU3
```

In certain database recovery scenarios involving a corrupted UNDO tablespace, you may have to use this technique to identify undo segments. This is just one example of how an Oracle DBA might have to use the strings command; the important thing to keep in mind is that this utility provides you with a way to look for text strings in binary files.

> ## DOES DATABASE WRITER WRITE TO DATAFILES IN BACKUP MODE?
>
> A misconception that exists with some DBAs is that the database writer stops writing to datafiles while a datafile's tablespace is in backup mode. The following example uses the `strings` command to verify that the database writer does indeed continue to write to datafiles, even while in backup mode. First verify that a string does not exist in a datafile:
>
> ```
> $ strings users01.dbf | grep -i denver
> ```
>
> Verify that nothing is returned by the previous command. Next create a table, and place it in the USERS tablespace:
>
> ```
> SQL> create table city(name varchar2(50)) tablespace users;
> ```
>
> Next alter a tablespace into backup mode:
>
> ```
> SQL> alter tablespace users begin backup;
> ```
>
> Now insert a string into the CITY table:
>
> ```
> SQL> insert into city values('Denver');
> ```
>
> Connect as a privileged schema, and run the following command several times:
>
> ```
> SQL> alter system switch logfile;
> ```
>
> From the operating system command line, search for the string of denver in the USERS database file:
>
> ```
> $ strings users01.dbf | grep -i denver
> ```
>
> You should see the following output:
>
> ```
> Denver
> ```
>
> This verifies that the database writer continues to write to datafiles, even while the corresponding tablespace is in backup mode. Don't forget to take your USERS tablespace out of backup mode.

5-25. Finding a Recently Modified File

Problem

You recently created a file but can't remember where on the server it is located. You want to find any files with a recent creation date.

Solution

Use the `find` command with the `-mmin` (modified minutes) option to find very recently modified files. This example finds any files that have changed in the last 30 minutes beneath the current working directory:

```
$ find . -mmin -30
```

To find all files that were modified more than 30 minutes ago, use the + sign instead of the - sign:

```
$ find . -mmin +30
```

How It Works

The find command with a time-related option is useful for locating files that have recently been updated or changed. This command can be useful when you can't remember where you've placed recently modified or downloaded files.

If you're using a version of find that does not support the -mmin option, then try the -ctime option instead. The following command locates any files that have changed on the server in the last day beneath the /home/oracle directory:

```
$ find /home/oracle -ctime -1
```

Many options are available when trying to find a file. For example, use the -amin (access minutes) option to find a file based on when it was last accessed. This next line of code finds all files that were accessed beneath the current working directory exactly 60 minutes ago:

```
$ find . -amin 60
```

Table 5-7 describes a subset of time-related options commonly used with the find command.

Table 5-7. *Commonly Used Time-Related Options to Find Files*

Option	Description
-amin	Finds files accessed more than +n, less than -n, or exactly n minutes ago
-atime	Finds files accessed more than +n, less than -n, or exactly n days ago
-cmin	Finds files changed more than +n, less than -n, or exactly n minutes ago
-ctime	Finds files changed more than +n, less than -n, or exactly n days ago
-mmin	Finds files modified more than +n, less than -n, or exactly n minutes ago
-mtime	Finds files modified more than +n, less than -n, or exactly n days ago
-newer <file>	Finds files modified more recently than <file>

A plethora of options are available with the find command. Use the man find command to display the options available on your Linux system.

5-26. Finding and Removing Old Files

Problem

You want to find and remove old database trace files.

Solution

Use the find command to locate files older than a certain age. Once the old files are identified, use the rm command to remove them. The following example identifies files greater than 14 days old and removes them all with one line of code:

```
$ find . -type f -mtime +14 -exec rm -f {} \;
```

The previous command finds all files (the option -type f indicates a regular file) in the current working directory and its subdirectories that are older than 14 days. The rm command is executed (-exec) once for each file name located by the find command. The function of {} is to insert each file returned (by find) into the rm -f command line. When using the -f (force) option, you will not be prompted if you really want to remove write-protected files (files without write permission enabled). The \; denotes the end of the exec command line.

How It Works

The Oracle Database will regularly produce trace files as part of its normal operations. These files often contain detailed information about potential problems or issues with your database. Usually you don't need to keep trace and audit files lying around on disk forever. As these files grow older, the information in them becomes less valuable.

DBAs will typically write a small shell script to clean up old files. This shell script can be run automatically on a periodic basis from a utility such as cron. See Chapter 7 for details on shell scripting and Chapter 11 for techniques for automating tasks through cron.

5-27. Finding the Largest Files

Problem

Your database is experiencing availability issues because a disk is 100 percent full. You want to locate the largest files in a directory tree.

Solution

Use the find command to locate files recursively in a directory tree. The following command sends the output of the find operation to the sort and head commands to restrict the output to just the five largest files located in any directory beneath the current working directory:

```
$ find . -ls | sort -nrk7 | head -5
```

Here is a sample of the output:

```
6602760 820012 -rw-r-----   1 oracle   oinstall 838868992 Jan 21 14:55
./RMDB1/undotbs01.dbf
6602759 512512 -rw-r-----   1 oracle   oinstall 524296192 Jan 21 14:55
./RMDB1/system01.dbf
6602758 51260 -rw-r-----  1 oracle   oinstall 52429312 Jan 20 22:00
./RMDB1/redo03a.log
6602757 51260 -rw-r-----  1 oracle   oinstall 52429312 Jan 19 06:00
./RMDB1/redo02a.log
6602756 51260 -rw-r-----  1 oracle   oinstall 52429312 Jan 21 14:55
./RMDcB1/redo01a.log
```

The -nrk7 option of previous sort command orders the output numerically, in reverse order, based on the seventh position. As shown in the output, the output is sorted largest to smallest. The top listing shows that largest file is about 800MB in size.

How It Works

You can also use the find command to look for certain types of files. To look for a file of a particular extension, use the -name option. For example, the following command looks for the largest files beneath the current working directory and subdirectories that have an extension of .log:

```
$ find . -name "*.log" -ls | sort -nrk7 | head
```

DBAs often create shortcuts (via shell functions or aliases) that encapsulate long strings of commands. Command shortcuts can save time and prevent typing errors. See recipe 2-7 for details on creating functions and aliases.

5-28. Finding a File of a Certain Size

Problem

You're running out of disk space, and you want to recursively locate all files beneath a directory that exceed a certain size.

Solution

Use a combination of the find command with the -size option to accomplish this task. This example uses the -size option to find any files more than 100MB in the current working directory and any subdirectories:

```
$ find . -size +100000k
```

Here's a small snippet of the output:

```
./RMDB1/sysaux01.dbf
./RMDB1/temp01.dbf
```

How It Works

You can use the -size option of the find command in a number of useful ways. For example, if you want to find a file less than a certain size, then use the - minus sign. This next line of code finds any files less than 20MB beneath the directory named /home/oracle:

```
$ find . -size -20000k
```

If you want to find a file of an exact size, then leave off the plus or minus sign before the size of the file designator. This example finds all files with the size of 16,384 bytes:

```
$ find . -size 16384c
```

5-29. Sorting Files by Size

Problem

You want to list the files from largest to smallest.

Solution

The ls -alS command will display the long listing of all files sorted from largest to smallest. The following example combines ls with the head command to display the largest files in the current working directory:

```
$ ls -alS
```

Here is a sample of the output:

```
total 4001584
-rwxr----- 1 oracle oinstall 2039488512 Jan 21 16:39 o1_mf_undotbs1_3gpysv9n_.dbf
-rwxr----- 1 oracle oinstall  983834624 Jan 21 16:37 o1_mf_sysaux_3gpystwj_.dbf
-rwxr----- 1 oracle oinstall  775954432 Jan 21 16:39 o1_mf_system_3gpysttv_.dbf
-rwxrwxr-x 1 oracle oinstall  176168960 Jan 21 02:31 o1_mf_temp_3gpz8s70_.tmp
```

How It Works

If there are many files in a directory, you can combine ls and head to just list the "top n" files in a directory. The following example restricts the output of ls to the first five lines:

```
$ ls -alS | head -5
```

■**Note** On some older Linux versions, the -S option may not be available. On older systems, use the ls -al | sort -rk5 command. The sort column may differ depending on the long listing of the output.

5-30. Finding the Largest Space-Consuming Directories

Problem

You have a mount point that is out of space, and you need to identify which directories are consuming the most space.

Solution

Use the du (disk usage) command to report on disk free space. The following example will report the top five directories consuming the most disk space beneath the current working directory:

```
$ du -S . | sort -nr | head -5
```

The -S (do not include size of subdirectories) option instructs du to report the amount of space used in each individual directory. Here's a sample of the output:

```
4001576 ./DB11G_BLLNX1/datafile
1500152 ./DB1TEST/datafile
307592  ./DB11G_BLLNX1/onlinelog
153800  ./DB1TEST/onlinelog
12044   ./DB11G_BLLNX1/controlfile
```

By default, the output of space used is reported in kilobytes. In the previous output, the largest directory beneath the current working directory is ./DB11G_BLLNX1/datafile, which uses 4GB of space.

If you want to report the sum of space consumed by a directory and its subdirectories, then leave off the -S option:

```
$ du . | sort -nr | head -5
```

Here is a sample of the output when aggregating the amount by directory and each directory's subdirectories:

```
5984872 .
4321220 ./DB11G_BLLNX1
4001576 ./DB11G_BLLNX1/datafile
1663604 ./DB1TEST
1500152 ./DB1TEST/datafile
```

When not using the -S option, the top directory will always report the most consumed space because it is an aggregate of its disk space plus any spaced used by its subdirectories.

■**Note** On some Unix systems, there may not be an -S option. For example, on Solaris the -o option performs the same feature as the Linux -S option. Use man du to list all options available on your database server.

How It Works

The du command recursively lists the amount of disk space used by directory and every subdirectory beneath it. If you don't supply a directory name as an argument, then du will by default start with the current working directory. The du command will report on one line the amount of space consumed and the name of the directory.

The du command has a plethora of useful options. For example, the -s (summary) option is used to report a grand total of all space used beneath a directory and its subdirectories. This command reports on the total disk space used beneath the /orahome directory:

```
$ du -s /orahome
3324160 /orahome
```

You can also use the -h option to make the output more readable:

```
$ du -sh /orahome
3.2G /orahome
```

5-31. Truncating an Operating System File

Problem

You have a large trace file that is being written to by a database process. You know that the trace file doesn't contain anything that needs to be retained. The trace file has filled up a disk, and you want to make the size of the file 0 bytes without removing the file because you know that a database process is actively writing to the file.

Solution

Copy the contents of /dev/null to the file. You can use either the cat command or the echo command to accomplish this. This example uses the cat command to make an existing log file 0 bytes in size:

```
$ cat /dev/null > listener.log
```

The other way to zero out the file is with the cp command. This example copies the contents of /dev/null to the trace file:

```
$ cp /dev/null listener.log
```

How It Works

One of us recently had a database that hung because one of the mount points was full and prevented Oracle from writing to disk and subsequently hung the database. Upon further inspection, it was discovered that an Oracle Net trace file had grown to 4GB in size. The file had grown large because a fellow DBA had enabled verbose tracing in this environment and had forgotten to monitor the file or inform the other DBAs about this new level of tracing.

In this case, there was an Oracle Net process actively writing to the file, so we didn't want to simply move or remove the file because we weren't sure how the background process would react. In this case, it's safer to make the file 0 bytes. The /dev/null device is colloquially called the *bit bucket*. It is often used for a location to send output when you don't need to save the output. It can also be used to make a file 0 bytes without removing the file.

■**Caution** Zeroing out a file will permanently delete its contents. Use the techniques in this recipe only if you're certain you do not need the information contained within the file.

5-32. Counting Lines and Words in a File

Problem

You want to count the number of lines and words in a shell script.

Solution

Use the wc (word count) command to count the number of lines and words in a file. This example counts the number of words in the rmanback.bash shell script:

```
$ wc rmanback.bash
434 1697 16260 rmanback.bash
```

The previous output indicates that there are 434 lines, 1,697 words, and 16,260 characters in the file.

How It Works

If you want to see only the number of lines in a file, then use wc with the -l option:

```
$ wc -l rmanback.bash
434 rmanback.bash
```

Similarly, if you want to display only the number of words, use the -w option:

```
$ wc -w rmanback.bash
1697 rmanback.bash
```

5-33. Creating a Second Name for a File

Problem

When performing a new install of the Oracle binaries, your initialization parameter file is located in an Oracle Flexible Architecture (OFA) directory such as /ora01/admin/DBS/pfile. When starting a database, Oracle will by default look for the initialization file in the ORACLE_HOME/dbs directory.

You don't want to maintain the initialization file in two separate directories. Instead, you want to create a link from the OFA directory to the default directory.

Solution

Use the ln -s command to create a soft link to another file name. The following creates a soft link for the physical file in /ora01/admin/DEV/pfile/initDEV.ora to the link of /ora01/product/10.2.0/dbs/initDEV.ora:

```
$ ln -s /ora01/admin/DEV/pfile/initDEV.ora /ora01/product/10.2.0/dbs/initDEV.ora
```

A long listing of the soft link shows it pointing to the physical file:

```
$ ls -altr /ora01/product/10.2.0/dbs/initDEV.ora
lrwxrwxrwx    1 oracle dba    39    Apr 15 15:58 initDEV.ora ->
/ora01/admin/DEV/pfile/initDEV.ora
```

How It Works

A *soft link* (also referred to as a *symbolic link*) creates a file that acts as a pointer to another physical file. Soft links are used by DBAs when they need a file to appear as if it is in two separate directories but physically resides in only one location.

The technique described in the solution of this recipe is commonly used by Oracle DBAs to manage the initialization file. This allows DBAs to view and edit the file from either the soft link name or the actual physical file name.

5-34. Creating a Second Name for a Directory

Problem

You want to physically move a datafile to a different disk location without having to change any of the Oracle metadata.

Solution

Use soft links to make a directory look like it exists, when it is really just a pointer to a physical location. This example shows how to move a tablespace datafile from one mount point to another, without having to change the datafile's name as it appears in the data dictionary. In this example, the datafile will be moved from /oradisk1/DBS to /oradisk2/DBS.

On this server, the following physical mount points exist:

```
/oradisk1/DBS
/oradisk2/DBS
```

A long listing shows the ownership of the mount points as follows:

```
$ ls -altrd /oradisk*
drwxr-xr-x  3 oracle oinstall 4096 Apr 15 19:17 /oradisk2
drwxr-xr-x  3 oracle oinstall 4096 Apr 15 19:19 /oradisk1
```

First, create the following soft link as the root user:

```
# ln -s /oradisk1 /oradev
```

Here's a simple test to help you understand what is happening under the hood. Change directories to the soft link directory name:

```
$ cd /oradev/DBS
```

Notice that if you use the built-in Bash pwd command, the soft link directory is reported:

```
$ pwd
/oradev/DBS
```

Compare that to the use of the Linux /bin/pwd command, which will report the actual physical location:

```
$ /bin/pwd
/oradisk1/DBS
```

■**Note** You can also make the Bash built-in pwd command display the physical location by using the -P (physical) option (see recipe 5-1 for more details).

Next create a tablespace that references the soft link directory. Here is an example:

```
SQL> CREATE TABLESPACE td01
     DATAFILE '/oradev/DBS/td01.dbf'
     SIZE 50M
     EXTENT MANAGEMENT LOCAL
     UNIFORM SIZE 128k
     SEGMENT SPACE MANAGEMENT AUTO;
```

A query from V$DATAFILE shows the soft link location of the datafile:

```
SQL> select name from v$datafile;
```

Here's the output pertinent to this example:

```
/oradev/DBS/td01.dbf
```

Next, shut down your database:

```
SQL> shutdown immediate;
```

Now move the datafile to the new location:

```
$ mv /oradisk1/DBS/td01.dbf /oradisk2/DBS/td01.dbf
```

Next (as root) remove the previously defined soft link:

```
# rm /oradev
```

Now (as root) redefine the soft link to point to the new location:

```
# ln -s /oradisk2 /oradev
```

Now (as oracle) restart the database:

```
SQL> startup
```

If everything goes correctly, your database should start. You have physically moved a datafile without having to change any data dictionary metadata information.

How It Works

Using soft links on directories gives you some powerful options when relocating datafiles. This technique allows you to make Oracle think that a required directory exists when it is really a soft link to a different physical location.

The techniques in the "Solution" section of this recipe are useful when duplicating databases to a remote server using RMAN. In this situation, you can use symbolic links to make the auxiliary database server look similar to the source database server filesystem. This provides a method for relocating databases to servers with different mount points from the original server in which you can make a mount point or directory look like it exists to Oracle when, in reality, it is a soft link.

CHAPTER 6

■ ■ ■

Archiving and Compressing Files

Most people who work with computers realize that the task of copying many files from one location to another is much easier if you can first bundle together the files and copy them as a single unit. This is especially true when copying hundreds or thousands of files from one location to another. For example, in a Windows environment, if you have hundreds of files in a folder, it's fairly easy to click and drag the folder (that contains the files) and copy it to a different location. This copy task would be time-consuming and error-prone if you individually copied each file within the folder.

In Linux, tar, cpio, and zip are utilities that DBAs often use to group files together into one file (like a Windows folder). Bundling a group of files together into one file is known as creating an *archive*. Archiving tools allow you to back up all files in a directory structure and preserve any file characteristics such as permissions, ownership, and contents. The archive file is used to move or copy the files as a single unit to a different location.

The tar utility was originally used to bundle (or archive) files together and write them to tape, which is why it's called *tape archive*, or, in shorthand, tar. Although tar was originally used to write files to tape, its bundling ability is mainly what DBAs use it for now.

The cpio utility gets its name from its ability to copy files in and out of archived files. This command-line utility is also widely used by database administrators to bundle and move files. Oracle often distributes its binaries packaged as cpio files.

The zip utility is another popular tool for bundling files. This utility is especially useful for moving files from one operating system platform to another. For example, you can use zip to bundle and move a group of files from a Windows server to a Linux server.

Network performance can sometimes be slow when moving large archive files from one server to another. In these situations, it's appropriate to compress large files before they are remotely transferred. Many compression programs exist, but the most commonly used in Linux environments are gzip and bzip2. The gzip utility is widely available on most Linux platforms. The bzip2 utility is a newer tool and has a more efficient compression algorithm than gzip. The zip utility is also used for compression, but it isn't as efficient at compressing files as gzip and bzip2.

In this chapter we'll also briefly show how to use the compress and uncompress utilities, even though we recommend you do not use compress. It's an older and less efficient compression utility. We mention it only because you might find yourself working with an older Linux server that has files that have been created with compress.

Most of the utilities described in this chapter are frequently used by DBAs. Which utility you use for the task at hand depends on variables such as personal preference, standards defined for your environment, and features of the utility. For example, when downloading Oracle installation files, these are usually bundled with cpio; this of course means that you must be familiar with cpio. In other situations, you might use tar because the person receiving the file has requested that the file be in the tar format.

DBAs spend a fair amount of time moving large numbers of files to and from database servers. To do your job efficiently, it's critical to be proficient with archiving and compression techniques. In this chapter, we cover common methods that database administrators utilize for bundling and compressing files. We also cover the basics of generating checksums and encrypting/decrypting files. We felt these topics were appropriate in this chapter because DBAs often use checksums and encryption when working with bundled files that are transferred to other database administrators.

6-1. Bundling Files Using tar

Problem

You want to package several database scripts into one file using the tar utility.

Solution

This first example uses the tar utility with the -cvf options to bundle all files ending with the string .sql that exist in the current working directory:

```
$ tar -cvf prodrel.tar *.sql
```

The -c (create) option specifies you are creating a tar file. The -v (verbose) option instructs tar to display the names of the files included in the tar file. The -f (file) option directly precedes the name of the tar archive file. The file that is created in this example is named prodrel.tar. It's standard to name the tar file with the extension of .tar.

If you want to include all files in a directory tree, then specify the directory name from where you want the tar utility to begin bundling. The following command bundles all files in the /orahome/scripts directory (and any files in its subdirectories):

```
$ tar -cvf script.tar /orahome/scripts
```

■**Note** A file created with tar is colloquially referred to as a *tarball*.

How It Works

Both DBAs and system administrators ubiquitously use the tar utility to bundle a large number of files together as one file. Once files have been packaged together, they can be easily moved as a unit to another location such as a remote server (see Chapter 14 for details on copying files over the network).

The tar command has the following basic syntax:

```
$ tar one_mandatory_option [other non-mandatory options] [tar file] [other files]
```

When running tar, you can specify only one mandatory option, and it must appear first on the command line (before any other options). Table 6-1 describes the most commonly used mandatory options.

Table 6-1. *Mandatory tar Options*

Option	Description
-c, --create	Create a new archive file.
-d, --diff, --compare	Compare files stored in one tar file with other files.
-r, --append	Append other files to tar file.
-t, --list	Display the names of files in tar file. If other files are not listed, then display all files in tar file.
-u, --update	Add new or updated files to tar file.
-x, --extract, --get	Extract files from the tar file. If other files is not specified, then extract all files from tar file.
-A, --catenate, --concatenate	Append a second tar file to a tar file.

There are three methods for formatting options when running the tar command:

- Short

- Old (historic)

- Mnemonic

The short format uses a single hyphen (-) followed by single letters signifying the options. Most of the examples in this chapter use the short format. This format is preferred because there is minimal typing involved. Here's an example of using the short format to create an archive of all files in the /ora01 directory (and its subdirectories):

```
$ tar -cvf ora01.tar /ora01
```

The old format is similar to the short format except that it doesn't use the hyphen. Most versions of tar still support the old syntax for backward compatibility with older Linux/Unix distributions.

The mnemonic format uses the -- double hyphen format followed by a descriptive option word. This format has the advantage that it's easier to understand which options are being used. For example, the next line of code clearly shows that you're creating a tar file, using the verbose output, for all files in the /ora01 directory (and its subdirectories):

```
$ tar --create --verbose --file ora01.tar /ora01
```

The -f or --file option must come directly before the name of the tar file you want to create. You'll receive unexpected results if you specify the f option anywhere but just before the name of the tar file. Look carefully at this next line of code and subsequent error message:

```
$ tar -cfv prod_rel.tar *.sql
tar: prod_rel.tar: Cannot stat: No such file or directory
```

The previous line of code will attempt to create a file named v and put in it a file named prod_rel.tar along with files in the current working directory ending with the extension of *.sql.

If you want to compress the files as you archive them, then use the -z option (for gzip) or the -j option (for bzip2). The next example creates a compressed archive file of everything beneath the /oracle/product/10.2 directory:

```
$ tar -cvzf orahome.tar /oracle/product/10.2
```

Depending on the version of tar, the previous command might not add an extension such as .gz to the name of the archive file. In that case, you can specify the file name with a .gz extension when creating the file, or you can rename the file after it has been created.

If you're using a non-GNU version of tar, then you may not have the z or j compression options available. In this case, you'll have to explicitly pipe the output of tar to a compression utility like gzip:

```
$ tar -cvf - /oracle/product/10.2 | gzip > orahome.tar.gz
```

You can also use tar to copy a directory from one location to another on a box. This next example uses tar to copy the scripts directory tree to the /ora01/backup directory:

```
$ tar -cvf - scripts | (cd /ora01/backup; tar -xvf -)
```

The previous line of code needs a bit of explanation. The tar command uses standard input (signified with a - as the tar file name. This is piped to the next set of commands. The cd command changes directories to /ora01/backup and then extracts to standard output (signified with a -). This essentially gives you a method for copying directories from one location to another without having to create an intermediary tarball file.

6-2. Unbundling Files Using tar

Problem

You want to retrieve files from a bundled tar file.

Solution

Use the -x option to extract files from a tar file. Usually it's a good idea to first create a new directory and extract the files in the newly created directory. This way you don't mix up files that might already exist in a directory with files from the archive.

This example creates a directory and then copies the tar file into the directory before extracting it:

```
$ mkdir tarball
$ cd tarball
$ cp ../mytar.tar .
$ tar -xvf mytar.tar
```

The previous example retrieves all files from the `mytar.tar` file into the directory named `tarball`.

How It Works

When extracting files, you can retrieve all files in the `tar` file, or you can provide a list of specific files to be retrieved. The following example extracts only two files from the `tar` file:

```
$ tar -xvf mytar.tar script1.sql script2.sql
```

You can also use pattern matching to retrieve files from a `tar` file. This example extracts all files that end in `*.bsh` from the `tar` file named `mytar.tar`:

```
$ tar -xvf mytar.tar *.bsh
```

If you don't specify any files to be extracted, then all files are retrieved:

```
$ tar -xvf mytar.tar
```

ABSOLUTE PATHS VS. RELATIVE PATHS

Some older, non-GNU versions of `tar` will use absolute paths when extracting files. The next line of code shows an example of specifying the absolute path when creating an archive file:

```
$ tar -cvf orahome.tar /home/oracle
```

Specifying an absolute path with non-GNU versions of `tar` can be dangerous. These older versions of `tar` will restore the contents with the same directories and file names from which they were copied. This means any directories and file names that previously existed on disk will be overwritten.

When using older versions of `tar`, it is much safer to use a relative pathname. This next example first changes directories to the `/home` directory and then creates an archive of the `oracle` directory (relative to the current working directory):

```
$ cd /home
$ tar -cvf orahome.tar oracle
```

The previous example uses the relative path name. With non-GNU versions of `tar`, using the relative path is much safer than using absolute paths.

You don't have to worry about absolute vs. relative paths on most Linux systems. This is because these systems use the GNU version of `tar`. This version will strip off the leading `/` and will restore files relative to where your current working directory is located.

Use the `man tar` command if you're not sure whether you have a GNU version of the `tar` utility. You can also use the `tar -tvf <tarfile name>` command to preview which directories and files will be restored to what locations.

6-3. Finding Differences in Bundled Files Using tar

Problem

You wonder whether there have been any changes to files in a directory since you last created a tar file.

Solution

Use the -d (difference) option of the tar command to compare files in a tar file to files in a directory tree. The following example finds any differences between the tar file backup.tar and the scripts directory:

```
$ tar -df backup.tar scripts
```

The previous command will display any differences with the physical characteristics of any of the files. Here is some sample output:

```
scripts/top.sql: Mod time differs
scripts/top.sql: Size differs
```

How It Works

If you find differences and want to update the tar file to make it current, then use the -u option. This feature will update and append any files that are different or have been modified since the tarball was created. The next line of code updates or appends to the tar file any changed or new files in the scripts directory:

```
$ tar -uvf backup.tar scripts
```

The output indicates that the top.sql has been updated:

```
scripts/
scripts/top.sql
```

6-4. Bundling Files Using cpio

Problem

You want to use cpio to bundle a set of files into one file.

Solution

When using cpio to bundle files, specify o (for out or create) and v (verbose). It's customary to name a bundled cpio file with the extension of .cpio. The following command takes the output of the ls command and pipes it to cpio, which creates a file named backup.cpio:

```
$ ls | cpio -ov > backup.cpio
```

If you want to bundle up a directory tree with all files and subdirectories, then use the `find` command on the target directory. The following pipes the output of the `find` command to `cpio`, which bundles all files and subdirectories beneath the current working directory:

```
$ find . -depth | cpio -ov > orahome.cpio
```

If you want to create a compressed file, then pipe the output of `cpio` to a compression utility like `gzip`:

```
$ find . -depth | cpio -ov | gzip > orahome.cpio.gz
```

The `-depth` option tells the `find` command to print the directory contents before the directory itself. This behavior is desirable especially when bundling files that are in directories with restricted permissions.

How It Works

The key to understanding on how to package files with `cpio` is that it accepts as input a piped list of files from the output of commands such as `ls` or `find`. Here is the general syntax for using `cpio` to bundle files:

```
$ [find or ls command] | cpio -o[other options] > filename
```

For example, if you wanted to back up all files in the `oracle` account's home directory tree, then run `cpio` as follows:

```
$ find /home/oracle | cpio -ov > orahome.cpio
```

You can also specify that you want only those file names that match a certain pattern. This example bundles all SQL scripts in the `scripts` directory:

```
$ find scripts -name "*.sql" | cpio -ov > mysql.cpio
```

6-5. Unbundling Files Using cpio

Problem

You just downloaded some Oracle software installation files. You notice that they are bundled as `cpio` files. You wonder how to retrieve files from the `cpio` archive.

Solution

Use `cpio` with the `idmv` options when unbundling a file. The i option instructs `cpio` to redirect input from an archive file. The d and m options are important because these instruct `cpio` to create directories and preserve file modification times, respectively. The v option specifies that the file names should be printed as they are extracted.

The following example first creates a directory to store the scripts before unbundling the `cpio` file:

```
$ mkdir Disk1
$ cd Disk1
```

After copying the archive file to the Disk1 directory, then use cpio to unpack the file:

```
$ cpio -idvm < linux10g_disk1.cpio
```

You can also pipe the output of the cat command to cpio as an alternative method to extract the file:

```
$ cat linux10g_disk1.cpio | cpio -idvm
```

You can also uncompress and unbundle files in one concatenated string of commands:

```
$ cat linux10g_disk1.cpio.gz | gunzip | cpio -idvm
```

The previous command allows you to easily uncompress and extract the Oracle distribution media.

How It Works

The cpio utility is used with the i option to extract archive files. Here is the general syntax to unbundled files using cpio:

```
$ cpio -i[other options] < filename
```

You can extract all files or a single file from a cpio archive. This next example uses the cpio utility to extract a single file named rman.bsh from a cpio file named dbascripts.cpio:

```
$ cpio -idvm rman.bsh < dbascripts.cpio
```

An alternative way to unpack a file is to pipe the output of cat to cpio. Here is the syntax for this technique:

```
$ cat filename | cpio -i[other options]
```

Also of note is that you can use cpio to unbundle tar files. This example uses cpio to extract files from a script named scripts.tar:

```
$ cpio -idvm < scripts.tar
```

6-6. Bundling Files Using zip

Problem

Your database design tool runs on a Windows box. After generating some schema creation scripts, you want to bundle the files on the Windows server and copy them to the Linux box. You wonder whether there is a common archiving tool that works with both Windows and Linux servers.

Solution

Use the zip utility if you need to bundle and compress files and transfer them across hardware platforms. This first example uses zip with the -r (recursive) option to bundle and compress all files in the oracle10g directory tree (this includes all files and subdirectories):

```
$ zip -r ora10g.zip oracle10g
```

You can also specify files that you want included in a `.zip` file. The following command bundles and compresses all SQL files in the current working directory:

```
$ zip myzip.zip *.sql
```

How It Works

The `zip` utility is widely available on Windows and Linux servers. Files created by `zip` on Windows can be copied to and extracted on a Linux box. The `zip` utility both bundles and compresses files.

The compression ratio achieved by `zip` is not nearly as efficient as `bzip2` or `gzip`. However, the `zip` and `unzip` utilities are popular because the utilities are portable across many platforms such as Linux, Windows, Unix, and Mac OS. If you need cross-platform portability, then use `zip` to bundle and `unzip` to unbundle.

■**Tip** Run `zip -h` at the command line to get help information on either a Windows or Linux server.

6-7. Unbundling Files Using zip

Problem

Your database-modeling tool runs on a Windows box. After generating some schema creation scripts, you want to bundle the files on the Windows server, copy them to the Linux box, and unbundle them.

Solution

To uncompress a zipped file, first create a target directory location, then move the `zip` file to the new directory, and finally use `unzip` to unbundled and uncompress all files and directories included in the `zip` file. The example in this solution performs the following steps:

1. Creates a directory named `march03`

2. Changes the directory to the new directory

3. Copies the zip file to the new directory

4. Unzips the zip file

   ```
   $ mkdir march08
   $ cd march08
   $ cp /mybackups/mvzip.zip .
   $ unzip mvzip.zip
   ```

You should see output indicating what directories are being created and what files are being extracted. Here's a small snippet of the output for this example:

```
inflating: mscd642/perf.sql
creating: mscd642/ppt/
inflating: mscd642/ppt/9inew_f.ppt
inflating: mscd642/ppt/brpreso.ppt
inflating: mscd642/ppt/chap01.ppt
inflating: mscd642/ppt/chap02.ppt
```

How It Works

The unzip utility will list, test, or extract files from a zipped archive file. You can use this utility to unzip files regardless of the operating system platform on which the zip file was originally created. This is handy because it allows you to easily transfer files between Linux and other operating systems such as Windows.

You can also use the unzip command to extract a subset of files from an existing zip archive. The following example extracts upgrade.sql from the upgrade.zip file:

```
$ unzip upgrade.zip upgrade.sql
```

Similarly, this example retrieves all files that ended with the extension of *.sql:

```
$ unzip upgrade.zip *.sql
```

Sometimes you run into situations where you want to add only those files that do exist in the source directory and do not exist in the target directory. First recursively zip the source directory. In this example, the relative source directory is orascripts:

```
$ zip -r /orahome/ora.zip orascripts
```

Then cd to the target location and unzip the file with the -n option. In this example, there is an orascripts directory beneath the /backup/scripts directory:

```
$ cd /backups/scripts
$ unzip -n /orahome/ora.zip
```

The -n option instructs the unzip utility to not overwrite existing files. The net effect is that you unbundle only those files that do exist in the source directory but do not exist in the target directory.

6-8. Listing the Contents of a Bundled File

Problem

You want to verify which files are contained within an archived file before extracting its contents.

Solution

Each of the bundling commands (tar, cpio, and zip) has a method for listing files within an archive file. Each technique is described briefly in its own subsection.

tar

Use the -tvf (table of contents, verbose, file) option to display the contents of a tar file. This example lists the contents of the orahome.tar file:

```
$ tar -tvf orahome.tar
```

If you want to view the contents of a compressed tar file, then use a z or j (gzip or b2zip, respectively). This example displays the contents of a tar file that has been compressed with gzip:

```
$ tar -tzvf orahome.tar.gz
```

Interestingly, you can use the cpio utility to work on tar files. This next example lists the contents of the orahome.tar tarball:

```
$ cpio -itv < orahome.tar
```

cpio

Use the -itv (input, table of contents, verbose) option to display the contents of a cpio-generated file. This example lists the contents of the dir.cpio file:

```
$ cpio -itv < dir.cpio
```

Here's an alternate way to view the contents of a cpio file using the cat command:

```
$ cat dir.cpio | cpio -itv
```

zip

To view the contents of a zip file, use the unzip command with the -l (list files) option:

```
$ unzip -l backup.zip
```

How It Works

It's almost always a good idea to first list the files contained in an archived file. This will show you which directories will be created and which files will be extracted. If you're ever unsure about the contents of a bundled file, then use one of the techniques described in the "Solution" section of this recipe for obtaining a listing of the bundled file's contents.

6-9. Bundling Files Using find

Problem

You want to find all trace files over a certain age and bundle them into an archive file.

Solution

You'll have to use a combination of commands to find and compress files. This next example finds all trace files that were modified more than two days ago and then bundles and compresses them:

```
$ find /ora01/admin/bdump -name "*.trc" -mtime +2 | xargs tar -czvf trc.tar.gz
```

This next example uses `cpio` to achieve the same result:

```
$ find /ora01/admin/bdump -name "*.trc" -mtime +2 | cpio -ov | gzip > trc.cpio.gz
```

■**Note** See recipe 5-25 for more details on using the `find` command with date and time options.

How It Works

Quite often you'll find yourself cleaning up old files on database servers. When dealing with log or trace files, sometimes it's desirable to first find, bundle, and compress the files and then at some later time physically delete the files after they're not needed anymore (see recipe 5-26 for examples of finding and removing files). We recommend you encapsulate the code in this recipe in a shell script and run it regularly from a scheduling utility such as `cron` (see Chapter 11 for details on automating jobs).

6-10. Adding to a Bundled File

Problem

You want to add one file to a previously created bundled archive.

Solution

Each of the bundling commands (`tar`, `cpio`, and `zip`) has a method for adding a file or a directory to an existing archive. Each technique is described briefly in its own section here.

tar

To add one file to a `tar` archive, use the `-r` (append) option:

```
$ tar -rvf backup.tar newscript.sql
```

This next example adds a directory named `scripts` to the `backup.tar` file:

```
$ tar -rvf backup.tar scripts
```

cpio

To add a file to a `cpio` bundle, use the `-A` (append) option. Also specify the F option to specify the name of the existing `cpio` file. This next example adds any files with the extension of `*.sql` to an existing `cpio` archive named `my.cpio`:

```
$ ls *.sql | cpio -ovAF my.cpio
```

To add a directory to an existing `cpio` file, use the `find` command to specify the name of the directory. This line of code adds the `backup` directory to the `my.cpio` file:

```
$ find backup | cpio -ovAF my.cpio
```

zip

Use the -g (grow) option to add to an existing zip file. This example adds the file script.sql to the my.zip file:

```
$ zip -g my.zip script.sql
```

You can also add a directory to an existing zip archive. This next line adds the directory backup to the my.zip file:

```
$ zip -gr my.zip backup
```

How It Works

If you deal with a lot of files, sometimes it's easier to add a file to an existing archive rather than re-creating the archive from scratch. In these situations, use one of the techniques in the "Solution" section of this recipe to append a file.

6-11. Compressing and Uncompressing Files

Problem

Before copying a large file over the network to a remote server, you want to compress it.

Solution

Several utilities are available for compressing and uncompressing files. The gzip, bzip2, and compress utilities are widely used in Linux and Unix environments. Each of them is briefly detailed in the following sections.

gzip and gunzip

This first example uses gzip to compress the scripts.tar file:

```
$ gzip scripts.tar
```

The gzip utility will add an extension of .gz to the file after it has been compressed. To uncompress a file compressed by gzip, use the gunzip utility:

```
$ gunzip scripts.tar.gz
```

The gunzip utility will uncompress the file and remove the .gz extension. The uncompressed file has the original name it had before the file was compressed.

Sometimes there is a need to peer inside a compressed file without uncompressing it. The following example uses the -c option to send the contents of the gunzip command to standard output, which is then piped to grep to search for the string error:

```
$ gunzip -c scrdv12_ora_19029.trc.gz | grep -i error
```

You can also use the zcat utility to achieve the same effect. The next command is identical to the previous command:

```
$ zcat scrdv12_ora_19029.trc.gz | grep -i error
```

bzip2 and bunzip2

Use bzip2 to compress files. By default, files compressed with bzip2 will be given a .bz2 extension. This example compresses the file exp.dmp:

```
$ bzip2 exp.dmp
```

To uncompress a bzip2 compressed file, use bunzip2. This utility expects a file to be uncompressed to be named with an extension of one of the following: .bz2, .bz, .tbz2, .tbz, or .bzip2. This example uncompresses a file named exp.dmp.bz2:

```
$ bunzip2 exp.dmp.bz2
```

The bzip2 utility will uncompress the file and remove the .bz2 extension. The uncompressed file has the original name it had before the file was compressed.

Sometimes you need to view the contents of a compressed file without uncompressing it. The following example uses the -c option to send the contents of the bunzip2 command to standard output, which is then piped to grep to search for the string error:

```
$ bunzip2 -c scrdv12_ora_19029.trc.bz2 | grep -i error
```

compress and uncompress

The compress utility is aptly named. Files compressed with this utility are given a .Z extension. This example compresses a large trace file:

```
$ compress dwrep_lgwr_1912.trc
```

To uncompress a compress compressed file, use uncompress:

```
$ uncompress dwrep_lgwr_1912.trc.Z
```

The uncompress utility will uncompress the file and remove the .Z extension. The uncompressed file has the original name it had before the file was compressed.

■**Tip** Generate a checksum before compressing a file, and compare it to the checksum after uncompressing. This allows you to validate that a file has not been corrupted by the compression utility. See recipe 6-12 for details on using Linux checksum utilities.

How It Works

DBAs often move files from one location to another. This frequently includes moving files to remote servers. Compressing files before transferring them is critical to being able to copy large files. Several compression utilities are available. The most commonly used are gzip, b2zip, and compress.

The gzip utility is widely available in the Linux and Unix environments. If you have scripts that need to be portable across many variants of Linux and Unix, then gzip and gunzip are excellent choices.

The bzip2 utility is a newer and more efficient compression algorithm than gzip. The bzip2 tool is CPU intensive but achieves high compression ratios. If you need good compression with large files, then use bzip2 to compress and bunzip2 to uncompress.

We recommend you use gzip or bzip2 instead of compress. The compress utility is an older tool and less efficient compression tool. We mention it in this chapter only because you may run into compress compressed files on an older Linux or Unix server. Every once in a while you may run into a shell script that a previous DBA wrote that uses the compress utility.

■**Tip** The best compression available is achieved with the rm (remove) command. A word of caution, though— your data is permanently irretrievable after using rm. As of the time this book was published, there is still no unrm (unremove) command available.

6-12. Validating File Contents

Problem

You just copied a file from one server to another. You need to verify that the destination file has the same contents as the source file.

Solution

Use a utility such as sum to compute a checksum on a file before and after the copy operation. This example uses the sum command to display the checksum and number of blocks within a file:

```
$ sum backup.tar
24092 78640
```

In the previous output, the checksum is 24092, and the number of blocks in the file is 78640. After copying this file to a remote server, run the sum command on the destination file to ensure that it has the same checksum and number of blocks. Table 6-2 lists the common utilities used for generating checksums.

■**Note** On some Linux/Unix platforms, the sum utility may compute a different checksum for a file depending on the version of the operating system.

How It Works

When moving files between servers or compressing and uncompressing, it's prudent to verify that a file contains the same contents as it did before the copy or compress/uncompress operation. The most reliable way to do this is to compute a checksum. This allows you to verify that a file wasn't inadvertently corrupted during a transmission or compress/uncompress.

A *checksum* is a value that is calculated that allows you to verify a file's contents. The simplest form of a checksum is a count of the number of bytes in a file. For example, when transferring a file to a remote destination, you can then compare the number of bytes between the source file and the destination file. This checksum algorithm is very simplistic and not entirely reliable. However, in many situations, counting bytes is the first step to determine whether a source and destination file contain the same contents. Fortunately, many standard Linux utilities are available to calculate reliable checksum values.

DBAs also compute checksums to ensure that important files haven't been compromised or modified. For example, you can use the md5sum utility to compute and later check the checksum on a file to ensure that it hasn't been modified in any way. This example uses md5sum to calculate and store the checksums of the listener.ora, sqlnet.ora, and tnsnames.ora files:

```
$ cd $TNS_ADMIN
$ md5sum listener.ora sqlnet.ora tnsnames.ora >net.chk
```

Then at some later time, you can use md5sum to verify that these files have not been modified since the last time a checksum was computed:

```
$ md5sum --check net.chk
listener.ora: OK
sqlnet.ora: FAILED
tnsnames.ora: OK
md5sum: WARNING: 1 of 3 computed checksums did NOT match
```

From the pervious output, the sqlnet.ora file has been modified sometime after the checksum was computed. This allows you to detect changes and ensure that important files have not been compromised.

Table 6-2. *Common Linux Utilities Available for Generating Checksum Values*

Checksum Utility	Description
sum	Calculates checksum and number of blocks
cksum	Computes checksum and count of bytes
md5sum	Generates 128-bit Message-Digest algorithm 5 (MD5) checksum and can detect file changes via --check option
sha1sum	Calculates 160-bit SHA1 (Secure Hash Algorithm 1) checksum and can detect file changes via --check option

6-13. Encrypting and Decrypting Files

Problem

You store sensitive DBA password information in a file on disk and want to encrypt the file before sharing it with other database administrators.

Solution

Use the gpg utility to encrypt a file. The first step is to generate public and private keys required by gpg:

```
$ gpg --gen-key
```

The previous command will prompt you for input such as what key type, size, lifetime, real name, and passphrase. Usually the default values are sufficient. You will need to remember the passphrase because that is required when you decrypt an encrypted file. You should see files created for you in the HOME/.gnupg directory.

After you have successfully generated the required keys, you can now encrypt files. In this example, the oracle user encrypts a file that contains sensitive passwords.

```
$ gpg --encrypt --recipient oracle passwords.txt
```

This creates a new file named passwords.txt.gpg. It does not remove the passwords.txt file. You can manually remove the passwords.txt file with the rm command.

The following line of code decrypts the passwords.txt.gpg file:

```
$ gpg --output passwords.txt --decrypt passwords.txt.gpg
```

You will be prompted for the passphrase. After entering the correct passphrase, an unencrypted file will be created for your perusal.

How It Works

The gpg (GNU Privacy Guard) utility is an encryption tool that is installed by default on most Linux servers. This utility allows you to encrypt and decrypt sensitive files. When you first use the tool, you must generate public and private keys via the --gen-key option.

To send an encrypted message, use the receiver's public key in combination with the sender's private key. In other words, before you can send an encrypted file, you must first obtain the recipient's public key and place it on your keyring. The follow steps illustrate this concept:

1. As the sender of the encrypted file, generate the public and private keys:

   ```
   $ gpg --gen-key
   ```

2. As the receiver of the encrypted file, generate the public and private keys, and export the public key:

   ```
   $ gpg --gen-key
   $ gpg --export > oracle@bllnx3.key
   ```

   If you're going to e-mail the key to the user sending the encrypted file, sometimes it's desirable to export the key as an ASCII file:

   ```
   $ gpg -a --export > oracle@bllnx3.key
   ```

3. As the receiver, send your exported key file to the user who will send the encrypted file. In this example, the file is oracle@bllnx3.key. You can scp the file to a location the sender can access or e-mail an ASCII key file to them.

4. As the sender of the encrypted file, import the exported key of the receiver:

```
$ gpg --import oracle@bllnx3.key
```

You can verify that the user to receive the encrypted file has been placed on the keyring:

```
$ gpg --list-keys
```

Here is a partial listing of the output:

```
pub   1024D/7EF416B7 2008-08-12 oracle@bllnx3 (oracle@bllnx3) <oracle@bllnx3>
sub   2048g/710EAC88 2008-08-12
```

5. As the sender, encrypt the file to be sent to the receiver. In this example, the receiver is oracle@bllnx3, and the file to be encrypted is password.txt:

```
$ gpg -e -r oracle@bllnx3 password.txt
```

Here is a partial snippet of the output from this command:

```
It is NOT certain that the key belongs to the person named
in the user ID.  If you *really* know what you are doing,
you may answer the next question with yes
Use this key anyway?
```

Enter y for "yes." An encrypted file with the extension .gpg should now be created for you. In this example, the encrypted file name is password.txt.gpg.

6. Now send the encrypted file to the recipient.

7. As the recipient, decrypt the file:

```
$ gpg password.txt.gpg
```

You should be prompted for a passphrase:

```
You need a passphrase to unlock the secret key for
user: oracle@bllnx (oracle@bllnx3) <oracle@bllnx3>"
```

As the receiver, enter your passphrase. After you successfully enter the correct passphrase, you should now have a decrypted password.txt file.

There are other encryption utilities such as openssl that you can use to protect sensitive files. This utility allows you to encrypt files without having to create keys. Before using openssl, first view the available ciphers available:

```
$ openssl list-cipher-commands
```

Here is a partial listing of the output:

```
aes-128-cbc
aes-128-ecb
aes-192-cbc
aes-192-ecb
aes-256-cbc
```

```
aes-256-ecb
base64
bf
bf-cbc
bf-cfb
```

Note A cipher is an algorithm used for encrypting and decrypting files.

Pick one of the ciphers from the previous list to use for encrypting a file. The following example uses the Advanced Encryption Standard (AES) 128-bit cipher in Cipher Block Chaining (CBC) mode:

```
$ openssl enc -aes-128-cbc -in passwords.txt -out passwords.enc
```

You should now be prompted for a password:

```
enter aes-128-cbc encryption password:
```

You will be prompted again for verification:

```
Verifying - enter aes-128-cbc encryption password:
```

To decrypt the file, use the -d option:

```
$ openssl enc -d -aes-128-cbc -in passwords.enc -out passwords.txt
```

After the password you entered is successfully authenticated, the file will be decrypted. The previous command will overwrite the file passwords.txt if it exits. If you don't specify an output file, the decrypted form of the encrypted file will be displayed on your terminal.

You can also specify a password on the command line when encrypting and decrypting via the -pass option of openssl. This encrypts the passwords.txt file using a password of foo:

```
$ openssl enc -aes-128-cbc -in passwords.txt -out passwords.enc -pass pass:foo
```

Similarly, use the -pass option when decrypting:

```
$ openssl enc -d -aes-128-cbc -in passwords.enc -out passwords.txt -pass pass:foo
```

Both openssl and gpg are considered to be robust encryption and decryption utilities. You may find the openssl utility a little easier to use because you don't have to generate keys when sharing encrypted files with other users.

CHAPTER 7

███

Shell Scripting

Shell scripting is an important expertise that every professional DBA must possess. Most DBAs use this coding technique to automate many critical database administration tasks such as database backups and monitoring. As part of your job, you'll be asked to maintain scripts that prior DBAs have written, and you'll also be required to write new shell scripts as unique needs arise. The better you are at scripting, the better you'll be able to perform your job.

To be effective at shell scripting, DBAs minimally need to be familiar with four types of tools:

- SQL application

- Text editor

- Shell interface

- Shell scripting

The most common tools that map to the previous list are SQL*Plus, the vi editor, and the Bash shell. The Bash shell is both a shell interface and a scripting language. The previous bulleted list is a minimal list of tools that you should be familiar with. You'll need to use a wide variety of Oracle database utilities in shell scripts such as RMAN, Export/Import, Data Pump, SQL*Loader, and so on.

As discussed in previous chapters, a shell is a command-line interface that allows you to interact with the Linux kernel. Some shells that are commonly used by DBAs in Linux environments are the Bourne Again shell (bash) and the Korn shell (ksh). As explained in Chapter 3, this book focuses on the Bash shell, so we won't rehash those details here.

A *shell script* is an operating system file that contains one or more commands that a shell can execute. Any command that the shell can execute can be placed in a shell script file. For example, a shell script can run other shell scripts, executable binary files (such as sqlplus or rman), or any Linux utility.

DBAs use shell scripts for critical tasks such as proactively monitoring the database and taking backups. These critical tasks need to be repeatable and testable. DBAs typically use shell scripts to run a series of commands that accomplish the desired task. DBAs like shell scripting because they don't need to be expert programmers to write shell scripts. With a base knowledge (and a good example), it's fairly quick and easy to create a shell script that performs the desired task.

The purpose of this chapter is to provide you with a core set of techniques to enable you to successfully write shell scripts. This chapter does not cover all the facets of shell scripting (that would take an entire book to accomplish). Rather, we provide you with the common approaches and shell scripting fundamentals that DBAs need to perform their jobs. Once you become adept at shell scripting, you'll be able to leverage these skills to automate critical database jobs (see Chapter 11 for details on automating tasks).

The first recipe of this chapter introduces you to the basics of how to write a shell script. If you're already familiar with the basics, then you can skip recipe 7-1.

Note One could argue that a database administrator might exclusively use a graphical user interface (GUI) or a browser user interface (BUI) tool to automate database tasks. We strongly recommend you learn how to write shell scripts to automate DBA tasks. If the GUI or BUI ever becomes inaccessible or doesn't do something you need it to do, then—for your job's sake—you had better know how to write and debug a shell script.

7-1. Writing a Simple Shell Script

Problem

You're new to shell programming, and you want to write a simple script to determine whether your database is accessible.

Solution

Use an editor to create a new file (see Chapter 4 for details on using the vi file editor). Place within the file the following text:

```
#!/bin/bash
ORACLE_SID=SCDEV
ORACLE_HOME=/orahome/oracle/product/10.2.0.1/db_1
PATH=$ORACLE_HOME/bin:$PATH
echo "select 'DB up' from dual;" | sqlplus -s system/foo
exit 0
```

Modify the previous code to match your ORACLE_SID and ORACLE_HOME variables and your system schema password. After you've created the file, you'll also need to modify the permissions on the file to be executable. In this example, the file name is dbcheck.bsh:

```
$ chmod u+x dbcheck.bsh
```

This changes the permission for the owner (u) of the file to executable (x). Now you should be able to successfully run the program:

```
$ dbcheck.bsh
```

If your database is up, you should receive a message like this:

```
'DBUP
-----
DB up
```

All of the checking within the script is performed with one line of code:

```
echo "select 'DB up' from dual;" | sqlplus -s system/foo
```

The echo command pipes a valid SQL statement to the sqlplus executable. The sqlplus executable will then attempt to log on with the system schema and run the statement.

BASH SHELL EXIT COMMAND

You can place an exit command at any location within a shell script to instruct the Bash shell to immediately terminate the program. A successful exit is normally specified with an exit or an exit 0. Exiting a shell script when a failure condition has been detected is indicated by a nonzero value, such as an exit 1. We recommend you explicitly place an exit 0 command within your shell script to indicate a successful completion. You should also use a nonzero value such as an exit 1 to indicate that some sort of an error condition has been detected.

Each Bash shell command that executes will also return an exit code. If a command executes successfully, it will terminate with a status of 0. If there has been some sort of a failure, the exit code will be nonzero. You can check the status of an exit code by inspecting the $? variable. The $? variable holds the exit value of the previously executed command. The nonsuccess value of an exit code will vary by each command. For example, the grep utility will return a 0 on successfully finding a match, a 1 if no matches are found, and a 2 if there has been some sort of a syntax error or missing input file.

How It Works

The first line of the shell script in the "Solution" section of this recipe needs a little more explanation. We've reproduced the line here for the discussion:

```
#!/bin/bash
```

The # character is normally used to comment out a line in a shell script. One exception to that rule is when #! appears as the first text in the shell script. When #! is placed on the first line, it can be then combined with a path and program name. The path and program name specify the location and name of the program that will interpret the commands within the script. This is important because it means you can have the script run with a designated shell regardless of the interactive shell you're using.

If you don't specify a #!/<path>/<program>, then the shell you're currently logged on to will be used to interpret the commands within the script. We recommend you specify the path and shell program on the first line of your script so that there is no ambiguity about which shell will be used to interpret the commands within the script.

On most Linux distributions, the bash interpreter is in the /bin directory. If you don't know the location of your bash executable, you can use the which or whereis command to locate it:

```
$ whereis bash
bash: /bin/bash
```

When you first attempt to run a shell script, you may receive an error similar to the following:

```
-bash: dbcheck.bsh: command not found
```

This means your PATH variable doesn't include the current working directory. To work around this, you can reset your PATH variable to include the current working directory. This example exports the PATH variable to include the current working directory:

```
$ export PATH=$PATH:.
```

Another method for ensuring that the Bash shell can locate a script is to include the complete directory path to where the script resides. In this example, the script is located in the directory /home/oracle and is run as shown here:

```
$ /home/oracle/dbcheck.bsh
```

You can also instruct the shell to look in the current working directory to determine the location of the script. You do this by placing a ./ before the script name:

```
$ ./dbcheck.bsh
```

Note Adding the file extension .sh, .bsh, or .bash to the end of a Bash shell script is a common industry practice. Keep in mind that file extensions are meaningless in Linux/Unix environments (other than helping you document the type of script). This is different from DOS where .exe, .com, and .bat indicate executable operating system files.

7-2. Checking Simple Conditions

Problem

You want to check for a condition such as whether a critical database background process is running and send an e-mail if there is a problem.

Solution

Use the if/then/else Bash control structure to check for a condition and perform an appropriate action. The following example uses an if/then/else structure to determine whether the Oracle system monitor process is running and sends an e-mail if the process is not detected:

```
#!/bin/bash
SID=SAND
critProc=ora_smon
ps -ef | grep -v 'grep' | grep ${critProc}_$SID
if [ $? -eq 0 ]; then
  echo "$SID is available."
else
  echo "$SID has issues." | mail -s "problem with $SID" bbill@gmail.com
fi
exit 0
```

The previous example uses the $? variable. This variable is often used after conditional statements to evaluate the success or failure of the previous command. The $? contains the status of the last executed command. If the previously executed command was successful, then the $? variable will contain a zero; otherwise, it will contain a nonzero value.

How It Works

The if/then/else control structure comes in three basic forms. The first one states that if a condition is true, then execute the following commands. Its syntax is as follows:

```
if condition ; then
  commands
fi
```

On the first line of code in the previous example, the keyword then is a separate command, so you must insert a semicolon to indicate the end line termination point of the if keyword. Another way of executing the previous bit of code would be as follows:

```
if condition
then
  commands
fi
```

The next form of the if/then/else structure states if a condition is true, execute the following commands. If the first condition is false, then execute a separate set of commands. Its syntax is as follows:

```
if condition ; then
  commands
else
  commands
fi
```

The third form of the if/then/else structure states that if a condition is true, then execute the first set of commands; otherwise, check for the next condition, and if it is true, execute the commands. This functionality is enabled with the elif keyword. You can have many elif conditions in this form. Its syntax is as follows:

```
if condition ; then
  commands
elif  condition
  commands
elif  condition
  commands
fi
```

7-3. Testing a Condition

Problem

You want to write a script that checks for certain conditions such as the number of parameters passed to a script. Based on the condition, you want to perform an action such as display an informational message or exit the script.

Solution

As shown in recipe 7-2, the if/then/else structure is an important programming technique. However, it is the combination of if/then/else with a condition that can be *tested* that gives you a much more powerful tool to automate DBA tasks. The test command gives you the ability to check a condition within an if command. Here is the basic syntax for the test command:

```
test operand1 operator operand2
```

The test command can also be written with the [ ] syntax. This syntax uses a left brace to start the command and then finishes the command with a right brace. Its syntax is as follows:

```
[ operand1 operator operand2 ]
```

Note The shell script examples in this chapter will use the [ ] form of the test command.

For some test conditions, an operand1 isn't required. The syntax for this condition is as follows:

```
[ operator operand2 ]
```

The previous test conditional checks will exit with a status of 0 (true) or 1 (false), depending on the evaluation of the condition. Ensure that you have a space between the operands, operators, and brackets. The space is how the shell knows where the operator and operand are separated. If there is no space between the operator, operand, and brackets, then the shell will interpret the value as one string, which will result in erroneous outcomes.

Verifying the Number of Parameters

To bring if/then/else and test together, you'll write a small—but useful—piece of code that checks to see whether the correct number of parameters are passed to a script. The script will use the $# parameter. The $# parameter automatically gets assigned to the number of positional parameters typed at the command line. The $# variable is handy when you want to check for the correct number of parameters passed to a script.

The following bit of code uses the -ne conditional check to determine whether the number of variables passed to the script is not equal to 1:

```
#!/bin/bash
if [ $# -ne 1 ]
then
  echo "Wrong number of parameters passed to script."
  exit 1
fi
```

The $0 parameter is often used in conjunction with the $# parameter to display the correct syntax required when invoking a script. Within a shell script, the $0 parameter contains the name of the shell script being executed. Here's a slight variation of the previous code that uses the $0 variable to display the name of the script:

```
if [ $# -ne 1 ]
then
  echo "Wrong number of parameters passed to script."
  echo "Usage: $0 ORACLE_SID"
  exit 1
fi
```

The -ne operator is an arithmetic operator and is used to test whether the operands are not equal. If the script is called without passing exactly one parameter to it, then the following output is displayed:

```
Wrong number of parameters passed to script.
Usage: ./ss.bsh ORACLE_SID
```

Notice that there is a ./ in front of the script name in the previous output. To scrape the ./ out of the output, use the basename command as follows:

```
Pgm=$(basename $0)
if [ $# -ne 1 ]
then
  echo "Wrong number of parameters passed to script."
  echo "Usage: $Pgm ORACLE_SID"
  exit 1
fi
```

In the previous piece of code, notice the first line of code uses a shell technique known as *command substitution*. Command substitution allows you to take the output of a command and load it into a variable. The basic syntax for doing this is as follows:

```
variable=$(shell commands)
```

Verifying the Amount of Physical Memory

Another arithmetic check that you may want to do is to verify the amount of physical memory on your database server. Here's a simple script that verifies that the database server memory is greater than 1 gigabyte:

```
#!/bin/bash
thresh=1048576
totMem=$(grep MemTotal /proc/meminfo | awk '{print $2}')
if [ $totMem -lt $thresh ]; then
  echo "Total Memory $totMem is less than: $thresh"
  exit 1
else
  echo "Total Memory is: $totMem"
fi
```

Several arithmetic operators are available with the Bash shell. Table 7-1 gives a brief description of each operator.

Table 7-1. *Arithmetic Operators*

Operator	Description
-eq	True if two integers are equal
-ne	True if two integers are not equal
-lt	True if operand1 is less than operand2
-le	True if operand1 is less than or equal to operand2
-gt	True if operand1 is greater than operand2
-ge	True if operand1 is greater than or equal to operand2

Checking the Name of User Running the Script

You can also use strings with test conditions. There are a wide variety of ways to use string comparisons. Table 7-2 lists test operations for strings and their descriptions. For example, you may want to check to ensure that you're logged on as a certain operating system user before you run commands in a script. This example checks to see whether the user running the script is oracle:

```
#!/bin/bash
checkUser=oracle
curWho=$(whoami)
if [ "$curWho" != "$checkUser" ]; then
  echo "You are currently logged on as: $curWho"
  echo "Must be logged in as $checkUser to run this script.."
  exit 1
fi
```

In the previous bit of code, the curWho variable is assigned to the name of the user running the script. That string variable is then checked to see whether it matches the string of oracle. If user doesn't match, then the script displays informational messages and exits the script.

Table 7-2. *String Operators*

String Operator	Description
-z string	True if the string is empty
-n string	True if the string is not empty
string1 = string2	True if the strings are equal
string1 != string2	True if the strings are not equal
string1 < string2	True if string1 sorts before string2
string1 > string2	True if string1 sorts after string2

Accepting Input from the Command Line

Another useful example of a string comparison is to read input from a user and verify an operation. Suppose you want to check the current Oracle SID variable before continuing to run more commands within the script. This is useful if you work with multiple databases contained on one physical server. This script displays the value of ORACLE_SID and asks whether you want to continue running the script:

```
#!/bin/bash
keepGoing=n
echo "Current value of ORACLE_SID: $ORACLE_SID"
echo -n "Do you want to continue? y/n "
read keepGoing
if [ "$keepGoing" = "y" ]; then
  echo "Continue to run script."
else
  echo "Exiting script"
  exit 1
fi
```

How It Works

In addition to arithmetic and string comparisons, you can also perform various tests on operating system files. The test command allows you to perform checks such as the availability of a file, the file type, and so on. Table 7-3 contains descriptions of the Bash shell tests for file operations.

For example, you may want to determine whether an error log file exists and, if it does, then send an e-mail to the appropriate support person. This script uses the -e parameter of the test command to determine this:

```
#!/bin/bash
checkFile=/home/trace/error.log
if [ -e $checkFile ]; then
  mail -s "errors" bbill@gmail.com <$checkFile
else
  echo "$checkFile does not exist"
fi
```

If you want your shell script to do nothing after checking for a condition, then use the colon (:) command (sometimes called *no-operation* or *null*). For example, the following bit of code does nothing if it detects that the given file exists:

```
#!/bin/bash
checkFile=/home/oracle/.bashrc
if [ -e $checkFile ]; then
  :
else
  echo "$checkFile does not exist"
fi
```

Table 7-3. *File Operators*

File Operator	Description
-a	True if file exists
-b	True if file is a block device file
-c	True if file is a character device file
-d	True if file is a directory
-e	True if file exists
-f	True if file exists and is a regular file
-g	True if file has set-group-id permission set
-h	True if file is a symbolic link
-L	True if file is a symbolic link
-k	True if file's sticky bit is set
-p	True if file is a named pipe
-r	True if the file is readable (by current user)
-s	True if file exists and is not empty
-S	True if file is socket
-u	True if file is set-user-id
-w	True if file is writable (by current user)
-x	True if file is executable
-O	True if file is effectively owned by current user
-G	True if file is effectively owned by current user's group
-N	True if file has been modified since it was last read
file1 -nt file2	True if file1 is newer than file2
file1 -ot file2	True if file1 is older than file2
file -ef file2	True if file1 is a hard link to file2

■**Tip** The test options will vary by vendor and version of Linux. For a complete listing of available test operations in your environment, use the `help test` command or the `man test` command.

7-4. Checking Complex Conditions

Problem

You need to perform a sophisticated set of checking for conditions. You wonder whether there is a structure more powerful than `if/then/else`.

Solution

In many cases (pun intended), a simple `if/then/else` construct is all you need to check a condition. However, as soon as you are presented with many different actions to take, the `if/then/else` syntax can become unwieldy and nonintuitive. In these situations, use a `case` statement instead. The basic syntax for a `case` statement is as follows:

```
case expression in
  pattern1)
     commands ;;
  pattern2)
     commands ;;
esac
```

The following bit of code uses a `case` statement to check for the percentage of free disk space in the archive log file location and e-mails the DBA a report:

```
#!/bin/bash
archLoc=/dev/sda2
usedSpc=$(df -h $archLoc | awk '{print $5}' | grep -v Use | cut -d "%" -f1 -)
#
case $usedSpc in
[0-9])
  arcStat="relax, lots of disk space: $usedSpc"
;;
[1-7][0-9])
  arcStat="disk space okay: $usedSpc"
;;
[8][0-9])
  arcStat="gulp, space getting low: $usedSpc"
;;
[9][0-9])
  arcStat="red alert, running out of space: $usedSpc"
;;
```

```
[1][0][0])
  arcStat="update resume, no space left: $usedSpc"
;;
*)
arcStat="huh?: $usedSpc"
esac
#
BOX=$(uname -a | awk '{print $2}')
echo $arcStat | mail -s "archive space on: $BOX" prodSupport@gmail.com
exit 0
```

In the prior bit of code, the usedSpc variable gets assigned a value that shows what percentage of disk space is used on a mount point. The case statement then examines usedSpc to determine which range the variable falls within. Lastly, it e-mails the production support alias an informational message.

If the device name being assigned to archLoc is longer than 21 characters, then the df command does not neatly display the output on one line (and thus breaks the previous script). If this is the situation on your server, then you can create a symbolic link name (see recipe 5-34 for details) to a name that is 21 characters or fewer.

How It Works

The code in the "Solution" section of this recipe compresses a wide variety of shell commands and coding techniques into a short amount of code. The result is a small but extremely useful script that monitors disk space. The third line of the script needs additional explanation. We repeat it here for convenience:

```
usedSpc=$(df -h $archLoc | awk '{print $5}' | grep -v Use | cut -d "%" -f1 -)
```

The output of the df (disk free) command is piped to the awk command, which extracts the fifth column. This in turn is passed to the grep command, which eliminates any output that contains the string Use. This output is piped to the cut command, which extracts the first field delimited by a % character. The resultant string should be the percentage of disk space used on the mount point in question.

On some Linux/Unix platforms, the output of the df command might not display the string Use. For example, on Solaris, the output from the df command uses the word Capacity to indicate the amount of disk space used. In those situations, you can modify the script to use egrep to filter out multiple strings. This example uses egrep to filter a line containing either use or capacity from the output:

```
usedSpc=$(df -h $archLoc|awk '{print $5}'|egrep -iv "use|capacity"|cut -d "%" -f1 -)
```

In the example in the "Solution" section of this recipe, the case statement performs a sophisticated set of string comparisons on the value stored in the usedSpc variable. The case statement will check each condition until it finds a match. When a condition is met, the case statement runs any statements within the matched section and then exits.

An example will help clarify this concept. Let's look at the first condition in the case statement in the "Solution" section of this recipe:

```
[0-9])
  arcStat="relax, lots of space: $usedSpc"
;;
```

In the previous snippet of code, the case statement checks the value of the variable to see whether it is a one-digit string that contains a value within the range of 0 through 9. If it matches, then it sets the arcStat variable to an appropriate message and exits the case statement.

Take a look at the second condition in the case statement:

```
[1-7][0-9])
  arcStat="space okay: $usedSpc"
;;
```

In the prior bit of code, the case statement checks for a two-digit number. The first character it's looking for must be in the range of 1 through 7. The second character can be any number from 0 to 9. If the pattern matches, the arcStat variable is set to an appropriate value, and the case statement exits.

The case statement will continue to attempt to find a match based on the specified pattern. If no match is made, then the catchall clause *) will be executed, and the case statement will be exited. The structure of the case statement allows you to perform complicated comparisons that would probably drive you crazy if you tried to code it using if/then/else statements. Table 7-4 lists common pattern matching characters used in case statements.

Table 7-4. *Common Character Matching Patterns*

Pattern	Description
a|b	Matches either an a or a b
*	Matches any string of characters, often used for a catchall
[abc]	Matches any character a, b, or c
[a-c]	Matches any character a, b, or c
[0-9]	Matches any character 0 through 9
"<string>"	Matches the string enclosed in the quotes

Case closed!

7-5. Repeating a Task

Problem

You want to repeatedly perform a task a specific number of times or for a specific number of arguments that are passed in a list.

Solution

A for loop allows you to rerun a section of code a fixed number of times. This control construct is particularly useful because DBAs often have a known set of databases or files that need to be operated on. The for loop syntax is as follows:

```
for name [in list]
do
  commands that can use $name
done
```

The following code illustrates the power of a for loop. In this environment, there are three databases that are being monitored for a critical background process. The for loop allows you to provide an input list and have the same code reexecuted for each database name in the input list:

```
#!/bin/bash
SID_LIST="dev1 dev2 dev3"
critProc=ora_smon
for curSid in $SID_LIST
do
  ps -ef | grep -v 'grep' | grep ${critProc}_$curSid
  if [ $? -eq 0 ]; then
    echo "$curSid is available."
  else
    echo "$curSid has issues." | mail -s "issue with $curSid" lellison@oracle.com
  fi
done
```

How It Works

The for loop iterates through each argument passed in to the parameter list. This control structure is ideal for (no pun intended) a fixed input list. Depending on which shell you use, the syntax may be slightly different from the one described in the "Solution" section.

You can use the built-in Bash shell $@ variable to pass a list to a for loop. The $@ variable contains a quoted list of arguments passed to the script. By default, a for loop will use $@ if no input list is provided. The previous code snippet can be slightly modified to take advantage of this technique, as shown here:

```
#!/bin/bash
critProc=ora_smon
for curSid in $@
do
  ps -ef | grep -v 'grep' | grep -i ${critProc}_$curSid
  if [ $? -eq 0 ]; then
    echo "$curSid is available."
  else
    echo "$curSid has issues." | mail -s "issue with $curSid" bbill@gmail.com
  fi
done
```

Assume that the previous bit of code is placed in a file named dbup.bsh. It can now be run from the command line to pass in a list of databases to check:

```
$ dbup.bsh dev1 dev2 dev3
```

7-6. Iterating Until a Condition Is Met

Problem

You want to perform an operation an unknown number of times until a certain condition is achieved.

Solution

The while and until flow control constructs allow a piece of code to iterate until a condition is met. In contrast to a for loop construct, the while and until loops are useful when the number of times needed to continue looping is not known beforehand. The while loop runs until a test condition has zero exit status. The syntax for the while loop is as follows:

```
while condition ; do
    commands
done
```

The until control construct is similar to the while loop. The until loop runs until a test condition has a nonzero exit status.

```
until condition ; do
  commands
done
```

Sometimes it's useful when debugging scripts to iterate through all arguments passed to a shell script and view the parameter values. This next snippet of code uses a while loop to display all parameters passed into a script:

```
while [ $# -ne 0 ]; do
  echo $1
  shift 1
done
```

How It Works

In the previous code sample in the "Solution" section, the shift command is used to move the positional parameters one position to the left. You can think of the positional parameters as an array of values, and (when invoked) the shift command (destructively) moves these values left in the array by the specified number of values.

An example will help clarify this shifty concept. Suppose there are three parameters passed into a program: A, B, and C. This means $1 will contain A, $2 will contain B, and $3 will contain C. When you issue the shift 1 command, $1 now contains B, $2 contains C, and $3 now contains nothing. Another shift will move C into $1, and $2 and $3 will now be empty, and so forth.

7-7. Displaying a Menu of Choices

Problem

You want to present a menu of choices for the shell script user to pick from.

Solution

The select command allows you to create a menu from an input list. If the input list is omitted, then the positional parameters (contained in the $@ variable) are used to construct the menu. The syntax of the select command is nearly identical to the for command:

```
select name in  [input list ]
do
  commands that use $name
done
```

Listed next is a shell script that uses the select command to query the contents of the /var/opt/oracle/oratab file and set your Oracle operating system variables depending on which value for ORACLE_SID that you chose.

```
#!/bin/bash
# Why:    Sets Oracle environment variables.
# Setup: 1. Put oraset file in /var/opt/oracle
#        2. Ensure /var/opt/oracle is in $PATH
# Usage: batch mode: . oraset <SID>
#        menu mode:  . oraset
#=====================================================
OTAB=/var/opt/oracle/oratab
if [ -z $1 ]; then
   SIDLIST=$(grep -v '#' ${OTAB} | cut -f1 -d:)
   # PS3 incidates the prompt to be used for the Bash select command.
   PS3='SID? '
   select sid in ${SIDLIST}; do
     if [ -n $sid ]; then
       HOLD_SID=$sid
       break
     fi
   done
else
   if grep -v '#' ${OTAB} | grep -w "${1}:">/dev/null; then
     HOLD_SID=$1
   else
     echo "SID: $1 not found in $OTAB"
   fi
   shift
fi
#
```

```
export ORACLE_SID=$HOLD_SID
export ORACLE_HOME=$(grep -v '#' $OTAB|grep -w $ORACLE_SID:|cut -f2 -d:)
export ORACLE_BASE=${ORACLE_HOME%%/product*}
export TNS_ADMIN=$ORACLE_HOME/network/admin
export PATH=$ORACLE_HOME/bin:/usr/ccs/bin:/opt/SENSsshc/bin/\
:/bin:/usr/bin:.:/var/opt/oracle
export LD_LIBRARY_PATH=/usr/lib:$ORACLE_HOME/lib
```

When you run the script, be sure to run it with the source command, or the . notation, in one of the following ways:

```
$ . oraset <database name>
```

Or you can run the script interactively and pick your database name from a menu as follows:

```
$ . oraset
```

How It Works

The . instructs the shell to *source* the script. Sourcing tells your current shell process to inherit any variables set within an executed script. If you don't use the . notation, then the variables set within the script are visible only within the context of the subshell that is spawned when the script is executed.

■**Note** In the Bash and C-shell shell, the source command and the . built-in are synonymous.

When running the oraset program, suppose the contents of your /var/opt/oracle/oratab file contains the following text:

```
BRDSTN1:/global/ORAHOME1/product/10.2:Y
DEV9:/global/ORAHOME1/product/9.2:Y
```

The names of the databases in the previous text are BRDSTN1 and DEV9. The paths to the each database's home directory is next in the line (separated from the database name by a :). The last column should contain a Y or an N and indicates whether you want the databases to automatically be restarted when the system reboots (see Chapter 11 for details).

When you run oraset from the command line, you should be presented with a menu like this:

```
1) BRDSTN1
2) DEV9
```

In this example, you can now type a 1 or a 2 to set the operating system variables required for the particular database for whichever database you want to use. This allows you to interactively set up OS variables regardless of the number of database installations on the server.

7-8. Running Commands Based on Success/Failure of the Previous Command

Problem

You want to run a command based on the success or failure of the previously run command.

Solution

Use the && and || control operators to conditionally execute a command based on the status of the previously run command. The && operator says that if the first command was successful (exits with an exit status of zero), then run the second command in the list. If the first command did not run successfully, then do not run the second command. For example, in this next line of code, an e-mail will be sent only if the grep command finds the string ORA-00600 in the alert.log file:

```
$ grep ORA-00600 alert.log && echo "DB prob" | Mail -s "ORA 600 error" lare@orc.com
```

The || control operator says that if the first command is not successful (runs with a nonzero exit status), then the next command should be run. This next command checks for the existence of a log file, and if it is not found, then an e-mail is sent:

```
$ ls alert.log || echo "no log" | Mail -s "log file error" larrye@oracle.com
```

The previous examples give you another shell scripting tool that you can use in creative ways to monitor for various activities and alert you if there are problems.

How It Works

Sometimes it's useful to have a command execute depending on the success or failure of the previous immediately run command. For example, you may want to check the status of a background process. If the background process is not running, then have the shell program e-mail you an appropriate message.

7-9. Modularizing Scripts

Problem

You want to make your scripts more modular and functional. You determine that shell functions will help accomplish this task.

Solution

Functions are commonly used in most programming languages. A function is a block of commands that perform an action. You can think of a function as a small script within another script that compartmentalizes a section of code. Using functions allows you to modularize your code and make it more reusable, readable, and maintainable.

Like variables, functions must be declared before you can use them. Not surprisingly, the `function` command is used to declare functions. To illustrate the use of functions, let's say you need to create a reusable bit of code that displays some debugging information. This example creates a function named `showMsg`:

```
#!/bin/bash
function showMsg {
  echo "---------------------------------------------"
  echo "You're at location: $1 in the $0 script."
  echo "---------------------------------------------"
} # showMsg
```

The function can now be referenced anywhere in the script after the point at which it was declared. For example, further down in the script this snippet of code invokes the `showMsg` function:

```
showMsg 1
# more code goes here...
showMsg 2
```

How It Works

Functions can also be declared and invoked directly from the operating system command line. From a DBA perspective, this gives you a *very* powerful tool that allows you to create and use any number of useful functions that can be run as if they were operating system commands. For example, create a file named `dbaFunk.bsh`, and place it in the following commands:

```
#!/bin/bash
#---------------------------------------------------------------------------#
# sshl : ssh with your login to remote host
  function sshl {
    echo "ssh -l $LOGNAME $*"
    ssh -l $LOGNAME $*
  } # sshl
#---------------------------------------------------------------------------#
# ssho : ssh with the oracle userid to remote host
  function ssho {
    echo "ssh -l oracle $*"
    ssh -l oracle $*
  } # ssho
#---------------------------------------------------------------------------#
# chkps: check for a process on the box
  function chkps {
    ps -ef | grep -i $1
  } # chkps
#---------------------------------------------------------------------------#
```

Now source the file as shown here:

```
$ . dbaFunk.bsh
```

You now have access to these functions—sshl, ssho, and chkps—from the operating system command line. To illustrate this, the chkps function is called while passing in the string of oracle to operate on:

```
$ chkps oracle
```

You'll most likely collect many functions in your DBA tool bag to alleviate having to type long, typo-prone shell commands. Yes, for the previous simple functions, you could create aliases to accomplish essentially the same task. However, functions give you the additional ability to combine several different commands, use parameters, and echo useful informational messages.

7-10. Passing Parameters to Scripts

Problem

You don't like hard-coding variables in your script. You want to change a script to set variables based on parameters passed to the script. This makes your code more reusable, flexible, and maintainable.

Solution

First, take a look at this script with hard-coded values in it for the database SID:

```
#!/bin/bash
ORACLE_SID=brdstn
rman target / <<EOF
backup database;
EOF
```

The << characters instruct the command running (in this case, the rman utility) to receive its input from anything that appears between the first EOF and the last EOF. You don't have to use EOF for start and finish markers; it can be any text string. It simply marks the beginning and end of where the shell directs the input for the command running.

If you want to use this script (as it is) to back up a different database, then you'll have to manually edit it and change the name of the database. That isn't very efficient. A better approach would be to modify the script so that it dynamically can be passed the name of the database to be backed up. Assume for this example that the script name is back.bsh. The script is modified as shown to accept as input the database name:

```
#!/bin/bash
ORACLE_SID=$1
rman target / <<EOF
backup database;
EOF
```

In the previous bit of code, $1 is a built-in variable in the Bash shell. The $1 variable holds the first parameter passed to the script when invoking it. Now the script can be run by passing in a database name. In this example, we pass in the name of devdb:

```
$ back.bsh devdb
```

How It Works

You can pass any number of arguments into a shell script. The first parameter is referenced inside the script as $1, the second parameter is referenced as $2, and so on. These shell variables are known as *positional parameters*.

Positional parameters are special variables that are set internally by the shell and are available for you to use within a script. The shell provides several special variables for you. Some of the more useful of these variables are described in Table 7-5. Examples of using these variables will be sprinkled throughout the chapter.

Table 7-5. *Special Shell Variables*

Name	Description
$1 - $n	Positional parameters that hold values for parameters passed to the script.
$?	The exit status of the last command. Contains a 0 for successfully executed commands. Contains a nonzero value for commands that failed. This nonzero value depends on what the command actually returned.
$0	Within a shell script, contains the name of the shell script being executed.
$#	The number of positional parameters passed to a script.
$$	The process number of the shell. Can be used to generate unique file names.
$!	The process number of the most recently executed background process.
$*	Contains all the positional parameters passed to the script.

If you pass in more than nine positional parameters to a script, you will have to use braces ({}) to wrap the number portion of the parameter with multidigit parameters. This is because $10 will be interpreted as the contents of $1 with a 0 concatenated to it, whereas ${10} will be interpreted as the contents of the tenth variable. An example will help illustrate this point; say you pass ten parameters to a script as shown here:

```
$ myscript.bsh a b c d e f g h i j
```

For illustration purposes, suppose this line of code is contained within the script:

```
echo $10
```

In this case, that will produce a result of a0, because it is echoing the contents of parameter 1 concatenated with a 0.

When the braces are used with the echo command:

```
echo ${10}
```

that will produce a j, which is the tenth parameter that was passed to the script. Remember to use the braces anytime you reference a multidigit parameter within a shell script, or you will probably not get the results you intended.

WORKING WITH VARIABLES

Most programming languages need variables. Variables allow you to manipulate data. Variables are symbolic names that you can assign values to and modify during the execution of a program. In the Bash shell, you define a variable in the following way:

```
mydir=/home/oracle
```

Be aware that when defining a variable, you cannot use spaces around the = sign like this:

```
mydir = /home/oracle
```

In the previous line of code, the shell will interpret this to be a command named mydir followed by two arguments, = and /home/oracle. In this case, there is no mydir command, and the following error is returned:

```
bash: mydir: command not found
```

Sometimes the need arises to concatenate a string to a variable value. For example, if you wanted to append the string xyz to the value stored in the variable mydir, you might attempt this:

```
$ echo "$mydirxyz"
```

This returns no value because the shell interprets this to echo the value of the variable mydirxyz (and not mydir concatenated with xyz). If you need a variable value appended by a string of characters, then use {} to accomplish this:

```
$ echo ${mydir}xyz
/home/oraclexyz
```

The curly braces instruct the shell to echo the value of the variable (contained within the braces) and to append a string that appears immediately after the variable.

7-11. Processing Parameters

Problem

You want to efficiently process parameters passed into a script for valid values.

Solution

Use the getopts function to process parameters. Here is a script that uses getopts to examine and act on parameters passed to an RMAN backup script:

```
#!/bin/bash
PRG=$(basename $0)
USAGE="Usage: $PRG -d SID [-c compress] [-h]"
if [ $# -eq 0 ]; then
  echo $USAGE
  exit 1
fi
```

```
# If char followed by :, then argument is expected, the argument
# should be separated from the option by a white space.
OPTSTRING=":d:c:h"
#
while getopts "$OPTSTRING" ARGS; do
  case $ARGS in
  d) ORACLE_SID=${OPTARG}
     ;;
  c) COMP_SWITCH=$(echo ${OPTARG} | tr '[A-Z]' '[a-z')
     if [ $COMP_SWITCH = "compress" ]; then
       COMP_MODE=" as compressed backupset "
     else
       echo $USAGE
       exit 1
     fi
     ;;
  h) echo $USAGE
     exit 0
     ;;
  *) echo "Error: Not a valid switch or missing argument."
     echo ${USAGE}
     exit 1
     ;;
  esac
done
#
echo rman backup
rman target / <<EOF
backup $COMP_MODE database;
EOF
#
exit 0
```

How It Works

The getopts (get options) utility provides you with an efficient way to inspect and process command-line switches. The getopts program ensures a standard interface is used for shell program parameter handling.

   The while getopts command will iterate through each character in the OPTSTRING. This next bulleted list describes how getopts handles characters in the string:

- When the first character in the string is a :, that instructs the shell script to generate error messages. If the first character is not a :, then the getopts command should handle processing errors.

- If an option character is followed by :, then an argument is expected on command line; the argument should be separated from the option by a space.

- If an option is missing an argument, ARGS is set to a :, and OPTARG is set to the option missing an argument.

- If an option is invalid, ARGS is set to a ? question mark, and OPTARG gets set to the invalid option passed in.

In the "Solution" section of the recipe, the string name is OPTSTRING and is defined as follows:

```
OPTSTRING=":d:c:h"
```

The OPTSTRING starts with a :, which specifies that the shell script should handle error conditions and generate any related error messages. If OPTSTRING does not start with a :, this instructs the getopts command to display any applicable error messages.

The d and c options are both followed by colons and therefore require arguments. The h option is not followed by a colon and therefore does not require an option.

Assume that the name of the script in the "Solution" section is named rman.bsh. The following is a valid way to invoke the script:

```
$ rman.bsh -d ORCL -c compress
```

If you attempt to run the script with an invalid option, an error is returned:

```
$ rman.bsh -g
Error: Not a valid switch or missing argument.
Usage: rman.bsh -d SID [-c compress] [-h]
```

For this shell script, the -d (database) switch signifies a valid database SID. The -c (compress) switch will specify whether compression should be used. The -h (help) switch will display the correct usage of the script.

■**Note** Linux also has a getopt command (no s on the end). This command is used in a similar fashion to getopts. View the man getopt documentation for more information.

7-12. Running Database Commands in Scripts

Problem

You want to run a database utility command within a shell script.

Solution

There are several techniques for running database commands from within shell scripts. These are two techniques commonly used:

- Running commands directly

- Capturing output in a variable

These techniques are described in the following sections.

Running a Command Directly

For example, here is a script that invokes the Oracle RMAN utility and takes a backup of the control file:

```
#!/bin/bash
ORACLE_SID=DEV_DB
rman target / <<EOF
backup current controlfile;
EOF
```

The `<<` characters instruct the command running (in this case the `rman` utility) to receive its input from anything that appears between the first `EOF` and the last `EOF`. You don't have to use `EOF` for start and finish markers, it can be any text string. It simply marks the beginning and end of where the shell directs the input for the command running.

This technique applies to any Oracle utility. The following runs a SQL*Plus command within a shell script:

```
#!/bin/bash
ORACLE_SID=RMDB1
sqlplus -s <<EOF
/ as sysdba
select sysdate from dual;
EOF
```

Capturing Output in a Variable

Capturing the output of a command within a variable is known as *command substitution*. DBAs use this technique often in shell scripts.

For example, a DBA task might be to determine whether some Oracle materialized views are refreshing on a daily basis. One way of doing this is to select a count from the Oracle data dictionary view `USER_MVIEWS` where the last refresh date is greater than one day.

```
#/bin/bash
critVar=$(sqlplus -s <<EOF
pdb_m/abc@papd
SET HEAD OFF FEED OFF
SELECT count(*) FROM user_mviews WHERE sysdate-last_refresh_date > 1;
EXIT;
EOF)
```

The script returns a value into the variable `critVar`, and then you can test to see whether the value is a 0:

```
if [ $critVar -ne 0 ]; then
mail -s "Problem with MV refresh" support@backend.com <<EOF
MVs not okay.
EOF
else
  echo "MVs okay."
fi
```

If the value isn't 0, the script will send an e-mail to the appropriate support e-mail address.

How It Works

You can put any commands that a shell can interpret inside a script. The basic technique for running database tasks is to invoke the database utility and run any specific commands that the utility can interpret. The database commands need to be enclosed by a "start of command" and "end of command" marker.

The following example uses EOF for the start and end of a SQL*Plus command that reports the names of objects created in the database in the last week:

```
#!/bin/bash
newobjs=$(sqlplus -s << EOF
fbar/invqi@INVQI
select object_name
from dba_objects
where created > sysdate - 7
and owner not in ('SYS','SYSTEM');
EOF)
echo $newobjs | mailx -s "new objects" support@backend.com
```

There are two techniques for achieving command substitution in a shell script:

- $(command)

- `command`

For example, if you wanted to return the name of a server into a variable, it could be accomplished with the following techniques:

```
$ BOX=$(uname -a | awk '{print$2}')
```

or the following:

```
$ BOX=`uname -a | awk '{print$2}'`
```

Either technique is a valid method. Depending on which shell you use, the $(command) command substitution technique might not be available.

If you're using a data dictionary view (within a shell script) that contains a dollar sign ($) as part of the view name, then you must escape the dollar sign within the shell script. For example, the following selects from the view V$DATAFILE the number of datafiles that have an OFFLINE status:

```
#!/bin/bash
nf=$(sqlplus -s << EOF
/ as sysdba
set head off
select count(*)
from v\$datafile
where status='OFFLINE';
EOF)
echo "offline count: $nf" | mailx -s "# files offline" prod@supp.com
```

If you don't escape the dollar sign, then the shell script interprets the view name as a shell variable. The backslash (\) in front of the dollar sign instructs the shell script to ignore the meaning of special characters.

7-13. Crafting a Robust DBA Shell Script

Problem

You want to write a flexible and reusable shell script that incorporates the techniques used by experienced shell writers.

Solution

Most shell scripts that DBAs use require the following functionality:

1. Set the shell.

2. Validate parameters passed to the script.

3. Set any special variables to be used in the script.

4. Set the Oracle environment variables.

5. Call the Oracle utility.

6. Capture the output in a unique log file name.

7. Send an e-mail indicating the success or failure of the job.

8. Exit the script.

Listed next is a basic shell script that uses these techniques to determine whether a SQL*Plus connection can be made to a database. The line numbers have been included for discussion purposes and should be taken out before attempting to run the script:

```
1   #!/bin/bash
2   PRG=$(basename $0)
3   #
4   # Validate parameters
5   USAGE="Usage: ${PRG} <database name> "
6   if [ $# -ne 1 ]; then
7      echo "${USAGE}"
8      exit 1
9   fi
10  #
11  # Set variables used in the script
12  SID=${1}
13  CONSTR=system/foo@${SID}
```

```
14   MAILX='/bin/mailx'
15   MAIL_LIST='dkuhn@sun.com'
16   LOG_DIR=/orahome/oracle/scripts
17   DAY=$(date +%F)
18   LOG_FILE=${LOG_DIR}/${PRG}.${DAY}.$$.log
19   LOC_SID=SCDEV
20   BOX=$(uname -a | awk '{print$2}')
21   #
22   # Source oracle variables
23   . /var/opt/oracle/oraset $LOC_SID
24   #
25   # Attempt to connect to database via SQL*Plus
26   crit_var=$(sqlplus -s <<EOSQL
27   $CONSTR
28   SET HEAD OFF FEED OFF
29   select 'success' from dual;
30   EOSQL)
31   #
32   # Write output to log file
33   echo ${crit_var} > $LOG_FILE
34   #
35   # Send status
36   echo $crit_var | grep success 2>&1 >/dev/null
37   if [[ $? -ne 0 ]]; then
38     $MAILX -s "Problem with ${SID} on ${BOX}" $MAIL_LIST <$LOG_FILE
39   else
40     echo "Success: ${SID} on ${BOX}" | \
41     $MAILX -s "Success: ${SID} okay on ${BOX}" $MAIL_LIST
42   fi
43   #
44   exit 0
```

■**Tip** If you're using vi for an editor, use the set number and set nonumber commands to toggle the viewing of line numbers (see recipe 4-11 for more details).

How It Works

The shell script in the "Solution" section of this recipe uses a wide variety of shell programming techniques. You can use these methods to automate a diverse assortment of DBA tasks. We included line numbers in the shell program so that we could describe the purpose of each line. Table 7-6 contains a brief description of each line of code.

Table 7-6. *Explanation of Shell Script to Check on Database Status*

Line Number	Explanation
1	Specifies the Bash shell command interpreter for this script.
2	Captures the name of the shell script in the PRG shell variable. The $0 variable contains the name of the program. The basename command strips off any directory text that is prepended to the program name.
3–4	Comments.
5	Construct an information string and place it in the USAGE variable.
6–9	If the number of parameters is not equal to 1, then display the script usage string and exit the program. See recipe 7-11 for an advanced discussion of processing variables.
10–11	Comments.
12	Set the SID variable to the parameter passed into the script.
13	Set the CONSTR variable to contain the SQL*Plus database connection string.
14	Set the MAILX variable to the path and name of the mail utility on the server.
15	Specify the e-mail address of the DBA(s) to receive the job status.
16	Set the LOG_DIR variable to the directory of the log files.
17	Set the DAY variable to the current date string.
18	Specify the LOG_FILE to be a combination of the program name and date. The $$ variable is a unique process identifier and allows you to generate multiple log files per day.
19	Set the LOC_SID to a local instance name on the box that the shell script is running on.
20	Set the BOX variable to contain the name of the local database server.
21–22	Comments.
23	Use a program to set the required operating system variables such as ORACLE_HOME. See recipe 7-7 for an example of a file that sets the Oracle variables.
24–25	Comments.
26	Capture in the crit_var variable the output of the SQL*Plus command. Initiate a connection to SQL*Plus. EOSQL specifies the starting point for the SQL*Plus commands.
27	Connect to SQL*Plus with the value in CONSTR.
28–29	Run the SQL*Plus formatting and SQL command.
30	The EOSQL specifies the end of the text to be interpreted as SQL.
31–32	Comments.
33	Write the contents of the crit_var variable to the log file.
34–35	Comments.

Table 7-6. *Explanation of Shell Script to Check on Database Status (Continued)*

Line Number	Explanation
36	Examine the contents of the crit_var variable for the string success that should have been returned from the SQL*Plus command.
37	The $? contains the status of the previously run command. Check to see whether the previous grep command found the string success. If the grep command succeeded, then $? will contain a 0. The $? variable will contain a nonzero value if the grep command does not find the string success in the crit_var variable.
38	Send an e-mail indicating there is a problem.
39–41	The $? is equal to 0; therefore, the grep command found the string success in the crit_var variable. Send an e-mail indicating the database is up.
42	The end if the if statement.
43	Blank comment line.
44	Exit the shell script with a success status (indicated by a 0).

CREATING A LOCK FILE

One common method for preventing simultaneous jobs from running is to create a lock file for a script. If the file exists, then the job is already running or previously terminated abnormally. Place the following code at the beginning of your script. Modify the LOCKFILE parameter to match your environment:

```
LOCKFILE=/ora01/oradata/BRDSTN/lock/rman.lock
if [ -f $LOCKFILE ]; then
  echo "lock file exists, exiting..."
  exit 1
else
  echo "DO NOT REMOVE, RMAN LOCKFILE" > $LOCKFILE
fi
```

At the end of your script, remove the lock file:

```
if [ -f $LOCKFILE ]; then
  rm $LOCKFILE
fi
```

The use of a lock file ensures that if the script is already running and is called again, it won't start a new job.

7-14. Running Scripts in the Background

Problem

You work in a distributed environment and have database servers in remote locations. You want to run a job in the background that will continue to run, even if there are network problems or you log off the box.

Solution

Use the ampersand (&) character to place a job in the background. This example runs the rman.bsh script in the background:

```
$ rman.bsh &
[1] 6507
```

From the previous output, the [1] indicates the job number, and 6507 is the process identifier. You can verify that the program is running in the background via the jobs command:

```
$ jobs
[1]+  Running                 rman.bsh &
```

On some older systems, you may be required to use the nohup (no hangup) command to ensure that the job will still execute even if you log off the server. If using an older shell, then use this syntax to place a job in the background:

```
$ nohup rman.bsh &
```

To stop a background job use the kill command. This next line of code stops job 1:

```
$ kill %1
```

How It Works

In today's global environment, DBAs may find themselves logging onto remote servers halfway around the planet. Sometimes DBAs find themselves running long jobs on a remote server from the command line. For example, you might encounter an issue with a backup job, and you want to kick it off manually so that you can baby-sit it. One issue that arises is that sometimes the network connection being used can be somewhat unstable, and it will terminate your session before the given job has completed.

By default, when you run a shell script from the command line, it will run in the foreground. To execute a job in the background, place an ampersand character at the end of the command string. Here is the general syntax:

```
$ <command> &
```

Using & ensures that a command will continue to run, even if you log off the box. On some older systems, you may be required to use the nohup command to achieve this functionality. In this example, the nohup command is used to run a shell script in the background:

```
$ nohup export_db.bsh &
```

By default, the output from a nohup command is written to a file named nohup.out. You can redirect the output to the file of your choice as follows:

```
$ nohup export_db.bash >exp.out &
```

You can interactively monitor the output of the previous job by viewing it with the tail -f command:

```
$ tail -f exp.out
```

Note If you want a job to consistently run in the background at a specified time, then use a scheduling utility like `cron`. See Chapter 11 for details on automating jobs.

The & and `nohup` commands are the traditional ways of keeping a job running in the background. You can use the Linux `screen` command to achieve the same result with significantly more functionality. The `screen` command starts a terminal session on your server that will persist for you even if there is unexpected network disruption.

To start a `screen` session, issue the following command:

```
$ screen
```

If you receive an error like "Cannot open terminal */dev/pts/1*," then as `root` change the permissions on that file:

```
# chmod a+rw /dev/pts/1
```

When you invoke `screen`, you are presented with a terminal from which you can type commands and run scripts. The difference between a `screen` session and a normal terminal session is that the `screen` session will continue to run even after you are detached.

For example, say you are at your work location and log on to a database box and start a `screen` session. You then start a long-running backup job in your `screen` session. After the job is started, you detach from the screen session by pressing Ctrl+A and then the D key. You can then drive home, remotely log on to the database server, and reattach to the `screen` session you started previously while you were at work and monitor the backup job as if you were looking at the same terminal you started at work.

Here's a simple example of how this works. Type `screen`, as shown here:

```
$ screen
```

Print the current working directory so that you have some output on the screen that you can recognize when you attach to this `screen` session from another terminal:

```
$ pwd
/home/oracle
```

Now press Ctrl+A and then the D key (that's pressing the Ctrl and the A key at the same time, releasing them, and then pressing the D key). This detaches you from the `screen` session. You should see the following message:

```
[detatched]
```

Now start a different terminal session, and log on to the database server. Issue the following command to display any detached `screen` sessions:

```
$ screen -ls
There is a screen on:
        31334.pts-1.rmougprd2    (Detached)
1 Socket in /tmp/uscreens/S-oracle.
```

You can reattach to any screen session using the -r (reattach) option followed by [[pid.]tty[.host]]. For this particular example, you can reestablish the screen connection by typing this:

```
$ screen -r 31334.pts-1.rmougprd2
```

You should now see the output of the previously entered pwd command. It's as if you never left the screen terminal session. This is a *very* powerful utility that can be used to start jobs and then monitor them from another remote terminal session. You can even share a screen session with other users.

To display screen online help, press Ctrl+A and then the ? key. (That's pressing the Ctrl key and the A key at the same time, releasing those keys, and then pressing the ? key.) To leave a screen session, use the exit command. This will stop your screen session.

7-15. Monitoring the Progress of a Script

Problem

You're executing a shell script and want to monitor its progress.

Solution

Sometimes you'll need to monitor the progress of a long-running shell script. You can use the Linux tail command with the f (follow) switch to display the output of a job as it is written to a log file. In this example, the output of a backup job is redirected to an output file named rmanback.out:

```
$ rmanback.bash >rmanback.out 2>&1
```

From another session, the output being written to the log file is interactively viewed with the tail -f command:

```
$ tail -f rmanback.out
```

Here is snippet of typical output that might be displayed to the screen:

```
channel ORA_DISK_2: starting archive log backupset
channel ORA_DISK_2: specifying archive log(s) in backup set
input archive log thread=1 sequence=868 recid=859 stamp=628426116
input archive log thread=1 sequence=869 recid=860 stamp=628426523
input archive log thread=1 sequence=870 recid=861 stamp=628466994
channel ORA_DISK_2: starting piece 1 at 21-JUL-07
```

How It Works

DBAs often used the tail command to monitor things like alert logs and view potential issues with the database as they are happening. In this example, we continuously follow the display of what's being written to an Oracle database alert.log file:

```
$ tail -f alert_BRDSTN.log
```

Here's a snippet of typical output written to the alert.log file:

```
Completed: ALTER DATABASE BACKUP CONTROLFILE TO TRACE
DBID: 2917656785
Fri Jul 20 23:13:09 2007
Thread 1 advanced to log sequence 71
Current log# 2 seq# 71 mem# 0: /ora01/oradata/BRDSTN/oradata/redo02a.log
```

When you want to discontinue viewing the contents of a log file, press Ctrl+C (press Ctrl and C keys at the same time) to break out of the tail command.

EXECUTION TIME

Another common task associated with monitoring is determining how long it takes to run a command. The time command runs a specified program and then reports timing statistics when the command finishes. The following bit of code shows timing statistics when running the du -sh command to display the total disk usage:

```
$ time du -sh /
12G     .
real    0m1.288s
user    0m0.158s
sys     0m1.130s
```

The default output contains three types of statistics. The *real time* is the amount of time the program took from start to finish. In the previous output, the real time is 0 minutes and 1.288 seconds. The *user time* is the amount of time spent executing application code. The *sys time* is the amount of time spent executing kernel code.

7-16. Debugging a Script

Problem

Your script isn't doing what you expected. You want to debug the script.

Solution

The Bash shell has several features that are useful for debugging and troubleshooting problems in scripts. The -n switch (no execution) allows you to check the syntax of a script before you run it. To check a Bash shell script for syntax errors, use the -n as shown here:

```
$ bash -n db.bash
```

If the script contains any errors, it will display a message such as this:

```
db.bsh: line 10: syntax error: unexpected end of file
```

Another useful debugging feature is the -o xtrace option. This instructs the Bash shell to display every command before it is executed. This option also shows any variable substitutions and expansions. This allows you to view the actual variable values used when the shell script executes. You can invoke the -o xtrace feature from the command line as follows:

```
$ bash -o xtrace <script name>
```

You'll notice that the output contains lines that don't seem to have anything to do with your code:

```
+ alias 'rm=rm -i'
+ alias 'cp=cp -i'
+ alias 'mv=mv -i'
+ '[' -f /etc/bashrc ']'
+ . /etc/bashrc
+++ id -gn
+++ id -un
+++ id -u
++ '[' root = root -a 0 -gt 99 ']'
++ umask 022
++ '[' '' ']'
+ export JAVA_HOME=/opt/java
```

That's because the first several lines in the output are from code executed in profile scripts that are in your Linux environment. Also of note, the plus signs in the output indicate the level of nesting of a command within the script.

How It Works

As shell scripts become longer and more complex, it can sometimes be problematic to squash the source of bugs within a script. This can be especially true when maintaining code that somebody else wrote.

If you just want to see the tracing for specific commands within the script, then embed set -o xtrace directly within your code at the desired location. In this example, tracing is turned on before the if statement and then turned off at the end:

```
set -o xtrace
if [ $? -eq 0 ]; then
  echo "$critProc is available."
else
  echo "$critProc has issues." | mail -s "problem with $critProc" bbill@gmail.com
fi
set +o xtrace
```

To enable a set command feature, you must use the minus (-) sign. This may seem counterintuitive. Equally counterintuitive, use a plus (+) sign to disable a set command feature.

■**Note** You can also use the set -x command to print each command's parameter assignments before they are executed. To turn off tracing, use set +x. This is identical to the set -o xtrace command.

CHAPTER 8

■ ■ ■

Analyzing Server Performance

The delineation of tasks between a system administrator and a DBA is often nebulous. This can be especially true in small shops where you find yourself wearing multiple hats. Even in large organizations with established roles and responsibilities, you'll still find yourself in an occasional "all-hands-on-deck" fire drill where you're expected to troubleshoot server issues. In these scenarios, you must be familiar with the operating system commands used to extract information from the server. An expert DBA does not diagnose database problems in a vacuum; you have to be server savvy.

Whenever there are application performance issues or availability problems, seemingly (from the DBA's perspective) the first question asked is, what's wrong with the database? Regardless of the source of the problem, the onus is often on the DBA to either prove or disprove whether the database is behaving well. This process sometimes includes determining server bottlenecks. The database and server have a symbiotic relationship. DBAs need to be well versed with techniques to monitor server activity.

This chapter covers techniques used to analyze the server's CPU, memory, disk I/O, and network performance. Take some time to familiarize yourself with the relevant commands covered in each section. Being able to quickly survey system activity will vastly broaden your database administrator skill set.

System administrators also heavily use the tools described in this chapter. Table 8-1 summarizes the operating system utilities described in this chapter. Being familiar with how these operating system commands work and how to interpret the output will allow you to better work in tandem with your system administration team when diagnosing server performance issues.

Table 8-1. *Performance and Monitoring Utilities*

Tool	Purpose
vmstat	Monitors processes, CPU, memory, or disk I/O bottlenecks.
watch	Periodically runs another command.
ps	Identifies highest CPU- and memory-consuming sessions. Used to identify Oracle sessions consuming the most system resources.
top	Identifies sessions consuming the most resources.
mpstat	Reports CPU statistics.
sar	Displays CPU, memory, disk I/O, and network usage, both current and historical.

Table 8-1. *Performance and Monitoring Utilities (Continued)*

Tool	Purpose
free	Displays free and used memory.
df	Reports on free disk space.
du	Displays disk usage.
iostat	Displays disk I/O statistics.
netstat	Reports on network statistics.

■**Note** Oracle recommends you install the sysstat package on your database server. This package includes performance-monitoring utilities such as mpstat, iostat, and sar. Several of the recipes in this chapter utilize these tools. See Chapter 10 for details on installing the sysstat package.

8-1. Identifying System Bottlenecks

Problem

The application users are reporting that the database seems slow. You want to determine whether there are any system resource bottlenecks on the database server.

Solution

The vmstat (virtual memory statistics) tool is intended to help you quickly identify bottlenecks on your server. The vmstat command displays real-time performance information about processes, memory, paging, disk I/O, and CPU usage. This example shows using vmstat to display the default output with no options specified:

```
$ vmstat
procs -----------memory---------- ---swap-- -----io---- --system-- ----cpu----
 r  b   swpd   free   buff  cache   si   so    bi    bo   in   cs us sy id wa
14  0  52340  25272   3068 1662704    0    0    63    76    9   31 15  1 84  0
```

Here are some general heuristics you can use when interpreting the output of vmstat:

- If the wa (time waiting for I/O) column is high, this is usually an indication that the storage subsystem is overloaded. See recipes 8-9 and 8-10 for identifying the sources of I/O contention.

- If b (processes sleeping) is consistently greater than 0, then you may not have enough CPU processing power. See recipe 8-2 for identifying Oracle processes and SQL statements consuming the most CPU.

- If so (memory swapped out to disk) and si (memory swapped in from disk) are consistently greater than 0, you may have a memory bottleneck. See recipe 8-5 for details on identifying Oracle processes and SQL statements consuming the most memory.

Note The Linux vmstat command does not count itself as a currently running process.

How It Works

If your database server seems sluggish, then analyze the vmstat output to determine where the resources are being consumed. Table 8-2 details the meanings of the columns displayed in the default output of vmstat.

Table 8-2. *Column Descriptions of vmstat Output*

Column	Description
r	Number of processes waiting for runtime
b	Number of processes in uninterruptible sleep
swpd	Total virtual memory (swap) in use (KB)
free	Total idle memory (KB)
buff	Total memory used as buffers (KB)
cache	Total memory used as cache (KB)
si	Memory swapped in from disk (KB/s)
so	Memory swapped out to disk (KB/s)
bi	Blocks read in (blocks/s) from block device
bo	Blocks written out (blocks/s) per second to block device
in	Interrupts per second
cs	Context switches per second
us	User-level code time as a percentage of total CPU time
sy	System-level code time as a percentage of total CPU time
id	Idle time as a percentage of total CPU time
wa	Time waiting for I/O completion

By default, only one line of server statistics is displayed when running vmstat (without supplying any options). This one line of output displays average statistics calculated from the last time the system was rebooted. This is fine for a quick snapshot. However, if you want to gather metrics over a period of time, then use vmstat with this syntax:

```
$ vmstat <interval in seconds> <number of intervals>
```

While in this mode, vmstat reports statistics sampling from one interval to the next. For example, if you wanted to report system statistics every two seconds for ten intervals, then issue this command:

```
$ vmstat 2 10
```

You can also send the vmstat output to a file. This is useful for analyzing historical performance over a period of time. This example samples statistics every 5 seconds for a total of 60 reports and records the output in a file:

```
$ vmstat 5 60 > vmout.perf
```

Another useful way to use vmstat is with the watch tool. The watch command is used to execute another program on a periodic basis. This example uses watch to run the vmstat command every five seconds and to highlight on the screen any differences between each snapshot:

```
$ watch -n 5 -d vmstat
Every 5.0s: vmstat                                  Thu Aug  9 13:27:57 2007
procs -----------memory---------- ---swap-- -----io---- --system-- ----cpu----
 r  b   swpd   free   buff  cache   si   so    bi    bo   in   cs us sy id wa
 0  0    144  15900  64620 1655100    0    0     1     7   16    4  0  0 99  0
```

When running vmstat in watch -d (differences) mode, you'll visually see changes on your screen as they alter from snapshot to snapshot. To exit from watch, press Ctrl+C.

One last note, the default unit of measure for the memory columns of vmstat is in kilobytes. If you want to view memory statistics in megabytes, then use the -S m (statistics in megabytes) option:

```
$ vmstat -S m
```

OS WATCHER

Oracle provides a collection of Linux/Unix scripts that gather and store metrics for CPU, memory, disk, and network usage. The OS Watcher tool suite automates the gathering of statistics using tools such as top, vmstat, iostat, mpstat, netstat, and traceroute. If you don't have these utilities installed, see Chapter 10 for details on installing the sysstat package.

You can obtain OS Watcher from Oracle's MetaLink web site. Search for document ID 301137.1 or for the document titled "OS Watcher User Guide." Navigate to the Contents page, and search for the Download link.

This utility also has an optional graphical component for visually displaying performance metrics. The OS Watcher utility is currently supported on the following platforms: Linux, Solaris, AIX, Tru64, and HP-UX.

8-2. Identifying CPU-Intensive Processes

Problem

You want to identify which Oracle session is consuming the most CPU on the database server. If it's an Oracle session running a SQL query, then you want to display the associated SQL.

Solution

Use the ps command to identify the process IDs of sessions consuming the most CPU on the server. This next ps command displays the top ten CPU-consuming statements and the associated process IDs:

```
$ ps -e -o pcpu,pid,user,tty,args | sort -n -k 1 -r | head
```

To limit the output to oracle processes, use this command:

```
$ ps -e -o pcpu,pid,user,tty,args | grep -i oracle | sort -n -k 1 -r | head
```

Here is a partial listing of the output:

```
99.6 15940 oracle ? oracleRMDB1 (DESCRIPTION=(LOCAL=YES)(ADDRESS=(PROTOCOL=beq)))
74.5 16022 oracle ? oracleRMDB1 (DESCRIPTION=(LOCAL=YES)(ADDRESS=(PROTOCOL=beq)))
 3.8 16014 oracle ? rman
 1.2 16019 oracle ? oracleRMDB1 (DESCRIPTION=(LOCAL=YES)(ADDRESS=(PROTOCOL=beq)))
 0.1 16026 oracle  pts/2    -bash
 0.1 16021 oracle ? oracleRMDB1 (DESCRIPTION=(LOCAL=YES)(ADDRESS=(PROTOCOL=beq)))
```

The first column is the percentage of CPU being consumed. The second column is the process ID. You can use the process ID from the previous output as an input to the following query to show information about the Oracle session:

```
SET LINESIZE 80 HEADING OFF FEEDBACK OFF
SELECT
  RPAD('USERNAME : ' || s.username, 80) ||
  RPAD('OSUSER   : ' || s.osuser, 80) ||
  RPAD('PROGRAM  : ' || s.program, 80) ||
  RPAD('SPID     : ' || p.spid, 80) ||
  RPAD('SID      : ' || s.sid, 80) ||
  RPAD('SERIAL#  : ' || s.serial#, 80) ||
  RPAD('MACHINE  : ' || s.machine, 80) ||
  RPAD('TERMINAL : ' || s.terminal, 80)
FROM v$session s,
     v$process p
WHERE s.paddr = p.addr
AND   p.spid  = '&PID_FROM_OS';
```

If you run the prior query and supply to it the process ID of 15940, you get the following output:

```
USERNAME : INVMGR
OSUSER   : oracle
PROGRAM  : sqlplus@rmugprd.rmug.com (TNS V1-V3)
SPID     : 15940
SID      : 529
SERIAL#  : 2564
MACHINE  : rmugprd.rmug.com
TERMINAL :
```

From the prior output, it's a SQL*Plus session that is consuming the most CPU resources. To identify the SQL statement that this process is running, you pass to this query the operating system process ID as input:

```
SET LINESIZE 80 HEADING OFF FEEDBACK OFF
SELECT
  RPAD('USERNAME : ' || s.username, 80) ||
  RPAD('OSUSER   : ' || s.osuser, 80) ||
  RPAD('PROGRAM  : ' || s.program, 80) ||
  RPAD('SPID     : ' || p.spid, 80) ||
  RPAD('SID      : ' || s.sid, 80) ||
  RPAD('SERIAL#  : ' || s.serial#, 80) ||
  RPAD('MACHINE  : ' || s.machine, 80) ||
  RPAD('TERMINAL : ' || s.terminal, 80) ||
  RPAD('SQL TEXT : ' || q.sql_text, 80)
FROM v$session s
    ,v$process p
    ,v$sql     q
WHERE s.paddr        = p.addr
AND    p.spid        = '&PID_FROM_OS'
AND    s.sql_address = q.address
AND    s.sql_hash_value = q.hash_value;
```

If you run the previous query for the process ID of 15940, you get the following output:

```
USERNAME : INVMGR
OSUSER   : oracle
PROGRAM  : sqlplus@rmugprd.rmug.com (TNS V1-V3)
SPID     : 15940
SID      : 529
SERIAL#  : 2564
MACHINE  : rmugprd.rmug.com
TERMINAL :
SQL TEXT : select  count(*) ,object_name from dba_objects,dba_segments
```

The previous queries in this solution allow you to quickly identify Oracle processes and SQL statements that are currently consuming the greatest CPU resources on your database server.

How It Works

When you run multiple databases on one server and are experiencing server performance issues, it can be difficult to identify which database and session are consuming the most system resources. In these situations, use the ps command to identify the highest-consuming process and correlate that to a database session.

Once you have identified the highest resource-consuming session, then you have the option of trying to tune the operation (whether it be SQL, RMAN, and so on), or you might want to terminate the process. See recipe 3-2 for details on how to kill a Linux process and/or stop a SQL session.

Another tool for identifying resource-intensive processes is the top command. Use this utility to quickly identify which processes are the highest consumers of resources on the server. By default, top will repetitively refresh (every three seconds) information regarding the most CPU-intensive processes. Here's the simplest way to run top:

```
$ top
```

Here's a fragment of the output:

```
top - 08:58:33 up 4 days, 13:30,  2 users,  load average: 20.52, 20.58, 19.79
Tasks: 129 total,  22 running, 107 sleeping,   0 stopped,   0 zombie
Cpu(s): 95.2% us,  4.8% sy,  0.0% ni,  0.0% id,  0.0% wa,  0.0% hi,  0.0% si
Mem:   2074904k total,  2045824k used,    29080k free,     3236k buffers
Swap:  4184924k total,    52512k used,  4132412k free,  1580060k cached

  PID USER      PR  NI  VIRT  RES  SHR S %CPU %MEM    TIME+  COMMAND
 1446 oracle    25   0  499m  26m  19m R   10  1.3  2:58.61 oracle
 1465 oracle    25   0  499m  26m  19m R   10  1.3  2:55.71 oracle
 1708 oracle    25   0  497m  23m  19m R   10  1.2  2:48.57 oracle
23444 oracle    25   0  539m  56m  21m R   10  2.8 20:33.85 oracle
23479 oracle    25   0  539m  56m  21m R   10  2.8 20:24.11 oracle
23499 oracle    25   0  515m  40m  21m R   10  2.0 20:34.25 oracle
```

The process IDs of the top-consuming sessions are listed in the first column (PID). Use the SQL queries in the "Solution" section of this recipe to map the operating system process ID to information in the Oracle data dictionary.

While top is running, you can interactively change its output. For example, if you type >, this will move the column that top is sorting one position to the right. Table 8-3 lists some key features that you can use to alter the top display to the desired format.

Table 8-3. *Commands to Interactively Change the top Output*

Command	Function
Spacebar	Immediately refreshes the output.
< or >	Moves the sort column one to the left or to the right. By default, top sorts on the CPU column.
d	Changes the refresh time.
R	Reverses the sort order.
z	Toggles the color output.
h	Displays help menu.
F or O	Chooses a sort column.

Type q or press Ctrl+C to exit top. Table 8-4 describes several of the columns displayed in the default output of top.

Table 8-4. *Column Descriptions of the top Output*

Column	Description
PID	Unique process identifier.
USER	OS username running the process.
PR	Priority of the process.
NI	Nice value or process. Negative value means high priority. Positive value means low priority.
VIRT	Total virtual memory used by process.
RES	Nonswapped physical memory used.
SHR	Shared memory used by process.
S	Process status.
%CPU	Processes percent of CPU consumption since last screen refresh.
%MEM	Percent of physical memory the process is consuming.
TIME	Total CPU time used by process.
TIME+	Total CPU time, showing hundredths of seconds.
COMMAND	Command line used to start a process.

You can also run top using the -b (batch mode) option and send the output to a file for later analysis:

```
$ top -b > tophat.out
```

While running in batch mode, the top command will run until you kill it (with a Ctrl+C) or until it reaches a specified number of iterations. You could run the previous top command in batch mode with a combination of nohup and & to keep it running regardless if you were logged onto the system. The danger there is that you might forget about it and eventually create a very large output file (and an angry system administrator).

If you have a particular process that you're interesting in monitoring, use the -p option to monitor a process ID or the -U option to monitor a specific username. You can also specify a delay and number of iterations by using the -d and -n options. The following example monitors the oracle user with a delay of 5 seconds for 25 iterations:

```
$ top -U oracle -d 5 -n 25
```

■**Tip** Use the man top or top --help commands to list all the options available with your operating system version.

USING THE /PROC/<PID> FILES TO MONITOR PROCESS ACTIVITY

For every Linux process that is running, a directory is created in the /proc virtual filesystem. For example, say you want to view some details about the operating process ID of 19576. You can navigate to the virtual /proc/19576 directory and do a long listing. You see several informational files and directories related to this running process:

```
$ cd /proc/19576
$ ls -l
```

Here is a partial listing of the output:

```
-r--r--r--  1 oracle oinstall 0 Jul  4 13:30 cmdline
lrwxrwxrwx  1 oracle oinstall 0 Jul  4 13:31 cwd -> /oracle/product/10.2/dbs
-r--------  1 oracle oinstall 0 Jul  4 13:31 environ
lrwxrwxrwx  1 oracle oinstall 0 Jul  4 13:31 exe
/oracle/product/10.2/bin/oracle
dr-x------  2 oracle oinstall 0 Jul  4 13:32 fd
-rw-r--r--  1 oracle oinstall 0 Jul  4 13:31 loginuid
-r--r--r--  1 oracle oinstall 0 Jul  4 13:31 maps
-r--r--r--  1 oracle oinstall 0 Jul  4 13:31 status
-rw-------  1 oracle oinstall 0 Jul  4 13:31 mem
```

The output tells us that this is an oracle process, and now you can analyze it further by looking at the memory usage maps file or the status file. Since these files do not exist on disk, use a utility such as cat to display their contents:

```
$ cat /proc/<PID>/maps
$ cat /proc/<PID>/status
```

8-3. Identifying CPU Bottlenecks

Problem

You want to monitor the system load on your CPUs.

Solution

As a DBA, you'll also need to periodically examine the load on CPUs to determine system bottlenecks. The mpstat (multiple processor statistics) utility displays statistics for processors on the server:

```
$ mpstat
Linux 2.6.9-55.0.6.ELsmp (rmugprd.rmug.com)  07/04/2008
12:39:52 PM  CPU    %user   %nice %system %iowait    %irq   %soft   %idle    intr/s
12:39:52 PM  all    35.21    0.06    0.71    0.24    0.00    0.00   63.78   1008.87
```

The default output of mpstat will show only one line of aggregated statistics for all CPUs on the server. You can also view CPU snapshots that report statistics accumulated between intervals. The following example uses the -P option to report only on processor 0; it displays output every 2 seconds for a total of 20 different reports:

```
$ mpstat -P 0 2 20
```

Here are a few lines of the output:

```
12:38:14 PM  CPU   %user   %nice %system %iowait    %irq   %soft   %idle   intr/s
12:38:16 PM   0    92.00    0.00    8.00    0.00    0.00    0.00    0.00  1002.50
12:38:18 PM   0    97.50    0.00    2.50    0.00    0.00    0.00    0.00  1002.00
12:38:20 PM   0    96.00    0.00    4.00    0.00    0.00    0.00    0.00  1002.50
12:38:22 PM   0    93.53    0.00    6.47    0.00    0.00    0.00    0.00   872.14
```

See Table 8-5 under "How It Works" for descriptions of the mpstat output. Here are some general guidelines for interpreting the output of the previous report:

- If %idle is high, then your CPUs are most likely not overburdened.

- If the %iowait output is a nonzero number, then you may have some disk I/O contention.

- If you identify that the CPUs are overloaded, see recipe 8-2 for techniques to pinpoint sessions consuming the most processor resources.

How It Works

Use the -P ALL options of the mpstat command to print on separate lines each CPU's statistics:

```
$ mpstat -P ALL
Linux 2.6.9-55.0.6.ELsmp (rmugprd.rmug.com)  07/04/2008
12:51:23 PM  CPU   %user   %nice %system %iowait    %irq   %soft   %idle   intr/s
12:51:23 PM  all   35.26    0.06    0.71    0.24    0.00    0.00   63.73  1008.94
12:51:23 PM    0   35.77    0.06    0.71    0.19    0.00    0.00   63.27   504.17
12:51:23 PM    1   34.74    0.07    0.72    0.29    0.00    0.00   64.18   504.77
```

The prior output shows that this server has two CPUs (indicated by a line for CPU 0 and a line for CPU 1). The %idle column is in the 60 percent range, indicating that there is some load on the CPUs on this box but not an inordinate amount. Table 8-5 describes the various statistics in the mpstat output.

Table 8-5. *Column Definitions for mpstat Processor Statistics*

Column	Description
CPU	Processor number. Starts at 0. The all row reports average statistics for all processors.
%user	Percentage of CPU utilization while executing at user level.
%nice	Percentage of CPU utilization while executing at user level with nice priority.
%system	Percentage of CPU utilization while executing at kernel level.

Table 8-5. *Column Definitions for* mpstat *Processor Statistics (Continued)*

Column	Description
%iowait	Percentage of time CPUs were idle during an outstanding disk I/O operation.
%irq	Percentage of time spent by CPUs servicing interrupts.
%soft	Percentage of time spent by CPUs to service software interrupts.
%idle	Percentage of time that CPUS were idle without outstanding disk I/O operations.
intr/s	Total number of interrupts received per second by CPU.

It's useful to compare the output of mpstat to that of vmstat (see recipe 8-1 for a discussion on using vmstat). Here you can confirm that the CPUs are 64 percent idle (id column) and there is no waiting on the I/O subsystem (wa column):

```
procs -----------memory---------- ---swap-- -----io---- --system-- ----cpu----
 r  b   swpd   free   buff   cache  si   so    bi    bo   in   cs us sy id wa
 3  0  87164  40520   2312 1811872   0    0    79    65   19    6 35  1 64  0
```

You can also save the output of mpstat to a file. This next example saves to a file all CPU activity reported every 10 seconds for 100 times:

```
$ mpstat -P ALL 10 100 > mpperf.perf
```

This allows you to save performance statistics so that you can analyze and contrast performance for different time periods. See recipe 8-4 for a discussion on how to use the sar command to display the historical CPU usage.

8-4. Analyzing Historical CPU Load

Problem

You want to view the CPU load over the past several days.

Solution

The sar (system activity reporter) command is useful for displaying both current and historical processor load. Use sar with the -u option to report on CPU statistics. By default, sar will report on the current day's activities:

```
$ sar -u
```

To report on the previous day's worth of CPU statistics, use the -f option. The files that sar uses to report on statistics for different days of the month are located in the /var/log/sa directory and have the naming convention of saNN, where NN is the two-digit day of the month. For example, to have sar display CPU statistics for the tenth day of the month, run it as follows:

```
$ sar -u -f /var/log/sa/sa10
```

Here is a partial snapshot of the output:

02:40:01 PM	CPU	%user	%nice	%system	%iowait	%idle
02:50:01 PM	all	0.22	0.00	0.24	0.00	99.54
03:00:01 PM	all	0.22	0.00	0.24	0.00	95.53
03:10:01 PM	all	0.22	0.00	0.23	0.00	99.55
03:20:01 PM	all	0.42	0.00	1.06	2.11	96.41
03:30:01 PM	all	0.24	0.00	1.22	0.01	92.54
Average:	all	0.19	0.00	0.19	0.07	99.55

The columns in the prior output have the same meaning as the `mpstat` output and are described in Table 8-5. A low `%idle` could be an indication that the CPUs are underpowered or indicative of a high application load.

Note When you install the `sysstat` package, two `cron` jobs will be instantiated to create files used by the `sar` utility to report on historical server statistics. You can view these `cron` jobs by looking in the `/etc/cron.d/sysstat` file.

The `%iowait` column displays the time waiting for I/O. It follows that a high `%iowait` time indicates that the I/O subsystem is a potential bottleneck. See recipes 8-9 and 8-10 in this chapter for details on analyzing I/O performance.

After you identify a time in the past that had poor CPU performance, you can then run an Oracle Automatic Workload Repository (AWR) report for the same time period to correlate the operating system load to database activity. By default, Oracle will store seven days worth of AWR snapshots with 24 snapshots per day.

Note For complete details on using the AWR utility, see the Oracle Database Performance Tuning Guide. All of Oracle's documentation is available at `http://otn.oracle.com`.

MANUALLY RUNNING AWR, ADDM, AND ASH REPORTS

The AWR report is extremely useful for diagnosing database performance issues. To manually run an AWR report, log on to SQL*Plus as a privileged database account, and run the following script:

```
SQL> @?/rdbms/admin/awrrpt.sql
```

You will be prompted for input such as the type of report (HTML or text), the number of days, and the snapshot interval. The question mark (?) in the previous SQL statement is translated by SQL*Plus to the value of the ORACLE_HOME operating system variable.

> The Automatic Database Diagnostic Monitor (ADDM) report is useful for tuning SQL statements. To manually run an ADDM report, log on to SQL*Plus as a privileged database schema, and run the following script:
>
> ```
> SQL> @?/rdbms/admin/addmrpt.sql
> ```
>
> Another useful report is the Active Session History (ASH) report. This report details recent active session activities. To run the ASH report, log into SQL*Plus as a privileged database schema, and run the following script:
>
> ```
> SQL> @?/rdbms/admin/ashrpt.sql
> ```
>
> See Chapter 11 for examples on how to automate the running of the previous reports for your environment.

How It Works

The sar utility is extremely useful because it allows you to analyze processor statistics for one of the three types of time periods:

- Real-time current statistics

- The current day's activities

- A previous day's activity

To use sar to report on real-time CPU statistics, specify a snapshot interval (in seconds) and the number of reports. The following displays current processor activity with a snapshot interval of 2 seconds for a total of 20 reports:

```
$ sar -u 2 20
```

To use sar to report on the current day's CPU activity, simply specify the -u option:

```
$ sar -u
```

To use sar to report on a previous day in the month, use the -f option. See the examples in the "Solution" section of this recipe for techniques for reporting on a previous day's statistics.

If you have multiple CPUs, you can view the output per CPU with the -P ALL options. You should now see one line per CPU in the output:

```
$ sar -u -P ALL
```

Here is a partial listing of the output:

```
04:30:01 PM        0     0.10     0.00     0.01     0.00     99.99
04:30:01 PM        1     0.11     0.00     0.01     0.00     99.98
```

8-5. Identifying Memory-Intensive Processes

Problem

You want to identify which Oracle session is consuming the most memory on the database server. If it's an Oracle session running a SQL query, then you want to display the associated SQL.

Solution

Use the ps command to identify the top memory-consuming Oracle processes and their associated process IDs:

```
$ ps -e -o pmem,pid,user,tty,args | grep -i oracle | sort -n -k 1 -r | head
```

Here is some sample output:

```
3.8    332 oracle ? oracleRMDB1 (DESCRIPTION=(LOCAL=YES)(ADDRESS=(PROTOCOL=beq)))
2.5 32092 oracle ? ora_mmon_RMDB1
2.4 32083 oracle ? ora_smon_RMDB1
1.6    329 oracle ? oracleRMDB1 (DESCRIPTION=(LOCAL=YES)(ADDRESS=(PROTOCOL=beq)))
1.5 32675 oracle ? oracleRMDB1 (DESCRIPTION=(LOCAL=YES)(ADDRESS=(PROTOCOL=beq)))
 1.3 32090 oracle    ?           ora_cjq0_RMDB1
```

From the second column in the previous output, the process with the ID of 332 is consuming 3.8 percent of the memory. Next you run the following query to identify Oracle-related details about process 332:

```
SET LINESIZE 80 HEADING OFF FEEDBACK OFF
SELECT
  RPAD('USERNAME : ' || s.username, 80) ||
  RPAD('OSUSER   : ' || s.osuser, 80) ||
  RPAD('PROGRAM  : ' || s.program, 80) ||
  RPAD('SPID     : ' || p.spid, 80) ||
  RPAD('SID      : ' || s.sid, 80) ||
  RPAD('SERIAL#  : ' || s.serial#, 80) ||
  RPAD('MACHINE  : ' || s.machine, 80) ||
  RPAD('TERMINAL : ' || s.terminal, 80) ||
  RPAD('SQL TEXT : ' || q.sql_text, 80)
FROM v$session s
    ,v$process p
    ,v$sql     q
WHERE s.paddr          = p.addr
AND    p.spid          = '&PID_FROM_OS'
AND    s.sql_address   = q.address(+)
AND    s.sql_hash_value = q.hash_value(+);
```

Here is the output for this example:

```
USERNAME : SYS
OSUSER   : oracle
PROGRAM  : rman@rmugprd.rmug.com (TNS V1-V3)
SPID     : 332
SID      : 538
SERIAL#  : 23
MACHINE  : rmugprd.rmug.com
TERMINAL :
SQL TEXT :
```

From the previous output, you can see that it is an RMAN backup job that is consuming the most memory resources. In this case, there is no associated SQL text with this job.

How It Works

The query in the "Solution" section of this recipe is a slight variation of the query presented in the "Solution" section of recipe 8-2. In this recipe, you outer join to the V$SQL view so the query will still return values even if there is no associated SQL query with the process being investigated.

This is useful for identifying oracle sessions that are consuming high amounts of system resources but are not related to a SQL query. These scenarios can occur if you're running Oracle utilities such as RMAN, Export/Import, Data Pump, and so forth.

8-6. Identifying Memory Bottlenecks

Problem

You want to view the current usage of memory on your database server.

Solution

Paging and swapping activity is an indicator of the efficiency of memory usage on your sever. In general, high amounts of paging and swapping indicate an inadequate amount of memory. Numerous utilities are available to monitor paging and swapping. For example, you can use vmstat (virtual memory statistics) to monitor the current memory usage. In this next line of code we generate vmstat reports every two seconds for a total of three reports:

```
$ vmstat 2 3
```

Here is some sample output:

```
procs -----------memory---------- ---swap-- -----io---- --system-- ----cpu----
 r  b   swpd   free   buff  cache   si   so    bi    bo   in   cs us sy id wa
 2  0  80708  22224   2768 1886272   0    0   142    81    5    8 36  1 63  0
 2  0  80708  22800   2764 1885244   0    4  9356  3138 1120  190 84  3  0 13
 2  0  80708  23888   2680 1884288   0    0  9134    16 1103  217 84  3  0 14
```

If you have a fairly recent version of Linux, you can also use the -a option, which displays active and inactive memory. Here is an example of running vmstat with the -a option:

```
$ vmstat -a 2 3
```

Here's what the output looks like with the additional columns:

```
procs -----------memory---------- ---swap-- -----io---- --system-- ----cpu----
 r  b   swpd   free  inact active   si   so    bi    bo   in   cs us sy id wa
 2  0  85924  30992 849720 1147696   0    0   143    81    5    8 36  1 63  0
 2  0  85920  30864 849752 1147796   2    0  2828   480 1072  249 87  6  0  7
 2  0  85920  30032 849764 1148828   0    0     0 13600 1156   33 74  5  0 21
```

If your server shows high amounts of memory swapped in from disk (si column) or the amount of memory swapped out to disk (so column), then you may have a memory bottleneck. If you identify memory as being a bottleneck, refer to the "Solution" section of recipe 8-5 for identifying specific oracle processes consuming the most memory on your system.

How It Works

One of the main indicators of memory health is the amount of paging and swapping that is occurring. If you read five different Linux performance-tuning white papers, you'll get five slightly different definitions of paging and swapping. We're not going to split hairs about the exact definitions of those terms. We're going to state that "in general, paging and swapping are the movement of the contents of memory to and from disk."

Paging and swapping occur when there isn't enough physical memory to accommodate all the memory needs of the processes on the server. When paging and swapping take place, performance usually suffers. This is because the process of copying memory contents to and from disk is an inherently slow activity.

You can also use the free command to display current memory used, both physical and virtual (swap):

```
$ free
              total       used       free     shared    buffers     cached
Mem:        2057876    2040168      17708          0      55668    1805760
-/+ buffers/cache:       178740    1879136
Swap:       2031608        144    2031464
```

From the previous output, this system has 2GB of RAM of which almost all of it is used. It has about 2GB of swap space of which almost none is used. Don't be too alarmed if your Linux system is using most of its physical memory; that's typical on many Linux servers.

■**Note** See Chapter 9 for details on using ipcs to view the memory and semaphores used by your database.

You can use the -s option to have the free command report output on a repeating interval. This example uses free to display memory usage in two-second snapshots and sends the output to a file:

```
$ free -s 2 > freemem.perf
```

Press Ctrl+C to exit from free when using the -s option. By default the free output reports memory usage in kilobytes. Use the -m to print in megabytes or the -g to display the output of free in gigabytes.

An effective way to use free is in combination with the watch command. The watch command is used to execute another program on a periodic basis. The next example uses watch to run the free utility every three seconds via the -n (interval) option. The -d (differences) option is used to have the output highlighted on the screen when there is a change in value from snapshot to snapshot:

```
$ watch -n 3 -d free
```

```
Every 3.0s: free                              Sun Aug  5 18:21:05 2007
                 total      used      free    shared    buffers    cached
Mem:           2057876   2038240     19636         0     89840   1703248
-/+ buffers/cache:        245152   1812724
Swap:          2031608       144   2031464
```

You should be able visually see any changes in memory activity on your screen when running in this mode. To exit from watch, press Ctrl+C.

You can also view the current characteristics of memory by viewing the /proc/meminfo file. You can use the file to display the current physical memory and swap space being used. This example uses the cat utility to display the current memory usage:

```
$ watch -d cat /proc/meminfo
```

By default, the watch command will refresh the screen every two seconds. You should visually see differences highlighted from interval to interval:

```
MemTotal:      2074904 kB
MemFree:         23520 kB
Buffers:          2832 kB
Cached:        1838380 kB
SwapCached:        108 kB
Active:        1703208 kB
Inactive:       298916 kB
HighTotal:     1179584 kB
HighFree:         1024 kB
LowTotal:       895320 kB
LowFree:         22496 kB
SwapTotal:     4184924 kB
SwapFree:      4126964 kB
```

If you see an unusual amount of swap space being used (low SwapFree), then this is an indication that your server needs more memory. To exit from watch, press Ctrl+C.

8-7. Analyzing Historical Memory Load

Problem

You want to view the memory load for a previous day in the week.

Solution

Use sar with the -f (file) option to report on memory statistics for different days of the month. The files that sar uses to report statistics for different days of the month are located in the /var/log/sa directory and have the naming convention of saNN, where NN is the two-digit day of the month. For example, to have sar display memory paging statistics for the first day of the month, run it with the -B (report paging statistics) and -f (file) options as follows:

```
$ sar -B -f /var/log/sa/sa01
```

Here is a partial listing of the report:

```
11:10:01 AM  pgpgin/s pgpgout/s   fault/s  majflt/s
11:20:01 AM      0.02     16.17     18.37      0.00
11:30:01 AM      3.49     21.68     74.15      0.04
11:40:01 AM   4182.58    439.44    320.94      0.68
11:50:02 AM   4960.03   1027.79   4384.73      0.51
12:00:02 PM   4542.48   1156.96   6459.71      0.14
```

The previous output shows that around 11:40 a.m., there was a substantial increase in paging in from disk (pgpgin/s), pages paged out to disk (pgpgout/s), and page faults per second (fault/s).

Similarly, you can use the -W (report swapping statistics) option to view memory swapping:

```
$ sar -W -f /var/log/sa/sa01
```

Here is a partial snippet of the output:

```
11:10:01 AM  pswpin/s pswpout/s
11:20:01 AM      0.00      0.00
11:30:01 AM      0.01      0.00
11:40:01 AM      1.08      1.45
11:50:02 AM      0.81      2.97
12:00:02 PM      0.52      6.75
```

Unusually high values of pages swapped in to memory per second (pswpin/s) and pages swapped out per second (pswpout/s) are indications of inadequate memory. From the previous output, the system began to swap memory at around 11:40 a.m.

Because the sar utility reports on events that have happened in the past, you'll need to determine what system activity was taking place that caused any unusual spikes in memory usage.

After you identify a time in the past that had poor memory performance, you can then run an Oracle Automatic Workload Repository (AWR) report for the same time period to correlate the operating system load to database activity. By default, Oracle will store seven days' worth of AWR snapshots with 24 snapshots per day.

■**Tip** For more details on using the AWR utility, see the Oracle Database Performance Tuning Guide. All of Oracle's documentation is available at http://otn.oracle.com.

How It Works

The sar utility is useful because you can use it to generate memory statistics in one of the following modes:

- Current real-time memory usage

- Current day's activity

- Previous day in the month

To report on real-time memory statistics, specify the -W option with an interval (in seconds) and the number of reports. This example generates current swapping statistics snapshots every three seconds for a total of ten reports:

```
$ sar -W 3 10
```

To report on the current day's worth of memory statistics, then do not provide sar with an interval or number of reports. The following example uses the -B option of sar to report on today's paging statistics:

```
$ sar -B
```

To report on a previous day's worth of memory statistics, use the -f option of sar. Refer to the "Solution" section of this recipe for examples on reporting on a previous day.

Several options are available with sar to report on memory. For example, the -r option will report extensive memory and swap utilization statistics:

```
$ sar -r
```

When run in this mode, the output can be wide and lengthy; it doesn't quite fit within the limits of this physical page. Refer to Table 8-6 for a description of each column.

```
02:40:01 PM kbmemfree kbmemused  %memused kbbuffers  kbcached kbswpfree kbswpused
%swpused  kbswpcad
02:50:01 PM     15460    2042416     99.25     64752   1654492   4031456       144
0.00         0
03:00:01 PM     15516    2042360     99.25     64772   1654472   4031456       144
0.00         0
```

Table 8-6. *Column Descriptions of the sar -r Output*

Column	Description
kbmemfree	Free memory in kilobytes
kbmemused	Amount of memory used in kilobytes
%memused	Percentage of used memory
kbbuffers	Amount of memory used as buffers in kilobytes
kbcached	Amount of memory used to cache data by the kernel in kilobytes
kbswpfree	Amount of free swap space in kilobytes
kbswpused	Amount of used swap space in kilobytes
%swpused	Percentage of used swap space
kbswpcad	Amount of cached swap memory in kilobytes

8-8. Monitoring Disk Space

Problem

You want to proactively monitor disk space so that you're not surprised in the middle of the night by a disk becoming full.

Solution

Use a shell script like the one listed next to proactively monitor disk space:

```
#!/bin/bash
#
inCheck='/dev/sda1 /dev/sda2'
for mntList in $inCheck
do
usedSpc=$(df -h $mntList|awk '{print $5}'|egrep -iv 'Use|Capacity'| \
cut -d "%" -f1 -)
#
case $usedSpc in
[0-9])
  diskStat="relax, lots of disk space: $usedSpc"
;;
[1-7][0-9])
  diskStat="disk space okay: $usedSpc"
;;
[8][0-9])
  diskStat="WARNING, disk space low: $mntList $usedSpc percent full"
;;
[9][0-9])
  diskStat="ALERT, running out of space: $mntList $usedSpc percent full"
;;
[1][0][0])
  diskStat="ERROR, no space left: $mntList $usedSpc percent full"
;;
*)
diskStat="huh?: $usedSpc"
esac
#
BOX=$(uname -a | awk '{print $2}')
sLine="Disk space issue on: $BOX, mount point $mntList"
echo $diskStat|egrep 'ALERT|ERROR' && echo $diskStat|mailx -s "$sLine" prd@spt.com
done
#
exit 0
```

You'll have to modify variables in the previous script to match your environment. For example, the inCheck variable should hold the mount points you are interested in monitoring.

Refer to Chapter 11 for details on how to automate the running of a script. See Chapter 7 for techniques used to create a shell script.

How It Works

The df (disk free) command is used frequently by DBAs to determine the amount of disk-free space on a server. The default output of df lists a disk's used and available space in kilobytes for all mounted filesystems:

```
$ df
```

```
Filesystem           1K-blocks      Used Available Use% Mounted on
/dev/mapper/VolGroup00-LogVol00
                     74699952    9304680  61600740  14% /
/dev/sda1              101086      14092     81775  15% /boot
none                 1028936          0   1028936   0% /dev/shm
```

The previous output can sometimes be difficult to read. Use the -h (human-readable) option of df to have the free space automatically displayed in kilobytes, megabytes, gigabytes, or terabytes. The df -h output will adjust the space amount abbreviation (K, M, G, T) depending on the size of each filesystem:

```
$ df -h
```

```
Filesystem           Size  Used Avail Use% Mounted on
/dev/mapper/VolGroup00-LogVol00
                      72G  8.9G   59G  14% /
/dev/sda1             99M   14M   80M  15% /boot
none                1005M     0 1005M   0% /dev/shm
```

You can also use df to view disk space on a particular mount point. For example, to check for free space in the /tmp mount point, use this:

```
$ df -h /tmp
```

```
Filesystem           size  used  avail capacity  Mounted on
swap                 15G   2.3M   15G     1%     /tmp
```

The du (disk usage) command is another extremely useful utility for monitoring disk space. When a filesystem fills up, the DBA needs to quickly determine what directories are using up what space. The du command helps you quickly determine where the disk space is being consumed.

By default, du will recursively display disk usage for each directory below a parent directory as well as show an aggregate amount of space usage of all directories beneath a parent. For example, to display the disk space usage of all directories below the /ora01 mount point, use du, as shown here:

```
$ du /ora01
```

Here's a partial listing of the output:

```
848      /ora01/10g/database/install
276      /ora01/10g/database/response
801668   /ora01/10g/database
1585268 /ora01/10g
12       /ora01/oraInventory/locks
40       /ora01/oraInventory/logs/results/db
```

The default output of du is displayed in kilobytes. Use the -h switch to make the output more readable and also display an appropriate space amount abbreviation (K, M, G, or T):

```
$ du -h /ora01
848K     /ora01/10g/database/install
276K     /ora01/10g/database/response
783M     /ora01/10g/database
1.6G     /ora01/10g
12K      /ora01/oraInventory/locks
40K      /ora01/oraInventory/logs/results/db
```

To report an aggregated disk space amount used in a directory and its subdirectories, use the -s option. This example uses -s and -h to print an aggregated total in human-readable form:

```
$ du -sh /ora01
4.6G     /ora01
```

Another clever way DBAs use du is to display the top directories and files that consume space below a given parent directory. This command will display the top five directories in terms of disk space used below a given directory:

```
$ du -s * | sort -nr | head -5
```

The previous command would get a little tedious to type in over and over again. To resolve this, create an alias that points to the command:

```
$ alias tn='du -s * | sort -nr | head -5'
```

An alternate technique to creating an alias is to create a function (see Chapter 4 for details). This next bit of code creates a Bash shell function to allow you to dynamically specify the top number of disk usage directories to be displayed. If you're not using the Bash shell, type the command bash to set your shell appropriately:

```
$ bash
```

Then create the function by typing the following lines:

```
$ function tnf {
> du -s * | sort -nr | head -$1
> }
```

•

The $1 variable holds the first parameter passed into the tnf function. You can call the tnf function directly from the command line and pass it in the number of top directories you want to view (in this example ten):

```
$ tnf 10
```

8-9. Monitoring I/O

Problem

You want to determine whether your disk storage is a bottleneck.

Solution

The iostat command can help you determine whether disk I/O is potentially a source of performance problems. The -x (extended) option used with the -d (device) option is a useful way to generate I/O statistics. This next example uses the -x and -d options to display extended device statistics every ten seconds:

```
$ iostat -xd 10
```

You need a really wide screen to view this output; here's a partial listing:

```
Device:    rrqm/s wrqm/s   r/s   w/s rsec/s wsec/s   rkB/s   wkB/s avgrq-sz
avgqu-sz  await svctm  %util
sda          0.01   3.31  0.11  0.31   5.32  28.97    2.66   14.49    83.13
0.06  138.44   1.89   0.08
```

■**Note** On some Linux/Unix distributions, the iostat output may report the disk utilization as %b (percent busy).

This periodic extended output allows you to view in real time which devices are experiencing spikes in read and write activity. To exit from the previous iostat command, press Ctrl+C. Table 8-7 describes the I/O-related columns in the iostat output.

When trying to determine whether device I/O is the bottleneck, here are some general guidelines when examining the iostat output:

- Look for devices with abnormally high blocks read or written per second.

- If any device is near 100 percent utilization, that's a strong indicator I/O is a bottleneck.

If the bottlenecked disks are used by Oracle, then you can query the data dictionary to identify sessions with high I/O activity. The following query is useful for determining which SQL statements generate the most read/write activity:

```
SELECT *
FROM
(SELECT
  parsing_schema_name
 ,direct_writes
 ,SUBSTR(sql_text,1,75)
 ,disk_reads
FROM v$sql
ORDER BY disk_reads DESC)
WHERE rownum < 20;
```

The next query is useful for determining which objects produce the heaviest I/O activity in the database:

```
SELECT *
FROM
(SELECT
  s.statistic_name
 ,s.owner
 ,s.object_type
 ,s.object_name
 ,s.value
  FROM v$segment_statistics s
  WHERE s.statistic_name IN
    ('physical reads', 'physical writes', 'logical reads',
     'physical reads direct', 'physical writes direct')
ORDER BY s.value DESC)
WHERE rownum < 20;
```

How It Works

If you execute iostat without any options, then you'll get a default report that displays averages since the system was last started:

```
$ iostat
avg-cpu:  %user   %nice    %sys %iowait   %idle
          18.91    0.04    1.20    0.15   79.70

Device:            tps   Blk_read/s   Blk_wrtn/s   Blk_read   Blk_wrtn
sda               7.14       398.01       409.52  164484368  169239542
sda1              0.00         0.00         0.00       1538        166
sda2             54.15       396.92       407.74  164032098  168505032
sda3              0.35         1.04         1.77     429820     733168
```

Notice that there are two sections in the prior iostat output. The first section is the CPU Utilization Report. The second section relates to disk I/O and is referred to as the Device Utilization Report. Table 8-7 describes the columns used for disk I/O. Use the -d option of iostat to display only device statistics.

Table 8-7. *Column Descriptions of* iostat *Disk I/O Output*

Column	Description
Device	Device or partition name.
tps	I/O transfers per second to the device.
Blk_read/s	Blocks per second read from the device.
Blk_wrtn/s	Blocks written per second to the device.
Blk_read	Number of blocks read.
Blk_wrtn	Number of blocks written.
rrqm/s	Number of read requests merged per second that were queued to device.
wrqm/s	Number of write requests merged per second that were queued to device.
r/s	Read requests per second.
w/s	Write requests per second.
rsec/s	Sectors read per second.
wsec/s	Sectors written per second.
rkB/s	Kilobytes read per second.
wkB/s	Kilobytes written per second.
avgrq-sz	Average size of requests in sectors.
avgqu-sz	Average queue length of requests.
await	Average time in milliseconds for I/O requests sent to the device to be served.
svctm	Average service time in milliseconds.
%util	Percentage of CPU time during which I/O requests were issued to the device. Near 100 percent indicates device saturation.

You can also instruct iostat to display reports at a specified interval. The first report displayed will report averages since the last server reboot; each subsequent reports shows statistics since the previously generated snapshot. The following example displays a device statistic report every three seconds:

```
$ iostat -d 3
```

To exit from the previous iostat command, press Ctrl+C. You can also specify a finite number of reports that you want generated. This is useful for gathering metrics to be analyzed over a period of time. This example instructs iostat to report every 2 seconds for a total of 15 reports:

```
$ iostat 2 15
```

When working with locally attached disks, the output of the iostat command will clearly show where the I/O is occurring. However, it is not that clear-cut in environments that use external arrays for storage. What you are presented with at the filesystem layer is some sort of a virtual disk that might also have been configured by a volume manager. Virtual disks are often referred to as *volumes* or *logical units* (LUNs). A LUN is a logical disk that physically comprises one or more physical disks. The LUN represents the virtualization layer between the physical disks and the applications running on the database server. Figure 8-1 illustrates at a high level the abstraction involved with virtual disks.

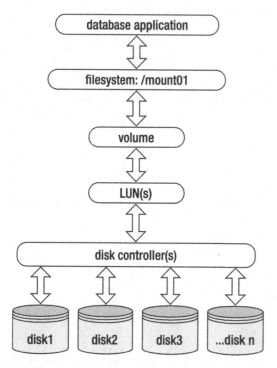

Figure 8-1. *Abstraction layers between database application and physical disks*

When working with virtual disks, the output from iostat will report on read/write activity at the virtual disk level, not the underlying physical disks. In these situations, there may be many layers of abstraction between the database application and physical disks. This can make it difficult to isolate the exact source of an I/O bottleneck. We recommend you work closely with your storage system administrator to determine whether a particular set of LUNs (and under-lying physical disks) are a source of poor I/O performance.

WHAT'S WRONG WITH THE DATABASE?

One of us was recently involved with a performance crisis with a production database system. A materialized view refresh job that used to take ten minutes was now taking four hours. The managers and system admin-istrators were asking the DBAs for answers.

One of the DBAs inspected the output from iostat and noticed the utilization (%util) for several disks was near 90 percent. Next, the DBA used the dd command to generate some large files on the Oracle file-system to get timings on a file creation:

```
$ time dd if=<database filename> of=<test filename>
```

The DBA performed this test on the production server and then executed the same test on a test box with a similar disk layout (as production). The time to create a large file was five times faster on the test box. This allowed the DBA to show the system administrators that something was wrong with I/O on the production box. The SAs reconfigured the disks in production, and the MV refresh job went back down to ten minutes.

8-10. Analyzing Historical I/O Load

Problem

You want to view disk I/O activity for the past several days.

Solution

Use the sar utility with the -f (file) option to report on statistics for different days of the month. This is a useful tuning and troubleshooting feature because it allows you to analyze metrics over a period of several days.

To report on historical statistics, the sar command uses files located in the /var/log/sa directory. These files have the naming convention of saNN, where NN is the two-digit day of the month. For example, to have sar display disk statistics for the tenth day of the month, run it with the -d and -f options as follows:

```
$ sar -d -f /var/log/sa/sa10
```

Here's a partial snippet of the output (this output may vary depending on your version of Linux and the sar command):

```
02:40:01 PM   DEV           tps    rd_sec/s  wr_sec/s
03:50:01 PM   dev1-14      0.00      0.00      0.00
03:50:01 PM   dev1-15      0.00      0.00      0.00
03:50:01 PM   dev8-0      30.02    642.39   2824.27
03:50:01 PM   dev9-0       0.00      0.00      0.00
```

The tps column shows the I/O operatings (transfers) per second to the device. The rd_sec/s is the number of sectors read from the device. The wr_sec/s is the number of sectors written to the device. Unusually high read and write rates indicate an overworked disk subsystem.

At the bottom of the sar report, the averages over the period of reporting time are displayed:

```
Average:      dev1-14      0.00      0.00      0.00
Average:      dev1-15      0.00      0.00      0.00
Average:      dev8-0      31.68   2331.40   1978.12
Average:      dev9-0       0.00      0.00      0.00
```

After you identify a time in the past that had a heavy I/O load, you can then run an Oracle AWR report for the same time period to correlate the operating system load to database activity. By default, Oracle will store 7 days' worth of AWR snapshots with 24 snapshots per day.

■**Tip** For more details on using the AWR utility, see the Oracle Database Performance Tuning Guide. All of Oracle's documentation is available at `http://otn.oracle.com`.

How It Works

The sar utility is powerful because you can use it to generate device I/O statistics in one of the following types of output:

- Current real-time memory usage

- Current day's activity

- Previous day of the month statistics

To report current real-time I/O statistics, use the -d option with an interval (in seconds) and the number of reports you want generated. The following syntax instructs sar to report disk statistics every 2 seconds for a total of 12 reports:

```
$ sar -d 2 12
```

While reporting on real-time statistics, use the -o (out) option to send output to a file:

```
$ sar -d 2 12 -o sarout.perf
```

This creates a binary output file that can later be used to analyze disk I/O metrics. At some later point you can use sar with the -f option to report on the contents of that file.

To report on the current day's worth of activity, specify the -d option with no time interval:

```
$ sar -d
```

To report device I/O statistics on a previous day of the month, see the "Solution" section of this recipe for an example.

8-11. Monitoring Network Traffic

Problem

You suspect that the network may be a bottleneck. You want to view network statistics.

Solution

Use the netstat (network statistics) command to display network traffic. Perhaps the most useful way to view netstat output is with the -ptc options. These options display the process ID and TCP connections, and they continuously update the output:

```
$ netstat -ptc
```

Press Ctrl+C to exit the previous command. Here's a partial listing of the output:

```
(Not all processes could be identified, non-owned process info
 will not be shown, you would have to be root to see it all.)
Active Internet connections (w/o servers)
Proto Recv-Q Send-Q Local Address  Foreign Address  State        PID/Program name
tcp      0      0 rmug.com:62386 rmug.com:1521    ESTABLISHED 22864/ora_pmon_RMDB
tcp      0      0 rmug.com:53930 rmug.com:1521    ESTABLISHED 6091/sqlplus
tcp      0      0 rmug.com:1521  rmug.com:53930   ESTABLISHED 6093/oracleRMDB1
tcp      0      0 rmug.com:1521  rmug.com:62386   ESTABLISHED 10718/tnslsnr
```

If the Send-Q (bytes not acknowledged by remote host) column has an unusually high value for a process, this may indicate an overloaded network. The useful aspect about the previous output is that you can determine the operating system process ID (PID) associated with a network connection. If you suspect the connection in question is an oracle session, you can use the techniques described in the "Solution" section of recipe 8-2 to map an operating system PID to an oracle process or SQL statement.

■**Note** The /proc/net directory stores information about current network settings and activity.

How It Works

When experiencing performance issues, usually the network is not the cause. Most likely you'll determine that bad performance is related to a poorly constructed SQL statement, inadequate disk I/O, or not enough CPU or memory resources. However, as a DBA, you need to be aware of all sources of performance bottlenecks and how to diagnose them. In today's highly inter-connected world, you must possess network troubleshooting and monitoring skills. The netstat utility is a good starting place for monitoring server network connections.

You can also use the sar command with the -n option to report on network statistics. The -n option takes as an argument one of the following: DEV (network devices), EDEV (error count), SOCK (sockets), or FULL (all). The following command displays the current day's network device statistics:

```
$ sar -n DEV
```

Here's a limited listing of the output:

```
12:00:01 AM  IFACE  rxpck/s txpck/s  rxbyt/s  txbyt/s  rxcmp/s  txcmp/s  rxmcst/s
12:10:01 AM    lo    0.00    0.00     0.00     0.00     0.00     0.00     0.00
12:10:01 AM    eth0  0.34    0.11    39.17    10.22     0.00     0.00     0.04
12:10:01 AM    eth1  0.00    0.00     0.00     0.00     0.00     0.00     0.00
12:10:01 AM    sit0  0.00    0.00     0.00     0.00     0.00     0.00     0.00
```

The previous output shows the number of packets transmitted and received per second, as well as the bytes and compressed packets. The sar -n output allows you to examine the current day's network traffic on snapshots taken on ten-minute intervals.

TROUBLESHOOTING DATABASE NETWORK CONNECTIVTY

Use these steps as guidelines when diagnosing Oracle database network connectivity issues:

1. Use `ping` to determine whether the remote box is accessible. If `ping` doesn't work, work with your system or network administrator to ensure you have server-to-server connectivity in place.

2. Use `tnsping` to determine whether Oracle Net is working. This utility will verify that an Oracle Net connection can be made to a database via the network. If `tnsping` can't contact the remote database, verify that the remote listener and database are both up and running. On the remote box, use the `lsnrctl status` command to verify that the listener is up. Verify that the remote database is available by establishing a local connection as a non-`SYS` account (`SYS` can often connect to a troubled database when other schemas will not work).

3. Verify that the `tns` information is correct. If the remote listener and database are working, then ensure that the mechanism for determining `tns` information (like the `tnsnames.ora` file) contains the correct information. Sometimes the client machine will have multiple `TNS_ADMIN` locations and `tnsnames.ora` files. One way to verify whether a particular `tnsnames.ora` file is being used is to rename it and see whether you get a different error when attempting to connect to the remote database.

If you're still having issues, examine the client `sqlnet.log` file and the remote server `listener.log` file. Sometimes these files will show additional information that will pinpoint the issue.

CHAPTER 9

■■■

Viewing and Configuring System Resources

As part of normal operations, Oracle database processes constantly coordinate and communicate with system server processes. In Linux, this type of process-to-process coordination is referred to as *interprocess communication* (IPC). Linux supports three types of interprocess communication mechanisms: semaphores, shared memory, and message queues. Oracle database applications typically require significant amounts of semaphore and shared memory resources to function properly. This chapter focuses on how to view and manage these critical system resources.

A *semaphore* is a construct used by the operating system to control what processes can have access to other server resources such as shared memory. The amount of operating system resources that a database application can consume is governed by several kernel parameters. Maintaining these values is described in detail in this chapter.

■**Note** The *kernel* is the core program of the operating system that manages access to operating system resources required by other processes on the system. The kernel is typically responsible for process, CPU, memory, and disk management activities.

Nowadays, just about any medium to large database can quickly exceed the default kernel settings for system resource limits. Therefore, most database vendors (Oracle, MySQL, DB2, PostgreSQL, and so on) have their own set of recommended values for the kernel parameters that govern the various required operating system resources.

Before you can install a database on a Linux server, it's prudent to first ensure that the kernel parameters are configured correctly. An incorrectly configured kernel usually results in either a nonoperative or poorly performing database. For example, when starting Oracle, if enough shared memory can't be allocated, then an error message like this will be thrown:

```
ORA-27123: unable to attach to shared memory segment
```

That's not good. Your boss will not be impressed. To avoid problems like this, a knowledgeable DBA *must* know how to view and set kernel parameters that impact database availability and performance. This chapter begins with a high-level overview of how to examine and modify kernel parameters and then dives into specific details for settings most critical for database applications.

9-1. Displaying Server Hardware and the Operating System

Problem

Sometimes it's necessary to determine certain characteristics of your server. For example, you might have the task of installing the Oracle database binaries, and before you download and install this software, you need to know the system architecture and operating system version of the target Linux box.

Solution

Use the uname (print system information) tool to display system details. This example uses the -a option to print all the information:

```
$ uname -a
Linux dv2.rmug.org 2.6.9-55.0.6.ELsmp #1 SMP Tue Sep 4 21:36:00 EDT 2007 i686 i686
i386 GNU/Linux
```

The previous output shows the kernel name (Linux), hostname (dv2.rmug.org), kernel release (2.6.9-55.0.6.ELsmp), kernel build (#1 SMP Tue Sep 4 21:36:00 EDT 2007), name of hardware (i686), processor type (i686), hardware platform (i386), and operating system (GNU/Linux).

How It Works

In today's global environment, you'll often find yourself connecting remotely to database servers located in dispersed data centers. In these situations, you'll find yourself constantly using the uname command with the -a option to verify what machine you're logged on to. Use the --help parameter to display all the choices available with uname in your environment:

```
$ uname --help
Usage: uname [OPTION]...
Print certain system information.  With no OPTION, same as -s.
  -a, --all              print all information, in the following order:
  -s, --kernel-name      print the kernel name
  -n, --nodename         print the network node hostname
  -r, --kernel-release   print the kernel release
  -v, --kernel-version   print the kernel version
  -m, --machine          print the machine hardware name
  -p, --processor        print the processor type
  -i, --hardware-platform  print the hardware platform
  -o, --operating-system   print the operating system
      --help     display this help and exit
      --version  output version information and exit
```

From the prior output, if you wanted to view only the kernel release version of your Linux server, you can use the -r option of the uname command, as shown here:

```
$ uname -r
2.6.9-55.0.6.ELsmp
```

In a Linux environment, you can also view server information by querying the virtual files in the /proc directory. For example, you can view the current version of the server by viewing the /proc/version file:

```
$ cat /proc/version
Linux version 2.6.9-55.0.6.ELsmp (mockbuild@builder4.centos.org) (gcc
version 3.4.6 20060404 (Red Hat 3.4.6-8)) #1 SMP Tue Sep 4 21:36:00
EDT 2007
```

THE /PROC VIRTUAL FILESYSTEM

The Linux /proc virtual filesystem acts as an interface for viewing and configuring kernel parameters. The /proc directory is a hierarchy of files and subdirectories that contain the current settings of kernel values. It is appropriately named /proc because this virtual filesystem sends information to other system processes.

The /proc filesystem is virtual because its files don't actually reside on disk. You'll note that most files beneath the /proc directory have a 0-byte size. The /proc virtual files are created dynamically in memory from kernel data when you access them.

For your convenience, the /proc filesystem is subdivided into directories that contain related parameters. For example, the /proc/sys subdirectory contains many of the parameters used to configure the kernel. Use the man proc command to view documentation on the /proc virtual filesystem for your server.

Interestingly, some utilities such as top and free extract information from the /proc virtual files and present it in a human-readable formatted fashion. Table 9-1 describes some of the virtual files in the /proc directory. Use your favorite file-viewing utility (cat, more, less, view, grep, and so on) to inspect these virtual files.

Table 9-1. *Descriptions of Virtual Files in the /proc Directory*

File Name	Contains Information Regarding
/proc/cpuinfo	CPU and system architecture.
/proc/meminfo	Free and used memory for both physical RAM and swap.
/proc/net	Directory containing network information.
/proc/mounts	All mounted filesystems.
/proc/diskstats	Disk I/O statistics for each disk.
/proc/devices	PCI devices.
/proc/filesystems	Filesystems compiled into the kernel.

Table 9-1. *Descriptions of Virtual Files in the* /proc *Directory (Continued)*

File Name	Contains Information Regarding
/proc/sys	Contains subdirectories and files pertaining to kernel variables. Some variables can be configured with the sysctl command.
/proc/cmdline	Parameters passed to the kernel at boot time.
/proc/version	Version of the operating system.

9-2. Listing CPUs

Problem

The Oracle installation documentation recommends installing the binaries on a server with powerful CPUs. You want to display the CPU characteristics on your Linux server.

Solution

You can quickly obtain in-depth information about the physical characteristics of the CPU(s) on a Linux server by viewing the virtual /proc/cpuinfo file:

```
$ cat /proc/cpuinfo
```

For multiple processor boxes, there will be a section in the output for each CPU. The first CPU on the box is identified as 0 and the next one as 1, and so on. Here's a partial listing of some typical output from /proc/cpuinfo:

```
processor       : 0
vendor_id       : GenuineIntel
cpu family      : 15
model           : 2
model name      : Intel(R) Xeon(TM) CPU 2.66GHz
stepping        : 5
cpu MHz         : 2667.494
cache size      : 512 KB
physical id     : 0
siblings        : 2
core id         : 0
cpu cores       : 1
```

How It Works

Sometimes you need to know whether the CPUs on your box are powerful enough to handle the database software being installed. If you have multiple CPUs on your server, then you'll see a listing for each CPU. Use the information in the /proc/cpuinfo file to determine whether your server meets Oracle's prerequisites for CPU minimum megahertz speed (this is usually the cpu MHz line in the /proc/cpuinfo file).

9-3. Displaying Physical Memory

Problem

Oracle's installation documentation recommends you have a certain minimal amount of memory installed on the Linux server. You want to verify you have enough memory on a box before you do a database installation.

Solution

With Linux, you can view the contents of the /proc/meminfo file with grep to check the total physical memory amount:

```
$ grep MemTotal /proc/meminfo
MemTotal:     2074904 kB
```

To view the total amount of swap memory, issue the following grep command:

```
$ grep SwapTotal /proc/meminfo
SwapTotal:    4184924 kB
```

Tip See Oracle's MetaLink Note 233753.1 for a detailed discussion of /proc/meminfo.

How It Works

When dealing with database servers, you have to be aware of two types of memory: physical RAM and virtual (swap). Depending on the software you install on a box, you are sometimes required to check to see whether there is sufficient RAM and swap memory on the target server. If you don't have enough physical or swap memory, usually the Oracle Universal Installer will alert you as to any inadequacies when attempting to perform the installation.

You can also view physical and swap memory by issuing the free command with no options. This command gives you a view of the currently free and consumed memory on the box:

```
$ free
             total       used       free     shared    buffers     cached
Mem:       2074904    2050512      24392          0      84704    1759792
-/+ buffers/cache:     206016    1868888
Swap:      4184924      74652    4110272
```

Additionally, if you want to view per-process memory consumption, use the following cat commands:

```
$ cat /proc/<PID>/maps
$ cat /proc/<PID>/status
```

TEMPOARARILY ADDING SWAP SPACE

If you're short on swap space, you can temporarily add a swap file to your server. As the `root` user, run the following commands to add approximately 1GB of swap space:

```
# dd if=/dev/zero of=tempswap bs=1k count=1000000
# chmod 600 tempswap
# mkswap tempswap
# swapon tempswap
```

Verify that the swap space was added with the `-s` option of the `swapon` command:

```
# swapon -s
```

To remove the temporary swap file, as `root` run the following commands:

```
# swapoff tempswap
# rm tempswap
```

After disabling the swap file, you should see the swap space in `/proc/meminfo` return to its original value.

9-4. Viewing Kernel Parameters

Problem

You're installing database binaries on a new Linux server and need to modify some kernel parameters per the installation documentation. Before you make the change, you first want to view all kernel parameters.

Solution

Run the following grep command as `root` to view the current kernel settings in the `/proc/sys/kernel` directory:

```
# grep . /proc/sys/kernel/*
```

The previous command instructs grep to print all strings contained in files located in the `/proc/sys/kernel` directory. Here is a partial listing of the output:

```
/proc/sys/kernel/real-root-dev:0
/proc/sys/kernel/sem:250          32000     100       128
/proc/sys/kernel/shmall:2097152
/proc/sys/kernel/shmmax:536870912
/proc/sys/kernel/shmmni:4096
/proc/sys/kernel/suid_dumpable:0
/proc/sys/kernel/sysrq:0
/proc/sys/kernel/tainted:0
/proc/sys/kernel/threads-max:32750
```

■**Note** You can view many files in the /proc virtual filesystem as a non-root account. However, you will need root access to view all virtual files.

You can also use grep to filter for a particular setting. The next example searches for the string sem in any files in the /proc/sys/kernel directory:

```
# grep . /proc/sys/kernel/* | grep sem
/proc/sys/kernel/sem:250          32000    100      128
```

If you want to save all the current kernel values in a file, then pipe the output of the grep command to a file:

```
# grep . /proc/sys/kernel/* >jul11_kernel_parms.txt
```

How It Works

Another way to display all kernel parameters is via the sysctl utility. This utility allows you to view and modify the kernel files found in the /proc/sys directory. Use the -a option of sysctl to view all kernel parameters:

```
# sysctl -a
```

Here is a small snippet of the large output of the previous command:

```
kernel.sysrq = 0
kernel.sem = 250          32000    100      128
kernel.msgmnb = 16384
kernel.msgmni = 16
kernel.msgmax = 8192
kernel.shmmni = 4096
kernel.shmall = 2097152
kernel.shmmax = 536870912
kernel.acct = 4 2        30
kernel.hotplug = /sbin/hotplug
```

You can save the output of the sysctl -a command to a text file, as shown here:

```
# sysctl -a > /root/kernelsysctl.txt
```

Inspect the output of the sysctl -a command. Notice that the kernel values are either a single value or an array of values. When just a single value is involved, it's fairly easy to determine the setting of the parameter. For example, from the output of sysctl -a, the maximum setting for shared memory (shmmax) is 536,870,912 bytes:

```
kernel.shmmax = 536870912
```

When the kernel settings are stored as an array, it becomes a bit more difficult to determine a particular value. For example, this array of four values shows the current kernel settings for sem (semaphores):

```
kernel.sem = 250    32000    100       128
```

When working with array values, it's important to know what element of the array maps to what kernel setting. In the previous output, the values of the semaphore array 250 32000 100 128 map to the following kernel parameters, respectively, semmsl, semmns, semopm, and semmni. For example, semmsl is set to 250 and defines the maximum number of semaphores in a semaphore array. The meanings of these semaphore parameters are discussed in detail in recipe 9-6 of this chapter.

9-5. Modifying Kernel Parameters

Problem

You're performing a database installation. The Oracle documentation specifies the recommending settings for several kernel parameters. You want to modify these kernel parameters.

Solution

There are several valid techniques for changing kernel parameters:

- Running sysctl

- Editing sysctl.conf

- Adding entries with echo

- Adding entries with cat

These methods are detailed in the next several sections.

Running sysctl

Use the sysctl command with the -w option to dynamically modify kernel parameters. The following command changes the kernel semaphore settings in the /proc/sys/kernel/sem virtual file:

```
# sysctl -w kernel.sem="250 32000 100 128"
```

Notice there are no spaces around the = sign. If you attempt to run the sysctl command with spaces around the = sign, you will receive an error like the following:

```
error: 'kernel.sem' must be of the form name=value
error: Malformed setting '='
error: '250 32000 100 128' must be of the form name=value
```

To make changes persist across system reboots, use your favorite editor (like vi) to add the parameters to the /etc/sysctl.conf file.

■**Tip** Use the man sysctl or sysctl --help command for all options available in your environment.

Editing sysctl.conf

You can also directly modify the /etc/sysctl.conf file and then use the sysctl -p command to make desired kernel parameter changes. This example uses vi to first edit the /etc/sysctl.conf file:

```
# vi /etc/sysctl.conf
# Add changes and then exit...
```

After you modify the /etc/sysctl.conf file, you can use the sysctl -p command to make the entries in the /etc/sysctl.conf file instantiated as the current values used by the Linux kernel:

```
# sysctl -p
```

The previous command loads into memory the values found in the /etc/sysctl.conf file. You can verify that the values were changed by using cat to view the corresponding virtual file.

When editing the sysctl.conf file, we recommend you first make a copy of the file with the date embedded into the file name. For example, before making any changes, create a copy of the file, as shown here:

```
# cp /etc/sysctl.conf  /etc/sysctl.conf.01_jan_08
```

Making a copy serves two purposes. First, it provides you with a copy of the parameters as they were before the change. This comes in handy if for any reason you want to revert to the previous settings. Second, this also gives you an audit trail of all kernel changes made via this file. You can then use commands like diff to display differences in file versions (see recipe 5-14 for details).

Adding Entries with echo

You can use the echo command to write the desired output to the specified virtual file. This example writes the values 250 32000 100 128 to the virtual /proc/sys/kernel/sem file using the echo command:

```
# echo 250 32000 100 128 > /proc/sys/kernel/sem
```

The previous command immediately changes the kernel settings for the sem (semaphores) parameter. If you want the change to persist across system reboots, then you also need to add an entry to the /etc/sysctl.conf file. This file is read when the system boots to determine the settings for kernel parameters. You can edit the /etc/sysctl.conf file directly (with an editor such as vi) and add the following line:

```
kernel.sem = 250 32000 100 128
```

Alternatively, you can use the echo command to add the desired parameters to the end of the /etc/sysctl.conf file, as shown here:

```
# echo "kernel.sem = 250 32000 100 128" >> /etc/sysctl.conf
```

Notice that the previous command uses >> to concatenate the desired entry to the bottom of the /etc/sysctl.conf file. You would not want to use just a single right arrow >, because that would overwrite the contents of /etc/sysctl.conf.

When you use echo and >> to write to the contents of the /etc/sysctl.conf file, no checks are performed to determine whether the kernel parameters you are writing to the file already exist. The echo and >> technique simply adds the values to the bottom of the file.

If there happen to be two entries in the /etc/sysctl.conf file that configure the same kernel parameter, the value that appears nearest to the bottom of the file will be the one that gets set. This is because the parameters are processed from top to bottom. For example, say you have the following two lines in the /etc/sysctl.conf file:

```
kernel.sem = 500 64000 200 500
kernel.sem = 250 32000 100 128
```

The bottom line in the previous listing will be set last and therefore will dictate the kernel setting for the kernel.sem value.

After you use echo to write to the /etc/sysctl.conf file, you can use the sysctl -p command to make the entries in the /etc/sysctl.conf file instantiated as the current values used by the Linux kernel:

```
# sysctl -p
```

Adding Entries with cat

The technique shown here is handy for adding several entries to the /etc/sysctl.conf file at the same time. First use the cat command to add entries to the /etc/sysctl.conf file. This example shows how to use cat to write typical kernel parameter settings for an Oracle database:

```
# cat >> /etc/sysctl.conf <<EOF
kernel.shmall = 2097152
kernel.shmmax = 536870912
kernel.shmmni = 4096
kernel.sem = 250 32000 100 128
fs.file-max = 65536
net.ipv4.ip_local_port_range = 1024 65000
net.core.rmem_default = 262144
net.core.rmem_max = 262144
net.core.wmem_default = 262144
net.core.wmem_max = 262144
EOF
```

The previous command uses cat to write to the /etc/sysctl.conf file all the values encapsulated between the two EOF markers. This allows you to add several parameters simultaneously to the /etc/sysctl.conf file. When using cat and >> to write parameters to the /etc/sysctl.conf file, there is no automatic checking to determine whether the parameters already exist in the file. Using cat and >> will simply write to the bottom of the file.

After the desired changes are made, use the sysctl -p command to make the entries in the /etc/sysctl.conf file the current values used by the Linux kernel, as shown here:

```
# sysctl -p
```

How It Works

One advantageous feature of Linux is that you can dynamically change many of the kernel settings while the system is running. The parameters take effect as soon as you change them, and you are not required to reboot the system. This is different from many other operating systems that require a server reboot for kernel changes to become instantiated.

The /proc/sys directory contains virtual files that correspond to kernel settings. You can change the /proc/sys files to dynamically configure kernel values. Hundreds of parameters exist that you can modify. Run the following find command to give you a rough idea of how many kernel files there are with your version of Linux:

```
# find /proc/sys -type f | wc -l
448
```

Not all virtual files in the /proc/sys directory can be modified. One quick way to determine whether a /proc/sys file can be altered is to check the permissions. Any file that shows the writable permission can be changed. This example uses the ls -altr command to view the /proc/sys/kernel file permissions:

```
# ls -altr /proc/sys/kernel
```

Here is a partial listing of the output. Notice that the first two files are not modifiable, but the last three can be modified (signified by the w write permission).

```
-r--r--r--  1 root root 0 Sep  4 16:32 version
-r--r--r--  1 root root 0 Sep  4 16:32 tainted
-rw-r--r--  1 root root 0 Sep  4 16:32 shmmni
-rw-r--r--  1 root root 0 Sep  4 16:32 shmmax
-rw-r--r--  1 root root 0 Sep  4 16:32 shmall
```

■**Caution** Be careful when modifying kernel values. Modifying a kernel parameter to an unusable value can cause the system to become unstable and require a restart with the boot disk.

9-6. Displaying Semaphores

Problem

The Oracle installation documentation recommends configuring the system semaphores to certain minimal values. Before you modify the settings, you want to view the semaphore parameters.

Solution

You can view semaphore information by displaying the contents of the /proc/sys/kernel/sem file. This example uses the cat command to view semaphore data (you don't have to be root to view these values):

```
$ cat /proc/sys/kernel/sem
250     32000   100     128
```

Notice that there are four values listed for semaphores in the previous output. Those numbers represent the value for the following semaphore kernel parameters: semmsl, semmns, semopm, and semmni, respectively. For example, the semmsl value is currently 250, semmns is 32000, and so forth.

How It Works

Before making changes to any kernel information, it's prudent to first view the current values. Table 9-2 details the meanings of the relevant Linux semaphore variables. Notice that all semaphore variable names aptly begin with the letters sem. These semaphore names may vary slightly depending on which version of the Linux/Unix operating system you're using.

Table 9-2. *Semaphore Kernel Parameters and Descriptions*

IPC Semaphore Parameter	Description
semmsl	Maximum number of semaphores per set (array)
semmns	Maximum number of semaphores on entire system
semopm	Maximum operations for semop system call
semmni	Maximum number of semaphore arrays on entire system
semvmx	Maximum value of a semaphore

Semaphores are locking mechanisms that are used to coordinate mutually exclusive access to sharable system resources. Semaphores act as gatekeepers to ensure that particular shared system resources are not accessed by multiple processes at the same time. Databases use semaphores to manage access to operating system resources such as shared memory.

Database background processes require semaphores to manage mutually exclusive access to shared resources. If there aren't enough semaphores available for all database processes, this could cause the database to not start or cause a runtime failure. If there are any semaphore-related problems, it's critical that DBAs know how to view and configure these kernel parameters.

RAILROAD SEMAPHORES

In the early days of the railroad, engineers quickly discovered the need for communicating the status of railway lines over long distances. Knowing in advance whether a railway line was in use had direct impact on survivability. To minimize collisions, railroad engineers devised techniques of signaling via signs visible over long distances.

The signs that the railways used consisted of moving mechanical arms or multicolored lights. These mechanical signs and lights—colloquially called *semaphores*—were utilized to communicate in advance whether a set of tracks was free from an obstruction (such as an oncoming train). In this way, the railway engineers ensured that only one train at a time used a single section of tracks.

Semaphores in computers function much like their railway counterparts. Semaphores signify whether a resource is busy (or not). These constructs are typically utilized to manage exclusive access to segments of shared memory. A database process that needs access to a shared memory segment must first check the status of the corresponding semaphore variable to guarantee that the section is not already in use. In this way, semaphores ensure that only one process at a time operates on a particular shared memory area.

9-7. Configuring Semaphores

Problem

You're installing Oracle software on a database server and need to modify the semaphore settings.

Solution

Before beginning, first check the current values in case they need to be referenced later. To view the current semaphore settings, use the cat command:

```
# cat /proc/sys/kernel/sem
250      32000   32       128
```

As noted in Table 9-2, the values in the previous output represent the settings for the following semaphore parameters in this order: semmsl, semmns, semopm, and semmni.

This next example uses the echo command to increase the maximum number of semaphore arrays (semmni) from 128 to 256:

```
# echo 250 32000 100 256 > /proc/sys/kernel/sem
```

■**Note** See recipe 9-5 for alternate ways of changing kernel parameters.

How It Works

After you change the semaphore settings, it's a good idea to use the cat command to verify that the changes took place:

```
# cat /proc/sys/kernel/sem
250      32000   100      256
```

If you want the changes to persist across a system reboot, then ensure that you modify the /etc/sysctl.conf file appropriately. In this example, an editor (like vi) is used to add the following entry to the /etc/sysctl.conf file:

```
kernel.sem = 250 32000 100 256
```

■**Note** Refer to Oracle's installation documentation for recommended settings of semaphores for your version of Oracle and Linux.

9-8. Viewing Shared Memory Settings

Problem

The Oracle installation documentation indicates you need a minimal amount of memory installed on the Linux box to run the database. You want to view the database server memory settings.

Solution

All the shared memory parameters appropriately begin with the string shm. Use the ls (list) command with the -1 (that's a number one) option to display which shared memory parameters are available on your Linux system:

```
$ ls -1 /proc/sys/kernel/shm*
```

You should see output similar to this:

```
/proc/sys/kernel/shmall
/proc/sys/kernel/shmmax
/proc/sys/kernel/shmmni
```

Next use the cat command to view individual shared memory settings. This example shows how to view the maximum size (in bytes) of a shared memory segment (shmmax) that can be created:

```
$ cat /proc/sys/kernel/shmmax
2147483648
```

How It Works

Table 9-3 describes the shared memory parameters. Some of these parameters may not be updatable on your particular Linux system.

Table 9-3. *Shared Memory Kernel Parameter Descriptions*

IPC Shared Memory Parameter	Description
shmmax	Maximum size (in bytes) for shared memory segment
shmmin	Minimum size (in bytes) of shared memory segment
shmall	Total amount of shared memory (in bytes or pages) that can be used at any time
shmseg	Maximum number of shared memory segments per process
shmmni	Maximum number of shared memory segments for the entire system

If you want to view the currently allocated shared memory segments, use the -m option of the ipcs command. This next example shows the shared memory segments in use on a server running an Oracle database:

```
$ ipcs -m
------ Shared Memory Segments --------
key        shmid    owner    perms    bytes      nattch    status
0xb3e36378 131072   oracle   640      421527552  17
```

Correctly sizing and configuring shared memory are important DBA tasks when building a new database server. Databases use shared memory as a holding area for data read from disk.

Database processes read and modify the data held in shared memory. The shared memory area uses semaphores (described in Table 9-2) to control exclusive access to memory segments.

A database will fail to start if there is not enough shared memory available to be allocated. Therefore, it's paramount that DBAs know how to manage shared memory because it has a direct impact on database availability and performance. These tasks are described in detail in recipe 9-9.

9-9. Modifying Shared Memory

Problem

You're installing Oracle software on a database server and need to modify the shared memory configuration.

Solution

You can use any of the techniques described in recipe 9-5 for changing the kernel parameters. This solution uses the echo command to modify the maximum shared memory segment size to approximately 500MB:

```
# echo 536870912 > /proc/sys/kernel/shmmax
```

The previous command will take effect immediately (without a system reboot). Use the cat command to verify the change:

```
# cat /proc/sys/kernel/shmmax
536870912
```

If you want the changes to persist across system reboots, then make sure you add them to the /etc/sysctl.conf file:

```
kernel.shmmax = 536870912
```

■**Note** Refer to Oracle's installation documentation for recommended settings for shared memory parameters for your version of Oracle and Linux.

How It Works

Before making on-the-fly changes to shared memory, it's a good idea to first view the overall amount of physical memory available on the box. You probably don't want to set your maximum shared memory size to a value that exceeds the total memory available on the server. Use the cat command with grep to view the contents of the virtual /proc/meminfo file, as shown here:

```
# cat /proc/meminfo | grep -i memtotal
MemTotal:       2057876 kB
```

The previous output shows that there are a total of 2GB of physical memory available on this server. If you don't filter the contents of /proc/meminfo with the grep command, then you will be presented with all the server memory information.

After you're comfortable with the overall size of physical memory on the box, you can change the shared memory settings by using either the echo command or the sysctl utility. On most Linux systems there are three memory parameters of interest: shmall, shmmax, and shmmni (see Table 9-3 for descriptions of these parameters).

■**Note** The shmmax parameter can have a significant impact on database performance. With Oracle databases, this parameter should be set to a value higher than the SGA size. If the shmmax value is too small, then you may not be able to start your Oracle instance.

9-10. Viewing Memory Structures

Problem

Your database has experienced a hard crash. You want to see whether there are any database-related memory structures that are still physically allocated on the server.

Solution

Use the ipcs (interprocess communication status) command without any options to view the current allocated physical memory, semaphores, and message queues:

```
$ ipcs
```

Here is some typical output:

```
------ Shared Memory Segments --------
key        shmid      owner      perms      bytes      nattch     status
0xb3e36378 131072     oracle     640        421527552  17
------ Semaphore Arrays --------
key        semid      owner      perms      nsems
0x288e2800 1146880    oracle     640        126
0x288e2801 1179649    oracle     640        126
0x288e2802 1212418    oracle     640        126
0x288e2803 1245187    oracle     640        126
0x288e2804 1277956    oracle     640        126
------ Message Queues --------
key        msqid      owner      perms      used-bytes  messages
```

The prior output has three sections. The oracle user has 421,527,552 bytes of shared memory allocated. There are five semaphore arrays allocated with 126 semaphores per array. There are no message queues allocated.

How It Works

The "Solution" section of this recipe demonstrates how to view in-memory structures currently allocated. To view the system limits imposed on memory and semaphores, use the -lms options of the ipcs command:

```
$ ipcs -lms
------ Shared Memory Limits --------
max number of segments = 4096
max seg size (kbytes) = 2097152
max total shared memory (kbytes) = 8388608
min seg size (bytes) = 1
------ Semaphore Limits --------
max number of arrays = 128
max semaphores per array = 250
max semaphores system wide = 32000
max ops per semop call = 100
semaphore max value = 32767
```

Compare the maximum memory values to the settings in the /proc/sys/kernel directory:

```
$ cat /proc/sys/kernel/shmall
2097152
$ cat /proc/sys/kernel/shmmax
2147483648
$ cat /proc/sys/kernel/shmmni
4096
```

Notice that the maximum total shared memory available to oracle is the product of the maximum number of segments (4,096) and the maximum size per segment (2,147,483,648).

To view all the options available with the ipcs command, use the -h (help) option:

```
$ ipcs -h
ipcs provides information on ipc facilities for which you have read access.
Resource Specification:
        -m : shared_mem
        -q : messages
        -s : semaphores
        -a : all (default)
Output Format:
        -t : time
        -p : pid
        -c : creator
        -l : limits
        -u : summary
-i id [-s -q -m] : details on resource identified by id
usage : ipcs -asmq -tclup
        ipcs [-s -m -q] -i id
        ipcs -h for help.
```

9-11. Removing In-Memory Structures

Problem

Your database unexpectedly crashed, and for some reason the semaphores and shared memory have not been released. Other databases are running on the server, so you cannot reboot the system to release the shared memory objects. You want to manually remove these orphaned memory structures.

Solution

First view the structures to be removed with the ipcs -sm command:

```
$ ipcs -sm
```

On this server there are two instances of Oracle running, each with one allocated shared memory segment and five sets of semaphore arrays:

```
------ Shared Memory Segments --------
key          shmid      owner     perms     bytes        nattch    status
0xb3e36378   32768      oracle    640       421527552    16
0x34525e84   65537      oracle    640       421527552    11


------ Semaphore Arrays --------
key          semid      owner     perms     nsems
0x288e2800   360448     oracle    640       126
0x288e2801   393217     oracle    640       126
0x288e2802   425986     oracle    640       126
0x288e2803   458755     oracle    640       126
0x288e2804   491524     oracle    640       126
0x3239d0e4   622597     oracle    640       126
0x3239d0e5   655366     oracle    640       126
0x3239d0e6   688135     oracle    640       126
0x3239d0e7   720904     oracle    640       126
0x3239d0e8   753673     oracle    640       126
```

■**Caution** If you're working on a server that has multiple Oracle instances running, ensure that you remove the correct memory structure. If you remove the wrong structure, you will inadvertently crash another database.

If you have multiple databases on one server, first verify which memory structures belong to the orphaned instance by running the Oracle sysresv utility (located in the ORACLE_HOME/bin directory). This command reports on memory structures that correspond to your current instance setting of ORACLE_SID. Run this command as the owner of the Oracle binaries (usually oracle):

```
$ sysresv
```

Here is the pertinent output:

```
IPC Resources for ORACLE_SID "RMDB2" :
Shared Memory:
ID              KEY
65537           0x34525e84
Semaphores:
ID              KEY
622597          0x3239d0e4
655366          0x3239d0e5
688135          0x3239d0e6
720904          0x3239d0e7
753673          0x3239d0e8
```

You can remove memory objects either by the key or by ID. This next example uses the -m option to remove a shared memory segment by its ID:

```
$ ipcrm -m 65537
```

This next example uses the -s option to remove semaphore arrays using IDs:

```
$ ipcrm -s 622597
$ ipcrm -s 655366
$ ipcrm -s 688135
$ ipcrm -s 720904
$ ipcrm -s 753673
```

You can verify that the memory structures have been removed by running sysresv again:

```
$ sysresv
IPC Resources for ORACLE_SID "RMDB2" :
Shared Memory
ID              KEY
No shared memory segments used
Semaphores:
ID              KEY
No semaphore resources used
Oracle Instance not alive for sid "RMDB2" ☹
```

How It Works

The ipcrm command uses either the key or the ID as its input for identifying what IPC object to remove. The basic syntax for using ipcrm is as follows:

```
$ ipcrm [ -M key | -m id | -Q key | -q id | -S key | -s id ]
```

In the previous syntax description, -M is used with a shared memory key, -m is used with a shared memory ID, -S is used with a semaphore key, and -s is used with a semaphore ID.

You may run into an occasional scenario where you have a database crash and for some reason the database semaphores or shared memory structures have not been released properly by the operating system. In these rare situations (if you don't have the luxury of rebooting the server), you will have to first identify the unreleased memory object with the `ipcs` and `sysresv` commands and then remove it with the appropriate `ipcrm` command.

9-12. Viewing Network Configuration Settings

Problem

The Oracle documentation recommends setting some network parameters to minimal values. You first want to inspect the current network settings.

Solution

The virtual /proc network files are usually located either in /proc/sys/net/core or in /proc/sys/net/ipv4. By using the `ls -altr` command, you can see that most of the virtual network files in /proc/sys/net/core are updatable:

```
# ls -altr /proc/sys/net/core
total 0
-rw-r--r--  1 root root 0 Sep  4 16:54 wmem_max
-rw-r--r--  1 root root 0 Sep  4 16:54 wmem_default
-rw-r--r--  1 root root 0 Sep  4 16:54 somaxconn
-rw-r--r--  1 root root 0 Sep  4 16:54 rmem_max
-rw-r--r--  1 root root 0 Sep  4 16:54 rmem_default
-rw-r--r--  1 root root 0 Sep  4 16:54 optmem_max
-rw-r--r--  1 root root 0 Sep  4 16:54 no_cong_thresh
-rw-r--r--  1 root root 0 Sep  4 16:54 no_cong
-rw-r--r--  1 root root 0 Sep  4 16:54 netdev_max_backlog
-rw-r--r--  1 root root 0 Sep  4 16:54 mod_cong
-rw-r--r--  1 root root 0 Sep  4 16:54 message_cost
-rw-r--r--  1 root root 0 Sep  4 16:54 message_burst
-rw-r--r--  1 root root 0 Sep  4 16:54 lo_cong
-r--r--r--  1 root root 0 Sep  4 16:54 divert_version
-rw-r--r--  1 root root 0 Sep  4 16:54 dev_weight
```

Use the `cat` command to view a particular virtual network file. This example uses `cat` to display the current setting for the `rmem_default` kernel parameter:

```
# cat /proc/sys/net/core/rmem_default
262144
```

How It Works

To view a complete listing of network settings, use the `sysctl` command and `grep` for the string net:

```
# sysctl -a | grep -i net
```

You'll be presented with a great deal of output. Table 9-4 lists some of the network kernel parameters that you may have to modify for database servers.

Table 9-4. *Network Kernel Parameter Descriptions*

Network Kernel Parameter	Location	Description
rmem_default	/proc/sys/net/core	Default socket receive buffer size (in bytes)
wmem_default	/proc/sys/net/core	Default socket send buffer size (in bytes)
rmem_max	/proc/sys/net/core	Maximum socket receive buffer size (in bytes)
wmem_max	/proc/sys/net/core	Maximum socket send buffer size (in bytes)
tcp_keepalive_time	/proc/sys/net/ipv4	Number of seconds a connection is idle before TCP starts sending keep-alive probes
tcp_keepalive_intvl	/proc/sys/net/ipv4	Interval (in seconds) between keep-alive probes
tcp_keepalive_probes	/proc/sys/net/ipv4	Number of unacknowledged probes sent before connection is terminated
tcp_retries1	/proc/sys/net/ipv4	Number of times TCP will attempt to transmit packet normally
tcp_retries2	/proc/sys/net/ipv4	Maximum number of times a TCP will attempt to transmit a packet
tcp_syn_retries	/proc/sys/net/ipv4	Maximum number of SYNs attempts to transmit
ip_local_port_range	/proc/sys/net/ipv4	Ports allowed for TCP and UDP traffic

VIEWING IP INFORMATION

You'll occasionally need to view aspects about your network such as the server's Internet Protocol (IP) address. Look in the /etc/hosts file, and view your hostname and IP information. The /etc/hosts file contains a cross-reference between IP addresses and server names. This example uses cat to display the contents of the /etc/hosts file:

```
$ cat /etc/hosts
```

Here's a sample of what you might find:

```
127.0.0.1           localhost.localdomain localhost
177.22.33.89        db123.cent.com    db123
```

You can also use hostname -i to view your server IP address, and you can use the hostname -d command to display domain information.

9-13. Configuring Network Settings

Problem

You're installing database software on a Linux server, and the Oracle documentation indicates you need to configure some network parameters.

Solution

Use the `echo` command to update the `/proc/sys/net/ipv4/ip_local_port_range` file. This example uses the `echo` command to change the first local port allowed for TCP and UPD traffic to 1024 and the last local port to 65000:

```
# echo  1024 65000 > /proc/sys/net/ipv4/ip_local_port_range
```

You can verify the changes with the `cat` command:

```
# cat  /proc/sys/net/ipv4/ip_local_port_range
1024    65000
```

You need to add these entries to the `/etc/sysctl.conf` file to have the changes persist across system reboots. Here's a sample entry in the `/etc/sysctl.conf` file:

```
net.ipv4.ip_local_port_range=1024 65000
```

How It Works

Before changing any network kernel parameters, make sure you first save a copy of the original values somewhere. This will allow you to change back to the old values in the event the new values cause undesirable results. In the next example, the value of the `ip_local_port_range` is first viewed with the `cat` command:

```
$ cat  /proc/sys/net/ipv4/ip_local_port_range
32768    61000
```

■**Note** Refer to the Oracle installation documentation for recommended settings for network kernel parameters for your version of Oracle and Linux.

9-14. Modifying System Open File Limits

Problem

The Oracle installation documentation recommends setting the system-wide open file limit for the server. You want to enable this restriction.

Solution

Use the echo command or the sysctl command to dynamically modify the /proc/sys/fs/file-max value. This next example uses the echo command to change the file-max value on the fly to 65536:

```
# echo 65536 > /proc/sys/fs/file-max
```

Use the cat command to verify that the change took place:

```
# cat /proc/sys/fs/file-max
65536
```

Here's an example of using sysctl -w to modify the maximum open file limit:

```
# sysctl -w fs.file-max=65536
```

Remember to add an entry to the /etc/sysctl.conf file to make the changes persist across system reboots.

How It Works

Linux imposes a limit on the overall number of files simultaneously open on the server. Servers that host database applications tend to have many simultaneously open files. If the default value for the maximum number of open files is too low, you most likely will have to increase it. You'll know that you've hit the maximum limit on the number of open files if you start seeing errors pertaining to "running out of file handles."

This maximum open file limit is governed by the Linux kernel /proc/sys/fs/file-max virtual file. You can also view the maximum number of file handles by viewing the contents of the /proc/sys/fs/file-nr virtual file:

```
# cat /proc/sys/fs/file-nr
885 0 65536
```

The previous output shows the current number of allocated file handles, the number of free file handles, and the maximum number of file handles, respectively.

9-15. Showing Shell Limits

Problem

You want to view system resource limits instantiated by your logon shell.

Solution

By default, the -a (all) option of the ulimit command will print the current soft limits for a process:

```
$ ulimit -a
core file size          (blocks, -c) 0
data seg size           (kbytes, -d) unlimited
file size               (blocks, -f) unlimited
pending signals                (-i) 1024
```

```
max locked memory        (kbytes, -l) 32
max memory size          (kbytes, -m) unlimited
open files                       (-n) 10000
pipe size               (512 bytes, -p) 8
POSIX message queues       (bytes, -q) 819200
stack size               (kbytes, -s) 10240
cpu time                (seconds, -t) unlimited
max user processes               (-u) 16375
virtual memory           (kbytes, -v) unlimited
file locks                       (-x) unlimited
```

The previous output displays the parameter, the units of measurement, the option used to manipulate the parameter, and its current setting. To view the hard limit resources, use the ulimit -aH command. If you want to view a soft or hard limit for a particular setting, specify its option. For example, to display the hard limit for the number of open files, use the -Hn option:

```
$ ulimit -Hn
20000
```

How It Works

Your logon shell will impose default maximum limits on various resources that a process can use such as the number of open files, processes per user, amount of memory allocated, and so on. These shell limits are defined by the ulimit command. Each resource has a soft limit setting and a hard limit setting. The soft limit setting establishes the default resource limit when a user logs on to the system. If the user process exceeds the soft limit setting for a resource, an error will be thrown. The user can manually increase the setting of the soft limit setting for a resource up to (but not exceeding) the value defined by the hard limit.

A user can modify the hard limit down but cannot modify the hard limit up. This means if you set a hard limit to a lower value, you cannot reset it to its original value. Only the root user can modify a hard limit to a higher value.

The default values for soft and hard limits on the server are established by adding entries into the /etc/security/limits.conf file. Database processes tend to consume more resources than what the default shell limits allow. Therefore, it's important you're familiar with viewing and modifying shell resource limits.

Note The Bash, Bourne, and Korn shells use the ulimit command to view and modify shell resource limits. If you are using the C shell, then use the limit command.

9-16. Changing Shell Limits

Problem

You're performing an Oracle installation on a new server and need to modify the shell limits per the installation instructions.

Solution

To alter the default shell limits for a user, as root edit the /etc/security/limits.conf file. This example shows how to change the number of processes and number of open files defined for the oracle user:

```
oracle soft nproc 2047
oracle hard nproc 16384
oracle soft nofile 1024
oracle hard nofile 65536
```

In the previous output, the first line defines the soft limit for the number of processes for the oracle user to 2047, and the second line sets the hard limit for the number of processes to 16384. The third and fourth lines set the soft and hard limits for the number of open files for the oracle user, respectively. These limits will be imposed on the oracle user when logging onto the server.

Caution Do not set the hard limit for a user resource to be higher than the system-wide limit. In particular, don't set the hard limit for the number of open files to be higher than the value defined in the /proc/sys/fs/file-max virtual file. If a process is able to open the maximum number of files that reaches the system-wide setting, this causes the system to run out of open files and could cause the system to become unstable. Not good.

How It Works

The ulimit command provides a way to view and limit resources used by a shell and the resources of subprocesses started by a shell. As a non-root user, you can change your soft limits up to the value defined by the hard limit. As the root user, you can modify hard limits to higher values.

For example, to adjust the soft limit of the number of open files to 15000, issue the following:

```
$ ulimit -Sn 15000
```

To view the change, then issue the command without a value:

```
$ ulimit -Sn
15000
```

If you exceed the value defined by the hard limit, you'll receive an error such as the following:

```
-bash: ulimit: open files: cannot modify limit: Invalid argument
```

When you add entries to the /etc/security/limits.conf file, this sets the default shell limit for the user process when they log on to the system. Table 9-5 shows the meanings of values you can change in /etc/security/limits.conf file.

Table 9-5. *Description of Limits Set via* /etc/security/limits.conf *Virtual File*

Parameter	Limits
core	Core file size (in KB)
data	Maximum data size (in KB)
fsize	Maximum filesize (in KB)
memlock	Maximum locked in memory address space (in KB)
nofile	Maximum number of open files
rss	Maximum resident set size (in KB)
stack	Maximum stack size (in KB)
cpu	Maximum CPU time (in minutes)
nproc	Maximum number of processes
as	Address space limit
maxlogins	Maximum number of logins for user
priority	Priority at which to run user process
locks	Maximum number of locks for user

When working with database applications, you may not want to ever have a database process constrained by a soft limit. Rather, you want only the hard limit to govern the amount of resources a database process uses. In this case, you can set the soft limit equal to the hard limit in the database user login profile file. For example, if the oracle user on your Linux box uses the Bash shell, then you would modify the .bash_profile login file (see recipe 2-5 for further details). The following entries are added to the oracle user's .bash_profile file to establish the soft limits equal to the hard limits:

```
ulimit -u 16384
ulimit -n 65536
```

When using the ulimit command, if you don't denote an -S (soft) or -H (hard) option, then this sets both the soft and hard limits to the value specified. Whenever the oracle user logs on, the soft and hard limits for the number of processes will be 16384, and the soft and hard limits for the number of open files will be 65536.

If you write an entry into the logon file that exceeds the hard limit, the user will receive an error such as this at logon time:

```
-bash: ulimit: open files: cannot modify limit: Operation not permitted
```

■**Note** The Bourne and Korn shells use the .profile initialization file for setting parameters on logon. The C shell uses the .login or .cshrc file.

## CHAPTER 10

Managing Server Software

Although more and more Fortune 500 companies are embracing Linux, its adoption still appears to be more prevalent in the small to medium (SMB) market. In companies that adopt Linux as a standard, DBAs often perform or share the system administration responsibilities. Often for budgetary constraints, DBAs in the SMB space have more involvement in operating system maintenance. For larger companies, a true delineation of roles and responsibilities exists. For DBAs who perform software management roles in the Linux world, in particular Red Hat and Oracle Enterprise Linux, this chapter is for you.

In this chapter, we will take a bare-bones Red Hat installation and register the Red Hat server to Oracle's Unbreakable Linux Network, leverage Oracle's validated install to load all the required RPMs to install an Oracle database, perform a silent installation of Oracle Database 11*g* software, perform a silent database creation, and complete the server build by setting up a silent network configuration. Silent mode installations are the foundations of creating an automated server installation procedure.

We will start by demonstrating how to install RPMs, switching to Oracle's Unbreakable Linux Network from the Red Hat Network, listing the contents of an RPM package, correlating operating system executables to RPMs, downloading RPMs, automating with Oracle's validated install, and removing RPMs.

The database software management portion of this chapter concentrates exclusively on silent installations. While learning how to set up a database server from a soup-to-nuts implementation, you will also learn about RPM and up2date management.

10-1. Installing Packages

Problem

You want to install software components on the Linux server.

Solution #1

One of the ways you can manage software on the Linux server is by executing the rpm command with the -i option (or --install) to install the package. Here's an example of installing the screen executable:

```
[root@rac5 up2date]# rpm -ihv screen-4.0.3-1.el5.i386.rpm
Preparing...                ########################################### [100%]
   1:screen                 ########################################### [100%]
```

The -h option displays hash marks during the installation. The -v option provides verbose output that reports the progress of the installation. The rpm executable can install packages from the local filesystem, CD, or remote server accessible by HTTP or FTP.

Solution #2

If you do not have a license with either Red Hat Network or Oracle's Unbreakable Linux Network, you can maintain your system with the rpm command. Instead of locating RPMs associated with the executable or determining the dependencies associated with an RPM, administrators can register up2date to pull the RPMs and associated dependencies down from the up2date repository. Here is an example of using up2date to install the screen executable:

```
# up2date screen

Fetching Obsoletes list for channel: el4_i386_latest...
########################################

Fetching Obsoletes list for channel: el4_i386_oracle...

Fetching Obsoletes list for channel: el4_i386_addons...

Fetching rpm headers...
########################################

Name                                    Version      Rel
---------------------------------------------------------
screen                                  4.0.2        5              i386


Testing package set / solving RPM inter-dependencies...
########################################
screen-4.0.2-5.i386.rpm:    ######################### Done.
Preparing                   ######################################## [100%]

Installing...
   1:screen                  ######################################## [100%]
```

With a single command, up2date downloaded the screen-4.0.2-5.i386.rpm package from the up2date repository and installed the software. If dependencies existed, up2date would have downloaded the dependent package(s) and installed the package(s) in the required order. You can imagine the potential time and frustration you save by not having to deal with dependency nightmares.

Oracle Database 10g/11g requires both 32-bit and 64-bit RPMs to be installed on a 64-bit architecture Linux server. To install 32-bit RPMs on a 64-bit machine with up2date, you can use the --arch option as shown here:

```
# up2date --arch=i386 glibc-devel
```

How It Works

In a nutshell, RPM is a package management system. RPM originally stood for Red Hat Package Manager because it was designed by Red Hat for Red Hat distributions. Since RPM was intended for Linux distributions and utilized by many Linux distributions, RPM now stands for RPM Package Manager.

The RPM system is composed of a local database, the rpm executable, and the RPM package files. The local RPM database is stored in the /var/lib/rpm directory, and it houses metadata information about installed packages including package prerequisites and file attributes. Since the local RPM database tracks all the packages and file attributes, removing a package becomes a relatively simple operation.

The RPM package file is composed of compressed archive files and dependency information. The package name or label contains the following attributes:

```
<name>-<version>-<release>.<architecture>.rpm
```

Here's an example of the package label:

```
unixODBC-2.2.11-7.1.i386.rpm
```

The unixODBC RPM is a required RPM for Oracle Database 11g. For this particular example, the version of the RPM is 2.2.11. The release of the RPM is 7.1. This particular RPM is designed for a 32-bit Intel IA32 (x86) CPU. The AMD64/Intel em64t RPM will have the architecture name x86_64.

RPMs that contain source code will have .src before the .rpm suffix. At times, you may not find binary RPMs associated with your architecture and flavor of Linux. An equivalent source code RPM may be available for another flavor of Linux. You can download the source and compile the RPM.

You will also notice that certain RPMs will have the .noarch extension in the file names to denote that the RPM does not have a dependency on the architecture of your system.

Note Optionally, you can install RPMs leveraging Yellowdog Updater, Modified (yum) or the Advanced Packaging Tool (apt). Unfortunately, neither Red Hat Network nor Oracle ULN provides support for downloading/installing RPMs with these executables. You can set up a local yum repository, but this topic is outside the context of this chapter. apt is considered to be one of Debian Linux's better features.

10-2. Switching to Oracle's Unbreakable Linux Network

Problem

You installed Red Hat Enterprise Linux 4 or 5 but want to leverage Oracle's Unbreakable Linux Network (ULN). You want to start performing updates from ULN instead of Red Hat Network (RHN).

Solution

Before you can start taking advantage of ULN, you must download and upgrade to the new version of the up2date and up2date-gnome packages from https://linux.oracle.com/switch.html for your version of Red Hat and server architecture. In addition, you must have a valid CSI and license for Oracle Enterprise Linux (OEL).

Installing Oracle's up2date

Once you download the up2date and up2date-gnome packages, you can upgrade the existing packages as the root user on your Red Hat system using the rpm -Uhv command, as shown here:

```
[root@rac5 Desktop]# rpm -Uhv up2date-5.10.1-40.8.el5.i386.rpm  \
                             up2date-gnome-5.10.1-40.8.el5.i386.rpm
warning: up2date-5.10.1-40.8.el5.i386.rpm: Header V3 DSA signature: NOKEY, key ID
 1e5e0159
Preparing...                ########################################### [100%]
   1:up2date               ########################################### [ 50%]
   2:up2date-gnome         ########################################### [100%]
```

If you do not have up2date-gnome installed, you can exclude that RPM. Once the RPMs are successfully installed, you must import Oracle's GPG keys by executing the import option:

```
rpm --import /usr/share/rhn/RPM-GPG-KEY
```

Registering with ULN

Now you are ready to register the Red Hat server with ULN. Once you register the Red Hat server, you will be able to start using the up2date command to automatically download and install/ upgrade packages on the Linux server. The single greatest feature of up2date is that all the dependencies are automatically resolved without the administrator's intervention. The biggest frustration with RPM management is dealing with a colloquialism referred to as *dependency hell*. For example, RPM X will have a dependency on RPMs A, B, and C. RPM B will have another dependency on L, M, and N. Not realizing the RPM dependencies, when you try to install RPM N, you encounter another dependency for RPM N that requires RPMs H and I. You simply wanted to install RPM X, but you stumble into a multitude of other RPM requirements, and the dependency requirements stack on top of each other. You will encounter situations where up2date will significantly simplify the management of a Linux server.

■**Note** The process to register a Red Hat server and an Oracle Enterprise Linux server with ULN is identical. Customers who implement OEL can also register with ULN with the same steps outlined next to start using up2date to maintain their systems.

To start the registration process, you can execute the following command:

```
up2date --register
```

■**Note** You can execute the command up2date --register --nox to launch up2date in non-GUI mode.

Without the --nox option, your DISPLAY parameter must be set to a valid X server or the VNC server. Initially, you will be presented with the Welcome to Unbreakable Linux Network Update Agent screen. Click the Forward button to be directed to the Unbreakable Linux Network Login screen. Since this is the first time you are logging in to up2date, you must provide all the credentials on the screen, including a login ID, a password (twice for verification), and a licensed CSI number, as shown in Figure 10-1.

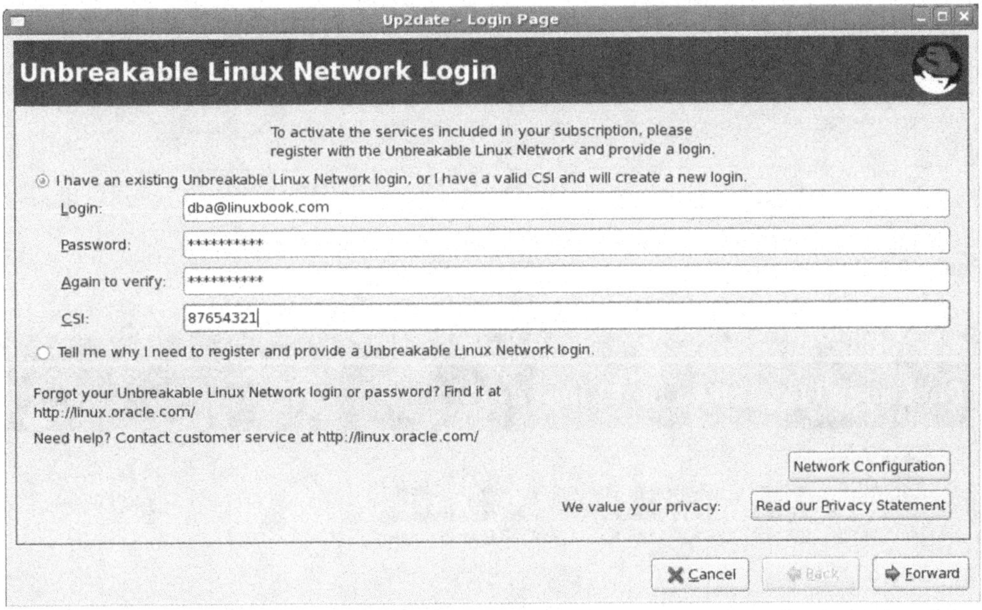

Figure 10-1. *Unbreakable Linux Network Login screen*

Once you enter all the required credentials, click the Forward button. All the information that is entered will be validated, and the login and CSI information will be validated with Oracle's ULN database. Next, you will be directed to the Activate screen, as shown in Figure 10-2, where you will be prompted to send hardware information and the package list to ULN. You will also have to confirm the name of the server to register. You can click the Details button to review the information that will be sent to ULN. Once you are satisfied with the information, click the Forward button.

A progress dialog box will pop up to display the progress of the information that is being transmitted to ULN. Once all the information is sent to ULN, you will be directed to the Channels screen. During the up2date registration, you can subscribe only to the channel containing the latest software for the architecture and OS revision of the system. You can specify a different channel using the web interface at https://linux.oracle.com, after you complete the register process. Click the Forward button to be routed to the Packages Flagged to Be Skipped screen, as displayed in Figure 10-3.

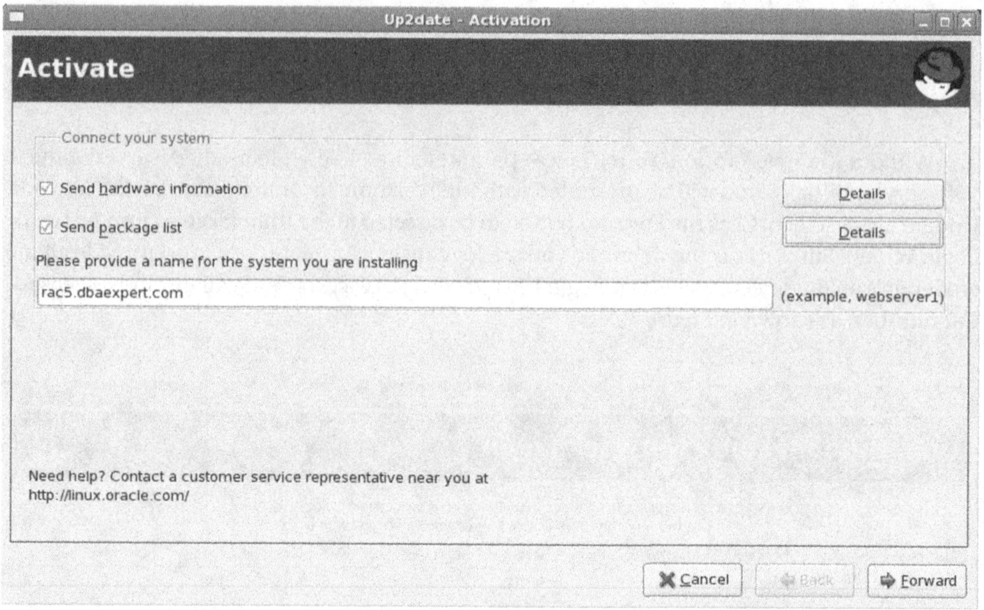

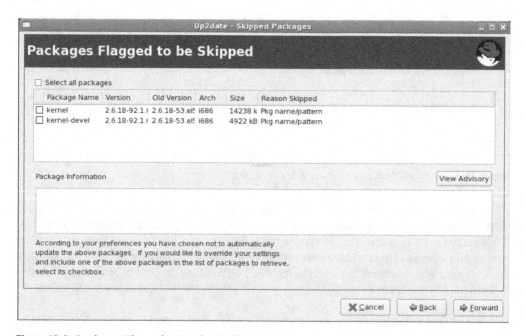

Figure 10-2. *Activate screen*

Figure 10-3. *Packages Flagged to Be Skipped screen*

You will want to skip updating the kernel and kernel-devel packages unless you plan on upgrading the operating system to a newer version. Leave the boxes unchecked, and click the Forward button. You will be directed to the Available Package Updates screen, as shown in Figure 10-4.

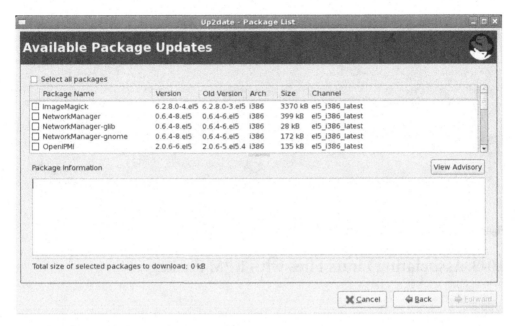

Figure 10-4. *Available Package Updates screen*

You can select one or more packages to update and click the Forward button. On this screen, you may opt to select all the package requirements to install Oracle Database 10*g* or 11*g*. up2date will download all the packages on the Retrieving Packages screen. When all the packages that you selected are downloaded, you can click the Forward button to take you to the Installing Packages screen. Once all the packages are successfully installed, click the Forward button again to be directed to the Finish screen. Finally, click the Finish button to exit.

How It Works

Switching from Red Hat Network to Oracle's ULN is straightforward. Once you purchase a license of OEL, you can start receiving support from Oracle MetaLink instead of Red Hat. You can start to receive support from a single front end for both the operating system and the database from Oracle MetaLink.

Once you have successfully registered your Red Hat server with ULN, you can access the ULN portal via https://linux.oracle.com. In the Login and Password fields, you can provide the login and password credentials that you supplied while registering your Red Hat server. Once you log in, you should be able to see your server, as displayed in Figure 10-5.

■**Note** Another major advantage of registering a server with Oracle's ULN is that you can execute up2date to download and install ASM-related RPMs. You do not have to investigate which ASM-related RPMs need to be downloaded based on the kernel level of your Linux server. up2date automatically determines which packages need to be downloaded for you.

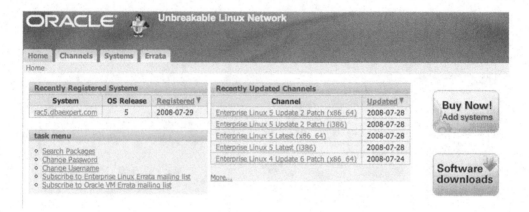

Figure 10-5. *Server confirmation on ULN*

10-3. Associating Linux Files with RPM Packages

Problem

You identified that one of the servers has an executable you need but another server does not. You want to identify the RPM package to install on the server.

Solution

Let's look at an example of the gedit executable and see which RPM delivers this executable:

```
[root@rac5 bin]# rpm -qf /usr/bin/gedit
gedit-2.16.0-5.el5
```

The -qf option also works for shared objects. If you happen to be curious about which package the libc.so file came from, you can issue the -qf option, as demonstrated here:

```
[root@rac5 lib]# rpm -qf libc.so
glibc-devel-2.5-18
```

How It Works

rpm provides features to query the RPM database to extract the owning package. You can correlate an executable or library from the operating system to an RPM. You can execute rpm with the -qf (-q for -query and -f for -file) option to determine which RPMs are associated with a specified file or executable.

10-4. Listing the Contents of an RPM Package

Problem

You want to look inside the .rpm file to view the contents of the package and peek at the destination where the files will be extracted.

Solution

You can execute rpm with the -qlp option to list the files in a package. Here's an example where the contents of the openmotif21 RPM is examined with HTTP:

```
[root@rac5 up2date]# rpm -qlp http://dbaexpert.com/rpms/openmotif21-2.1.30-
11.RHEL4.6.i386.rpm
warning: http://dbaexpert.com/rpms/openmotif21-2.1.30-11.RHEL4.6.i386.rpm: Header
V3 DSA signature: NOKEY, key ID b38a8516
/usr/X11R6/lib/libMrm.so.2
/usr/X11R6/lib/libMrm.so.2.1
/usr/X11R6/lib/libUil.so.2
/usr/X11R6/lib/libUil.so.2.1
/usr/X11R6/lib/libXm.so.2
/usr/X11R6/lib/libXm.so.2.1
/usr/share/doc/openmotif21-2.1.30
/usr/share/doc/openmotif21-2.1.30/COPYRIGHT.MOTIF
/usr/share/doc/openmotif21-2.1.30/README
/usr/share/doc/openmotif21-2.1.30/RELEASE
/usr/share/doc/openmotif21-2.1.30/RELNOTES
```

As mentioned in a previous recipe, you can execute the previous rpm command against a file on the local filesystem, CD, or remote server with HTTP or FTP access.

How It Works

The rpm command has a myriad of options. The -p option allows you to view information directly from the package. The two commonly executed options with -p are -qip and -qlp. The -qlp option lists all the files that make up the package.

The -qip option provides detailed information about the package. Here we're executing the same command as previously, except with the -qip option:

```
[root@rac5 rpm]# rpm -qip http://dbaexpert.com/rpms/openmotif21-2.1.30-
11.RHEL4.6.i386.rpm
warning: http://dbaexpert.com/rpms/openmotif21-2.1.30-11.RHEL4.6.i386.rpm: Header
V3 DSA signature: NOKEY, key ID b38a8516
Name        : openmotif21              Relocations: /usr/X11R6
Version     : 2.1.30                        Vendor: (none)
Release     : 11.RHEL4.6                Build Date: Sat 07 Oct 2006 08:45:00
AM CDT
Install Date: (not installed)          Build Host: ca-build10.us.oracle.com
Group       : System Environment/Libraries  Source RPM: openmotif21-2.1.30-
11.RHEL4.6.src.rpm
Size        : 2249149                      License: Open Group Public License
Signature   : DSA/SHA1, Mon 09 Oct 2006 08:24:28 PM CDT, Key ID 2e2bcdbcb38a8516
URL         : http://www.opengroup.org/openmotif/
Summary     : Compatibility libraries for Open Motif 2.1.
Description :
This package contains the compatibility libraries for running Open Motif 2.1
applications.
```

Notice that the -qip option provides additional details about the packages such as when the package was built, from what machines, the source RPM, the size, the signature, and even a description of what the package is about. You can also combine these options as -qlip, which shows both the detailed information about the package and the list of all files in the package.

10-5. Downloading RPMs

Problem

You want to download RPMs from the Linux terminal.

Solution

By far, the easiest way to download RPMs is by executing the up2date command with the -d option (or --download). Here's an up2date example to download the perl RPM from ULN:

```
[root@rac5 up2date]# up2date -d perl

Fetching Obsoletes list for channel: el5_i386_latest...

Fetching rpm headers...
########################################

Name                              Version        Rel
------------------------------------------------------------
perl                              5.8.8          10.0.1.el5_2.3    i386


Testing package set / solving RPM inter-dependencies...
########################################
perl-5.8.8-10.0.1.el5_2.3.i ######################### Done.
```

Notice that the channel that this server subscribes to happens to be the el5_i386_latest channel. You have options to subscribe to other channels from Oracle's ULN: http://linux. oracle.com.

Let's assume you do not want to download the latest RPMs for a particular server. Instead, you may opt to download only from a specific update patch. You can unsubscribe the latest channel and subscribe to the el5_u2_i386_base channel. The el5_u2_i386_base channel provides all packages released on the Enterprise Linux 5 update 2 (i386) installation media but does not contain updates. For a complete listing of all the channels you are subscribed to, you can pass the --show-channels option to the up2date command, as displayed here:

```
# up2date --show-channels
el5_i386_latest
el5_i386_ocfs2
el5_i386_oracle
```

How It Works

By default, up2date downloads all the RPMs in the /var/spool/up2date directory. In the /var/spool/up2date directory, you can confirm that up2date downloaded the perl header and package:

```
[root@rac5 /]# cd /var/spool/up2date
[root@rac5 up2date]# ls -l perl*
-rw-r--r-- 1 root root   288104 Jul 29 16:51 perl-5.8.8-10.0.1.el5_2.3.i386.hdr
-rw-r--r-- 1 root root 12159555 Aug  2 14:47 perl-5.8.8-10.0.1.el5_2.3.i386.rpm
```

You can change the temporary location of the download directory using the --tmpdir option. Here's another example of the up2date command using the --tmpdir option to download the screen RPM to the /tmp directory:

```
up2date --download screen --tmpdir=/tmp
```

■ **Note** You can also download .rpm files from either Red Hat Network or Oracle's Unbreakable Linux Network by logging in to one of their network web sites using a valid login. up2date provides the flexibility of remaining in the Linux terminal and downloading specific packages.

10-6. Automating with Oracle Validated Install

Problem

You do not want to spend time researching RPM requirements to install Oracle Database 10g/11g. You want to take advantage of Oracle's preconfigured validated installation process.

Solution

If you are running on Oracle Enterprise Linux or Red Hat Linux and subscribe to Oracle's ULN, you can fully leverage Oracle's validated installation processes. Oracle's validated install automates the download of all the required RPMs, the installation of RPMs including dependency requirements, the setup of the Linux kernel parameters, the creation of the oracle user in the /etc/passwd file, and the creation of entries in the /etc/group file for dba and oinstall. To take advantage of Oracle's validated install, the server must be set up with up2date with Oracle's Linux Network. Once the up2date registration is complete, you can execute up2date with the --install option, as shown here:

```
[root@rac5 ~]# up2date --install oracle-validated

Fetching Obsoletes list for channel: el5_i386_latest...

Fetching rpm headers...
########################################
```

```
Name                            Version        Rel

------------------------------------------------------------

oracle-validated                1.0.0          8.el5              i386


Testing package set / solving RPM inter-dependencies...
#########################################
oracle-validated-1.0.0-8.el ######################### Done.
compat-db-4.2.52-5.1.i386.r ######################### Done.
compat-gcc-34-3.4.6-4.i386. ######################### Done.
compat-gcc-34-c++-3.4.6-4.i ######################### Done.
compat-libstdc++-33-3.2.3-6 ######################### Done.
enterprise-release-5-0.0.9. ######################### Done.
libXp-1.0.0-8.1.el5.i386.rp ######################### Done.
libaio-devel-0.3.106-3.2.i3 ######################### Done.
sysstat-7.0.2-1.el5.i386.rp ######################### Done.
unixODBC-2.2.11-7.1.i386.rp ######################### Done.
unixODBC-devel-2.2.11-7.1.i ######################### Done.
Preparing              ########################################### [100%]


Installing...
   1:unixODBC            ########################################### [100%]
   2:compat-gcc-34       ########################################### [100%]
   3:compat-gcc-34-c++   ########################################### [100%]
   4:unixODBC-devel      ########################################### [100%]
   5:sysstat             ########################################### [100%]
   6:libaio-devel        ########################################### [100%]
   7:libXp               ########################################### [100%]
   8:enterprise-release  ########################################### [100%]
   9:compat-libstdc++-33 ########################################### [100%]
  10:compat-db           ########################################### [100%]
  11:oracle-validated    ########################################### [100%]
The following packages were added to your selection to satisfy dependencies:


Name                            Version        Release

------------------------------------------------------------

compat-db                       4.2.52         5.1
compat-gcc-34                   3.4.6          4
compat-gcc-34-c++               3.4.6          4
compat-libstdc++-33             3.2.3          61
enterprise-release              5              0.0.9
libXp                           1.0.0          8.1.el5
libaio-devel                    0.3.106        3.2
sysstat                         7.0.2          1.el5
unixODBC                        2.2.11         7.1
unixODBC-devel                  2.2.11         7.1
```

As mentioned earlier, the validated install process also modifies the /etc/sysctl.conf kernel configuration file. The following entries are added:

```
fs.file-max=327679
kernel.msgmni=2878
kernel.msgmax=8192
kernel.sem=250 32000 100 142
kernel.shmmni=4096
kernel.shmall=3279547
kernel.sysrq=1
net.core.rmem_default=262144
# For 11g recommended value for net.core.rmem_max is 4194304
net.core.rmem_max=4194304
# For 10g uncomment the following line, comment other entries for this parameter
# and re-run sysctl -p
# net.core.rmem_max=2097152
net.core.wmem_default=262144
net.core.wmem_max=262144
fs.aio-max-nr=3145728
net.ipv4.ip_local_port_range=1024 65000
kernel.shmmax=536870912
```

In addition, the validated install process adjusts the /etc/passwd file to include the oracle user and creates the /home/oracle directory:

```
oracle:x:500:500::/home/oracle:/bin/bash
```

Furthermore, entries for dba and oinstall are added to the /etc/group file:

```
dba:x:500:
oinstall:x:501:oracle
```

How It Works

Many DBAs do not realize that the validated installation option exists. If you are licensed for Oracle Enterprise Linux and have set up up2date with ULN, you can execute up2date with the --install oracle-validated option to automatically install required packages by the Oracle Universal Installer. Executing the command can single-handedly prepare your Linux server to install Oracle Database, Grid Control, or Oracle Application Server. Most important, the oracle-validated installation also sets up the oracle user and required groups and adjusts the kernel parameters suitable for housing an enterprise database. You can review the /etc/sysconfig/oracle-validated/results/orakernel.log Oracle Validated Configuration RPM log file to review system configuration changes.

10-7. Upgrading Packages

Problem

You realize that you have older versions of software components. You want to upgrade some of the older packages to the newest release.

Solution

To upgrade an existing package, you can execute rpm with the -Uhv option (or --upgrade). For this particular solution, you will upgrade the perl RPM. Before you upgrade the perl RPM, let's query the RPM database and determine the current version and release of the perl RPM:

```
[root@rac5 tmp]# rpm -qa perl
perl-5.8.8-10
```

Now, let's upgrade the perl package to 10.0.1 release. You will execute the rpm executable with the -Uhv option to upgrade the perl package:

```
[root@rac5 up2date]# rpm -Uhv  perl-5.8.8-10.0.1.el5_2.3.i386.rpm
Preparing...              ######################################### [100%]
   1:perl                 ######################################### [100%]
```

Next, you will query the RPM database to display the new perl package release:

```
[root@rac5 up2date]# rpm -qa perl
perl-5.8.8-10.0.1.el5_2.3
```

By invoking the rpm executable, we just demonstrated how to upgrade the perl package from version 5.8.8 release 10 to version 5.8.8 release 10.0.1.

■**Note** Alternatively, you can upgrade RPMs by executing the up2date command with the -u (--update) option.

How It Works

You can take advantage of the -Uhv option to upgrade an existing package. Behind the scenes, the original package will be removed, and the new package will be installed. The original configuration file will remain but will be renamed with the .rpmsave extension. Because the -U option removes and installs the package(s), you can utilize the -U option to install packages also. If the package does not exist, the packaged will be installed.

■**Tip** If you have a requirement to upgrade a large quantity of packages (or even apply upgrades to all the existing packages), you can utilize the -F option (or --freshen). The -F option will not install packages if the packages do not already exist.

10-8. Removing Packages

Problem

You want to remove a package from the Linux server.

Solution

To remove a package, you can execute rpm with the -e option (or --erase). To remove the screen package, you can execute the following syntax:

```
rpm -e screen
```

How It Works

Software is removed from the server with the -e option. You must provide the installed package name as the second parameter. You do not provide the package file name. For the example in the solution, the screen package is removed from the system. Often, you will not be able to remove an RPM because of dependency requirements. You will have to know the dependency order to remove the designated RPM. Although we do not recommend it, you can avoid the dependency check with the --nodeps option.

10-9. Checking RPM Requirements to Install Oracle Database

Problem

You want to make sure your database software installation goes as smoothly as possible. You want to check to see whether the Linux server has all the required list of packages as specified by Oracle to install Oracle Database 10*g* or Oracle Database 11*g*.

Solution

You can execute the following provided shell script called rpm_check4.ksh to check to see whether the Linux server complies with the package requirements required to install and configure a database:

```
cat rpm_check4.ksh
function rpmcheck
{
export rpm_module=$1
#echo ""
echo "Found:"
rpm -qa $rpm_module --queryformat "%{NAME}-%{VERSION}.%{RELEASE} (%{ARCH})\n"
}


rpmcheck binutils
echo "Checking to see if the server has at least: binutils-2.15.92.0.2-18.x86_64.
rpm "

rpmcheck compat-db
echo "Checking to see if the server has at least: compat-db-4.1.25-9.i386.rpm"
echo "Checking to see if the server has at least: compat-db-4.1.25-9.x86_64.rpm"

rpmcheck control-center
echo "Checking to see if the server has at least: control-center-2.8.0-
12.x86_64.rpm"
```

```
rpmcheck gcc
echo "Checking to see if the server has at least: gcc.3.4.3-22.1.x86_64.rpm"

rpmcheck gcc-c\+\+
echo "Checking to see if the server has at least: gcc-c++-3.4.3-22.1.x86_64.rpm"

rpmcheck glibc
echo "Checking to see if the server has at least: glibc-2.3.4-2.9.i686.rpm"
echo "Checking to see if the server has at least: glibc-2.3.4-2.9.x86_64.rpm"

rpmcheck glibc-common
echo "Checking to see if the server has at least: glibc-common-2.3.4-2.9.x86_64.rpm"

rpmcheck gnome-libs
echo "Checking to see if the server has at least: gnome-libs-1.4.1.2.90-44.1.x86_64"

rpmcheck libstdc\+\+
echo "Checking to see if the server has at least: libstdc++-3.4.3-22.1.x86_64"

rpmcheck libstdc\+\+-devel
echo "Checking to see if the server has at least: libstdc++-devel-3.4.3-22.1.x86_64"

rpmcheck make
echo "Checking to see if the server has at least: make-3.80-5.x86_64.rpm"

rpmcheck pdksh
echo "Checking to see if the server has at least: pdksh-5.2.14-30.x86_64.rpm"

rpmcheck sysstat
echo "Checking to see if the server has at least: sysstat-5.0.5-1.x86_64.rpm"

rpmcheck xscreensaver
echo "Checking to see if the server has at least: xscreensaver-4.18-
5.rhel4.2.x86_64.rpm"

echo ""
echo "Found:"
rpm -qa --queryformat "%{NAME}-%{VERSION}.%{RELEASE} (%{ARCH})\n"
  |grep -i compat-libstdc
echo "Checking to see if the server has at least: compat-libstdc++-33-3.2.3-
47.3.x86_64.rpm"
echo "Checking to see if the server has at least: compat-libstdc++-33-3.2.3-
47.3.i386.rpm"

rpmcheck glibc-kernheaders
echo "Checking to see if the server has at least: glibc-kernheaders-2.4-
9.1.87.x86_64.rpm"
```

```
rpmcheck glibc-headers
echo "Checking to see if the server has at least: glibc-headers-2.3.4-
2.9.x86_64.rpm"

rpmcheck libaio
echo "Checking to see if the server has at least: libaio-0.3.103-3.i386.rpm"
echo "Checking to see if the server has at least: libaio-0.3.103-3.x86_64.rpm"

rpmcheck libgcc
echo "Checking to see if the server has at least: libgcc-3.4.3-22.1.i386.rpm"

rpmcheck glibc-devel
echo "Checking to see if the server has at least: glibc-devel-2.3.4-2.9.x86_64.rpm"
echo "Checking to see if the server has at least: glibc-devel-2.3.4-2.9.i386.rpm"

rpmcheck xorg-x11-deprecated-libs
echo "Checking to see if the server has at least: xorg-x11-deprecated-libs-6.8.2-
1.EL.13.6.i386.rpm"

echo "# ----------------------------------------------------------------------- #"
echo "# For GC "
echo "# ----------------------------------------------------------------------- #"
rpmcheck openmotif21
echo "Checking to see if the server has at least: openmotif21-2.1.30-11"

rpmcheck setarch
echo "Checking to see if the server has at least: setarch-1.6-1"

echo "# ----------------------------------------------------------------------- #"
echo "# For Oracle Database 11g "
echo "# ----------------------------------------------------------------------- #"
rpmcheck unixODBC
echo "Checking to see if the server has at least: unixODBC-2.2.11"

rpmcheck unixODBC-devel
echo "Checking to see if the server has at least: unixODBC-devel-2.2.11"

rpmcheck elfutils-libelf
echo "Checking to see if the server has at least: elfutils-libelf-0.97-5"

rpmcheck elfutils-libelf-devel
echo "Checking to see if the server has at least: elfutils-libelf-devel-0.97-5"

rpmcheck libaio-devel
echo "Checking to see if the server has at least: libaio-devel-0.3.105-2"
```

How It Works

If you are planning to run Oracle databases on a 64-bit Linux operating system, you will need to check for both 32-bit and 64-bit packages. For example, you need to install both 32-bit and 64-bit components of the compat-db package. You can specify the -qf option (or --queryformat) followed by format options to manipulate the display of the output. The query string format consists of static strings similar to the printf syntax.

In this solution, we specified the "%{NAME}-%{VERSION}.%{RELEASE} (%{ARCH})\n" format to display the architecture. If the output displays (x86_64), you can confirm that the 64-bit package is installed. If the output displays (i386), you have confirmation that the 32-bit version of the package is installed. Here's a sample output from the rpm4_check.ksh script:

```
# ./rpm4_check.ksh
Found:
binutils-2.15.92.0.2.22 (x86_64)
Checking to see if the server has at least: binutils-2.15.92.0.2-18.x86_64.rpm
Found:
compat-db-4.1.25.9 (x86_64)
compat-db-4.1.25.9 (i386)
Checking to see if the server has at least: compat-db-4.1.25-9.i386.rpm
Checking to see if the server has at least: compat-db-4.1.25-9.x86_64.rpm
Found:
control-center-2.8.0.12.rhel4.5 (x86_64)
Checking to see if the server has at least: control-center-2.8.0-12.x86_64.rpm
Found:
gcc-3.4.6.8.0.1 (x86_64)
Checking to see if the server has at least: gcc.3.4.3-22.1.x86_64.rpm
Found:
gcc-c++-3.4.6.8.0.1 (x86_64)
Checking to see if the server has at least: gcc-c++-3.4.3-22.1.x86_64.rpm
Found:
glibc-2.3.4.2.36 (x86_64)
glibc-2.3.4.2.36 (i686)
Checking to see if the server has at least: glibc-2.3.4-2.9.i686.rpm
Checking to see if the server has at least: glibc-2.3.4-2.9.x86_64.rpm
Found:
glibc-common-2.3.4.2.36 (x86_64)
Checking to see if the server has at least: glibc-common-2.3.4-2.9.x86_64.rpm
Found:
gnome-libs-1.4.1.2.90.44.2 (x86_64)
Checking to see if the server has at least: gnome-libs-1.4.1.2.90-44.1.x86_64
Found:
libstdc++-3.4.6.8.0.1 (x86_64)
libstdc++-3.4.6.8.0.1 (i386)
Checking to see if the server has at least: libstdc++-3.4.3-22.1.x86_64
```

Found:
libstdc++-devel-3.4.6.8.0.1 (x86_64)
libstdc++-devel-3.4.6.8.0.1 (i386)
Checking to see if the server has at least: libstdc++-devel-3.4.3-22.1.x86_64
Found:
make-3.80.6.EL4 (x86_64)
Checking to see if the server has at least: make-3.80-5.x86_64.rpm
Found:
pdksh-5.2.14.30.3 (x86_64)
Checking to see if the server has at least: pdksh-5.2.14-30.x86_64.rpm
Found:
sysstat-5.0.5.14.rhel4 (x86_64)
Checking to see if the server has at least: sysstat-5.0.5-1.x86_64.rpm
Found:
xscreensaver-4.18.5.rhel4.12 (x86_64)
xscreensaver-4.18.5.rhel4.14.0.1 (x86_64)
Checking to see if the server has at least: xscreensaver-4.18-5.rhel4.2.x86_64.rpm

Found:
compat-libstdc++-296-2.96.132.7.2 (i386)
compat-libstdc++-33-3.2.3.47.3 (i386)
compat-libstdc++-33-3.2.3.47.3 (x86_64)
Checking to see if the server has at least: compat-libstdc++-33-3.2.3-
47.3.x86_64.rpm
Checking to see if the server has at least: compat-libstdc++-33-3.2.3-47.3.i386.rpm
Found:
glibc-kernheaders-2.4.9.1.100.EL (x86_64)
Checking to see if the server has at least: glibc-kernheaders-2.4-9.1.87.x86_64.rpm
Found:
glibc-headers-2.3.4.2.36 (x86_64)
Checking to see if the server has at least: glibc-headers-2.3.4-2.9.x86_64.rpm
Found:
libaio-0.3.105.2 (x86_64)
libaio-0.3.105.2 (i386)
Checking to see if the server has at least: libaio-0.3.103-3.i386.rpm
Checking to see if the server has at least: libaio-0.3.103-3.x86_64.rpm
Found:
libgcc-3.4.6.8.0.1 (i386)
libgcc-3.4.6.8.0.1 (x86_64)
Checking to see if the server has at least: libgcc-3.4.3-22.1.i386.rpm
Found:
glibc-devel-2.3.4.2.36 (i386)
glibc-devel-2.3.4.2.36 (x86_64)
Checking to see if the server has at least: glibc-devel-2.3.4-2.9.x86_64.rpm
Checking to see if the server has at least: glibc-devel-2.3.4-2.9.i386.rpm

```
Found:
xorg-x11-deprecated-libs-6.8.2.1.EL.13.37.5.1 (i386)
xorg-x11-deprecated-libs-6.8.2.1.EL.18.0.1 (x86_64)
xorg-x11-deprecated-libs-6.8.2.1.EL.13.37.5.1 (x86_64)
xorg-x11-deprecated-libs-6.8.2.1.EL.18.0.1 (i386)
Checking to see if the server has at least: xorg-x11-deprecated-libs-6.8.2-
1.EL.13.6.i386.rpm
# ------------------------------------------------------------------------ #
# For GC
# ------------------------------------------------------------------------ #
Found:
openmotif21-2.1.30.11.RHEL4.6 (i386)
Checking to see if the server has at least: openmotif21-2.1.30-11
Found:
setarch-1.6.1 (x86_64)
Checking to see if the server has at least: setarch-1.6-1
# ------------------------------------------------------------------------ #
# For Oracle Database 11g
# ------------------------------------------------------------------------ #
Found:
unixODBC-2.2.11.1.RHEL4.1 (i386)
unixODBC-2.2.11.1.RHEL4.1 (x86_64)
Checking to see if the server has at least: unixODBC-2.2.11
Found:
unixODBC-devel-2.2.11.1.RHEL4.1 (x86_64)
Checking to see if the server has at least: unixODBC-devel-2.2.11
Found:
elfutils-libelf-0.97.1.4 (i386)
elfutils-libelf-0.97.1.4 (x86_64)
Checking to see if the server has at least: elfutils-libelf-0.97-5
Found:
elfutils-libelf-devel-0.97.1.4 (x86_64)
Checking to see if the server has at least: elfutils-libelf-devel-0.97-5
Found:
libaio-devel-0.3.105.2 (x86_64)
Checking to see if the server has at least: libaio-devel-0.3.105-2
```

You still have to review the output to ensure that what the script finds meets or exceeds the level of the package expected. The primary purpose of this script is to provide a single consolidated output to review all the RPMs compared to what is required by Oracle to install and configure a database.

The output to the rpm4_check.ksh script has three sections. The first section lists all the RPMs to install Oracle Database 10g, the second section lists the packages to install Grid Control, and the last section lists the additional packages to install Oracle Database 11g.

Please stay tuned to future updates to the rpm4_check.ksh script and even to the rpm5_check.ksh script for Red Hat 5/OEL 5 at the http://blog.dbaexpert.com web site.

10-10. Checking RPM Requirements for Grid Control and E-Business Suite

Problem

You want to check to see whether Red Hat 4 ES/AS or Oracle Enterprise Linux (OEL) 4 has all the required packages as specified by Oracle to install Grid Control or E-Business Suite Release 12.

Solution

You can execute the rpm command with the -qa option followed by the package name. Please note that the package name provided to the -qa option does not have the version or release. Each of the packages needs to be at the level specified or higher than what is listed here to install Grid Control:

```
xscreensaver-4.18-5.rhel4.2
glibc-2.3.4-2.9
make-3.79
binutils-2.15.92.0.2-13
gcc-3.4.3-22.1
libaio-0.3.96
glibc-common-2.3.4-2.9
setarch-1.6-1
pdksh-5.2.14-30
openmotif21-2.1.30-11
sysstat-5.0.5-1
gnome-libs-1.4.1.2.90-44.1
libstdc++-3.4.3-22.1
libstdc++-devel-3.4.3-22.1
compat-libstdc++-296-2.96-
compat-db-4.1.25-9
control-center-2.8.0-12
```

Similarly, you must meet or exceed each of the following package requirements to install Oracle E-Business Suite Release 12:

```
glibc-2.3.4-2.25
glibc-common-2.3.4-2.25
binutils-2.15.92.0.2-21
compat-libstdc++-296-2.96-132.7.2
gcc-3.4.6-3
gcc-c++-3.4.6-3
libgcc-3.4.6-3
libstdc++-3.4.6-3
libstdc++-devel-3.4.6-3
openmotif21-2.1.30-11.RHEL4.6**
pdksh-5.2.14-30.3
setarch-1.6-1
```

```
make-3.80-6.EL4
gnome-libs-1.4.1.2.90-44.1
sysstat-5.0.5-11.rhel4
compat-db-4.1.25-9
control-center-2.8.0-12.rhel4.5
xscreensaver-4.18-5.rhel4.11
libaio-0.3.105-2
libaio-devel-0.3.105-2
```

■**Note** The openmotif package version must match the exact version that is specified in the previous RPM requirement list.

For specific RPM requirements for other 32-bit Linux operating systems, please review Oracle MetaLink Note 402310.1. In addition to the previously mentioned RPMs, you must also have ar, gcc, g++, ld, ksh, and make executables installed and available in your PATH environment variable on the Linux server.

How It Works

The last thing you want to experience is not being able to install an Oracle product because the server is missing the required packages. Meeting the minimal version and release of all the required RPMs for a Grid Control or E-Business Suite installation is one of the major hurdles to a successful implementation. You can execute the rpm -qa command followed by the package name and compare the output with the expected version and release numbers. Another way to list all the required RPMs is by typing all the required RPMs in a single command. Here's an example:

```
rpm -qa xscreensaver glibc make binutils gcc \
        libaio glibc-common setarch pdksh openmotif21 \
        sysstat gnome-libs libstdc\+\+ libstdc\+\+-devel \
        compat-libstdc\+\+ compat-db control-center
```

10-11. Performing Silent Oracle Software Installation

Problem

You need to do an install of the Oracle binaries on a remote server. You suspect that the network bandwidth will cause issues when trying to run the graphical installer. You instead want to do a silent install of the Oracle binaries with a response file.

Solution

This solution assumes you have successfully copied and unbundled the Oracle install software on your database server. After unbundling the installation software, you should see a directory named response in the database directory:

```
$ cd database
$ ls
doc  install  response  runInstaller  stage  welcome.html
```

First, change directories to the response directory, and list the files:

```
$ cd response
$ ls
```

You should see several response files:

```
custom.rsp emca.rsp netca.rsp dbca.rsp enterprise.rsp standard.rsp
```

This example demonstrates how to perform an enterprise-level silent installation. Before you modify the enterprise.rsp response file, make a backup copy of the file. Now, open the enterprise.rsp response file with an editor such as vi, and provide valid values for your environment for these variables within the response file:

```
UNIX_GROUP_NAME
FROM_LOCATION
ORACLE_BASE
ORACLE_HOME
ORACLE_HOME_NAME
n_configurationOption
```

Here's an example of what the parameters can be set to in a typical installation:

```
UNIX_GROUP_NAME=oinstall
FROM_LOCATION="/apps/oracle/software/database/stage/products.xml"
ORACLE_BASE=/apps/oracle
ORACLE_HOME=/apps/oracle/product/11.1.0/DB
ORACLE_HOME_NAME=11gDBHome1
n_configurationOption=3
```

The UNIX_GROUP_NAME is usually either dba or oinstall. The FROM_LOCATION variable must point to the products.xml file that is located under the stage directory where you unbundled the Oracle software. The ORACLE_HOME directory must point to the correct setting for your environment. This should match the value in your oratab file (usually located in the /etc directory) for your installation. The oratab file contains entries for databases that run locally on the server. Each line of the oratab file consists of three parameters: the database name, the location of the database software (also known as ORACLE_HOME), and the startup flag. The last parameter plays a significant role in automating database startups. If the value of the last parameter is set to Y, then the dbstart shell script located in the $ORACLE_HOME/bin directory will include the database to start when the server reboots.

The ORACLE_HOME_NAME is a unique name for the home of this installation. The n_configurationOption variable must be set to 3, which specifies the installer to just install the software. Valid values for n_configurationOption are 1 to create a database, 2 to configure an ASM instance, and 3 to install software only.

Change directories to where the runInstaller file is located. This is one directory up from where the enterprise.rsp file is located:

```
$ cd ..
$ ls
doc  install  response  runInstaller  stage  welcome.html
```

Make sure your operating system variables such as ORACLE_HOME match what you have
entered in the response file. Now you can install the binaries by running the runInstaller
program using the following command-line syntax:

```
./runInstaller -ignoreSysPrereqs -force -silent -responseFile <path>/rspfilename.rsp
```

In this solution, the -ignoreSysPrereqs parameter is specified to have the runInstaller
program ignore system prerequisite checks. For additional insight into this option, please
review recipe 10-12. The -force option allows the silent install into a nonempty directory.
When in doubt, you can always specify the -help option to list all the possible arguments.

Make sure you specify the full path and correct name for the response file. In our environment, the command looks like this:

```
$ ./runInstaller -ignoreSysPrereqs -force -silent -responseFile \
 /apps/oracle/software/database/response/enterprise.rsp
```

Next you'll see a lot of output (if things go OK). Here is a partial snippet of the output:

```
Starting Oracle Universal Installer...

Checking Temp space: must be greater than 80 MB.   Actual 116391 MB    Passed
Checking swap space: must be greater than 150 MB.   Actual 1023 MB    Passed
Preparing to launch Oracle Universal Installer from /tmp/OraInstall2008-07-30_02-24-
59PM. Please wait ...[oracle@rac5 database]$ Oracle Universal Installer,
Version 11.1.0.6.0 Production
Copyright (C) 1999, 2007, Oracle. All rights reserved.

You can find the log of this install session at:
 /home/oracle/oraInventory/logs/installActions2008-07-30_02-24-59PM.log
.................................................................... 100%
 Done.



Loading Product
Information.............................................................. 100%
 Done.



Starting execution of Prerequisites...
Total No of checks: 14

Performing check for CertifiedVersions
Checking operating system requirements ...
Expected result: One of enterprise-4,enterprise-5,Red Hat-4,Red Hat-5,SuSE-
```

```
10,asianux-2,asianux-3
Actual Result: enterprise-5
Check complete. The overall result of this check is: Passed


Check complete: Passed
==========================================================
```

As you can see from the output, a total of 14 checks will be performed. Initially, Oracle performs a check for certified versions to ensure that the operating system is running one of the following certified operating systems:

```
enterprise-4,enterprise-5,Red Hat-4,Red Hat-5,SuSE-10,asianux-2,asianux-3
```

Next, packages will be checked to see whether all the required RPMs are installed:

```
Performing check for Packages
Checking operating system package requirements ...
Checking for make-3.81; found make-1:3.81-1.1-i386.     Passed
Checking for binutils-2.17.50.0.6; found binutils-2.17.50.0.6-5.el5-i386.
Passed
Checking for gcc-4.1.1; found gcc-4.1.2-14.el5-i386.     Passed
[ … ]
```

Next, kernel parameters will be evaluated to make sure they are in accordance with the required settings. After checking kernel settings, other settings are scrutinized, including the glibc version, total memory, swap space, DHCP, path for other ORACLE_HOMEs, temp space, LD_LIBRARY_PATH, ORACLE_BASE, space for ORACLE_HOME, invalid ASM HOME, and ORACLE_HOME incompatibilities.

If all checks are passed, then you will see the progress and status of the installation:

```
Installation in progress (Wed Jul 30 14:25:25 CDT 2008)
...........................................................     7% Done.
...........................................................     14% Done.
...........................................................     21% Done.
...........................................................     28% Done.
...........................................................     35% Done.
...........................................................     43% Done.
...........................................................     50% Done.
...........................................................     57% Done.
...........................................................     64% Done.
...........................................................     71% Done.
...........................................................     78% Done.
...................................     83% Done.
Install successful

Linking in progress (Wed Jul 30 14:30:54 CDT 2008)
..     83% Done.
Link successful
```

```
Setup in progress (Wed Jul 30 14:32:39 CDT 2008)
................................                    100% Done.
Setup successful

End of install phases.(Wed Jul 30 14:32:50 CDT 2008)
WARNING:A new inventory has been created in this session. However, it has not yet
been registered as the central inventory of this system.
To register the new inventory please run the script
'/home/oracle/oraInventory/orainstRoot.sh' with root privileges.
If you do not register the inventory, you may not be able to update or patch the
products you installed.
The following configuration scripts need to be executed as the "root" user.
#!/bin/sh
#Root script to run
/home/oracle/oraInventory/orainstRoot.sh
/apps/oracle/product/11.1.0/DB/root.sh
To execute the configuration scripts:
     1. Open a terminal window
     2. Log in as "root"
     3. Run the scripts

The installation of Oracle Database 11g was successful.
Please check '/home/oracle/oraInventory/logs/silentInstall2008-07-30_02-24-59PM.log'
for more details.
```

Once the installation completes successfully, as root run both the orainstRoot.sh and root.sh scripts. In this example, the orainstRoot.sh script resides in the /home/oracle/ oraInventory directory, and the root.sh script resides in the /apps/oracle/product/11.1.0/DB directory:

```
$ su -
Password:
# /home/oracle/oraInventory/orainstRoot.sh
# /apps/oracle/product/11.1.0/DB/root.sh
```

You can now start using this new installation of the Oracle software and create a database.

How It Works

Using a response file allows you to fully automate the installation and configuration of Oracle software. The Oracle Universal Installer reads the values you specify in the response file to perform an installation. This technique is desirable in several scenarios. For example, if you often perform remote installs across a wide area network with limited bandwidth, then using the graphical installer may not be an option (because of extremely slow response times and network hang-ups).

You can easily customize the response file for database options required for your environment. You can then reuse the same response file for multiple installations. The silent installation technique allows you to perform repeatable and standardized Oracle installations and upgrades. You can document the exact steps required and have junior DBAs and/or system administrators install the oracle binaries using a response file.

As a surprise to some DBAs, you can create your own custom response file with the runInstaller program and the -record option. In essence, your selections during the runInstaller session will be recorded into the specified response file name. The syntax to create a custom response file looks like this:

```
./runInstaller -record -destinationFile /tmp/custom_db_install.rsp
```

The -destinationFile option specifies the location of the target response file. You do not have to actually perform an install to create a response file. As long as you navigate to the Summary screen of the installation process, the response file will be created.

Troubleshooting Installation

If you encounter errors using a response file, 95 percent of the time it is probably an issue with how you set the variables within the response file. Inspect those variables carefully, and ensure they are set correctly. Also, if you don't correctly specify the command-line path to the response file, then you'll receive errors such as this:

```
OUI-10203: The specified response file 'enterprise.rsp' is not found.
```

Here is another common error when the path or name of the response file is incorrectly specified:

```
OUI-10202:No response file is specified for this session.
```

Listed next is the error message you can expect if you enter a wrong path to your products.xml file within the response file's FROM_LOCATION variable:

```
OUI-10133:Invalid staging area
```

Also, ensure that you provide the correct command-line syntax when running a response file. If you incorrectly specify or misspell an option, then you could receive a red herring error such as "DISPLAY not set." When using a response file, you don't need to have your DISPLAY variable set. This message is confusing because in this scenario the error is caused by an incorrectly specified command-line option and has nothing to do with the DISPLAY variable.

Another common issue is when specifying an ORACLE_HOME and the silent installation thinks that the given home already exists:

```
Check complete: Failed <<<<
Problem: Oracle Database 10g Release 2 can only be installed in a new Oracle Home
Recommendation: Choose a new Oracle Home for installing this product.
```

Make sure that the value you specify for ORACLE_HOME_NAME doesn't conflict with an already existing home in the oraInst.loc file. Usually this file is located in the /etc directory or the /var/opt/oracle directory.

Performing an Upgrade of Oracle Software

You can also take advantage of the response file to upgrade your Oracle software. For example, say you want to upgrade from 10.2.0.1 to 10.2.0.4. The good news is that the steps are identical to those documented in the "Solution" section of this recipe.

In this scenario, you first need to download the 10.2.0.4 upgrade software from Oracle's MetaLink website. Once you have downloaded and unbundled the upgrade software, then you can modify the response file and perform the binary upgrade as specified in the "Solution" section of this recipe.

10-12. Ignoring System Prerequisites

Problem

You are trying to install Oracle Database 10*g* Release 2 on a new Red Hat or OEL server but cannot get past the operating system check error.

Solution

When attempting to install Oracle Database 10*g* Release 2, you instantly receive an error from runInstaller indicating that the version of Red Hat or OEL is not supported, as shown here:

```
$ ./runInstaller
Starting Oracle Universal Installer...

Checking installer requirements...

Checking operating system version: must be redhat-3, SuSE-9, redhat-4, UnitedLinux-
1.0, asianux-1 or asianux-2
                        Failed <<<<

Exiting Oracle Universal Installer, log for this session can be found at
/home/oracle/oraInventory/logs/installActions2008-09-05_01-45-15AM.log
```

If you look at the release of the Linux server by viewing the /etc/redhat-release file, you can determine the version of Red Hat or OEL that the server is running:

```
$ cat /etc/redhat-release
Enterprise Linux Enterprise Linux Server release 5.2 (Carthage)
```

In this solution, we are deploying Red Hat 5 that has been migrated to OEL 5 ULN. If you utilize the -ignoreSysPrereqs option, the OUI will ignore the operating system check failure and continue with the installation, as demonstrated here:

```
$ ./runInstaller -ignoreSysPrereqs
Starting Oracle Universal Installer...

Checking installer requirements...

Checking operating system version: must be redhat-3, SuSE-9, redhat-4, UnitedLinux-
1.0, asianux-1 or asianux-2
                        Failed <<<<

>>> Ignoring required pre-requisite failures. Continuing...
```

```
Preparing to launch Oracle Universal Installer from /tmp/OraInstall2008-09-05_01-45-
40AM. Please wait
Oracle Universal Installer, Version 10.2.0.1.0 Production
Copyright (C) 1999, 2005, Oracle. All rights reserved.
```

Now, the operating system prerequisite error will be ignored and will proceed to display the OUI screen to the target of the DISPLAY parameter.

How It Works

The -ignoreSysPrereqs parameter is commonly used when you have a newer release of an operating system that is not on the list of supported versions. You can use this parameter on other Oracle products. In this recipe, this operating system check error is encountered simply because Red Hat 5 or OEL 5 was not available at the time Oracle Database 10g Release 2 became generally available as a production product.

10-13. Creating a Database with a Response File

Problem

You cannot launch the Database Configuration Assistant (DBCA) in GUI mode because your network connectivity is extremely slow or because you are behind multiple firewalls in an extremely secure data center. You want to create a database with the DBCA in silent mode.

Solution

The good news is that you can create a database in silent mode too after you modify the dbca.rsp response file to your desired configuration. For this particular solution, we will demonstrate the simplicity of creating a database after modifying a minimal number of parameters in the dbca.rsp response file. At a minimum, the parameters GDBNAME, SID, SYSPASSWORD, SYSTEMPASSWORD, SYSMANPASSWORD, DBSNMPPASSWORD, DATAFILEDESTINATION, STORAGETYPE, CHARACTERSET, and NATIONALCHARACTERSET should be modified. In this example, we modified all the previously mentioned parameters in the dbca.rsp file after backing up the original file to dbca.rsp.BKUP. Once you make the appropriate changes to the dbca.rsp response file, you can execute the diff command to identify changes that were made to the dbca.rsp file. Here's the output of the diff command:

```
$ diff dbca.rsp dbca.rsp.BKUP |grep "<"
< GDBNAME = "DEV.dbaexpert.com"
< SID = "DEV"
< SYSPASSWORD = "DigitalSignal123"
< SYSTEMPASSWORD = "DigitalSignal123"
< SYSMANPASSWORD = "oracle123"
< DBSNMPPASSWORD = "oracle123"
< DATAFILEDESTINATION = "/apps/oradata"
< STORAGETYPE=FS
< CHARACTERSET = "AL32UTF8"
< NATIONALCHARACTERSET= "UTF8"
```

The less-than sign (<) indicates that the changes are from the first file of the diff command, the dbca.rsp file. Now, let's launch dbca in silent mode from $ORACLE_HOME/bin. In this solution, dbca is launched with the -silent parameter and the -responseFile parameter followed by the location of the response file:

```
[oracle@rac5 bin]$ ./dbca -silent -responseFile
/apps/oracle/software/database/response/dbca.DEV.rsp

Copying database files
1% complete
3% complete
37% complete
Creating and starting Oracle instance
40% complete
45% complete
50% complete
55% complete
56% complete
60% complete
62% complete
Completing Database Creation
66% complete
70% complete
73% complete
77% complete
88% complete
100% complete
Look at the log file "/apps/oracle/cfgtoollogs/dbca/DEV/DEV.log" for further
details.
```

dbca in silent mode provides a progress status to notify you where in the database creation process it is at. During the initial phase, Recovery Manager (RMAN) performs a restore of the datafiles. Once the restore is complete, dbca creates and starts the instance. Finally, post-database configuration steps are executed. After the database is created, you can view the log file in the $ORACLE_BASE/cfgtoollogs/dbca/$ORACLE_SID directory. You will also notice an entry in the /etc/oratab file for the new database named DEV:

```
#
DEV:/apps/oracle/product/11.1.0/DB:N
```

How It Works

Nowadays, creating databases with the Database Configuration Assistant is a standard in many organizations. Many DBAs launch the DBCA and configure databases in GUI mode, but a few exploit the options available to them using the response file.

With effective utilization of the dbca.rsp response file, you can automate database creation and create databases consistently across the organization. You can modify the dbca.rsp file to build databases on ASM and even create RAC databases. You can control just about every aspect of the response file similar to launching the DBCA in GUI mode. Your DBA organization should seriously consider standardizing on creating databases in silent mode using the dbca.rsp response file.

10-14. Creating a Network Configuration with a Response File

Problem

You cannot launch netca in GUI mode because your network connectivity is extremely slow or because you are behind multiple firewalls in an extremely secure data center. You want to create a database listener with netca in silent mode.

Solution

You can launch netca in silent mode using a response file. Here's a sample response file with modifications called netca.DEV.rsp:

```
[GENERAL]
RESPONSEFILE_VERSION="11.1"
CREATE_TYPE= "CUSTOM"
LOG_FILE=""/tmp/netca.log""
[Session]
ORACLE_HOME="/apps/oracle/product/11.1.0/DB"
[oracle.net.ca]
INSTALLED_COMPONENTS={"server","net8","javavm"}
INSTALL_TYPE=""custom""
LISTENER_NUMBER=1
LISTENER_NAMES={"LISTENER"}
LISTENER_PROTOCOLS={"TCP;1521"}
LISTENER_START=""
NAMING_METHODS={"LDAP","TNSNAMES","HOSTNAME"}
NSN_PROTOCOLS={"TCP;HOSTNAME;1521"}
NSN_NUMBER=3
NSN_NAMES={"DEV","DBATOOLS","RMANPROD"}
NSN_SERVICE = {"DEV","DBATOOLS","RMANPROD"}
NSN_PROTOCOLS={"TCP;rac5.dbaexpert.com;1521","TCP;rac6.dbaexpert.com;1521","TCP;rac7
.dbaexpert.com;1521"}
```

Executing netca in silent mode with the modified response file yields this output:

```
[oracle@rac5 response]$ netca /silent /responsefile $PWD/netca.DEV.rsp

Sun Aug 03 21:50:12 CDT 2008 Oracle Net Configuration Assistant
Parsing command line arguments:
    Parameter "silent" = true
    Parameter "responsefile" = /apps/oracle/software/database/response/netca.DEV.rsp
    Parameter "log" = /tmp/netca.log
Done parsing command line arguments.
Oracle Net Services Configuration:
Configuring Listener:LISTENER
```

```
Listener configuration complete.
Oracle Net Listener Startup:
    Running Listener Control:
      /apps/oracle/product/11.1.0/DB/bin/lsnrctl start
    Listener Control complete.
    Listener started successfully.
Default local naming configuration complete.
    Created net service name: DEV
Default local naming configuration complete.
    Created net service name: DBATOOLS
Default local naming configuration complete.
    Created net service name: RMANPROD
Profile configuration complete.
Oracle Net Services configuration successful. The exit code is 0
```

Notice that netca utilizes / as the parameter prefix. dbca and runInstaller accept - as parameter prefixes. Behind the scenes, netca created three files in the $ORACLE_HOME/network/admin directory: sqlnet.ora, tnsnames.ora, and listener.ora.

How It Works

DBAs can fully configure Oracle's network topology by launching the Network Configuration Assistant. DBAs often do not realize the potential of automation through response files. With the proper standardization in directory structures and naming conventions, DBAs can script and manipulate the network configuration response files leveraging executables like awk and sed.

You can specify an alternate location for the netca log file by modifying the LOG_FILE parameter. Similar to the other silent installations, you must specify a valid ORACLE_HOME directory. The other portions of the netca response file that require explanation are the NSN_ parameters (NSN stands for number of service names). The parameter NSN_PROTOCOLS defines the protocol and associated parameters for each service name. The parameter NSN_NUMBER defines the number of service names to create. For this particular solution, the response file defines three service names to create in the tnsnames.ora file. The names of the TNSNAMES connect strings are defined to be DEV, RMANPROD, and DBATOOLS. All three of the TNSNAMES connect strings leverage service names. For this particular solution, you want every server to have entries for DBATOOLS and RMANPROD. Here are the contents of the tnsnames.ora file:

```
# tnsnames.ora Network Configuration File:
/apps/oracle/product/11.1.0/DB/network/admin/tnsnames.ora
# Generated by Oracle configuration tools.

RMANPROD =
  (DESCRIPTION =
    (ADDRESS_LIST =
      (ADDRESS = (PROTOCOL = TCP)(HOST = rac7.dbaexpert.com)(PORT = 1521))
    )
    (CONNECT_DATA =
      (SERVICE_NAME = RMANPROD)
    )
  )
```

```
DEV =
  (DESCRIPTION =
    (ADDRESS_LIST =
      (ADDRESS = (PROTOCOL = TCP)(HOST = rac5.dbaexpert.com)(PORT = 1521))
    )
    (CONNECT_DATA =
      (SERVICE_NAME = DEV)
    )
  )

DBATOOLS =
  (DESCRIPTION =
    (ADDRESS_LIST =
      (ADDRESS = (PROTOCOL = TCP)(HOST = rac6.dbaexpert.com)(PORT = 1521))
    )
    (CONNECT_DATA =
      (SERVICE_NAME = DBATOOLS)
    )
  )
```

Likewise, netca generated the following entries in the listener.ora file:

```
# listener.ora Network Configuration File:
/apps/oracle/product/11.1.0/DB/network/admin/listener.ora
# Generated by Oracle configuration tools.

LISTENER =
  (DESCRIPTION_LIST =
    (DESCRIPTION =
      (ADDRESS = (PROTOCOL = TCP)(HOST = rac5.dbaexpert.com)(PORT = 1521))
      (ADDRESS = (PROTOCOL = IPC)(KEY = EXTPROC1521))
    )
  )
```

Finally, netca produces the sqlnet.ora file which contains this single entry to define the directory path:

```
NAMES.DIRECTORY_PATH= (LDAP, TNSNAMES, HOSTNAME)
```

10-15. Applying Interim Patches

Problem

You need to apply a patch to resolve a database issue or eradicate a bug you encountered in your database.

Solution

Most of the time, applying a patch is simple with the opatch command-line interface. opatch accepts numerous arguments. The syntax for opatch is as follows:

```
opatch command  [options>] [-h[elp]]
```

Commonly supplied `opatch` arguments are as follows:

- `apply`

- `lsinventory`

- `rollback`

- `version`

Let's take, for example, patch number 6455659 to fix stored outlines in Oracle Release 11.1.0.6. We downloaded the patch file `p6455659_111060_LINUX.zip` to our download directory. We will extract the compressed archived file with the `unzip` command. If you want to see the contents of the `.zip` file without extracting the file, you can pass the `-l` argument to the `unzip` command. The `unzip` command will create a directory called `6455659` and extract all the files into the directory.

You should always read the `README.txt` file located in the base directory of the patch, which is the `6455659` directory in this case. The `README.txt` file will have explicit directions on how to apply the patch. Although the majority of patches require a simple `apply` parameter, some patches have prerequisite and postpatch steps. Some patches may even require multiple patches to be executed.

The `README.txt` file indicates that this patch application is straightforward. Let's proceed and apply patch 6455659. As a general rule, prior to applying any patch, the database must be shut down. Oracle does provide what is known as an *online patch* where the database does not have to be shut down for high availability considerations. You must examine the `README.txt` file to see whether a particular patch qualifies as an online patch. Since this particular patch requires the database to be shut down, we will incur an outage window to apply the patch.

The `opatch` executable is located in the `$ORACLE_HOME/OPatch` directory. The easiest way to apply a patch is to include the `opatch` executable to your `PATH` environment variable. To do so, simply export your `PATH` environment variable as `$ORACLE_HOME/OPatch:$PATH`.

We have already changed our directory to the 6455659 directory. Based on the `README.txt` file, we can apply this patch with the command `opatch apply`.

■**Note** You need to make sure to run the command `opatch apply` as the `oracle` account from the uncompressed patch subdirectory. Also, the OS environment variable `ORACLE_HOME` needs to be set accordingly before running `opatch`.

Let's see the `opatch` process in action relative to this patch:

```
$ opatch apply
Invoking OPatch 11.1.0.6.0

Oracle Interim Patch Installer version 11.1.0.6.0
Copyright (c) 2007, Oracle Corporation.  All rights reserved.
```

```
Oracle Home        : /apps/oracle/product/11.1/DB02
Central Inventory  : /home/oracle/oraInventory
   from            : /etc/oraInst.loc
OPatch version     : 11.1.0.6.0
OUI version        : 11.1.0.6.0
OUI location       : /apps/oracle/product/11.1/DB02/oui
Log file location  : /apps/oracle/product/11.1/DB02/cfgtoollogs/opatch/opatch2008-09-
05_10-27-17AM.log
```

ApplySession applying interim patch '6455659' to OH '/apps/oracle/product/11.1/DB02'

Running prerequisite checks...

OPatch detected non-cluster Oracle Home from the inventory and will patch the local
system only.

Please shutdown Oracle instances running out of this ORACLE_HOME on the local
system.
(Oracle Home = '/apps/oracle/product/11.1/DB02')

Is the local system ready for patching? [y|n]
y
User Responded with: Y
Backing up files and inventory (not for auto-rollback) for the Oracle Home
Backing up files affected by the patch '6455659' for restore. This might take a
while...
Backing up files affected by the patch '6455659' for rollback. This might take a
while...

Patching component oracle.rdbms, 11.1.0.6.0...
Updating archive file "/apps/oracle/product/11.1/DB02/lib/libserver11.a" with
"lib/libserver11.a/qol.o"
Running make for target ioracle
ApplySession adding interim patch '6455659' to inventory

Verifying the update...
Inventory check OK: Patch ID 6455659 is registered in Oracle Home inventory with
proper meta-data.
Files check OK: Files from Patch ID 6455659 are present in Oracle Home.

The local system has been patched and can be restarted.

OPatch succeeded.

Notice that the patching process prompts you to confirm that the local system is ready for
patching. You can alternatively supply the -silent parameter to apply this patch in silent

mode. The -silent parameter suppresses the user prompt to confirm that the system is ready. Here's a snippet of the opatch output utilizing the -silent parameter:

```
[ …]


Please shutdown Oracle instances running out of this ORACLE_HOME on the local
system.
 (Oracle Home = '/apps/oracle/product/11.1/DB02')


Is the local system ready for patching? [y|n]
Y (auto-answered by -silent)
User Responded with: Y
Backing up files and inventory (not for auto-rollback) for the Oracle Home
[ … ]
```

Notice that the Y answer is autoanswered from the -silent parameter. Now, let's check the inventory to see whether the patch exists. To view the patch list, pass the lsinventory argument to the opatch command, as shown here:

```
[oracle@rac5 6455659]$ opatch lsinventory
Invoking OPatch 11.1.0.6.0

Oracle Interim Patch Installer version 11.1.0.6.0
Copyright (c) 2007, Oracle Corporation.  All rights reserved.


Oracle Home       : /apps/oracle/product/11.1/DB02
Central Inventory : /home/oracle/oraInventory
   from           : /etc/oraInst.loc
OPatch version    : 11.1.0.6.0
OUI version       : 11.1.0.6.0
OUI location      : /apps/oracle/product/11.1/DB02/oui
Log file location : /apps/oracle/product/11.1/DB02/cfgtoollogs/opatch/opatch2008-09-
05_10-34-54AM.log

Lsinventory Output file location :
/apps/oracle/product/11.1/DB02/cfgtoollogs/opatch/lsinv/
lsinventory2008-09-05_10-34-54AM.txt


--------------------------------------------------------------------------------
Installed Top-level Products (1):

Oracle Database 11g                                          11.1.0.6.0
There are 1 products installed in this Oracle Home.
```

Interim patches (1) :

Patch 6455659   : applied on Fri Sep 05 10:27:56 CDT 2008
   Created on 17 Oct 2007, 23:22:33 hrs PST8PDT
   Bugs fixed:
     6455659

OPatch succeeded.

   You can execute the command opatch lsinventory -detail to produce a detailed output
of all the patches.

How It Works

OPatch is a collection of Perl scripts and Java classes providing the capability to apply and roll
back interim (one-off) patches to an Oracle database environment. opatch is the primary driver
that calls the Perl modules and Java classes. Although the minimum perl requirement is 5.005_03,
Oracle recommends the perl version to be at least 5.6 or greater. You can download OPatch
from MetaLink from the Patches & Updates tab by performing a simple search on *patchset
6880880*. For additional information, please review the MetaLink Note 224346.1.

   OPatch requires a Java Runtime Environment (JRE) to be available on the Linux server. In
addition, OPatch also has requirements for system commands such as jar, fuser, ar, and make on
the Linux servers. Patch information and backups reside in the $ORACLE_HOME/.patch_storage/
{patch_file} directory.

   Just like you can install a patch with the apply parameter, you can uninstall a patch with
the rollback parameter. The rollback parameter accepts an additional parameter, -id, to
specify the patch number to roll back. In our next example, we will roll back the same patch
that we applied in our solution:

```
$ opatch rollback -id 6455659
Invoking OPatch 11.1.0.6.0

Oracle Interim Patch Installer version 11.1.0.6.0
Copyright (c) 2007, Oracle Corporation.  All rights reserved.



Oracle Home       : /apps/oracle/product/11.1/DB02
Central Inventory : /home/oracle/oraInventory
   from           : /etc/oraInst.loc
OPatch version    : 11.1.0.6.0
OUI version       : 11.1.0.6.0
OUI location      : /apps/oracle/product/11.1/DB02/oui
Log file location : /apps/oracle/product/11.1/DB02/cfgtoollogs/opatch/opatch2008-09-
05_10-35-34AM.log
```

```
RollbackSession rolling back interim patch '6455659' from OH
'/apps/oracle/product/11.1/DB02'

Running prerequisite checks...

OPatch detected non-cluster Oracle Home from the inventory and will patch the local
system only.

Please shutdown Oracle instances running out of this ORACLE_HOME on the local
system.
(Oracle Home = '/apps/oracle/product/11.1/DB02')


Is the local system ready for patching? [y|n]
y
User Responded with: Y
Backing up files affected by the patch '6455659' for restore. This might take a
while...

Patching component oracle.rdbms, 11.1.0.6.0...
Updating archive file "/apps/oracle/product/11.1/DB02/lib/libserver11.a"  with
"lib/libserver11.a/qol.o"
Running make for target ioracle
RollbackSession removing interim patch '6455659' from inventory

The local system has been patched and can be restarted.


OPatch succeeded.
```

Oracle provides its infamous quarterly critical patch updates (CPUs) to address security vulnerabilities to the database and application server products. Often nonsecurity patches are included in the CPU because they are dependent patches. You probably receive e-mail updates as to when they are available for download and application. We recommend you closely scrutinize the quarterly CPUs and apply them in a timely manner.

Oracle also offers what is known as *merge label request* (MLR) patches. Basically, MLRs are multiple patches for multiple bugs that have been bundled together and presented as a single patch. In the RAC world, Oracle also provides what it calls *CRS bundle patches*. CRS bundle patches are collections of patches specifically intended for Oracle Clusterware. For a list of all CRS bundle patches, please refer to MetaLink Note 405820.1. CRS bundle patches are more complex to apply because numerous steps have to be executed as the root user and as the oracle user. With thorough analysis and careful execution, though, you can easily apply the CRS bundle patch to your RAC environment.

10-16. Attaching an Oracle Home

Problem

Your company continues to copy the Oracle Home binaries from one server to another. You encounter upgrade issues because the Oracle Home is not registered in oraInventory.

Solution

If you happen to be one of the DBAs who still creates tar copies of the Oracle binaries, you can continue to, as the saying goes, have your cake and eat it too. It's much easier to copy the Oracle binaries than it is to install the software from the CD or unzipped media software. You can accomplish in one command what could possibly take hours if you have a slow wide area network (WAN) connectivity between your desktop and the Linux server. If you are not comfortable with the silent installation option, you also need to find an X server or VNC server to set the DISPLAY environment variable to. In this solution, we show you how to attach an Oracle Home after you transfer the binaries from another server using the rcp/scp, tar, or rsh/ssh command. You must first set your ORACLE_HOME environment variable to the new directory you just copied over. For example, the ORACLE_HOME environment variable for this solution is set to /apps/oracle/product/11.1.0/ASM. Next, change your directory to the oui/bin subdirectory:

```
cd $ORACLE_HOME/oui/bin
```

From the oui/bin directory, execute the runInstaller command as shown here to attach the new Oracle Home to oraInventory:

```
./runInstaller -silent -attachHome -invPtrLoc /etc/oraInst.loc \
ORACLE_HOME="/apps/oracle/product/11.1.0/ASM" ORACLE_HOME_NAME="11gASM"
```

Upon a successful attach of the Oracle Home, you will receive a message stating that AttachHome was successful, as shown here:

```
Starting Oracle Universal Installer...

Checking swap space: must be greater than 500 MB.   Actual 952 MB      Passed
Preparing to launch Oracle Universal Installer from /tmp/OraInstall2008-09-05_02-01-
20PM. Please wait ...
[oracle@rac5 txt]$ The inventory pointer is located at /etc/oraInst.loc
The inventory is located at /home/oracle/oraInventory
'AttachHome' was successful.
```

The invPtrLoc parameter specifies the fully qualified file name that contains the location of the oraInventory. The oraInst.loc file is located in the /etc directory in the Linux operating system and looks like this:

```
inventory_loc=/home/oracle/oraInventory
inst_group=oinstall
```

By default, the inventory_loc will point to the $HOME directory of the oracle user account. As a precautionary measure, we recommend you back up the oraInventory directory prior to attaching an Oracle Home.

You can even attach RAC Oracle Homes. For RAC Oracle Homes, you must specify an additional parameter called CLUSTER_NODES. This parameter needs to be enclosed by curly brackets, as shown here:

```
CLUSTER_NODES={rac3,rac4}
```

You just need to execute the runInstaller command with the -attachHome option from one RAC node. oraInventory will be updated across all the RAC nodes.

How It Works

DBAs still continue to tar and un-tar the Oracle binaries from one server to another. In some companies, especially in non-RAC environments, DBAs copy the binaries from development database servers to quality assurance (QA) and production database servers with a command such as tar piped to ssh. Here's a popular one-liner script that you can leverage to copy Oracle binaries from one directory level above the Oracle Home to the target node:

```
tar cvf - {DIR_NAME} |ssh {target_node} "cd /apps/oracle/product/11.1.0; tar xvf -"
```

The tar command piped to ssh ensures that symbolic links get copied over as symbolic links. The best thing about this approach is that you do not have to incur double storage to store a local and remote copy of the tar archive.

Once you have successfully attached the new Oracle Home, you can view the contents of the /home/oracle/oraInventory/ContentsXML/inventory.xml file to confirm that the new Oracle Home is listed. Here's what the inventory.xml file looks like:

```
<?xml version="1.0" standalone="yes" ?>
<!-- Copyright (c) 1999, 2006, Oracle. All rights reserved. -->
<!-- Do not modify the contents of this file by hand. -->
<INVENTORY>
<VERSION_INFO>
   <SAVED_WITH>11.1.0.6.0</SAVED_WITH>
   <MINIMUM_VER>2.1.0.6.0</MINIMUM_VER>
</VERSION_INFO>
<HOME_LIST>
<HOME NAME="11gDBHome1" LOC="/apps/oracle/product/11.1.0/DB" TYPE="O" IDX="1"/>
<HOME NAME="11gDBHome2" LOC="/apps/oracle/product/11.1/DB02" TYPE="O" IDX="2"/>
<HOME NAME="11gASM" LOC="/apps/oracle/product/11.1.0/ASM" TYPE="O" IDX="3"/>
</HOME_LIST>
</INVENTORY>
```

You can see that 11gASM HOME_NAME is listed as a member in the XML inventory file.

## CHAPTER 11

Automating Jobs

In almost every type of Linux environment—from development to production—database administrators rely heavily on automating tasks such as database backups, monitoring, and maintenance. For highly available systems, it's often an absolute requirement to automate tasks such as the startup and shutdown of the Oracle database and listener. Automating routine tasks allows DBAs to be much more effective and productive. Automated environments inherently run smoother and more efficiently than manually administered systems.

This chapter starts by showing you how to automate the startup/shutdown of your database in the event of a system reboot. We next focus on showing you how to leverage the cron job scheduler. The cron utility is a scheduling tool universally available on most Linux/Unix systems. It's readily available, simple, and easy to use. For these reasons, this ubiquitous utility is frequently used by DBAs to automate database jobs.

This chapter builds heavily on your knowledge of Linux operating system commands, editing files, and shell scripting. You'll need this eclectic skill set to automate your database surroundings. The last several recipes in this chapter show you how to implement several real-world DBA jobs such as performance reporting, monitoring, and operating system file maintenance. You should be able to extend these recipes to meet the automation requirements of your environment.

11-1. Automating Database Shutdown and Startup

Problem

You want to automatically shut down and start up both your database and your listener when the server is rebooted.

Solution

Follow the next several steps to automate your database and listener shutdown and startup:

1. Edit the /etc/oratab file, and place a Y at the end of the entry for the databases you want to automatically restart when the system reboots. You might need root privileges to edit the file:

   ```
   # vi /etc/oratab
   ```

   Place within the file a line similar to this for your environment:

   ```
   RMDB1:/oracle/product/10.2:Y
   ```

In the previous line, RMDB1 is the database name, and /oracle/product/10.2 specifies ORACLE_HOME.

2. As root, navigate to the /etc/init.d directory, and create a file named dbora:

```
# cd /etc/init.d
```

```
# vi dbora
```

3. Place the following lines in the dbora file. Make sure you change the values of variables ORA_HOME and ORA_OWNER to match your environment:

```
#!/bin/bash
# chkconfig: 35 99 10
# description: Starts and stops Oracle processes
ORA_HOME=/oracle/product/10.2
ORA_OWNER=oracle
case "$1" in
  'start')
    su - $ORA_OWNER -c "$ORA_HOME/bin/lsnrctl start"
    su - $ORA_OWNER -c $ORA_HOME/bin/dbstart
  ;;
  'stop')
    su - $ORA_OWNER -c "$ORA_HOME/bin/lsnrctl stop"
    su - $ORA_OWNER -c $ORA_HOME/bin/dbshut
  ;;
esac
```

4. Change the group of the dbora file to match the group assigned to the operating system owner of the Oracle software (usually oinstall or dba):

```
# chgrp oinstall dbora
```

5. Change the permissions on the dbora file to 750:

```
# chmod 750 dbora
```

6. Run the following chkconfig command:

```
# /sbin/chkconfig --add dbora
```

■Tip If you want to automatically stop and start (on system reboots) other processes such as the Intelligent Agent, Management Server, and the HTTP Server, see Oracle MetaLink Note 222813.1 for details.

How It Works

Automating the shutdown and startup of your Oracle database will vary depending on whether you're using tools like cluster software or ASM. The solution in this recipe demonstrates the typical steps to implement the shutdown and startup of your database in the scenarios where you don't have other software that manages this task.

In step 1 from the solution, the format of the /etc/oratab file is as follows:

```
<SID>:<ORACLE_HOME>:Y
```

The Y on the end of the string signifies that the database can be started and stopped by the ORACLE_HOME/bin/dbstart and ORACLE_HOME/bin/dbshut scripts.

■**Note** With some Unix systems (such as Solaris), the oratab file is usually located in the /var/opt/ oracle directory.

In step 3 from the solution, ensure that you modify the dbora script to have values for ORA_HOME and ORA_OWNER that match your environment. Also, the following lines in the dbora file are mandatory:

```
# chkconfig: 35 99 10
# description: Starts and stops Oracle processes
```

The previous two lines describe the service characteristics of the script. The 35 means the service will be started in runlevels 3 and 5. The 99 indicates that the service will be started near the end of the init processing. The 10 signifies that the service will be stopped near the beginning of the init processing.

■**Note** A Linux *runlevel* is a logical container for specifying which services will run when the system is started.

In step 4, modify the group of the file so that the owner of the Oracle software (usually oracle) can view the dbora file. In step 5, make the script executable and readable.

In step 6, the chkconfig command registers the service script. This also creates the appropriate symbolic links to files beneath the /etc/rc.d directory.

Use the --list option to display whether a service is on or off for each runlevel:

```
# chkconfig --list | grep dbora
dbora           0:off   1:off   2:off   3:on    4:off   5:on    6:off
```

The previous output indicates the dbora service is on for runlevels 3 and 5. If you need to delete a service, use the --del option of chkconfig.

■**Note** If you are attempting to implement this shutdown/startup script on a non-Linux system (that is, Solaris, AIX, and so on), then see Oracle's installation documentation specific to that operating system for the details on required symbolic links.

To test whether the dbora script is working, as root run the following to stop your database and listener:

```
# /etc/init.d/dbora stop
```

To test the startup of your database and listener, as root issue the following command:

```
# /etc/init.d/dbora start
```

If you have the opportunity to reboot your system, we recommend you do that to ensure that the database stops and restarts correctly. There are log files created in your ORACLE_HOME directory named startup.log and shutdown.log. You can inspect the contents of these to verify that the shutdown and startup are working as expected.

LINUX SYSTEM V INIT RUNLEVELS

A Linux *service* is an application that typically runs in the background (conceptually similar to a Windows service). A *runlevel* is used to configure which services are running on a box. Typically there are seven runlevels (0–6). The chkconfig command manages which services you want running in which runlevel(s).

When Linux starts up, the /sbin/init program reads the /etc/inittab file to determine the runlevel to which it should run at. The following is a snippet from /etc/inittab that shows the runlevels used by Red Hat (these are similar to runlevels in other Linux distributions):

```
#   0 - halt (Do NOT set initdefault to this)
#   1 - Single user mode
#   2 - Multiuser, without NFS (The same as 3, if you do not have networking)
#   3 - Full multiuser mode
#   4 - unused
#   5 - X11
#   6 - reboot (Do NOT set initdefault to this)
```

To set the default runlevel, specify N in the id:<N>:initdefault line in the /etc/inittab file. The following example sets the default runlevel to 5:

```
id:5:initdefault:
```

The runlevel of 1 is used by system administrators (SAs) when performing maintenance and repairs. The runlevel of 5 will start the Linux server with a graphical login screen at the console plus networking capabilities. However, if you have a problem running the display manager at the console, such as due to a video driver issue, then you can start in runlevel 3 instead, which is command-line-based but still has networking services.

Most SAs who are security conscious operate their servers on runlevel 3. With the wide acceptance of VNC, SAs oftentimes do not see the benefit of running on runlevel 5. If an SA wants to take advantage of graphical utilities, they'll just use VNC (or a similar tool). Do not, by the way, attempt to set initdefault to either 0 or 6, because your Linux server will never start.

To determine the current runlevel, you can run who -r or runlevel as follows:

```
# runlevel
N 5
# who -r
         run-level 5   Jun 17 00:29                        last=S
```

> A given runlevel governs which scripts Linux will run when starting. These scripts are located in the directory /etc/rc.d/rc<N>.d, where <N> corresponds to the runlevel. For runlevel 5, the scripts are in the /etc/rc.d/rc5.d directory. For example, when Linux starts up in runlevel 5, one of the scripts it will run is /etc/rc.d/rc5.d/S55sshd, which is actually a softlink to /etc/rc.d/init.d/sshd.

11-2. Automating the Shutdown and Startup of Oracle Application Server

Problem

You want to automate the shutdown and startup of Oracle Application Server.

Solution

You can implement the appsora and oas_init.bash scripts to shut down and start up Oracle Application Server. Here's the content of the appsora script in the /etc/init.d directory:

```
#!/bin/sh
# File Name:  /etc/init.d/appsora
# Description: Oracle Application Server auto start-stop script.
#
# Set ORA_DB_HOME to be equivalent to the $ORACLE_HOME
#
# Set ORA_OWNER to the user id of the owner of the
# Oracle software in ORA_DB_HOME
#
ORA_DB_HOME=/apps/oracle/product/ias10g
SH=/var/opt/oracle/sh
ORA_OWNER=oracle

export ORA_DB_HOME SH ORA_OWNER

#
case "$1" in
    'start')
        # Start the Oracle databases:
        # The following command assumes that the oracle login
        # will not prompt the user for any values
        su - $ORA_OWNER -c "$SH/oas_init.bash start" > /tmp/start_ias.log 2>&1
        ;;
    'stop')
        # Stop the Oracle databases:
        # The following command assumes that the oracle login
        # will not prompt the user for any values
        su - $ORA_OWNER -c "$SH/oas_init.bash stop" > /tmp/shutdown_ias.log 2>&1
        ;;
esac
```

The appsora script merely calls the oas_init.bash script in the /var/opt/oracle/sh directory. The contents of the oas_init.bash script are as follows:

```
#!/bin/bash
# File Name: oas_init.bash
# Description:  Script called by /etc/init.d/appsora to actually startup
# or shutdown the application server.
#
export START_SHUTDOWN_FLAG=$1
# ------------------------------------------------------------------------------
# INITIAL SETUP
# ------------------------------------------------------------------------------
FN=`echo $0 | sed s/\.*[/]//`
export ORACLE_BASE=/apps/oracle
export BINDIR=/var/opt/oracle/sh
#-----------------------------------------------
export FILENAME=$(basename $0 |awk -F"." {'print $1'})
export CONFIG_FILE="${SH}"/"${FILENAME}".conf
export CONTROL_FILE="${SH}"/"${FILENAME}".ctl
export FN=`print $0 | sed s/\.*[/]//`
#----------------------------------------------------------------------
# Setup the Oracle Environment and pass the ORACLE_SID
#----------------------------------------------------------------------
export PATH=$PATH:/usr/local/bin
export ORAENV_ASK=NO
export ORACLE_SID=ias10g
. oraenv
[ "$START_SHUTDOWN_FLAG" = "" ] &&
{
  echo "No startup or shutdown flag specified!"
  echo "Aborting!"
  exit 1;
}
#
[ "$START_SHUTDOWN_FLAG" = "start" ] &&
{
export MODE="startall"
cd $ORACLE_HOME/opmn/bin
./opmnctl $MODE
emctl start agent
}
#
[ "$START_SHUTDOWN_FLAG" = "stop" ] &&
{
```

```
export MODE="stopall"
cd $ORACLE_HOME/opmn/bin
./opmnctl $MODE
}
#
emctl $START_SHUTDOWN_FLAG iasconsole
```

You can enable automatic startup and shutdown by creating symbolic links to the appsora file for start and kill actions. To create the symbolic links, execute the ln -s command as specified here from the /etc/rc.d/rc3.d directory:

```
ln -s ../init.d/appsora S99appsora
ln -s ../init.d/appsora K09appsora
```

The symbolic links associated with appsora should look like this in the /etc/rc.d/rc3.d directory:

```
lrwxrwxrwx  1 root root 17 Oct 26  2007 S99appsora -> ../init.d/appsora
lrwxrwxrwx  1 root root 17 Oct 26  2007 K09appsora -> ../init.d/appsora
```

The keyword stop or start will be passed on the command line to the symbolically linked files, depending on whether the server is booting up or shutting down. Usually the startup and kill files will link to the same file in the /etc/init.d directory. During the system startup processes, the S99appsora script will be executed as one of the last scripts. On the flip side, during the system shutdown process, K09appsora will be executed as one of the initial scripts.

How It Works

OPMN is Oracle Application Server's Process Monitor and Notification (OPMN) server. Oracle provides a command-line interface called opmnctl to control and monitor Oracle Application Server components. Using the opmnctl executable, you can start all the components of Oracle's Application Server except for the Oracle Enterprise Manager (OEM) 10g Application Server Control Console. The opmnctl interface accepts two parameters, startall and stopall, to start and shut down all the OPMN-managed processes for Oracle Application Server. Since you cannot manage OEM 10g Application Server Control Console with opmnctl, the oas_init.bash startup script invokes the emctl executable to start and shut down the OEM's iAS Console.

11-3. Enabling Access to Schedule Jobs

Problem

As the oracle operating system user, you're attempting to add an entry to the cron table via the crontab utility, and you receive the following error message:

```
You (oracle) are not allowed to use this program (crontab)
```

You want to grant access to the oracle user to use the crontab utility.

Solution

As the root user, add oracle to the /etc/cron.allow file with the echo command:

```
# echo oracle >> /etc/cron.allow
```

Once the oracle entry is added to the /etc/cron.allow file, you can use the crontab utility to schedule a job.

Note   You can also use an editing utility (such as vi) to add an entry to this file.

How It Works

The root user can always schedule jobs with the crontab utility. Other users must be listed in the /etc/cron.allow file. If the /etc/cron.allow file does not exist, then the operating system user must not appear in the /etc/cron.deny file. If neither the /etc/cron.allow nor the /etc/cron.deny file exists, then only the root user can access the crontab utility.

Note   On some Unix operating systems (such as Solaris), the cron.allow and cron.deny files are located in the /etc/cron.d directory.

The cron program is a job-scheduling utility that is ubiquitous in Linux/Unix environments. This tool derives its name from *chronos* (the Greek word for time). The cron (the geek word for scheduler) tool allows you to schedule scripts or commands to run at a specified time and repeat at a designated frequency.

When your Linux server boots up, a cron background process is automatically started that manages all cron jobs on the system. The cron background process is also known as the cron daemon. This process is started on system startup by the /etc/init.d/crond script. You can check to see whether the cron daemon process is running with the ps command:

```
$ ps -ef | grep crond | grep -v grep
root      3049     1  0 Aug02 ?        00:00:00 crond
```

You can also check to see whether the cron daemon is running using the service command:

```
$ /sbin/service crond status
crond (pid 3049) is running...
```

The root user uses several files and directories when executing system cron jobs. The /etc/crontab file contains commands to run system cron jobs. Here is a typical listing of the contents of the /etc/crontab file:

```
SHELL=/bin/bash
PATH=/sbin:/bin:/usr/sbin:/usr/bin
MAILTO=root
HOME=/
# run-parts
01 * * * * root run-parts /etc/cron.hourly
02 4 * * * root run-parts /etc/cron.daily
22 4 * * 0 root run-parts /etc/cron.weekly
42 4 1 * * root run-parts /etc/cron.monthly
```

This /etc/crontab file uses the run-parts utility to run scripts located in the following directories: /etc/cron.hourly, /etc/cron.daily, /etc/cron.weekly, and /etc/cron.monthly. If there is a system utility that needs to run other than on an hourly, daily, weekly, or monthly basis, then it can be placed in the /etc/cron.d directory.

Each user can create a crontab (also known as a cron table) file. This file contains the list of programs that you want to run at a specific time and interval (see recipe 11-4 for details). This file is usually located in the /var/spool/cron directory. For every user who creates a cron table, there will be a file in the /var/spool/cron directory named after the user. As root, you can list the files in that directory:

```
# ls /var/spool/cron
oracle  root
```

The cron background process is mostly idle. It wakes up once every minute and checks /etc/crontab, /etc/cron.d, and the user cron table files and determines whether there are any jobs that need to be executed.

Table 11-1 summarizes the purpose of the various files and directories used by cron. Knowledge of these files and directories will help you troubleshoot any issues as well as understand cron in more detail.

Table 11-1. *Descriptions of Files and Directories Used by the cron Utility*

File	Purpose
/etc/init.d/crond	Starts the cron daemon in system boot.
/var/log/cron	System messages related to the cron process. Useful for troubleshooting problems.
/var/spool/cron/<username>	User crontab files are stored in the /var/spool/cron directory.
/etc/cron.allow	Specifies users who can create a cron table.
/etc/cron.deny	Specifies users who are not allowed to create a cron table.
/etc/crontab	The system cron table that has commands to run scripts located in the following directories: /etc/cron.hourly, /etc/cron.daily, /etc/cron.weekly, and /etc/cron.monthly.
/etc/cron.d	A directory that contains cron tables for jobs that need to run on a schedule other than hourly, daily, weekly, or monthly.

Table 11-1. *Descriptions of Files and Directories Used by the cron Utility (Continued)*

File	Purpose
/etc/cron.hourly	Directory that contains system scripts to run on an hourly basis.
/etc/cron.daily	Directory that contains system scripts to run on a daily basis.
/etc/cron.weekly	Directory that contains system scripts to run on a weekly basis.
/etc/cron.monthly	Directory that contains system scripts to run on a monthly basis.

11-4. Scheduling a Job to Run Automatically

Problem

You want to have a backup script run automatically at 11:05 p.m. every night.

Solution

This solution details how to schedule a job using the cron utility. To schedule a job, you must add a line in your cron table specifying the time you want the job to execute. There are two methods for adding entries in your cron table:

- Editing the cron table file directly

- Loading the cron table from a file

These two techniques are described in the following sections.

Editing the cron Table Directly

You can edit your cron table directly with the -e (editor) option of the crontab command:

```
$ crontab -e
```

When issuing the previous command, you will be presented with a file to edit (see the "How It Works" section of this recipe for a discussion on the default editor). This file is known as your cron table (or crontab). To schedule a script named backup.bsh to run daily at 11:05 p.m., enter the following line into your cron table:

```
5 23 * * * /home/oracle/bin/backup.bsh
```

Exit the cron table file. If your default editor is vi, then type :wq to exit. When you exit crontab, your cron table is saved for you. To view your cron entries, use the -l (list) option of the crontab command:

```
$ crontab -l
```

To completely remove your cron table, use the -r option:

```
$ crontab -r
```

Before running the previous command, we recommend you save your cron table in a text file:

```
$ crontab -l > saved.cron
```

That way you can refer to the saved file in the event that you didn't really mean to delete your cron table.

Loading the cron Table from a File

The other way to modify your cron table is to load it directly with a file name using the following syntax:

```
$ crontab <filename>
```

In the previous line of code, the crontab utility will load the contents of the specified file into your cron table. We recommend you perform the following steps when modifying your cron table with this method:

1. First create a file with the contents of your existing cron table:

   ```
   $ crontab -l > mycron.txt
   ```

2. Make a copy of your cron table before you edit it. This allows you to revert to the original in the event you introduce errors and can't readily figure out what's incorrect. This also provides you with an audit trail of changes to your cron table:

   ```
   $ cp mycron.txt mycron.jul29.txt
   ```

3. You can now edit the mycron.txt file with your favorite text editor:

   ```
   $ vi mycron.txt
   ```

To schedule a script named backup.bsh to run daily at 11:05 p.m., enter the following into the file:

```
5 23 * * * /home/oracle/bin/backup.bsh
```

4. When you are finished making edits, load the crontab back, as shown here:

   ```
   $ crontab mycron.txt
   ```

If your file doesn't conform to the cron syntax, you'll receive an error such as the following:

```
"mycron.txt":6: bad day-of-week
errors in crontab file, can't install.
```

In this situation, either correct the syntax error or reload the original copy of the cron table.

■**Note** You can use the at command to schedule a job to run once at a specified point in the future.

How It Works

The default editor invoked to modify the cron table is dependent on the value of your VISUAL operating system variable. In our environment, the VISUAL variable is set to vi:

```
$ echo $VISUAL
vi
```

If the VISUAL operating system variable isn't set, then the value of EDITOR is used to define the default editor. Make sure that either VISUAL or EDITOR is set to your editor of choice. If neither VISUAL nor EDITOR is set, your system will default to the ed editor. In this scenario, you'll be presented with the following prompt:

```
26
<blank prompt>
```

Press the Q key to exit from ed. You can have the VISUAL or EDITOR variable automatically set for you when you log on to the system (see recipe 2-5 for additional details). You can also manually set the editor with the export command. The following sets the default editor to vi:

```
$ export EDITOR=vi
```

Formatting cron Table Entries

Your cron table is a list of numbers and commands that the cron background process (cron daemon) will run at a specified time and schedule. The crontab utility expects entries to follow a well-defined format. We recommend you add a comment line at the beginning of your crontab file that documents the required format:

```
# min(0-59) hr(0-23) dayMonth(1-31) monthYear(1-12) dayWeek(0/7-6) commandOrScript
```

In the previous line, the number (#) sign in a cron file represents the start of a comment. Any text entered after # is ignored by cron.

Each entry in the crontab is a single line comprised of six fields. The first five fields specify the execution time and frequency. These entries can be separated by commas or hyphens. A comma indicates multiple values for an entry, whereas a hyphen indicates a range of values. An entry can also be an asterisk (*), which indicates that all possible values are in effect. Here's an example to help clarify. The following entry sends an e-mail saying "Wake up" every half hour, from 8 a.m. to 4:30 p.m., on Monday through Friday:

```
0,30 8-16 * * 1-5 echo "wake up" | mailx -s "wake up" larry@oracle.com
```

On some Linux systems, you can skip a value within a range by following the entry with /<integer>. For example, if you wanted to run a job every other minute, use 0-59/2 in the minute column. You can also use a slash (/) with an asterisk to skip values. For example, to run a job every fourth minute, use */4 in the minute column.

The sixth field in the crontab can be one or more Linux commands or a shell script. Or put another way, the sixth column can be any combination of commands or a script that you can run on one line from the Linux command line.

The cron utility has a few quirks that need further explanation. The fifth column is the day of the week. Sunday is designated by either a 0 or a 7, Monday by a 1, Tuesday by a 2, and so forth, to Saturday, which is indicated with a 6.

The hour numbers in the second column are in military time format ranging from 0 to 23. The fourth column (month of year) and fifth column (day of week) can be represented with numeric values or by three-letter character abbreviations. For example, the following entry in the crontab uses three-letter character abbreviations for months and days:

```
0,30 8-16 * Jan-Dec Mon-Fri echo "wake up" | mailx -s "get up" larry@oracle.com
```

There also appear to be overlapping columns such as the third column (day of the month) and the fifth column (day of the week). These columns allow you to create flexible schedules for jobs that need to run on schedules such as the 1st and 15th day of the month or on every Tuesday. Put an asterisk in the column that you're not using. If you need to run a job on the 1st and 15th and every Tuesday, then fill in both columns.

If you're running a shell script from cron that contains a call to an Oracle utility such as sqlplus or rman, ensure that you instantiate (source) any required operating system variables such as ORACLE_SID and ORACLE_HOME. If you don't source these variables, you'll see errors such as the following when your shell script runs from cron:

```
sqlplus: command not found
```

When cron runs a script as a user, it doesn't run the user's startup or login files (like .bashrc). Therefore, any script (being run from cron) needs to explicitly set any required variables. You can directly set the variables within the script or call another script (such as Oracle's oraenv script) that exports these variables.

Tip Try not to schedule every job that you enter in cron to run at the same time every day. Rather, spread them out so as not to bog down cron or the system at any particular time.

Redirecting cron Output

You can specify that any output generated by a cron entry be redirected to a file. The following example writes standard output and standard error to a file named bck.log:

```
11 12 * * * /home/oracle/bin/backup.bsh 1>/home/oracle/bin/log/bck.log 2>&1
```

In the previous line, 1> redirects standard output, and 2>&1 specifies that the standard error should go to the same location that the standard output is located (see recipe 2-9 for more details on redirecting output). If you don't redirect the output for a cron job, then any output from the job will be e-mailed to the user who owns the cron job. You can override this by specifying the MAILTO variable directly within the cron table. In this next example, we want to aggravate the system administrator and send cron output to the root user:

```
MAILTO=root
11 12 * * * /home/oracle/bin/backup.bsh
```

If you don't want the output to go anywhere, then redirect it to the proverbial bit bucket. The following entry sends the standard output and standard error to the /dev/null device:

```
11 12 * * * /home/oracle/bin/backup.bsh 1>/dev/null 2>&1
```

Troubleshooting cron

If you have a cron job that isn't running correctly, follow these steps to troubleshoot the issue:

1. Copy your cron entry, paste it to the operating system command line, and manually run the command. Often a slight typo in a directory or file name can be the source of the problem. Manually running the command will highlight errors like this.

2. If the script runs Oracle utilities, ensure that you *source* (set) the required operating system variables within the script such as ORACLE_HOME and ORACLE_SID. Oftentimes these variables are set by startup scripts (like HOME/.bashrc) when you log on. Since cron doesn't run a user's startup scripts, any required variables must be set explicitly within the script.

3. Ensure that the first line of any shell scripts invoked from cron specifies the name of the program that will be used to interpret the commands within the script. For example, #!/bin/bash should be the first entry in a Bash shell script. Since cron doesn't run a user's startup scripts (like HOME/.bashrc), you can't assume that your operating system user's default shell will be used to run a command or script evoked from cron.

4. Ensure that the cron background process is running. Issue a ps -ef | grep crond to verify.

5. Check your e-mail on the server. The cron utility will usually send an e-mail to the operating system account when there are issues with a misbehaving cron job.

6. Inspect the contents of the /var/log/cron file for any errors. Sometimes this file has relevant information regarding a cron job that has failed to run.

11-5. Automating Oracle Performance Reports

Problem

You want to automate the distribution of Oracle performance reports such as the Automatic Workload Repository (AWR) report. You're thinking about using cron to do this task.

Solution

On your Linux database server, navigate to the ORACLE_HOME/rdbms/admin directory, and then follow these steps:

1. Make a copy of the ORACLE_HOME/rdbms/admin/awrrpti.sql file:

```
$ cd $ORACLE_HOME/rdbms/admin
$ cp awrrpti.sql awrcustom.sql
```

2. Modify the SQL in the awrcustom.sql file, as shown here:

```
$ vi awrcustom.sql
```

3. At the top of the report, replace the "Customer-customizable reporting settings" section with the following SQL code:

```
DEFINE num_days=0;
DEFINE report_type='text';
--
COL bsnap NEW_VALUE begin_snap
COL esnap NEW_VALUE end_snap
--
select max(snap_id) bsnap from dba_hist_snapshot
where begin_interval_time < sysdate-1;
--
select max(snap_id) esnap from dba_hist_snapshot;
--
COL idname NEW_VALUE dbid
COL dname  NEW_VALUE db_name
COL inum   NEW_VALUE inst_num
COL iname  NEW_VALUE inst_name
--
select d.dbid idname, lower(d.name) dname,
i.instance_number inum, i.instance_name iname
from v$database d, v$instance i;
--
-- Set the name for the report
DEFINE report_name='/orahome/scripts/awrrpt.&&db_name..txt'
```

The previous code defines variables that allow you to report on the prior 24 hours worth of statistics in your database. To automate the running of the awrcustom.sql script, create a shell script, as shown in step 4.

4. Create a Bash shell script named awr.bsh that calls awrcustom.sql:

```
#!/bin/bash
# source oracle OS variables; see recipe 7-7 for an example of oraset script,
# otherwise hardcode the values of ORACLE_HOME, ORACLE_SID, and PATH
. /var/opt/oracle/oraset RMDB1
#
for DB in proddb prod2db; do
sqlplus -s << EOF
system/foo@${DB}
@?/rdbms/admin/awrcustom.sql
exit
EOF
#
mail -s "AWR Rpt: ${DB}" larry@orc.com </orahome/scripts/awrrpt.${DB}.txt
#
done # for DB in...
exit 0
```

5. Call the report from `cron`:

```
0 6 * * * /orahome/scripts/awr.bsh 1>/orahome/scripts/log/awr.log 2>&1
```

The previous `cron` job runs the custom script daily at 6 am. The standard output and standard error are written to a file named /orahome/scripts/log/awr.log.

When using this script, ensure that you modify the shell script to reflect databases used in your environment; the operating system variables such as ORACLE_HOME, ORACLE_SID, and PATH; and the password for your DBA schema.

How It Works

The "Solution" section of this recipe combines the power of SQL, shell scripts, `cron`, and `mail` to automate a task such as sending daily performance reports. You should be able to extend these methods to automate any type of DBA task.

With any type of automation task, first you need to create a script that encapsulates the job that will be automated. Once you're confident that the script is ready, then schedule the job to run from `cron`. We recommend you send the output to a log file. This allows you to check to make sure job is running as intended.

11-6. Monitoring Jobs Using the Data Dictionary

Problem

You want to monitor whether the RMAN database backups have been running by checking the last backup date in V$RMAN_BACKUP_JOB_DETAILS.

Solution

First create a shell script that has the desired logic within it. We have added line numbers to the following shell script for discussion purposes. You'll need to take the line numbers out before you attempt to run the script. This script checks to see whether the RMAN backups have run within the last 24 hours:

```
1   #!/bin/bash
2   #
3   if [ $# -ne 2 ]; then
4     echo "Usage: $0 SID threshold"
5     exit 1
6   fi
7   # source oracle OS variables; see recipe 7-7 for an example of oraset script
8   . /var/opt/oracle/oraset $1
9   crit_var=$(sqlplus -s <<EOF
10  system/foo
11  SET HEAD OFF FEEDBACK OFF
12  SELECT COUNT(*) FROM
13  (SELECT (sysdate - MAX(end_time)) delta
14   FROM v\$rman_backup_job_details WHERE status='COMPLETED') a
```

```
15  WHERE a.delta > $2;
16  EXIT;
17  EOF)
18  if [ $crit_var -ne 0 ]; then
19    echo "rman backup problem with $1" | mailx -s "rman problem" chuck@orc.com
20  else
21    echo "rman ok"
22  fi
23  exit 0
```

■**Tip** See recipe 4-11 for details on displaying line numbers in a file that is edited via `vi`.

Now schedule the job via `cron` to run once a day. Ideally this job would run soon after your RMAN backups are finished. In this example, the previous code is contained within a script named `rman_chk.bsh`. This script is run once a day from `cron` at 5:25 a.m.; two parameters are passed to the script: DWREP (the database name) and 1 (for one day):

```
#---------------------------------------------------
# RMAN check
25 5 * * * /orahome/bin/rman_chk.bsh DWREP 1 1>/orahome/bin/log/rman_chk.log 2>&1
#---------------------------------------------------
```

In the previous `cron` entry, the `rman_chk.bsh` script is located in the `/orahome/bin` directory, and the standard output and standard error are written to the `/orahome/bin/log/rman_chk.log` file.

How It Works

The script in the "Solution" section of this recipe is very simplistic and checks to see only whether there has been one valid RMAN backup created within the last day. You can extend this script to meet the requirements of your environment. We kept the script as simple as possible to illustrate this point. This type of monitoring technique works well when you have a date-related column that is updated in the data dictionary when an event occurs. When using Oracle tools such as RMAN or materialized views, you can easily check the appropriate data dictionary view date column to validate whether the given event has occurred.

Line 1 sets the shell interpreter for the script. Lines 3 through 6 check to see whether two parameters have been passed to the script. In this case, the first parameter should be the database name. The second parameter is a threshold number. Passing in 1 for this parameter will instruct the script to check to see whether backups have occurred in the last day. If you passed in 2, then it would check to see whether a backup had occurred in the last two days.

Line 8 runs a script to source the operating system variables such as ORACLE_SID, ORACLE_HOME, and PATH. These variables need to be set to the appropriate values before you can access Oracle utilities like SQL*Plus. It is possible to hard-code those variables directly in the shell script like this (change these to reflect values in your environment):

```
ORACLE_SID=DWREP
ORACLE_HOME=/oracle/product/11.0.1
PATH=$ORACLE_HOME/bin:$PATH
```

However, we recommend you not hard-code those inside the script and instead source those variables through a called script (see recipe 7-7 for details). In the shell script in the "Solution" section of this recipe, we call a script named oraset that sets the previously listed variables. This script uses the oratab file to determine the location of ORACLE_HOME. This approach is more flexible and portable (than hard-coding values).

On line 10, you'll have to change the schema name and password in the script that works with a DBA account in your environment.

Lines 12 through 15 query the data dictionary to see whether a backup has occurred in the last n number of days, where n is the value of the second variable passed to the script.

Look at line 14. There's a reference to the following data dictionary view:

```
v\$rman_backup_job_details
```

Why is there a backslash (\) in front of the dollar sign ($)? If the data dictionary view you are referencing contains $, it must be escaped with a backslash because the dollar sign is a special Linux character that signifies a variable. The backslash placed before the dollar sign tells the Bash script to ignore the special meaning of the dollar sign variable. If you didn't do this, then the Bash shell would interpret the line to mean the value of v concatenated with the contents of a variable named rman_back_job_details.

If you set your NLS_DATE_FORMAT in the ORACLE_HOME/sqlplus/admin/glogin.sql script, this will cause the script to fail because the message "Session altered." gets displayed when logging into SQL*Plus and then subsequently is embedded into the crit_var variable. To work around this, set feedback off in glogin.sql, as shown here:

```
set feedback off;
alter session set nls_date_format='dd-mon-rr hh24:mi:ss';
set feedback on;
```

11-7. Monitoring Tablespace Fullness

Problem

You want to have a job automatically check and e-mail you if a tablespace is getting full.

Solution

Create a script similar to the one shown in this solution. Line numbers have been added for explanation purposes, so you'll have to take the line numbers out before you attempt to run this script:

```
1   #!/bin/bash
2   #
3   if [ $# -ne 2 ]; then
4     echo "Usage: $0 SID threshold"
5     exit 1
```

```
6  fi
7  # source oracle OS variables; see recipe 7-7 for an example of oraset script
8  . /var/opt/oracle/oraset $1
9  #
10  crit_var=$(
11  sqlplus -s <<EOF
12  system/foo
13  SET HEAD OFF TERM OFF FEED OFF VERIFY OFF
14  COL pct_free FORMAT 999
15  SELECT (f.bytes/a.bytes)*100 pct_free,'% free',a.tablespace_name||','
16  FROM
17  (SELECT NVL(SUM(bytes),0) bytes, x.tablespace_name
18   FROM dba_free_space y, dba_tablespaces x
19   WHERE x.tablespace_name = y.tablespace_name(+)
20   AND x.contents != 'TEMPORARY' AND x.status != 'READ ONLY'
21   GROUP BY x.tablespace_name) f,
22  (SELECT SUM(bytes) bytes, tablespace_name
23   FROM dba_data_files
24   GROUP BY tablespace_name) a
25  WHERE a.tablespace_name = f.tablespace_name
26  AND  (f.bytes/a.bytes)*100 <= $2
27  ORDER BY 1;
28  EXIT;
29  EOF)
30  if [ "$crit_var" = "" ]; then
31    echo "space okay"
32  else
33    echo "space not okay"
34    echo $crit_var
35    echo $crit_var | mailx -s "tbsp getting full on $1" unclarry@orc.com
36  fi
37  exit 0
```

Tip See recipe 4-11 for details on displaying line numbers in a file that is edited via vi.

In this example, the code is contained in a script named tbsp_chk.bsh. Here we cron the job to run every hour (at nine minutes after the hour) of every day:

```
#------------------------------------------------------
# Tbsp check
9 * * * * /orahome/bin/tbsp_chk.bsh DWREP 30 1>/orahome/bin/log/tbsp_chk.log 2>&1
#------------------------------------------------------
```

In the previous cron entry, the tbsp_chk.bsh script is located in the /orahome/bin directory, and the standard output and standard error are written to the /orahome/bin/log/tbsp_chk.log file.

How It Works

The script in the "Solution" section contains the underpinnings for most of what you would need to check to see whether a tablespace is filling up. You can take that code and extend it for any additional requirements in your environment.

Lines 3 through 6 check to ensure that two parameters are passed to the script. In this case, the script needs an Oracle SID name and a threshold limit. The threshold limit is the amount below which a tablespace percent of free space is considered to be low. For example, if you passed the script 15, then any tablespace that had less than 15 percent free space would be considered to be low on space.

Line 8 runs a script to source the operating system variables such as ORACLE_SID, ORACLE_HOME, and PATH. These variables need to be set to appropriate values before you can access Oracle utilities such as SQL*Plus. It is possible to hard-code those variables directly in the shell script like this (change these to reflect values in your environment):

```
ORACLE_SID=DWREP
ORACLE_HOME=/oracle/product/11.0.1
PATH=$ORACLE_HOME/bin:$PATH
```

However, we recommend you not hard-code those inside the script and instead source those variables through a called script (see recipe 7-7 for details). In the shell script in the "Solution" section of this recipe, we call a script named oraset that sets the previously listed variables. This script uses the oratab file to determine the location of ORACLE_HOME. This approach is more flexible and portable (than hard-coding the values).

Lines 11 through 29 run a SQL*Plus script that queries the data dictionary and determines the percentage of free space in each tablespace. You'll have to modify this script on line 12 to contain a valid username and password for your environment.

Lines 17 through 21 constitute an inline view that determines the amount of free space in a tablespace. The DBA_TABLESPACES is outer-joined to DBA_FREE_SPACE because DBA_FREE_SPACE will not return a row when there is no free space left in a datafile. On line 20 we exclude tablespaces that have a content type of TEMPORARY and a status of READ ONLY.

Lines 22 through 24 determine the amount of space allocated to a tablespace. Line 26 checks to see whether the amount of free space divided by the allocated bytes is less than the threshold value passed into the script.

On line 30, if there is no value returned from the query into the variable crit_var, then none of the tablespaces is less than the designated percentage free, and therefore there is no reason to send an e-mail alert. On line 35, an e-mail is sent if there is a value returned to the crit_var variable.

Here we run the script manually and pass an Oracle SID of DWREP and a threshold value of 30:

```
$ tbsp_chk.bsh DWREP 30
```

Listed next is a typical line denoting the contents of crit_var when several tablespaces are less than a 30 percent free threshold value:

```
space not okay
6 % free UNDOTBS1, 19 % free SYSAUX, 28 % free MV_DATA,
```

The output indicates that the UNDOTBS1 tablespace has only 6 percent of free space, the SYSAUX tablespace has 19 percent free space, and the MV_DATA tablespace has 28 percent of space free in its allocated datafiles.

Note You can also use Enterprise Manager tablespace alerts to monitor either percent full or percent free. These alerts can be enabled via the DBMS_SERVER_ALERT PL/SQL package.

11-8. Automating File Maintenance

Problem

You want to automate a job such as compressing and moving the alert.log file and deleting old compressed files.

Solution

Create a script similar to the one shown in this solution. Line numbers have been added for explanation purposes, so you'll have to take the line numbers out before you attempt to run this script:

```
1 #!/bin/bash
2 DAY=$(date '+%m.%d:%H:%M:%S')
3 SID=RMDB1
4 RMCMP='+14'
5 #--------------------
6 # source oracle OS variables; see recipe 7-7 for an example of the oraset script
7 . /var/opt/oracle/oraset $SID
8 #
9 TARGDIR=$(sqlplus -s <<EOF
10 system/foo
11 SET HEADING OFF FEEDBACK OFF
12 SELECT value FROM v\$parameter WHERE name='background_dump_dest';
13 EXIT;
14 EOF)
15 #
16 # Move and compress the alert.log file
17 if [ -f $TARGDIR/alert_${SID}.log ]; then
18   mv $TARGDIR/alert_${SID}.log $TARGDIR/${DAY}_alert_${SID}.log
19   gzip -f $TARGDIR/${DAY}_alert_${SID}.log
20 fi
21 # Remove old compressed files
22 find $TARGDIR -name "*.gz" -type f -mtime $RMCMP -exec rm -f {} \;
23 #
24 exit 0
```

> ■**Tip** See recipe 4-11 for details on displaying line numbers in a file that is edited with vi.

In this example, the code is contained in a script named rm_old.bsh. Here we cron the job to run every day at 3:35 a.m.:

```
#------------------------------------------------------
# Tbsp check
35 3 * * * /orahome/bin/rm_old.bsh 1>/orahome/bin/log/rm_old.log 2>&1
#------------------------------------------------------
```

In the previous cron entry, the rm_old.bsh script is located in the /orahome/bin directory, and the standard output and standard error are written to the /orahome/bin/log/rm_old.log file.

> ■**Tip** See recipe 11-9 or Appendix B for an example of using the logrotate utility to rename, compress, and delete log files.

How It Works

The script in the "Solution" section is a typical job that will find files, compress them, and remove files older than a certain age. DBAs use scripts like this to manage files on the operating system. You can take the code and modify it so that it works in your environment.

Line 1 specifies that the script runs in the Bash shell. The second line populates the DAY variable in a date format that will be used to create a uniquely named log file for a day. Line 3 contains the name of the target database name. Line 4 contains the variable that determines the number of days after which a file will be deleted.

Line 7 sources the oracle operating system variables. See recipe 7-7 for details on using a file like oraset to source variables such as ORACLE_SID, ORACLE_HOME, and so on.

Lines 9 through 14 query the data dictionary for the location of the background dump destination. On line 10 you'll need to change the script to contain a valid username and password for your environment.

Lines 17 through 20 check for the existence of an alert.log file, and if one is found, then it is renamed and compressed. Line 22 finds and removes any old compressed files that are more than 14 days old (defined by the RMCMP variable on line 4). Line 24 exits the shell script.

11-9. Rotating Your Log Files

Problem

You want to rename, compress, save, and/or remove the alert.log file before it grows to an unmanageable size.

Solution

Use the `logrotate` utility to perform tasks such as renaming, compressing, and removing old log files. Here are the steps for setting up a job to rotate the `alert.log` file of an Oracle database:

1. Create a configuration file named `alert.conf` in the directory `/home/oracle/config` (create the directory if it doesn't already exist):

```
/oracle/RMDB1/admin/bdump/*.log {
daily
missingok
rotate 7
compress
mail oracle@localhost
}
```

In the previous configuration file, the first line specifies the location of the log file. The asterisk (a wildcard) tells `logrotate` to look for any file with the extension of `.log` in that directory. The `daily` keyword specifies that the log file should be rotated on a daily basis. The `missingok` keyword specifies that `logrotate` should not throw an error if it doesn't find any log files. The `rotate 7` keywords specify the number of times to rotate a log file before it is removed. The `compress` keyword compresses the rotated log file. Last, a status e-mail is sent to the local `oracle` user on the server.

2. Create a `cron` job to automatically run the job on a daily basis:

```
0 9 * * * /usr/sbin/logrotate -s /home/oracle/config/alrotate.status
/home/oracle/config/alert.conf
```

The previous two lines of code should be one line in your `cron` table (it didn't fit nicely on this page on one line). The `cron` job runs the `logrotate` utility every day at 9 a.m. The `-s` (status) option directs the status file to the specified directory and file. The configuration file used is `/home/oracle/config/alert.conf`.

3. Manually test the job to see whether it rotates the `alert.log` correctly. Use the `-f` switch to force `logrotate` to do a rotation:

```
$ /usr/sbin/logrotate -f -s /home/oracle/config/alrotate.status \
/home/oracle/config/alert.conf
```

As shown in the previous steps, you can use the `logrotate` utility to easily set up log rotation jobs.

Note If you need to troubleshoot issues with your `logrotate` job, use the `-d` (debug) or `-v` (verbose) option.

How It Works

The process of copying, renaming, compressing, and deleting log files is colloquially known as *log rotation*. In Linux, it's fairly easy to enable log rotation via the `logrotate` utility. The `logrotate` utility is sometimes perceived as a utility only for system administrators. However, any user on the system can utilize logrotate to rotate log files for applications that they have read/write permissions on the specified log files.

You can also use the logrotate utility to manage log files such as the listener.log file. This file has some special considerations. For example, if you attempt to rename the listener.log file, the listener process will continue to write to the renamed file. If you remove the file, then a new one won't be written to until you stop and start the listener process. In this scenario, use the copytruncate option of logrotate to make a copy of the file, and then truncate it (see Table 11-2 for descriptions of commonly used logrotate options). In this situation, use a configuration file similar to this:

```
/oracle/product/10.2/network/log/listener.log {
weekly
copytruncate
rotate 7
mail oracle@localhost
}
```

In this example, the previous lines of code are placed in a file named listener.conf. Here we schedule the job to run in cron once a week on Sunday at 5:20 a.m.:

```
20 5 * * 0 /usr/sbin/logrotate -s /home/oracle/config/alrotate.status
/home/oracle/config/listener.conf
```

The previous two lines of code should be one line of code in your cron table (this amount of output did not fit nicely on one line on this page).

Note The copytruncate command is appropriate for any log file in which the logging activity cannot be temporarily halted.

Table 11-2. *Descriptions of Commonly Used logrotate Options*

Option	Purpose
compress	Compresses old versions of log files with gzip
copy	Copies the log file but doesn't change the original
copytruncate	Copies the log file and then truncates the original
daily	Rotates the log files daily
mail	Mails any deleted log files to the specified account
monthly	Rotates the log files only the first time logrotate is executed in a month
olddir <directory>	Moves the log files to the specified directory
rotate n	Rotates the logs n times before deleting
size n	Rotates the log file when it is greater than n bytes
weekly	Rotates the log files if more than a week has passed since the last rotation

11-10. Scheduling a Job using DBMS_SCHEDULER

Problem

You want to run an RMAN backup. You want to use the Oracle DBMS_SCHEDULER PL/SQL package to do this.

Solution

First create a shell script that performs an RMAN backup. This example creates a file named rmanback.bsh and places it in the /home/oracle/bin directory:

```
#!/bin/bash
# source oracle OS variables; see recipe 7-7 for an example of the oraset script
. /var/opt/oracle/oraset  RMDB1
rman target / <<EOF
spool log to '/home/oracle/bin/log/rmanback.log'
backup database;
spool log off;
EOF
exit 0
```

Next create a DBMS_SCHEDULER job. Run the following as SYS (from the SQL*Plus):

```
BEGIN
DBMS_SCHEDULER.CREATE_JOB(
job_name => 'RMAN_BACKUP',
job_type => 'EXECUTABLE',
job_action => '/home/oracle/bin/rmanback.bsh',
repeat_interval => 'FREQ=DAILY;BYHOUR=18;BYMINUTE=45',
start_date => to_date('16-SEP-08'),
job_class => '"DEFAULT_JOB_CLASS"',
auto_drop => FALSE,
enabled => TRUE);
END;
/
```

The previous example creates a daily RMAN backup job that runs at 6:45 p.m. Before you use the previous script, you'll need to modify the start date and schedule parameters to meet the requirements of your environment. If you want to view details about the job, you can query the DBA_SCHEDULER_JOBS and DBA_SCHEDULER_JOB_RUN_DETAILS views:

```
SELECT
  job_name
 ,status
 ,error#
 ,actual_start_date
FROM dba_scheduler_job_run_details
WHERE job_name='RMAN_BACKUP';
```

```
SELECT
  job_name
 ,last_start_date
 ,last_run_duration
 ,next_run_date
FROM dba_scheduler_jobs
WHERE job_name='RMAN_BACKUP';
```

If you want to delete a job, use the DROP_JOB procedure:

```
BEGIN
dbms_scheduler.drop_job(job_name=>'RMAN_BACKUP');
END;
/
```

How It Works

It's beyond the scope of this chapter or book to describe all the characteristics of DBMS_SCHEDULER. The example in the "Solution" section of this recipe barely scratches the surface of the wide variety of features available with this package.

DBAs often debate whether they should use DBMS_SCHEDULER or cron for scheduling and automating tasks. Listed next are some of the benefits that DBMS_SCHEDULER has over cron:

- Can make the execution of a job dependent on the completion of another job

- Robust resource balancing and flexible scheduling features

- Can run jobs based on a database event

- DBMS_SCHEDULER syntax works the same regardless of the operating system

- Can run status reports using the data dictionary

- If working in clustered environment, no need to worry about synchronizing multiple cron tables for each node in the cluster

Listed next are some of the advantages of using cron:

- Easy to use, simple, tried and true

- Almost universally available on all Linux/Unix boxes; for the most part, runs nearly identically regardless of the Linux/Unix platform (yes, there are minor differences)

- Database agnostic; operates independently of the database and works the same regardless of the database vendor or database version

- Works whether the database is available or not

These bulleted lists aren't comprehensive, but they should give you a flavor of the uses of each tool. See Chapters 26, 27, and 28 of the Oracle Database Administrator's Guide 11*g* and Oracle Database PL/SQL Packages Reference documentation for details on how to use DBMS_SCHEDULER. This documentation is available on Oracle's website (http://otn.oracle.com). See recipe 11-4 for details on how to use cron.

CHAPTER 12

■■■

Implementing Automatic Storage Management on Linux

Since Oracle announced Automatic Storage Management (ASM) as a new feature in Oracle Database 10g, advocates of Oracle technology quickly realized that the filesystem as they knew it for storing database files may be replaced by ASM. DBAs and system administrators alike asked the same question: What is the benefit of ASM? You should consider ASM for your corporate infrastructure for a number of reasons. ASM, in a nutshell, provides an integrated filesystem and volume management in the database kernel. Here are the most important reasons why you should consider ASM:

- Raw device performance

- Logical volume management

- Consolidation of storage management

- Mirroring/triple mirroring equivalence

- Striping

- Mirroring across heterogeneous storage arrays

- Mirroring across different storage vendors

- Real application cluster support

ASM over the years has become a gray area between system administrators and database administrators. Because ASM involves SQL*Plus, system administrators often take minimal ownership over this technology stack. At the same time, DBAs lack knowledge in the storage administration and often struggle with setup, configuration, and/or performance issues. ASM, although introduced as a DBA topic, often requires savvy system administration and knowledge.

Often storage vendors portray a negative image of ASM. Storage vendors lose revenue when ASM replaces the license cost associated with the vendor's logical volume management software. Furthermore, storage vendors also lose out on revenue associated with disk management and monitoring.

Obviously, we cannot cover all of ASM in a single chapter. This chapter focuses on core ASM components applicable to the Linux environment. This chapter will cover ASMLIB, how to install and configure ASM, and then how to migrate to ASM from the operating system. Finally, we'll cover the ASM command-line interface to demonstrate how you can master ASM outside SQL*Plus.

12-1. Installing RPMs for ASMLIB

Problem

You want to install packages for Oracle's ASM libraries (ASMLIB). During the installation, you encounter dependency errors as you attempt to apply ASMLIB Linux packages.

Solution

Installing Oracle's ASMLIB has dependency requirements. You must install the RPMs in the following order:

1. `oracleasm-support`

2. `oracleasm`

3. `oracleasmlib`

If you attempt to apply RPMs in a different order than listed here, you will encounter the "Error: Failed dependencies" message. In the following example, ASMLIB RPMs will be installed and configured in the correct dependency order:

```
[root@gc oracle]# rpm -ihv oracleasm-support-2.0.3-1.i386.rpm
Preparing... ######################################### [100%]
1:oracleasm-support ######################################### [100%]

[root@gc oracle]# rpm -ihv oracleasm-2.6.9-55.0.2.EL-2.0.3-1.i686.rpm
Preparing... ######################################### [100%]
1:oracleasm-2.6.9-55.0.2.######################################### [100%]

[root@gc oracle]# rpm -ihv oracleasmlib-2.0.2-1.i386.rpm
Preparing... ######################################### [100%]
1:oracleasmlib ######################################### [100%]
```

How It Works

Oracle announced ASMLIB as a generic storage management interface concept to address disk management, discovery, and provisioning. ASMLIB was intended as an API for storage and operating system vendors to extend their storage core strengths and features such as performance and greater data integrity. Since the introduction of ASMLIB, Oracle released Oracle's ASMLIB libraries only for the Linux operating system. ASMLIB is available for the following flavors of Oracle Unbreakable Linux:

- SUSE Linux Enterprise Server 10

- Red Hat Enterprise Linux 5 AS

- Red Hat Enterprise Linux 4 AS

- SUSE Linux Enterprise Server 9

- Red Hat Enterprise Linux 3 AS

- SUSE Linux Enterprise Server 8 SP3

- Red Hat Advanced Server 2.1

The ASMLIB software is composed of three essential RPMs:

- `oracleasmlib`, which is the core package

- `oracleasm-support`, which provides the command-line interfaces

- `oracleasm`, which is the kernel driver and is dependent on the version of the Linux kernel

The simplistic implementation would be to list all three RPMs in a single command, as shown here:

```
[root@gc oracle]# rpm -ihv oracleasm-2.6.9-55.0.2.EL-2.0.3-1.i686.rpm \
oracleasmlib-2.0.2-1.i386.rpm \
oracleasm-support-2.0.3-1.i386.rpm

Preparing... ######################################### [100%]
1:oracleasm-support ######################################### [ 33%]
2:oracleasm-2.6.9-55.0.2.######################################### [ 67%]
3:oracleasmlib ######################################### [100%]
```

By listing all the RPMs on a single command-line syntax, administrators do not have to be cognitive of dependency order.

We recommend that RPMs for ASMLIB 2.0 be downloaded from Oracle's website: http://www.oracle.com/technology/software/tech/linux/asmlib/index.html. When downloading RPMs, administrators must carefully select the appropriate RPMs specific for their Linux kernel version and architecture. You can use the `uname -r` command to determine the exact version of the Linux kernel specific to your environment. You can download RPMs specific to Red Hat 4 from the following website:

http://www.oracle.com/technology/software/tech/linux/asmlib/rhel4.html

12-2. Installing ASMLIB from Oracle's Unbreakable Linux Network

Problem

You are licensed for Oracle Enterprise Linux and want to take advantage of the up2date feature to download and install the ASMLIB RPMs from Oracle's Unbreakable Linux Network.

Solution

Here's the command and output to install the latest ASM libraries on your system:

```
# up2date -i oracleasm-support oracleasmlib oracleasm-`uname -r`

Fetching Obsoletes list for channel: el5_i386_latest...

Fetching Obsoletes list for channel: el5_i386_ocfs2...
########################################

Fetching Obsoletes list for channel: el5_i386_oracle...
########################################

Fetching rpm headers...
########################################

Name                            Version       Rel
------------------------------------------------------------
oracleasm-2.6.18-53.el5         2.0.4         1.el5         i686
oracleasm-support               2.0.4         1.el5         i386
oracleasmlib                    2.0.3         1.el5         i386


Testing package set / solving RPM inter-dependencies...
########################################
oracleasm-2.6.18-53.el5-2.0 ######################### Done.
oracleasm-support-2.0.4-1.e ######################### Done.
oracleasmlib-2.0.3-1.el5.i3 ######################### Done.
Preparing              ########################################### [100%]

Installing...
   1:oracleasm-support     ######################################### [100%]
   2:oracleasm-2.6.18-53.el5######################################### [100%]
   3:oracleasmlib          ######################################### [100%]
```

You must subscribe to the "Oracle Software for Enterprise Linux" channel to install the oracleasmlib RPM.

How It Works

If you are deploying Oracle Enterprise Linux, you can take advantage of up2date to download and install the ASMLIB RPMs just like any other RPMs. Once you successfully register the database server with the Unbreakable Linux Network (ULN), you can subscribe to the "Oracle Software for Enterprise Linux" channel and leverage up2date to download the ASM libraries.

■**Note** If you are upgrading your Linux operating system, you must update the oracleasm package since it is kernel-version-specific. You can upgrade the oracleasm package using the up2date -u command.

12-3. Autostarting the Non-RAC ASM Instance After a Reboot

Problem

For Real Application Cluster (RAC) databases, the ASM instance autostarts fine after a server reboot. For non-RAC implementations, the ASM instance does not start when the system is bounced for maintenance activities or during a planned outage window.

Solution

Oracle does not provide scripts to start the ASM instance during the reboot processes. You can take advantage of the dbstart shell script in $ORACLE_HOME/bin since this script has been redesigned to start the ASM instance first. For non-RAC databases, executing dbstart will start the ASM instance and all the databases listed in the /etc/oratab file with the autostart flag set to Y.

Customers can customize the system autostartup scripts in the /etc/rc[x].d directory since requirements may vary from system to system. Autostartup scripts are typically configured with the chkconfig command in Linux. As best practices, the driver script that initiates the autostartup scripts should be placed in the /etc/init.d directory.

Here's a simple script, /etc/init.d/dbora, that will restart the ASM instance and database after a server reboot:

```
#!/bin/sh
# chkconfig: 345 99 10
# Description: Oracle auto start-stop script.
# Name:  dbora
#
DB_HOME=/apps/oracle/product/11.1.0/DB
OWNER=oracle
export DB_HOME OWNER

case "$1" in
'start')
  # -- Sleep for 120 per Oracle Bug #:  3458327
  sleep 120;
  su - $OWNER -c "$DB_HOME/bin/dbstart $DB_HOME" > /tmp/dbstart.log 2>&1
  su - $OWNER -c "export ORAENV_ASK=NO; export ORACLE_SID=DBAPROD;. oraenv;
                 lsnrctl start" > /tmp/listener_start.log 2>&1
  ;;
'stop')
  # Stop the Oracle databases:
```

```
    su - $OWNER -c "export ORAENV_ASK=NO; export ORACLE_SID=DBAPROD;. oraenv;
                lsnrctl stop" > /tmp/listener_stop.log 2>&1
    su - $OWNER -c $DB_HOME/bin/dbshut >/tmp/dbshut.log 2>&1
    ;;
esac
```

How It Works

The dbora script can potentially satisfy the majority of the company's database startup requirements. The dbora script simply executes the dbstart script from $ORACLE_HOME/bin when the server starts and executes the dbshut script prior to the system shutdown process. Oracle's dbstart script loops through the /etc/oratab twice. In the first iteration, entries that start with a + sign are filtered out since the + sign denotes an ASM instance. If the ASM instance has a Y flag at the end of the colon-delimited parameters, the dbstart script will start the ASM instance. During the second loop iteration of the /etc/oratab file, dbstart starts all the databases that are designated to autostartup.

Despite efforts to autostart the databases, ASM instances will not autostart because of reported bug number 3458327. MetaLink Note 264235.1, which is titled "ORA-29701 On Reboot When Instance Uses Automatic Storage Management (ASM)," indicates that the dbstart script will not start the ASM instance. Indeed, the ASM instance will result in the following error:

```
ORA-29701 unable to connect to Cluster Manager.
```

The workaround to address this problem is to move the last line of the /etc/inittab file that respawns the init.cssd daemon between rc2 and rc3, as shown here:

```
l2:2:wait:/etc/rc.d/rc 2
h1:35:respawn:/etc/init.d/init.cssd run >/dev/null 2>&1 </dev/null
l3:3:wait:/etc/rc.d/rc 3
l4:4:wait:/etc/rc.d/rc 4
l5:5:wait:/etc/rc.d/rc 5
l6:6:wait:/etc/rc.d/rc 6
```

12-4. Configuring ASMLIB

Problem

You want to take full advantage of Oracle ASMLIB since you are running Linux. After successfully installing all the required packages for the ASMLIB, you want to configure ASMLIB to address disk permissions, to start the Oracle ASM library, and to set the disk ownership to oracle during system boot processes.

Solution

After you have successfully installed all the required RPMs, you can initiate ASMLIB configuration by issuing the /etc/init.d/oracleasm configure command. The oracleasm shell script will prompt you to do the following:

- Set up the ASMLIB driver owner

- Set up group permissions

- Set up driver boot options

- Load the oracleasm module into the kernel

- Scan the header of the disk to search for oracleasm disk members

The following example displays the configuration steps:

```
[root@rac3 init.d]# ./oracleasm configure
Configuring the Oracle ASM library driver.

This will configure the on-boot properties of the Oracle ASM library
driver.  The following questions will determine whether the driver is
loaded on boot and what permissions it will have.  The current values
will be shown in brackets ('[]').  Hitting <ENTER> without typing an
answer will keep that current value.  Ctrl-C will abort.

Default user to own the driver interface [oracle]: oracle
Default group to own the driver interface [dba]: dba
Start Oracle ASM library driver on boot (y/n) [n]: y
Fix permissions of Oracle ASM disks on boot (y/n) [n]: y
Writing Oracle ASM library driver configuration:          [  OK  ]
Loading module "oracleasm":                               [  OK  ]
Mounting ASMlib driver filesystem:                        [  OK  ]
Scanning system for ASM disks:                            [  OK  ]
```

How It Works

When you successfully install the RPMs required for ASMLIB, the primary command-line interface shell script called oracleasm is installed in the /etc/init.d directory. The oracleasm script is designed to start the ASM library, load the oracleasm kernel module, fix the disk permissions, mount the oracleasmfs filesystem, and scan the disk headers of each ASM disk. Executing /etc/init.d/oracleasm with the configure option prompts the administrator to respond to the values designated in brackets, as in [ ]. When responding to the oracleasm script, you should designate the owner of the driver interface to be the oracle user and set the default group ownership to be dba. Likewise, the startup of the Oracle ASM library should be set to start on system reboot and to correct the permissions for the Oracle ASM disks.

All the ASMLIB parameters and configuration information is recorded in the /etc/sysconfig/oracleasm file. Here are the parameters defined in the oracleasm configuration file:

```
#
# This is a configuration file for automatic loading of the Oracle
# Automatic Storage Management library kernel driver.  It is generated
# By running /etc/init.d/oracleasm configure.  Please use that method
# to modify this file
#
```

```
# ORACLEASM_ENABELED: 'true' means to load the driver on boot.
ORACLEASM_ENABLED=true

# ORACLEASM_UID: Default user owning the /dev/oracleasm mount point.
ORACLEASM_UID=oracle

# ORACLEASM_GID: Default group owning the /dev/oracleasm mount point.
ORACLEASM_GID=dba

# ORACLEASM_SCANBOOT: 'true' means fix disk perms on boot
ORACLEASM_SCANBOOT=true

# ORACLEASM_CLEARBOOT: 'true' means clean old disk perms on boot
ORACLEASM_CLEARBOOT=true

# ORACLEASM_SCANORDER: Matching patterns to order disk scanning
ORACLEASM_SCANORDER=

# ORACLEASM_SCANEXCLUDE: Matching patterns to exclude disks from scan
ORACLEASM_SCANEXCLUDE=
```

As you can see, answers that were supplied during the /etc/init.d/oracleasm configure command are captured in this file. This library configuration file is read during the automatic loading of the ASMLIB kernel driver.

12-5. Labeling Disks with ASMLIB

Problem

After the storage administrator provides you with the disk for the database and presents the disk to the server, you want to stamp the disks as ASMLIB disks using the oracleasm createdisk command.

Solution

Let's start with creating the ASMLIB disk. You invoke the same /etc/init.d/oracleasm script to create an ASMLIB disk. The createdisk command accepts two arguments: the disk name that you want to assign, which is limited to 30 characters, and the fully qualified device path name. In the following example, you will create four ASMLIB disks, DATA1 to DATA4:

```
[root@rac3 dev]# /etc/init.d/oracleasm createdisk DATA1 /dev/sdc1
Marking disk "/dev/sdc1" as an ASM disk:                    [  OK  ]
[root@rac3 dev]# /etc/init.d/oracleasm createdisk DATA2 /dev/sdc2
Marking disk "/dev/sdc2" as an ASM disk:                    [  OK  ]
[root@rac3 dev]# /etc/init.d/oracleasm createdisk DATA3 /dev/sdc3
Marking disk "/dev/sdc3" as an ASM disk:                    [  OK  ]
[root@rac3 dev]# /etc/init.d/oracleasm createdisk DATA4 /dev/sdc4
Marking disk "/dev/sdc4" as an ASM disk:                    [  OK  ]
```

How It Works

Once the disks are presented to the database server, you can create ASMLIB disks by marking the disk header with the `oracleasm` shell script. Marking the disk involves writing ASMLIB information on the disk header of the disk.

ASMLIB is concerned with only two portions of the disk header: the disk marker (also referred to as the *tag*) and the label. Successful creation of the DATA1 disk via ASMLIB will stamp the tag ORCLDISK and add the label DATA1 to the disk header.

■Note The tag ORCLDISK can be stamped by ASMLIB or by the ASM instance after the disk becomes a member of a diskgroup. All ASM disks will have the tag ORCLDISK on the disk header. The tag ORCLDISK indicates that the disk is provisioned for use by ASM or is already a member of an ASM diskgroup.

When ASMLIB scans the disks after a reboot, ASMLIB will detect the tag ORCLDISK and the label DATA1.

You can take advantage of the od command to dump the disk header information to retrieve the ASM disk label and/or diskgroup information. Using the dd command to extract just the 128 bytes of the disk header and piping the output to the od command to dump the output in octal format, you can view the named characters with the "--format=a" option. The od output should resemble something similar to what you see here:

```
[root@rac4 ~]# dd if=/dev/sdc1 bs=128 count=1 |od --format=a
1+0 records in
1+0 records out
0000000 nul nul nul nul nul nul nul nul nul nul nul nul   u   A   T   A
0000020 nul nul nul nul nul nul nul nul nul nul nul nul nul nul nul nul
0000040   O   R   C   L   D   I   S   K   D   A   T   A   1 nul nul nul
0000060 nul nul nul nul nul nul nul nul nul nul nul nul nul nul nul nul
*
0000200
```

You will notice that the disk header of /dev/sdc1 is marked with ORCLDISKDATA1 to denote that this is tagged as an ASM or ASMLIB disk and has a label called DATA1. When you assign the ASM disk to a diskgroup in recipe 12-15, additional information will be marked in the disk header.

ASM can discover ASMLIB disks by scanning the disk header. Even if the device name changes after a reboot, ASM still identifies the disk as an ASMLIB disk by reading the disk header. For example, what is /dev/hdc1 after a reboot may become /dev/sdh1. With ASMLIB, ASM does not care about device names surviving a reboot.

If a raw or block device is not configured to be an ASMLIB disk, the disk will not have a label at all. The label will in essence have an empty value. When ASMLIB scans a non-ASMLIB disk, it may detect the disk as an ASM disk if it has the ORCLDISK tag but will not recognize it as an ASMLIB disk since it has no label.

In a RAC configuration, you will execute only the oracleasm createdisk command on one RAC node. The remaining nodes will scan the disk header and pick up the label information using the oracleasm scandisks command.

12-6. Unmarking ASMLIB Disks

Problem

You want to delete the existing ASM disk label. You want to redistribute the disk for other purposes.

Solution

Before you delete the ASM disk label, you need to drop the disk from the ASM diskgroup. You can leverage the /etc/init.d/oracleasm deletedisk command to remove the disk header information. The oracleasm deletedisk command accepts one parameter, the ASM disk name. To delete the DATA2 ASM disk label, here's the syntax:

```
[root@rac4 ~]# /etc/init.d/oracleasm deletedisk data2
Removing ASM disk "DATA2":                              [  OK  ]
```

■**Note** All options to the oracleasm script that are not read-only actions require root privileges to execute. Such options include commands to configure, create, delete, and rename.

How It Works

The oracleasm deletedisk command deletes the disk label that identifies the disk as the ASMLIB disk. Before deleting the DATA2 disk label, you can see the DATA2 disk label on the header of the disk, as shown here:

```
[root@rac4 ~]# dd if=/dev/sdc2 bs=128 count=1 |od --format=a
1+0 records in
1+0 records out
0000000 nul nul nul nul nul nul nul nul nul nul nul nul   v   A   T   A
0000020 nul nul nul nul nul nul nul nul nul nul nul nul nul nul nul nul
0000040   O   R   C   L   D   I   S   K   D   A   T   A   2 nul nul nul
0000060 nul nul nul nul nul nul nul nul nul nul nul nul nul nul nul nul
*
0000200
```

After issuing the oracleasm deletedisk command, the disk header dump shows that the ORCLDISKDATA2 disk header is changed to ORCLCLRD:

```
[root@rac4 ~]# dd if=/dev/sdc2 bs=128 count=1 |od --format=a
1+0 records in
1+0 records out
0000000 nul nul nul nul nul nul nul nul nul nul nul nul   v   A   T   A
0000020 nul nul nul nul nul nul nul nul nul nul nul nul nul nul nul nul
0000040   O   R   C   L   C   L   R   D nul nul nul nul nul nul nul nul
0000060 nul nul nul nul nul nul nul nul nul nul nul nul nul nul nul nul
*
0000200
```

You can also use the dd command to clear out the headers of the ASM disks. A simple way is the write over the headers plus some extra space by copying over the /dev/zero special file. Here's an example of the dd command to clear out the first 10MB of the disk header:

```
$ sudo dd if=/dev/zero of=/dev/sdc1 bs=10240000 count=1
1+0 records in
1+0 records out
rac4.dbaexpert.com:/home/oracle
[ … ]
rac4.dbaexpert.com:/home/oracle
+ASM > sudo dd if=/dev/zero of=/dev/sdc4 bs=10240000 count=1
1+0 records in
1+0 records out
```

12-7. Changing the Disk Label of Member Disks

Problem

You want to change the disk label of an existing member of an ASM diskgroup without losing data.

Solution

You can use the force-renamedisk option to change the disk label of a disk. The force-renamedisk option can be leveraged to migrate from a block device to an ASMLIB disk. You can execute the /etc/init.d/oracleasm shell script, provide the script with the force-renamedisk option, and provide two parameters: the block device name and the ASM disk name you want to name it to. In the following example, we will rename the /dev/sdc4 block device to the FRA_1 ASM disk:

```
$ sudo /etc/init.d/oracleasm force-renamedisk /dev/sdc4 FRA_1
Renaming disk "/dev/sdc4" to "FRA_1":                      [  OK  ]
```

Likewise, you can rename an ASMLIB disk using the force-renamedisk option, as shown here:

```
$ sudo /etc/init.d/oracleasm force-renamedisk data1 data10
Renaming disk "data1" to "DATA10":                        [  OK  ]
```

How It Works

If you have not implemented ASMLIB, you may want to migrate to ASMLIB to take advantage of native features such as device persistency, device ownership, and permissions management. To migrate to ASMLIB, you must change the label of your existing disks by renaming the disks to an ASMLIB disk.

When you rename a block device or an ASM disk, you are simply altering the disk header information. You can rename a block device or an ASM disk but may not migrate a raw device to an ASMLIB disk. If you want to migrate a raw device, you must associate the block device rather than the raw device as the parameter to the force-renamedisk option. Attempting to directly migrate a raw device will yield an error message similar to what you see here:

```
# /etc/init.d/oracleasm force-renamedisk /dev/raw/raw1 data1
asmtool: Unable to open device "/dev/raw/raw1": Block device required
Renaming disk "/dev/raw/raw1" to "DATA1":                    [FAILED]
```

Note You should rename a disk only while the ASM instance is down. If you attempt to rename a disk while the ASM instance is up and running, you assume the risk of data corruption.

Most ASM administrators will first initiate the renaming of the ASM disk with the renamedisk option. The renamedisk operation will fail and will prompt you to use the force-renamedisk command instead, as shown here:

```
$ sudo /etc/init.d/oracleasm renamedisk /dev/sdc4 FRA_1
WARNING: Changing the label of an disk marked for ASM is a very dangerous
         operation.  If this is really what you mean to do, you must
         ensure that all Oracle and ASM instances have ceased using
         this disk.  Otherwise, you may LOSE DATA.
If you really wish to change the label, rerun with the force-renamedisk command.
Renaming disk "/dev/sdc4" to "FRA_1":                    [FAILED]
```

12-8. Listing ASMLIB Disks

Problem

You want to view all the disks incorporated into ASMLIB and correlate the ASMLIB disks to the block devices.

Solution

To view a list of all your ASMLIB disks, simply execute the /etc/init.d/oracleasm listdisks command. You can see in the example here that the oracleasm listdisks command provides an output of all the ASMLIB disks:

```
$ sudo /etc/init.d/oracleasm listdisks
DATA10
DATA3
FRA1
FRA2
FRA3
FRA4
```

Querying the disks individually using the oracleasm querydisk command provides the major and minor numbers of the device name. For example, querying the ASMLIB disk labeled DATA10 produces the following output:

```
$ sudo /etc/init.d/oracleasm querydisk DATA10
Disk "DATA10" is a valid ASM disk on device [8, 33]
```

How It Works

Every disk created using the `oracleasm createdisk` command will create an entry in the /dev/oracleasm/disks directory. ASM disk entries in the /dev/oracleasm/disks directory correlate to the major and minor numbers in the /dev directory:

```
[root@rac4 ~]# ls -l /dev/oracleasm/disks
total 0
brw-rw----  1 oracle dba 8, 33 May 22 23:01 DATA10
brw-rw----  1 oracle dba 8, 35 May 22 17:19 DATA3
brw-rw----  1 oracle dba 8, 49 May 22 17:13 FRA1
brw-rw----  1 oracle dba 8, 50 May 22 17:13 FRA2
brw-rw----  1 oracle dba 8, 51 May 22 17:13 FRA3
brw-rw----  1 oracle dba 8, 52 May 22 17:13 FRA4
```

Simply executing an `ls` command against the /dev directory, you can match the ASM disk to the block device. For example, ASM disk DATA10 maps to /dev/sdc1, as shown here:

```
[root@rac4 ~]# ls -l /dev |grep "8,  33"
brw-rw----  1 root    disk     8, 33 May 22 17:13 sdc1
```

Alternatively, you can leverage `oracleasm querydisk` using the device name. Instead of providing the ASMLIB disk as the parameter, you can specify the device name, and the script will return the ASMLIB disk associated with the device name. Querying the device name /dev/sdc1, you will notice the correlation back to DATA10:

```
$ sudo /etc/init.d/oracleasm querydisk /dev/sdc1
Disk "/dev/sdc1" is marked an ASM disk with the label "DATA10"
```

If you query a device name that is not an ASMLIB disk, you will get a message indicating that the disk is not marked as an ASMLIB disk:

```
$ sudo /etc/init.d/oracleasm querydisk /dev/sdc4
Disk "/dev/sdc4" is not marked an ASM disk
```

Another way to check the identity of the ASMLIB disk is to query the V$ASM_DISK view. You will notice that the V$ASM_DISK view has a LIBRARY, a LABEL, and a PATH column:

```
  1  select path, label, library from v$asm_disk
  2* order by 1,2
SQL> /


PATH        LABEL     LIBRARY
----------- --------- ------------------------------
/dev/sdc4             System
ORCL:DATA10 DATA10    ASM Library - Generic Linux, v
                      ersion 2.0.2 (KABI_V2)

[...]
ORCL:FRA4   FRA4      ASM Library - Generic Linux, v
                      ersion 2.0.2 (KABI_V2)

7 rows selected.
```

You can clearly see that the device /dev/sdc4 is not an ASMLIB disk. You will also see that all ASMLIB disks have path names that start with ORCL: followed by the label name.

12-9. Troubleshooting ASMLIB

Problem

For some unexpected reason, you encounter error(s) while trying to configure Oracle ASMLIB, or you cannot create a diskgroup using the ASMLIB disks.

Solution

If you have issues loading the oracleasm module, you will see errors in the /var/log/messages file that look similar to what is shown here:

```
Apr 24 22:24:42 gc modprobe: FATAL: Module oracleasm not found.
Apr 24 22:24:42 gc oracleasm: Unable failed
```

Unfortunately, many DBAs and system administrators do not realize the significance of ASMLIB. Because ASMLIB is an optional feature, administrators often do not spend a lot of time resolving ASMLIB issues. When complications arise while configuring ASMLIB, administrators tend to bypass ASMLIB and create ASM diskgroups using block devices. If you are deploying RAC and/or ASM environments on a Linux operating system, we strongly recommend that you implement ASMLIB. ASMLIB is an alternative interface to discover and access block devices. ASMLIB provides native features such as device naming and permission persistency.

The database is able to read and write to the ASM instance through the oracleasmfs filesystem. As part of the ASMLIB configuration process, ASMLIB creates an entry in the /proc/filesystems file and mounts the oracleasmfs filesystem. To confirm, you can view the contents of the /proc/filesystems file to ensure an entry exists for oracleasmfs:

```
# cat /proc/filesystems |grep -i asm
nodev   asmdisk
nodev   oracleasmfs
```

Next, you can confirm that the oracleasm filesystem is successfully mounted to /dev/oracleasm using the df -ha command, as shown here:

```
# df -ha
Filesystem          Size  Used Avail Use% Mounted on
/dev/hda1           16G   3.8G  11G  26% /
none                 0    0     0    -  /proc
[…]
/dev/hda2           31G   26G  3.6G  88% /apps
none               1014M  166M 849M  17% /dev/shm
/dev/hda5           4.0G   41M  3.7G  2% /tmp
/dev/mapper/vgmax-lvolsoft
                    126G  101M 120G   1% /soft
oracleasmfs          0    0     0    -  /dev/oracleasm
```

■**Note** The -h option designates a human-readable format that typically yields output in gigabytes instead of kilobytes. The -a option designates the output to display dummy filesystems that include empty filesystems (those with zero blocks).

The last line of the output should have the virtual oracleasmfs filesystem mounted to /dev/oracleasm. You can also check the files created in /dev/oracleasm/disks and make sure the ownership and permissions on the files are set to oracle:dba.

Another troubleshooting effort is to confirm that the oracleasm kernel module loaded successfully using the lsmod command:

```
# lsmod |grep -i asm
oracleasm              48020  1
```

At times, the oracleasm kernel module must be loaded manually. To load the oracleasm kernel module, change your directory to the /lib/modules/$(uname -r) directory, and issue the find command, as shown here:

```
# find . -name 'oracleasm.*'
./kernel/drivers/addon/oracleasm/oracleasm.ko
# insmod ./kernel/drivers/addon/oracleasm/oracleasm.ko
```

Once the kernel module is successfully loaded, you can continue with the ASMLIB configuration steps.

12-10. Checking ASMLIB Status

Problem

You want to verify that ASMLIB is running and ensure that it is enabled to autostart.

Solution

You can check the status of ASMLIB by specifying the oracleasm status command:

```
[root@rac4 ~]# /etc/init.d/oracleasm status
Checking if ASM is loaded:                              [  OK  ]
Checking if /dev/oracleasm is mounted:                  [  OK  ]
```

You can make sure that the ASMLIB is enabled at boot time:

```
[root@rac4 ~]# /etc/init.d/oracleasm enable
Writing Oracle ASM library driver configuration:        [  OK  ]
Scanning system for ASM disks:                          [  OK  ]
```

How It Works

The command oracleasm status checks to see that the ASM kernel module is loaded and confirms that the /dev/oracleasm filesystem is mounted. The oracleasm enable command simply writes to the configuration file to autostart ASMLIB. You can disable ASMLIB as part of the reboot process by using the `oracleasm disable` command.

12-11. Installing ASM Software on a Non-RAC Implementation

Problem

You want to install Oracle ASM software. You are not running RAC in your environment.

Solution

The steps involved to install ASM software do not differ from installing the database software. You install the base software version first and then upgrade the software to the latest release of Oracle. For example, to install Oracle version 10.2.0.3/10.2.0.4, you would have to download and install the Oracle release 10.2.0.1 software binaries from OTN and then upgrade to Oracle release 10.2.0.3 or 10.2.0.4 downloaded from MetaLink. To download the latest software release from MetaLink, you must have a valid CSI number and registration.

Note We recommend installing ASM in a separate Oracle Home from your Oracle Database software. Allocating a separate Oracle Home just for ASM is considered a best practice and prepares your implementation for future rolling upgrades.

This solution will focus on Oracle Database 11g. To install Oracle Database 11g software in preparation for using it to run an ASM instance, you can follow the detailed steps outlined here:

1. First, as the `root` user, create a Unix group called `asmadmin` using the `groupadd` command:

   ```
   # groupadd asmadmin
   ```

2. Assign the `oracle` user as a member of the `asmadmin` group in the `/etc/group` file, as shown here:

   ```
   [...]
   dba:x:500:
   oinstall:x:501:oracle
   screen:x:84:
   asmadmin:x:502:oracle
   ```

   If the `oracle` user is already logged in the Linux server, log out and log back in. If you print the user identify information with the `id` command, you should see the `asmadmin` group assignment:

   ```
   $ id
   uid=500(oracle) gid=500(dba) groups=500(dba),501(oinstall),502(asmadmin)
   ```

3. Set `DISPLAY=IP_ADDRESS:0.0` or `HOSTNAME:0.0` of the valid X server.

4. Execute ./runInstaller to install Oracle version 11.1.0.6.

   If you meet the minimal prerequisite requirements such as validation of 80MB availability in temp space, 150MB availability in swap space, and minimum 256 colors support, the Oracle Universal Installer screen will display on the designated X server.

   On the Select Installation Method screen, you have the option to choose either Basic Installation or Advanced Installation.

5. Select the Advanced Installation option, and click the Next button.

6. On the Select Installation Type screen, choose the installation type based on what you are licensed for at your environment. The majority of the customers will choose Enterprise Edition (3.18GB). If you want to customize the product to be installed, choose the Custom radio button.

7. Click the Next button.

   On the Install Location screen, your ORACLE_BASE field should already be populated. If you did not specify the $ORACLE_BASE environment variable prior to the installation, it will be set to the HOME directory of the Oracle user.

8. Set ORACLE_BASE to /apps/oracle (if you want to modify it).

9. Specify a name for your ORACLE_HOME. For example, enter **11gASMHome**.

10. Set the path for the ORACLE_HOME. For example, enter **/apps/oracle/product/11.1.0/ASM**.

11. Click the Next button.

12. On the Product-Specific Prerequisite Checks screen, the Oracle Universal Installer will validate that the minimum system requirements for installing Oracle Database 11*g* including the kernel parameters, swap space requirements, physical memory, glibc version, package requirements, PATH and LD_LIBRARY_PATH environment variable checks, validation of the Oracle base location, and network configuration requirements. You should correct all the errors on this screen. After all the issues are resolved, the very last line should read as follows:

    Check complete. The overall result of this check is: Passed.

13. Once you pass the system requirement checks, click the Next button.

14. On the Select Configuration Option screen, you have the option to create a starter database, configure ASM, or install software only. Choose the Install Software Only option, and click the Next button.

15. On the Privileged Operating System Groups screen, you will see the options to set the sysdba and sysoper privileges you're familiar with. Oracle now recommends you create the new system privilege called sysasm for enabling the management of ASM. Oracle also recommends you create a new Unix/Linux group, called asmadmin, for ASM administrators. Your screen should resemble Figure 12-1.

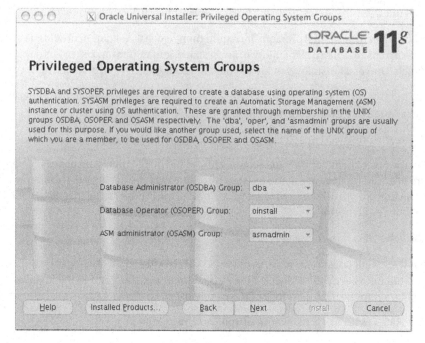

Figure 12-1. *Privileged Operating Systems Groups screen*

16. Click the Next button to be routed to the Summary screen. On the Summary screen, the Oracle Universal Installer summarizes the components of the installation. Review the software components, and click the Install button.

17. On the Install page, you'll see the progress of the installation. Once the installation finishes successfully, as root, execute root.sh, and accept all default options.

18. Navigate back to the Oracle Universal Installer, and exit it by first clicking Exit and then clicking Yes.

19. As root, execute localconfig add from the $ORACLE_HOME/bin directory. Executing the localconfig add command will create the Oracle Cluster Registry (OCR) keys, copy scripts to the /etc/init.d and /etc/rc directories, and initialize the Clusterware Synchronization Services (CSS) daemon (which is a lightweight, scaled-down version of the Oracle Clusterware software). The output of this script should look like this:

```
/apps/oracle/product/11.1.0/ASM/bin
[root@rac3 bin]# ./localconfig add
Successfully accumulated necessary OCR keys.
Creating OCR keys for user 'root', privgrp 'root'..
Operation successful.
Configuration for local CSS has been initialized
```

```
Cleaning up Network socket directories
Setting up Network socket directories
Adding to inittab
Startup will be queued to init within 30 seconds.
Checking the status of new Oracle init process...
Expecting the CRS daemons to be up within 600 seconds.
Cluster Synchronization Services is active on these nodes.
        rac3
Cluster Synchronization Services is active on all the nodes.
Oracle CSS service is installed and running under init(1M)
```

Once this script executes successfully, you will be able to create an ASM instance in a non-RAC environment. The CSS services must be up in order for the database instances to be able to communicate with the ASM instance. For RAC environments, this step is not needed since the CSS daemon is started as part of the cluster.

To check to see whether the CSS daemon is up and running, you can use the `crsctl` command from the $ORACLE_HOME/bin directory:

```
+ASM > ./crsctl check cssd
Cluster Synchronization Services appears healthy
```

How It Works

The ASM software is the same set of binaries that's installed with the Oracle Database Home. You do not have to create a separate Oracle Home for ASM, and in fact, you can optionally share the same binaries from the Oracle Database Home. However, we strongly recommend installing the ASM binaries to a separate Oracle Home rather than sharing the binaries from the Oracle Database Home.

You should separate the Oracle database software binaries from your ASM software binaries, for several compelling reasons. The primary reason for separating the Database Home from the ASM Home is to be able to apply patches without disturbing all the databases that share the same Oracle Home. Starting in Oracle Database 11g, you can perform rolling upgrades for ASM. The ability to perform rolling upgrades is available only for Oracle Database 11g and newer databases.

12-12. Creating the ASM Instance

Problem

All the disks are set up using ASMLIB or as block devices. You want to create the ASM instance.

Solution

Basically, you can create the ASM instance in two ways: by setting up Database Control using the Database Configuration Assistant (DBCA) or by creating an initialization file and manually starting the instance. This recipe will focus on how to create an ASM instance from the operating system command-line interface. To start the ASM instance, set up the initialization file or spfile located in the $ORACLE_HOME/dbs directory. You can set up the ASM instance by simply creating a file $ORACLE_HOME/dbs/init+ASM.ora for a stand-alone non-RAC implementation. Here's a sample initialization file:

```
###############################################################################
# ASM Init.ora parameter
###############################################################################

###########################################
# Diagnostics and Statistics
###########################################
background_dump_dest=/apps/oracle/admin/+ASM/bdump
core_dump_dest=/apps/oracle/admin/+ASM/cdump
user_dump_dest=/apps/oracle/admin/+ASM/udump

###############################################
# Instanct Type
# There are two possible instance types:
# ASM or RDBMS (regular database)
###############################################
instance_type=asm

###############################################
# Pools
###############################################
large_pool_size=12M

###############################################
# Security
###############################################
remote_login_passwordfile=exclusive

#  The default asm_diskstring is null
#  A null asm_diskstring actually specifies the combination of
#    '/dev/raw/*' and 'ORCL:*' values
#asm_diskstring='/dev/raw/raw*','/dev/sdc*'

#  When you first start your ASM instance, you should specify the asm_diskgroup
#  with a null value.  If you have two diskgroups such as DATA and FRA, you need
#  to separate them with commas enclosed by single apostrophes
#  Here's an example:
#  asm_diskgroups='DATA','FRA'
#asm_diskgroups=''
```

To start the ASM instance, you connect with the SQL*Plus tool using the sysasm role. To connect to the ASM instance, you would simply type the following:

```
sqlplus / as sysasm
```

Note In Oracle Database 10*g*, you would log on to the ASM instance using `sqlplus / as sysdba`. For ASM, the `sysdba` role is deprecated in Oracle Database 11*g*. You can continue to log on using the `sysdba` role, but error messages in the alert log file will appear indicating that the `sysdba` role is deprecated.

Once you have connected using SQL*Plus, you can issue the command `startup nomount` or `startup mount`. The `startup mount` command will result in an error because the initialization parameter file does not have the `asm_diskgroups` parameter set.

How It Works

Simply stated, the ASM instance is composed of memory structures and background processes similar to the logical volume manager daemons. The ASM instance is configured using the initialization file and has background processes that make it appear like a database instance. Contrary to what many DBAs believe, the ASM instance does not have a database to write records to. What differentiates an ASM instance from a database instance is the `INSTANCE_TYPE` initialization parameter. Two acceptable values for the `INSTANCE_TYPE` parameter are ASM and RDBMS.

The primary background processes that make up the ASM instance include the following:

- ARBn is responsible for performing the rebalance of data extents by moving extents. There can be numerous ARB0, ARB1, and so on, processes running at one time.

- ASMB (ASM background) primarily runs on the database instance that has one or more open ASM diskgroups. ASMB also runs on the ASM instances and manages storage and provides statistics.

- GMON is the diskgroup monitor and maintains disk memberships in the ASM diskgroups.

- RBAL (ASM rebalance master) runs on both database and ASM instances. RBAL performs a global open of ASM disks for the database instances. RBAL also coordinates rebalance activity for diskgroups on the ASM instance.

In addition to these background processes, the ASM instance also runs the standard database background processes, database writer process (DBWn), log writer process (LGWR), Process Monitor process (PMON), and System Monitor process (SMON).

12-13. Connecting to a Remote ASM Instance

Problem

You want to log in and manage an ASM instance on a remote server. You do not want to have to log on to remote servers to manage your ASM instances.

Solution

You can connect to a remote node's ASM instance using SQL*Plus. You can connect using Oracle's so-called easy connect naming method. The easy connect naming method does not require an entry in the TNSNAMES.ORA file. Here's how you can connect to an ASM instance using the easy connect naming method:

```
$ sqlplus /nolog

SQL*Plus: Release 11.1.0.6.0 - Production on Mon Oct 6 22:53:10 2008

Copyright (c) 1982, 2007, Oracle.  All rights reserved.

SQL> connect sys/oracle123@rac3:1521/+ASM AS SYSASM
Connected.
SQL>
```

The syntax for the easy connect naming method is as follows:

```
CONNECT username/password@host[:port][/service_name]
```

Note If your SQL*Plus client or target ASM instance is Oracle Database 10*g*, you must specify the connection with the "as sysdba" syntax since the sysasm role is available starting in Oracle Database 11*g*.

Once you are connected as sys on the ASM instance through the sysasm role, you can perform all the maintenance tasks as if you were connected locally. You can perform maintenance tasks such as mounting diskgroups:

```
SQL> alter diskgroup data mount;

Diskgroup altered.

SQL> alter diskgroup fra mount;

Diskgroup altered.
```

How It Works

You can log on remotely to another ASM instance if the password file is set up correctly on the remote ASM instance. You must set up the password file using the orapwd executable from the $ORACLE_HOME/bin directory. The orapwd executable writes the file to the $ORACLE_HOME/dbs directory if the file name does not have a fully qualified path to the location of the password file. The following example creates a password file with the password of oracle123 for the sys user account:

```
$ > orapwd file=orapw+ASM entries=25 ignorecase=true password=oracle123
```

The ignorecase option is a new feature for Oracle Database 11*g* that specifies whether the passwords can be case sensitive. A value of true specifies that the password will revert to the Oracle Database 10*g* specification, making the passwords case insensitive. In addition to the password file, the ASM instance must be participating as a service on the local database listener.

12-14. Creating an ASM Diskgroup

Problem

You want to create a diskgroup based on the disks that are allocated to the database server.

Solution

You can create a diskgroup called DATA using the ASMLIB disks. The create diskgroup syntax looks like this:

```
SQL> create diskgroup data
  2  external redundancy
  3  disk
  4  'ORCL:DATA1', 'ORCL:DATA2',
  5  'ORCL:DATA3', 'ORCL:DATA4';

Diskgroup created.
```

Notice the reference to the ORCL:DATA1 to ORCL:DATA4 disks. Remember that ASMLIB disk names start with ORCL:. If you have not set up ASMLIB disks, you can qualify the block device names instead. The syntax to create the DATA diskgroup using block device names resembles something like this:

```
  1  create diskgroup PRDATA external redundancy
  2  disk
  3  '/dev/sdc1', '/dev/sdc2',
  4* '/dev/sdc3', '/dev/sdc4'
SQL> /

Diskgroup created.
```

Once the ASM diskgroup(s) are created, please make sure to modify the ASM_DISKGROUPS initialization parameter so that the diskgroup will automount when the ASM instance is started.

How It Works

A diskgroup is a logical collection of disks and is equivalent to the LVM's volume group. An ASM's filesystem layer exists within the diskgroup. There are three kinds of ASM diskgroups: external redundancy (no redundancy at the ASM layer), normal redundancy (mirroring by ASM), and high redundancy (triple mirroring or twice mirroring by ASM). Normal and high redundancy requires additional disk space. Normal redundancy requires double the amount of raw disk space. The amount of usable space will equate to exactly half the allocated raw space. Similar logic applies to high redundancy. With high redundancy, you will have to provide triple the amount of raw disk space.

When you define a diskgroup and specify the keywords external redundancy, you are telling ASM that you are relying on your storage array to provide disk protection. All SAN arrays nowadays support the common protection levels that are widely used in the database community: RAID 1 (mirroring) and RAID 5 (parity-bit protection).

Normal and high redundancies require failure groups to be set up. Failure groups can be on the local SAN array or on a separate SAN array. Failure groups can also be on different SAN arrays too. For example, the primary diskgroup can be on an EMC Symmetrix, while the failure group can be on a Hitachi USP 1000. With Oracle Database 11*g* preferred read capability, the failure groups can also be located miles away at the remote site. Each site can read a local copy of the failure group instead of having to go across the WAN. This technology will greatly enhance what is known in the RAC community as *stretch clusters*. The syntax to create a diskgroup with normal redundancy is slightly different. The code example here uses the keywords normal redundancy and failgroup to specify additional mirrored disks:

```
1  create diskgroup nrdata
2  normal redundancy
3    failgroup fg1 disk
4      'ORCL:NRDATA1A' name ndata1a,
5      'ORCL:NRDATA1B' name ndata1b
6    failgroup fg2 disk
7      'ORCL:NRDATA2A' name nrdata2a,
8*     'ORCL:NRDATA2B' name nrdata2b
SQL> /

Diskgroup created.
```

The majority of the ASM implementations can be managed by two diskgroups, one for data and the other for the flash recovery area (FRA). When different hard drive speeds or different-sized disks or LUNs are introduced, you will have to create additional diskgroups. You should never mix different-sized disks or a different speed of disks in the same diskgroup. When you have multiple RAID levels, you will have additional diskgroups. For example, you should not mix RAID 5 with RAID 1 or RAID 5 with RAID 1+0 in a single diskgroup. You should place all RAID 5 disks in their own diskgroup and all RAID 1+0 disks on their own diskgroup.

Having two diskgroups provides you with the level of protection you need. The controlfiles should be placed on both the DATA and FRA diskgroups. Online redo logs should also be multiplexed in the DATA and FRA diskgroups. The FRA diskgroup can be designated for archive logs, flashback logs, and backup area. The DATA diskgroup can house all the data and index datafiles. Since ASM provides even I/O distribution, you do not have to worry about placing the datafiles on a separate filesystem or diskgroup and placing the index datafiles on a separate filesystem or diskgroup.

12-15. Adding Disks to an Existing Diskgroup

Problem

Your monitoring scripts or Grid Control sends you an alert that the DATA diskgroup is about to run out of space. You need to add space to the DATA diskgroup.

Solution

Adding disk space to an existing diskgroup is straightforward using the alter diskgroup command, as shown here:

```
1  alter diskgroup fra
2  add disk
3  'ORCL:FRA3', 'ORCL:FRA4'
4* rebalance power 11 wait
SQL> /

Diskgroup altered.
```

How It Works

Executing the alter diskgroup command, you specify the new disks that you want to add to an existing diskgroup. The last line (line 4) becomes an important line if you are dealing with a very large database (VLDB). If you are adding large amount of disk space, we recommend you shut down the ASM instance and manually force the rebalance of extents using a power limit setting of 5 or greater. The power limit setting specifies the intensity of the disk extent rebalancing. The default setting for the power limit parameter is 1. The higher the power limit setting, the more CPU and I/O utilization will be noticed on your server. The last option, wait, specifies to ASM not to relinquish control back to the client until the rebalance activity is done. If you add multiple terabytes to an existing diskgroup, the rebalance activity can take up to half a day or more.

12-16. Dropping an ASM Diskgroup

Problem

You realized that you created too many diskgroups. You want to drop the diskgroup called FRA2 because you already have a diskgroup designated as the flashback recovery area and want to reallocate the dropped disks to other diskgroups or to other ASM instances.

Solution

To drop an existing diskgroup, you simply execute the drop diskgroup command, as shown here, with the diskgroup name:

```
SQL> drop diskgroup fra2;

Diskgroup dropped.
```

How It Works

If the diskgroup you are attempting to drop has database files, you must specify the including contents clause. In Oracle Database 11g, you can specify the drop diskgroup command with the force option if not all the disks in the diskgroup are available.

12-17. Invoking the ASM Command Shell

Problem

You want to invoke the ASM command shell and look inside ASM.

Solution

You must satisfy two requirements to be able to connect to asmcmd in interactive mode. First, your ORACLE_SID must point to a valid ASM instance such as +ASM or +ASM# for RAC implementations. In a RAC environment, you will have one ASM instance per RAC node. The first RAC node will call the ASM instance +ASM1; the second ASM instance will be called +ASM2. Second, your ORACLE_HOME must point to an ORACLE_HOME that houses the asmcmd executable. To connect to the asmcmd command-line interface, you simply type asmcmd from the operating system. asmcmd has one special parameter, the -p parameter, which is equivalent to the PS1 environment variable in Linux.

Let's connect to the ASM instance using asmcmd. If not already, you should have the +ASM instance entry in the /etc/oratab file that looks something like this:

```
+ASM:/apps/oracle/product/11.1.0/ASM:Y
```

You can source the oraenv file and change your environment to the +ASM instance, as shown here:

```
$ . oraenv
ORACLE_SID = [DBATOOLS] ? +ASM
$
```

Now that your environment variables point to the +ASM instance, you can connect to the ASM instance using the asmcmd shell. Using the -p option, you will connect to the ASM instance:

```
$ asmcmd -p
ASMCMD [+] >
```

How It Works

As the ASM administrator, you do not want to have to log in to SQL*Plus or have to log in to Grid Control to view ASM disk or diskgroup information. In addition, you want to maximize your usage of the ASM command shell, which is invoked through the asmcmd command.

Note You can create an alias, asmcmd='asmcmd -p', so that every time you type asmcmd, the -p option will always be set.

12-18. Displaying Online Manual Pages

Problem

You want to leverage what is equivalent to Unix man pages for ASM commands.

Solution

You can display the online manual pages with the help command at the ASMCMD [+] > prompt. The output of the help command will list all the commands available for the asmcmd command-line interface, as shown here:

```
ASMCMD [+] > help
        asmcmd [-v] [-a <sysasm|sysdba>] [-p] [command]

        The environment variables ORACLE_HOME and ORACLE_SID determine the
        instance to which the program connects, and ASMCMD establishes a
        bequeath connection to it, in the same manner as a SQLPLUS / AS
        SYSDBA.  The user must be a member of the SYSDBA group.

        [...]

        Type "help [command]" to get help on a specific ASMCMD command.

        commands:
        --------
        help

        cd
        cp
        du
        find
        ls
        lsct
        lsdg
        mkalias
        mkdir
        pwd
        rm
        rmalias

        md_backup
        md_restore

        lsdsk
        remap
```

The help command without any other parameters will list all the commands available to the asmcmd utility. You can pass a parameter, the command you want help on, to the help command. For example, let's obtain some help on the rm command:

```
ASMCMD [+] > help rm
        rm [-rf] <name1 name2 . . .>

        If <nameN> is an empty directory, then rm removes it.  It is equivalent
        to ALTER DISKGROUP <dg_name> DROP DIRECTORY <name1, name2, . . .> in
        SQL.  Note that rm cannot remove system-created or non-empty
        directories.  Otherwise, rm treats <nameN> as files and deletes them,
        removing both system-created filenames and user-defined aliases.
        It is equivalent to ALTER DISKGROUP <dg_name> DROP FILE
        <name1, name2, . . .> in SQL.

        If using a wildcard, then rm deletes all matches with the exception
        of system-created directories and non-empty directories.

        If using the -r flag, then all entries under the specified <nameN> are
        deleted recursively.  Note that rm does not specifically issue the
        DROP DIRECTORY SQL command to drop system-created directories.  However,
        these are removed automatically by ASM once they are empty.

        If using the -r flag or wildcard matching, then rm prompts the user to
        confirm the deletion before proceeding, unless the user also specifies
        the -f flag.

        Warning!  Removing an user-defined alias removes the system-created
        filename as well, and vice versa.  This rule applies even when you
        use wildcard or the -r option!  The wildcard needs to match only one
        of the two, and both are deleted.  For -r, only one of the two needs
        to be under the directory to be deleted, and both are deleted.

        For instance, if you have an user-defined alias "+dg/dir1/file.alias"
        that points to "+dg/ORCL/DATAFILE/System.256.1", doing a
        "rm -r +dg1/dir1" will remove System.256.1 as well, even though it
        is not technically under "+dg/dir1".
```

How It Works

The help command is similar to the man pages available in the Unix operating system. You can obtain help for just about every command available in the asmcmd command-line interface. The asmcmd command-line interface is similar to the Korn shell or Bourne Again shell (Bash). Lots of the commands that are available in the Unix shell are available in the asmcmd command-line interface. Although not complete in terms of providing a shell access, asmcmd does provide a substantial amount of interaction to the ASM filesystem. Table 12-1 lists the majority of the commands provided by asmcmd.

Table 12-1. *ASM Commands*

Command	Description
cd	Changes the current directory to the specified directory.
du	Displays the total disk space occupied by ASM files in the specified ASM directory and all its subdirectories, recursively.
find	Lists the paths of all occurrences of the specified name (with wildcards) under the specified directory.
ls +data/testdb	Lists the contents of an ASM directory, the attributes of the specified file, or the names and attributes of all diskgroups.
lsct	Lists information about current ASM clients.
lsdg	Lists all diskgroups and their attributes.
mkalias	Creates an alias for a system-generated file name.
mkdir	Creates ASM directories.
pwd	Displays the path of the current ASM directory.
rm rm -f	Deletes the specified ASM files or directories. The -f option is to force delete a file. The -rf command is used similarly to how you would perform a recursive delete to delete all the files/subdirectories of a directory.
rmalias	Deletes the specified alias, retaining the file to which the alias points.
lsdsk	Lists disks visible to ASM.
md_backup	Creates a metadata backup of all the mounted diskgroups.
md_restore	Restores diskgroups from a backup.
mkalias	Creates an alias for system-generated file names.
remap	Repairs a range of physical blocks on a disk.
cp	Copies files into and out of ASM: ASM diskgroup to OS filesystem OS filesystem to ASM diskgroup ASM diskgroup to another ASM diskgroup on the same server ASM disk group to ASM diskgroup on a remote server

12-19. Removing Files or Directories for a Database with asmcmd

Problem

You want to delete database files or directories from the asmcmd command-line interface.

Solution

You can remove database files or directories using the rm command. Here's an rm example to delete all the files associated with the DBADEV database:

```
ASMCMD> cd +data
ASMCMD> rm -rf DBADEV
ASMCMD> cd +fra
ASMCMD> rm -rf DBADEV
```

The rm command also accepts wildcards to delete files or directories. In the next example, you will see in action the rm command prompting a response from the administrator while deleting a file with a wildcard:

```
ASMCMD [+data/dbatools/datafile] > ls
TOOLS.270.655646559
docs_d_01.dbf
ASMCMD [+data/dbatools/datafile] > rm docs*
You may delete multiple files and/or directories.
Are you sure? (y/n) y
```

How It Works

The rm command in asmcmd is similar to the rm command in the Unix operating system. You can specify the -f option to force delete files. Similarly to the Unix counterpart command, you can specify the -r option to remove subdirectories.

Note The rm command is particularly important when you run out of space in the archivelog destination. You can cd to the archivelog destination and remove old or backed-up archivelogs from the ASM instance. Here's another way to delete all the archive logs for a specific day and for a specific thread from the operating system:

```
asmcmd rm +DATA/DBATOOLS/archivelog/2008_03_10/thread_1*
```

12-20. Reviewing Disk Usage with asmcmd

Problem

You want to review ASM diskgroup disk space usage from the asmcmd command-line interface.

Solution

Another useful command in the asmcmd command-line interface is the du command. The du command will display the disk usage information for a specified directory. For example, if you want to know how much space is consumed for the DBATOOLS database in the +DATA diskgroup, you can view that information like this:

```
ASMCMD [+] > du +data/dbatools
Used_MB      Mirror_used_MB
    102              102
```

You can specify the full path of the subdirectory with the du command to determine the sizes of the tempfile(s) for a database, the size of all the datafiles for a database, or the size of the controlfile(s) for a database. In the following examples, the du command checks the size of the tempfiles, datafiles, and controlfile in the +DATA diskgroup:

```
ASMCMD [+data/dbadev] > du +data/dbadev/tempfile
Used_MB      Mirror_used_MB
   4002               4002

ASMCMD [+data/dbadev] > du +data/dbadev/datafile
Used_MB      Mirror_used_MB
   6312               6312

ASMCMD [+data/dbadev] > du +data/dbadev/controlfile
Used_MB      Mirror_used_MB
     24                 24
```

How It Works

The du command reports the total space used for files in a specified directory. The default is the current directory. The command reports two values: the megabytes of used space and the megabytes of used space in a normal or high redundancy diskgroup. If you have implemented the external redundancy, the values from both of these columns will always be the same.

12-21. Locating Files in ASM with asmcmd

Problem

You want to search for files in a directory structure from the asmcmd command-line interface.

Solution

You can exploit the find command in the ASM command-line interface to search for files. The find command has the following pattern:

```
find [-t <type>] <dir> <pattern>
```

The -t option specifies the type of file and is queried from the TYPE column in the V$ASM_FILE view. You can also specify the starting directory for the find command to search from. The last option is the pattern for the find command to match on. You can use either the percent sign (%) or the asterisk (*) as a wildcard character. Let's take a look at the find command to locate all the files in the data diskgroup that have the file names sys somewhere in the file name:

```
ASMCMD [+] > find -t datafile +data *sys*
+data/DBADEV/DATAFILE/SYSAUX.257.655588275
+data/DBADEV/DATAFILE/SYSTEM.258.655588211
```

If you want to locate all the online redo logs in the +DATA diskgroups, you can use the -t option and specify onlinelog as the parameter with the * wildcard for the pattern, as shown here:

```
ASMCMD [+] > find -t onlinelog +data *
+data/DBADEV/ONLINELOG/group_1.264.655587995
+data/DBADEV/ONLINELOG/group_2.263.655588025
+data/DBADEV/ONLINELOG/group_3.262.655588055
+data/DBADEV/ONLINELOG/group_4.261.655588099
+data/DBADEV/ONLINELOG/group_5.260.655588129
+data/DBADEV/ONLINELOG/group_6.259.655588177
```

You can use the find command to locate all the files associated with a database for a given diskgroup. You can specify a subdirectory to the find command with a wildcard for the pattern, as you can see here:

```
find +data/DBADEV %
```

How It Works

The find command is a powerful utility in the Unix arena and is also a powerful command in the asmcmd command-line interface. The find command in the asmcmd command-line interface does not have all the options you will find in Unix. The -t option for the find command allows you to search for types of files. To see all the types of files, you can query for distinct values from the TYPE column in the V$ASM_FILE view.

12-22. Listing Currently Connected Clients

Problem

You want to list all the databases connected to the ASM instance.

Solution

You can execute the lsct command in the ASM command interface to view all the database clients. In the example here, you can see that the DBATOOLS and DBADEV databases are connected to the ASM instance:

```
ASMCMD [+] > lsct -g
Instance_ID  DB_Name   Status      Software_Version  Compatible_version
   Instance_Name  Disk_Group
        1  DBADEV    CONNECTED      11.1.0.6.0         11.1.0.0.0  DBADEV
       DATA
        1  DBADEV    CONNECTED      11.1.0.6.0         11.1.0.0.0  DBADEV
       FRA
        1  DBATOOLS  CONNECTED      11.1.0.6.0         11.1.0.0.0  DBATOOLS
       DATA
```

How It Works

Another important command worth mentioning is the lsct command. The lsct command lists all the clients connected to the ASM instance. If you are in a RAC environment, you can use the -g option to list the instance number of the RAC instances.

12-23. Retrieving Diskgroup Information with asmcmd

Problem

You want to view the diskgroup properties of an ASM instance from the asmcmd command-line interface.

Solution

The lsdg command will list all the diskgroup information from the V$ASM_DISKGROUP view. The -g parameter, available in Oracle Database 11g, will list the instance ID information, as shown here:

```
ASMCMD [+] > lsdg -g
Inst_ID  State     Type    Rebal  Sector  Block       AU  Total_MB  Free_MB
  Req_mir_free_MB  Usable_file_MB  Offline_disks  Name
      1  MOUNTED   EXTERN  N         512    4096  1048576     61056    48729
               0           48729                0  DATA/
      1  MOUNTED   EXTERN  N         512    4096  1048576     61056    59169
               0           59169                0  FRA/
```

How It Works

The lsdg command lists all diskgroups and their attributes. The lsdg command can be an important ally when you are looking for space utilization information. The lsdg command also provides a Rebal column to inform the DBAs if a rebalance activity is taking place. The information produced from the lsdg command is extracted from the V$ASM_DISKGROUP_STAT or V$ASM_DISKGROUP view.

12-24. Retrieving Disk Information with asmcmd

Problem

You want to view all the disk properties of an ASM instance from the asmcmd command-line interface.

Solution

Starting in Oracle Database 11g, you can utilize the lsdsk command to list the disks available for an ASM instance. Here's the output of the lsdsk command without any parameters:

```
ASMCMD [+] > lsdsk
Path
ORCL:DATA1
ORCL:DATA2
ORCL:DATA3
ORCL:DATA4
ORCL:FRA1
ORCL:FRA2
ORCL:FRA3
ORCL:FRA4
```

If you type lsdsk without any parameters, the output will display all the disks in the ASM instance. In the next example, you can specify a -d option to limit the output to a specific diskgroup:

```
ASMCMD [+] > lsdsk -d data
Path
ORCL:DATA1
ORCL:DATA2
ORCL:DATA3
ORCL:DATA4
```

The -k option displays the TOTAL_MB, NAME, FAILGROUP, and PATH column information from the V$ASM_DISK view in the output:

```
ASMCMD [+] > lsdsk -k
Total_MB  Free_MB  OS_MB  Name   Failgroup  Library
                   Label  UDID   Product  Redund    Path
   15264    12180  15264  DATA1  DATA1        ASM Library - Generic Linux, version
2.0.2 (KABI_V2)  DATA1                 UNKNOWN  ORCL:DATA1
   15264    12184  15264  DATA2  DATA2        ASM Library - Generic Linux, version
2.0.2 (KABI_V2)  DATA2                 UNKNOWN  ORCL:DATA2
   15264    12184  15264  DATA3  DATA3        ASM Library - Generic Linux, version
2.0.2 (KABI_V2)  DATA3                 UNKNOWN  ORCL:DATA3
   15264    12181  15264  DATA4  DATA4        ASM Library - Generic Linux, version
2.0.2 (KABI_V2)  DATA4                 UNKNOWN  ORCL:DATA4
   15264    14791  15264  FRA1   FRA1         ASM Library - Generic Linux, version
2.0.2 (KABI_V2)  FRA1                  UNKNOWN  ORCL:FRA1
   15264    14795  15264  FRA2   FRA2         ASM Library - Generic Linux, version
2.0.2 (KABI_V2)  FRA2                  UNKNOWN  ORCL:FRA2
   15264    14790  15264  FRA3   FRA3         ASM Library - Generic Linux, version
2.0.2 (KABI_V2)  FRA3                  UNKNOWN  ORCL:FRA3
   15264    14793  15264  FRA4   FRA4         ASM Library - Generic Linux, version
2.0.2 (KABI_V2)  FRA4                  UNKNOWN  ORCL:FRA4
```

The -t option provides important information in terms of when the disk was added to the diskgroup, when it was mounted, how long the repair timer is, and the path of the disk. Here's an output of the lsdsk command with the -t option:

```
ASMCMD [+] > lsdsk -t
Create_Date  Mount_Date  Repair_Timer  Path
24-MAY-08    25-MAY-08   0             ORCL:DATA1
24-MAY-08    25-MAY-08   0             ORCL:DATA2
24-MAY-08    25-MAY-08   0             ORCL:DATA3
24-MAY-08    25-MAY-08   0             ORCL:DATA4
24-MAY-08    25-MAY-08   0             ORCL:FRA1
24-MAY-08    25-MAY-08   0             ORCL:FRA2
24-MAY-08    25-MAY-08   0             ORCL:FRA3
24-MAY-08    25-MAY-08   0             ORCL:FRA4
```

You can take advantage of the -s option to view statistical information about each of the disks. You can view read time, write time, bytes read, and bytes written to at the disk level. You can correlate the output from the -s option to find busy disks. Here's an output of the lsdsk command with the -s option:

```
ASMCMD [+] > lsdsk -s
Reads   Write  Read_Errs  Write_Errs  Read_time  Write_Time  Bytes_Read
Bytes_Written  Path
 2790   1622          0           0     14.507      5.644     27713536
ORCL:DATA1
 2614    754          0           0     13.302      5.912     30078976
ORCL:DATA2
 3959   1694          0           0     10.938      8.385     51269632
ORCL:DATA3
 4539    869          0           0     12.748      6.782     64300544
ORCL:DATA4
  700   1015          0           0       .696      2.312      2864128
ORCL:FRA1
  688    347          0           0       .636      2.361      2814464
ORCL:FRA2
  702    336          0           0       .819      4.097      2871808
ORCL:FRA3
  692    263          0           0       .767      2.135      2823680
ORCL:FRA4
```

How It Works

The lsdsk command lists all the visible disks for an ASM instance and is new to Oracle Database 11g. Valid options for lsdsk are as follows:

```
lsdsk [-ksptcgHI] [-d <diskgroup_name>] [pattern]
```

The pattern keyword restricts the output to only those disks that match the pattern. Wild-card characters and slashes (/ or \) can be part of the pattern.

12-25. Migrating to ASM from the Filesystem

Problem

Your company decided to standardize on ASM. Now, you want to migrate to ASM in as painless and safe a way as possible.

Solution #1 (Preferred)

Two options are available to migrate from the filesystem to ASM. The first method, and the one we recommend, involves using RMAN and is applicable to Oracle Database 10g. Oracle Database 10g updated the copy command to be able to back up at the database level. Instead of copying files or tablespaces, you can back up the entire database using the backup as copy database syntax.

Note The `backup as copy` command is available starting in Oracle Database 10*g*. For Oracle 9*i*, you can use the `copy` command to make image copies at the tablespace and datafile levels. The `copy` command has been deprecated as of Oracle Database 10*g* in favor of the new `backup as copy` command. The new `backup as copy` syntax allows the DBAs to make images copies at the database level.

You can specify the format to the location of the diskgroup while allocating a channel to the data disk group. The following code example demonstrates how to perform an image copy of the database to the DATA diskgroup:

```
RMAN> @backup_copy_asm.sql
RMAN> run
2> {
3> allocate channel d1 type disk format '+data';
4> backup as copy database;
5> release channel d1;
6> }
allocated channel: d1
channel d1: SID=154 device type=DISK

Starting backup at 12-MAY-08
channel d1: starting datafile copy
input datafile file number=00001 name=/data/oracle/DBATOOLS/system01.dbf
output file name=+DATA/dbatools/datafile/system.256.654520605
tag=TAG20080512T111635 RECID=2 STAMP=654520833
channel d1: datafile copy complete, elapsed time: 00:03:56
channel d1: starting datafile copy
[…]
input datafile file number=00004 name=/data/oracle/DBATOOLS/users01.dbf
output file name=+DATA/dbatools/datafile/users.261.654521041
tag=TAG20080512T111635 RECID=7 STAMP=654521042
channel d1: datafile copy complete, elapsed time: 00:00:01
Finished backup at 12-MAY-08

released channel: d1

RMAN>
RMAN> **end-of-file**
```

After the successful database backup, you must update the controlfile to point to the new location of the datafiles. The easiest way to update the controlfile is to use the `switch` command, as shown here:

```
RMAN> switch database to copy;
datafile 1 switched to datafile copy "+DATA/dbatools/datafile/system.256.654520605"
[..]
datafile 5 switched to datafile copy "+DATA/dbatools/datafile/example.258.654521005"
```

Although you successfully migrated the database files to ASM, your work is not complete yet. You still have controlfiles, temporary tablespaces, and online redo logs to migrate to ASM. Again, you have two options to migrate the controlfile to ASM:

- Rebuilding the controlfile from trace

- Restoring the controlfile using RMAN

■**Note** Using RMAN is the recommended approach to migrating the controlfiles to ASM. In this chapter, we will demonstrate how you can migrate controlfiles to ASM using RMAN.

To start the migration of controlfiles to ASM, you need to shut down the database and restart the instance in nomount mode. Once the database is up in nomount mode, you will perform the restore twice, once to the DATA diskgroup and the second time to the FRA diskgroup, as shown here:

```
RMAN> restore controlfile to '+data' from '/data/oracle/DBATOOLS/control01.ctl';
RMAN> restore controlfile to '+fra' from '/data/oracle/DBATOOLS/control01.ctl';
Starting restore at 12-MAY-08
using channel ORA_DISK_1

channel ORA_DISK_1: copied control file copy
Finished restore at 12-MAY-08
```

Restoring the controlfiles to the two alternate locations adheres to ASM best practices and provides additional redundancy.

Notice that the RMAN output does not include the location of the restored controlfiles. To locate the controlfiles, leverage the asmcmd command-line interface, execute the find command, and traverse through the +DATA and +FRA diskgroups to find the controlfile types using the -t option, as shown here:

```
ASMCMD> find -t controlfile + *
+DATA/DBATOOLS/CONTROLFILE/current.260.654527045
+FRA/DBATOOLS/CONTROLFILE/current.256.654527065
```

■**Note** The -t option specifies the type of file. The + sign indicates the command to start from the root directory. The + by itself is equivalent to doing a find /.

You located the controlfiles in ASM, so now you must modify either the init.ora file or the spfile file. Either way, the CONTROL_FILES initialization parameter must reflect the changes, as you see here:

```
control_files='+DATA/DBATOOLS/CONTROLFILE/current.260.654527045',
              '+FRA/DBATOOLS/CONTROLFILE/current.256.654527065'
```

Once you make the necessary change, you must bounce the database for the changes to take effect. Once the database is available, you can confirm the new location of the controlfiles:

```
SQL> show parameter control_file
```

NAME	TYPE	VALUE
control_file_record_keep_time	integer	7
control_files	string	+DATA/dbatools/controlfile/cur rent.260.654527045, +FRA/dbato ols/controlfile/current.256.65 4527065

The next task will be to move the temporary tablespace to ASM. The steps involved in moving the temp tablespace are relatively straightforward:

1. Create a staging temp tablespace (temp2).

2. Set the new database default to the staging temp directory (temp2).

3. Drop the original temp tablespace (temp).

4. Create the original temp tablespace in ASM (temp).

5. Set the new database default to temp.

6. Drop the staging temp tablespace.

You can use the following code example to migrate your temp tablespace from the operating system to ASM:

```
create temporary tablespace temp2 tempfile '+data' size 4g autoextend on;
alter database default temporary tablespace temp2;
drop tablespace temp;
create temporary tablespace temp tempfile '+data' size 4g autoextend on;
alter database default temporary tablespace temp;
drop tablespace temp2;
```

Last but not least, you must move the online redo logs to ASM. To move the online redo logs, you can add log file groups, as shown here:

```
  1* alter database add logfile group 10 ('+data', '+fra') size 100m
SQL> /
```

Database altered.

Since you started with four redo groups, you need to create three more groups. You can repeat the alter database add logfile command three more times for group numbers 11, 12, and 13. Once the additional online redo logs are added, you can delete all the members that reside on the operating system filesystem. To find the group number to delete the online redo logs, you can query the V$LOGFILE dictionary view, as you see here:

```
  1* select group#, member from v$logfile
SQL> /

  GROUP# MEMBER
---------- -----------------------------------------------------------
       4 /data/oracle/DBATOOLS/redo04.log
       3 /data/oracle/DBATOOLS/redo03.log
       2 /data/oracle/DBATOOLS/redo02.log
       1 /data/oracle/DBATOOLS/redo01.log
      10 +DATA/dbatools/onlinelog/group_10.262.654528555
      10 +FRA/dbatools/onlinelog/group_10.257.654528555
      11 +DATA/dbatools/onlinelog/group_11.264.654528583
      11 +FRA/dbatools/onlinelog/group_11.258.654528583
      12 +DATA/dbatools/onlinelog/group_12.263.654528599
      12 +FRA/dbatools/onlinelog/group_12.259.654528599
      13 +DATA/dbatools/onlinelog/group_13.266.654528613
      13 +FRA/dbatools/onlinelog/group_13.260.654528623

12 rows selected.
```

Before you start dropping redo groups, switch through all the redo logs as displayed here:

```
alter system archive log current;
alter system switch logfile;

SQL> alter database drop logfile group 1;

Database altered.
```

Repeat the `alter database drop logfile` syntax for group numbers 2, 3, and 4. Now, everything is in ASM!

How It Works #1

RMAN continues to be the proven method to move datafiles in and out of ASM as of Oracle Database 11*g* Release 1. Although you can use the `DBMS_FILE_TRANSFER` PL/SQL APIs to move datafiles to ASM from the operating system, the PL/SQL APIs do not compare to the performance of RMAN. Additional options to move the datafiles to ASM include the WebDAV `ftp` and `http`. You can move the datafiles using either FTP or HTTP, but a staging database with XMLDB enabled must be online and must own all the database-related files. The newest approach, the `asmcmd` copy command (`cp`), is available starting in Oracle Database 11g. We will discuss the new `asmcmd cp` approach in the next section.

Solution #2

An alternative approach to migration is to use the `asmcmd` command-line interface to copy files from your operating system's filesystem into ASM. Your target directory in ASM will be +data/dbatools/datafile. Before starting the copy to the +data/dbatools/datafile directory, create the subdirectories, since you have not placed any files there yet.

```
ASMCMD [+data] > mkdir dbatools
ASMCMD [+data] > cd dbatools
ASMCMD [+data/dbatools] > mkdir datafile
```

Next, you will copy the docs_d_01.dbf file to the DATA diskgroup after you put the docs_d tablespace offline. You will start by offlining the docs_d tablespace:

```
SQL> alter tablespace docs_d offline;
```

Tablespace altered.

Next, you will copy the docs_d_01.dbf file from the operating system to the +data diskgroup:

```
ASMCMD [+] > cp '/data/oracle/DBATOOLS/docs_d_01.dbf' '+data/dbatools/datafile'
source /data/oracle/DBATOOLS/docs_d_01.dbf
target +data/dbatools/datafile/docs_d_01.dbf
copying file(s)...
copying file(s)...
copying file(s)...
copying file(s)...
file, +DATA/dbatools/datafile/docs_d_01.dbf, copy committed.
```

Note The DBMS_DISKGROUP package provides APIs to copy datafile(s) out of ASM. You can add the DBMS_DISKGROUP package to your arsenal to even manually extract a raw block from a datafile stored in the ASM diskgroup. The ASM cp command in Oracle Database 11*g* leverages the DBMS_DISKGROUP package.

The multiple lines of copying file(s)... output is a progress bar of the copy process. Once the datafile is copied, you must rename the datafile using the alter database rename file command, as shown here:

```
SQL> alter database rename file '/data/oracle/DBATOOLS/docs_d_01.dbf' to
    '+data/dbatools/datafile/docs_d_01.dbf';
```

Database altered.

In this last step, you will put the tablespace back online:

```
SQL> alter tablespace docs_d online;
```

Tablespace altered.

Since the system tablespace cannot be offlined, you can shut down the database and put the database in mount mode. While in mount mode, you can copy the system tablespace datafile(s) to an ASM diskgroup and rename the system datafile with the same syntax as what was provided to rename the docs_d_01.dbf datafile.

How It Works

The cp command is a command that the DBA community has been waiting for since ASM was introduced in Oracle Database 10g Release 1. You can copy all the files that ASM supports: datafiles, online redo logs, archive logs, flashback logs, controlfiles, temporary files, tracking files, data pump exports, and spfile files. The caveat is that ASM will create an alias for the copied file. You can think of an alias as like a symbolic link in the Unix world. In the world of ASM, though, if you delete the alias, ASM will also delete the original file to which the alias is pointing.

In Oracle Database 11g Release 1, the copied file will belong to the ASMTESTING database identifier for the database subdirectory. You can see here that the docs_d_01.dbf datafile that was copied earlier is an alias to the TESTING file in the ASMTESTING/DATAFILE subdirectory:

```
ASMCMD [+DATA/DBATOOLS/DATAFILE] > ls -ltr
Type      Redund   Striped  Time            Sys  Name
DATAFILE  UNPROT   COARSE   MAY 28 10:00:00  Y    TOOLS.270.655646559
                                             N    docs_d_01.dbf =>
+DATA/ASMTESTING/DATAFILE/TESTING.271.655899281
```

■**Note** Notice the TESTING file name and ASMTESTING directory name for the database instance. The file and directory names are reported as a bug (Bug 5998102), which is supposed to be fixed in the 11.2 release. The next release should reflect the correct database instance instead of the ASMTESTING and file alias of TESTING.

If aliases for ASM copied files are acceptable, you can migrate from the filesystem to ASM using the asmcmd cp command. Additionally, you can use the cp command to copy files from ASM to the filesystem, from ASM to a remote ASM diskgroup, or from one diskgroup to another.

12-26. Creating a Database in ASM

Problem

You need to create a database and place all its files within ASM. You want to create the database using the create database script.

Solution

In this solution, you will see how to create a database using custom scripts. Before you create the database, you need to perform some preliminary tasks. First, the initialization parameter file needs to be created. Second, the Optimal Flexible Architecture (OFA)–compliant directory structures must be created in advance on the filesystem that comply with the initialization parameters. Here's a comprehensive example of the create database script:

```
create database  DBADEV
user sys identified by oracle123
user system identified by oracle123
  maxdatafiles  1021
    maxinstances  4
    maxlogfiles   16
    character set WE8MSWIN1252
    national character set AL16UTF16
    datafile
        '+DATA'       size 1000M
          autoextend off extent management local
    sysaux datafile '+DATA' size 1000m
    default temporary tablespace temp
    tempfile '+DATA' size 4000m
    uniform size 1m
    undo tablespace undo_rbs
    datafile '+DATA' size 4000m
    logfile
        ('+DATA'
         ,'+FRA')        size 300M,
        ('+DATA'
         ,'+FRA')        size 300M,
        ('+DATA'
         ,'+FRA')        size 300M,
        ('+DATA'
         ,'+FRA')        size 300M;
```

How It Works

When you create a database, you can place all the files in the DATA and FRA diskgroups. We recommend you multiplex your online redo logs to the DATA and FRA diskgroups. Even though you may already be mirroring at the hardware level, we recommend you multiplex your redo logs again. Also, we recommend you have at least one controlfile in each diskgroup for added protection.

The create database script in this solution places all the datafiles in the DATA diskgroup. The only components of the database at database creation time that is strategically placed in the FRA diskgroup are the mirrored redo logs and controlfiles. The file sizes for the SYSTEM, SYSAUX, TEMP, and UNDO tablespaces are sized for the larger databases.

After the database is created, you can run additional scripts such catalog.sql, catproc.sql, and catexp.sql from the $ORACLE_HOME/rdbms/admin directory. You may opt to execute additional scripts depending on your specific database requirements.

12-27. Creating/Adding Database Files in ASM

Problem

You need to create a new tablespace or add space to an existing tablespace.

Solution

To create a tablespace, you can simply type the following command:

```
create tablespace [tablespace_name];
```

By default, Oracle will create a 100MB datafile in the DB_CREATE_FILE_DEST location since the datafile clause is not specified. To add 1GB of space to an existing tablespace, you can issue the following syntax:

```
alter tablespace [tablespace_name] add datafile '+data' size 1g;
```

How It Works

The Oracle Managed File (OMF) feature was introduced in Oracle 9*i*. The primary purpose of OMF was to simplify the administration of Oracle database files. To use ASM intrinsically means you have to use OMF. All files will be managed by OMF even if you try to create a database file with a fully qualified name. The OMF concept can be a major challenge for DBAs who have religiously practiced OFA with fully qualified file names on the filesystems. If DBAs plan to implement ASM, they had better plan to accept OMF naming conventions.

Several initialization parameter influence how files are placed in the ASM diskgroup. The following initialization parameters are the key parameters that DBAs should be interested in relative to databases with ASM:

```
*.control_files='+DATA/visk/controlfile/control1.ctl',
                '+FRA/visk/controlfile/control2.ctl'
*.db_create_file_dest='+DATA'
*.db_create_online_log_dest_1='+DATA'
*.db_recovery_file_dest='+FRA'
*.log_archive_dest_1='LOCATION=USE_DB_RECOVERY_FILE_DEST'
*.log_file_name_convert='+DATA/VISKDR','+DATA/VISK'  ## added for Data Guard
```

The parameter db_create_file_dest='+DATA' specifies that all new datafiles will be created in the DATA diskgroup if the datafile clause is not specified. This parameter makes creating datafiles simple. If you want to specify a larger file, you can use the datafile clause to specify the location and size parameters. For example, if you want to create a 4GB datafile for the docs_i tablespace, here's how you would create the tablespace in the DATA diskgroup:

```
SQL> create tablespace docs_i datafile '+data' size 4g;
```

For DBAs who have to add an enormous amount of space to an existing tablespace, being on OMF really pays off. For example, say you have to add 200GB of a datafile for a given tablespace. And imagine that your company standard stipulates a maximum size of a database file to be 10GB. Based on the calculations, the DBA has to create twenty 10GB datafiles. With the db_create_file_dest parameter set to the DATA diskgroup, you merely have to issue the following command:

```
alter tablespace docs_i add datafile '+data' size 10g;
```

You can create the remaining 190GB of datafiles by typing the / command followed by the Enter key 19 times.

The parameter db_create_online_log_dest_1='+DATA' specifies that the online redo logs will be created in the DATA diskgroup if the location is not specified. Here's an example of creating the online redo group to the default ASM diskgroup:

```
SQL> alter database add logfile group 11;
```

The parameter *.db_recovery_file_dest='+FRA' will place flashback logs and backups to the FRA diskgroup. Last, the parameter *.log_archive_dest_1='LOCATION=USE_DB_RECOVERY_ FILE_DEST' will place all the archive logs in the FRA diskgroup. We recommend you place the archive logs in the FRA diskgroup for additional redundancy. By placing the archive logs, flashback logs, and backup sets in the FRA, the database will have extra layer of protection just in case you happen to lose the DATA diskgroup. You will have everything you need in the FRA to restore and roll forward the database to the exact point in time before the database crash.

In the earlier example, we created a tablespace called doc_i and added a 10GB datafile. The datafiles that were created reside in the OMF-compliant +DATA/DBATOOLS/DATAFILE directory. Here's the naming convention to which the directory structure adheres:

- +DATA is the DATA diskgroup.

- DBATOOLS is the name of the database.

- DATAFILE is the type of file this file is.

Note Other directories can be CHANGETRACKING, CONTROLFILE, ONLINELOG, TEMPFILE, FLASHBACK, PARAMETERFILE, AUTOBACKUP, BACKUPSET, and ARCHIVELOG.

Let's change the directory to the location of the datafiles. Listing all the files, the output looks like this:

```
ASMCMD [+DATA/DBATOOLS/DATAFILE] > ls -ltr
Type       Redund  Striped  Time              Sys  Name
DATAFILE   UNPROT  COARSE   MAY 28 10:00:00   Y    TOOLS.270.655646559
                                             N    docs_d_01.dbf =>
 +DATA/ASMTESTING/DATAFILE/TESTING.271.655899281
DATAFILE   UNPROT  COARSE   MAY 28 13:00:00   Y    DOCS_I.273.655912167
DATAFILE   UNPROT  COARSE   MAY 28 14:00:00   Y    DOCS_I.274.655913213
```

You will notice a strange naming convention for the files. Obviously, you can recognize the tablespace name embedded in the file names. The tablespace name portion of the file name is also referred to as the *tag name* of the datafile. Other tag names include group_# for online redo logs and log_# for flashback logs. Following the tag name, the first set of numbers correspond to the FILE_NUMBER column of the V$ASM_FILE view. The second set of numbers is known as the *incarnation number* and is a derivative of the timestamp when the file was created.

Archive logs follow a different naming convention. Archive logs are created in the date stamp subdirectory typically in the format of +FRA/[DB]/ARCHIVELOG/YYYY_MM_DD. Each day a new subdirectory is created following this format. The naming convention of the archive logs is the thread number followed by the sequence number followed by the file number followed by the incarnation number.

A sample listing of the archive log directory looks like this:

```
ASMCMD [+fra/dbadev/ARCHIVELOG/2008_05_28] > ls
thread_1_seq_4.263.655919409
thread_1_seq_5.264.655919415
```

CHAPTER 13

■ ■ ■

Implementing Real Application Clusters on Linux

Many customers around the world rely heavily on Oracle Real Application Clusters (RAC) for high availability, scalability, and system uptime. In the database world, Oracle RAC has no competition in this space. IBM UDB DB2 and Microsoft SQL Server are slowly catching up to Oracle, but Oracle is still the only vendor that truly provides an active/active real-time configuration between multiple nodes. Oracle dominates in the database cluster technologies.

Different DBAs have different schools of thought about implementing RAC. Some believe that just about every application can be converted to RAC. Some believe that RAC poses too many technological challenges and difficulties for their organization to introduce. Experienced DBAs will accept the challenge but will not embrace the technology until implementations can be a repeatable process and thoroughly tested with their application.

Contrary to what some vendors may state, Oracle RAC can scale horizontally. With Oracle Database 10g Release 2, RAC can scale up to 100 nodes. Given that the majority of Oracle's customers are in the range of 2- to 16-node RAC implementations, few companies have dared to stretch Oracle RAC to beyond 16 nodes.

In today's downturn economy, companies are slowly migrating away from large IBM, HP, or Sun servers and migrating to commodity hardware running Linux. Also, with the readily available quad-core Intel and AMD CPUs at affordable prices, companies can run eight CPU Linux servers at a fraction of the cost of enterprise Unix servers on IBM, Sun, and HP. More important, flavors of Linux such as SUSE, Red Hat, and Oracle Enterprise Linux have proven to be rock-solid operating systems that provide utmost reliability similar to their counterpart Unix operating systems such as Sun Solaris, HP/UX, and IBM AIX.

If your company has a new implementation of Oracle applications deployed on Oracle's Unbreakable Linux Network and has requirements for high availability or scalability, you should consider RAC. This chapter will focus on installing and configuring RAC on Linux. Obviously, we cannot cover all facets of RAC deployment on Linux in a single chapter. We will concentrate on the topics we consider to be the most relevant surrounding RAC deployments on a Linux operating system.

13-1. Architecting a RAC Environment

Problem

You are new to RAC and want to architect a RAC solution according to industry best practices. You want to make sure that hardware requirements are met and all the vested parties are on the same page as to how RAC is architected from the engineering side.

Solution

A typical RAC configuration with Automatic Storage Management (ASM) looks like Figure 13-1.

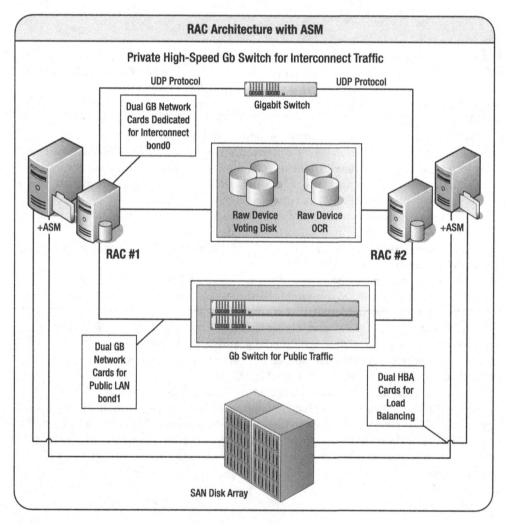

Figure 13-1. *Typical RAC configuration*

How It Works

A RAC configuration must have at least two network interface cards (NICs)—one dedicated to the private interconnect traffic and another NIC card dedicated to the public network. Oracle RAC architected for performance and reliability will incorporate at least four network cards per RAC node. Two of the NICs will be bonded or paired into a single interface (for example, bond0) for interconnect traffic. The other two network cards will be bonded to service the public network (for example, bond1).

RAC implementations with ASM will also have host bus adapters (HBAs). Again, a well-designed RAC architecture will require two HBAs for load balancing and failover. In addition, HBAs can also be aggregated for performance too. If you are implementing RAC on ASM, you will typically have HBAs and Fibre Channel on the storage area network.

Oracle RAC configurations require gigabit switches in the architecture. Because of the bonding requirements of the NICs for interconnect and public network, you will have to invest in switches that support NIC bonding. Again, your architecture should include two switches for load balancing and failover.

Oracle RAC can be implemented on numerous storage arrays and on multiple filesystem types. Depending on your company requirements, you may be leveraging one of the following file storage types; all support a clustered database:

- Oracle Clustered File System (OCFS) v1 for Linux 2.4 kernels or OCFS v2 for Linux 2.6 kernels

- Network File System (NFS)

- Third-party clustered filesystem such as Veritas Clustered FS

- ASM

- Raw devices

RAC implementations on NFS or OCFS tend to be easier for DBAs to configure than on ASM with raw devices for voting disks and Oracle Cluster Registry (OCR). Please keep in mind this comes at a cost of performance, as NFS and OCFS do not perform as well as ASM. The reason is simply because system administrators (SAs) will have presented the shared storage to all the RAC nodes, formatted the disks, and created a clustered/networked filesystem before presenting the storage to the DBAs. The SAs will have done the preliminary testing of the clustered filesystem prior to releasing the filesystems. DBAs at this point do not have to struggle from raw devices not being formatted with fdisk, clearing the disks with dd, or dealing with permission issues of the raw device.

Oracle RAC implementations on Linux require the installation of Oracle Clusterware software. Oracle Clusterware, formerly called Cluster Ready Services (CRS), provides the cluster management software for nodes to communicate with each other and establish a cluster.

Note As mentioned, as of Oracle Database 10*g* Release 2 (10.2), CRS is now Oracle Clusterware.

Oracle Clusterware, at a high level, is a product that manages high availability resources in a RAC configuration such as databases, instances, services, and listeners. In a typical RAC implementation, Oracle Clusterware should be installed and configured before the ASM/database software. Oracle Clusterware must be installed on a separate ORACLE_HOME. The Oracle Clusterware software home directory is also known as $ORA_CRS_HOME.

The OCR houses all the RAC configuration details and must be accessible by all the nodes in the cluster. The OCR contains information such as database names, status of the database, instances associated with the database, services, node applications, and services. In Linux, the location of the OCR is housed in the /etc/ocr.loc file.

The *voting disk*, formerly known as the *quorum disk*, stores the heartbeat of the RAC nodes and must be available to all the nodes in the cluster. The voting disks determine which nodes are available in the RAC cluster. The voting can be a single point of failure in a RAC configuration; thus, we strongly recommend you follow Oracle's best practices to have at least three voting disks in your RAC environment.

13-2. Setting Up the Linux Kernel Parameters for RAC

Problem

Before installing and configuring RAC on Red Hat or Oracle Enterprise Linux (OEL), you want to properly set the appropriate kernel parameters for database implementations.

Solution

The following kernel parameters in the /etc/sysctl.conf file are applicable for Red Hat and OEL distributions:

```
kernel.shmall              = 2097152
kernel.shmmax              = 2147483648
kernel.shmmni              = 4096
kernel.sem                 = 250 32000 100 128
fs.file-max                = 65536
net.ipv4.ip_local_port_range = 1024 65000
net.core.rmem_default      = 262144
net.core.rmem_max          = 262144
net.core.wmem_default      = 262144
net.core.wmem_max          = 262144
```

For the previously mentioned Linux distributions, you can modify the /etc/sysctl.conf file and reload the kernel parameters without incurring a server reboot by executing the sysctl -p command as root. To view the relevant parameters for Oracle databases, you can execute the /sbin/sysctl command provided here:

```
sysctl -a |egrep "shmmax|shmall|shmmni|sem|file-max|ip_local_port_range|rmem|wmem"
```

How It Works

The majority of the kernel parameters for stand-alone databases and RAC databases will be similar. You probably will not notice net.core.* parameters in the stand-alone database implementations. The net.core.* parameters are important to RAC since these parameters establish the UDP buffers required by Oracle Global Cache Services (GCS) for cache fusion traffic. Oracle interconnect utilizes UDP to transfer messages and data blocks between the instances. The Oracle recommended setting of 256KB should be sufficient to support the majority of database applications. The default value for net.core.rmem_default and net.core.wmem_default is 64KB. The default value for net.core.rmem_max and net.core.wmem_max is 128KB. Not setting appropriate values for the net.core.* parameters will generate errors while installing Oracle software.

Often, the net.core.*max parameters have to be adjusted to 1MB or greater to support a high number of concurrent blocks.

13-3. Installing the cvuqdisk Package

Problem

You want to check for shared disk availability before installing Oracle Clusterware.

Solution

The cvuqdisk package discovers and checks the accessibility of shared storage for SCSI disks. The cvuqdisk package is located in the installation media. You can change your directory to the clusterware/rpm directory after you unzip the Clusterware software and install the cvuqdisk package with the rpm -ihv command:

```
$ sudo rpm -ihv cvuqdisk-1.0.1-1.rpm
Preparing...                ########################################### [100%]
   1:cvuqdisk               ########################################### [100%]
```

How It Works

If the cvuqdisk package is not installed, you will receive an error as part of the runcluvfy.sh output indicating that the cluster verify utility could not determine the "sharedness" of a disk during the shared storage accessibility (SSA) component check:

```
Unable to determine the sharedness of /dev/sda on nodes:
     rac3,rac4
```

If you have a previous version of the cvuqdisk package, you should remove the previous version using the rpm -e command before installing the latest version. We recommend that Cluster Verification Utility (CVU) be run before and after CRS install as well as database install. CVU can be downloaded from OTN under the Clusterware page.

13-4. Setting Up the /etc/hosts File

Problem

You want to modify the /etc/hosts file for RAC. For example, you want to add the public, private, and virtual IP addresses of your RAC nodes.

Solution

The /etc/hosts file must be modified to reflect the interconnect private network IP addresses, public IP addresses, and virtual IP addresses (VIPs). A sample /etc/hosts file will have entries that resemble what you see here for a two-node RAC system:

```
172.16.201.132      rac3.dbaexpert.com           rac3
172.16.201.134      rac4.dbaexpert.com           rac4
172.16.201.232      rac3-vip.dbaexpert.com       rac3-vip
172.16.201.234      rac4-vip.dbaexpert.com       rac4-vip
192.168.2.3         rac3-priv.dbaexpert.com      rac3-priv
192.168.2.4         rac4-priv.dbaexpert.com      rac4-priv
```

The DNS server should also hold entries for the hostname and the virtual hostnames.

How It Works

In the sample /etc/hosts file entries, you will notice that a separate entry exists for the hostname, the virtual hostname, and the private hostname. For each RAC node, three entries must exist in the /etc/hosts file. In addition, the entries must be in the following format:

```
IP Address    hostname.domain_name    hostname
```

The /etc/hosts format in the previous example is Oracle's standard across the majority of its product line including Oracle Database, Grid Control, E-Business Suite, and Collaboration Suite. System administrators often have their own standard of making entries to the /etc/hosts file that do not coincide with Oracle's mandated format.

The virtual hostnames play an important role in the RAC world. The virtual hostnames are what DBAs in the RAC world refer to as *VIPs*. VIPs are leveraged for client side connectivity as well for fast client side failover. VIPs are leveraged to configure the database's listener.ora and tnsnames.ora files. You can also take advantage of VIPs to configure local and remote listeners.

■**Caution** A common mistake that DBAs and SAs make when configuring RAC for the first time is to set up the network interface for the VIP. Oracle VIP Configuration Assistant (VIPCA) is responsible for configuring the VIP network interfaces. Prior to the Clusterware installation, you must not be able to ping the VIPs. In addition, the output of the ifconfig -a command should not list an entry for the VIP.

Furthermore, a separate IP address for interconnect traffic is required on each host. Interconnect IP addresses often start with 192.xx or 10.xx octals. Interconnect hostnames should not be listed in the DNS servers.

13-5. Setting Up User Equivalence

Problem

You want to configure ssh so that the oracle Unix account can log on to the other RAC nodes without being prompted for a password.

Solution

To set up user equivalence, you must first generate the secure token key using the ssh-keygen Unix command. The ssh-keygen command accepts prompts for several input options. In this solution, you will specify the command to generate an RSA key and accept all default options. The output of the ssh-keygen command will look like this:

```
$ ssh-keygen -t rsa
Generating public/private rsa key pair.
Enter file in which to save the key (/home/oracle/.ssh/id_rsa):
Enter passphrase (empty for no passphrase):
Enter same passphrase again:
Your identification has been saved in /home/oracle/.ssh/id_rsa.
Your public key has been saved in /home/oracle/.ssh/id_rsa.pub.
The key fingerprint is:
21:bf:46:5a:a8:19:91:ea:6d:d1:e2:7c:18:57:e8:79 oracle@rac3.dbaexpert.com
```

The public key (id_rsa.pub file) is created in the $HOME/.ssh directory of the user. You can use the cat command to view the contents of this file from the /home/oracle/.ssh directory, as shown here:

```
$ cat id_rsa.pub
ssh-rsa AAAAB3NzaC1yc2EAAAABIwAAAIEAuvyW56fXOU+3Qm1LOcD+iE+QReloBVOK72sGuPVvH33WOiY9
H7ueJkrHErDqK2V2U9zAMkNysDX+pTIziiwbP9cFC94TYeWbwMz8a7tiWhNIANT8D6TAX1ZVncxjMSRoqYb8
XgpuokCgyUhAu3yo9LZc6mhAM2llq/A+jMnr/Us= oracle@rac3.dbaexpert.com
```

You can copy this file to the remote server and during the file transfer rename the file to something like id_rsa.pub.[hostname], or you can copy the contents of the id_rsa.pub file to your operating system buffer. Either way, you must copy the contents of the id_rsa.pub file to the $HOME/.ssh/authorized_keys file on the other RAC nodes. In this case, the authorized_keys file will be /home/oracle/.ssh/authorized_keys.

Once the entry to the other RAC node's authorized_keys file is made, you can secure shell to the RAC node without a password prompt.

■**Note** However, if you supplied a passphrase when running the command ssh-keygen -t rsa to create the public key, then you will be prompted for that passphrase when connecting to the other RAC nodes. Please review recipe 14-6 for details on how to configure a promptless login.

The first time you secure shell to a remote node, you will be prompted to confirm the authenticity of the server to which you are attempting to connect. The following example establishes a connection to rac4 for the first time:

```
$ ssh rac4
The authenticity of host 'rac4 (172.16.201.134)' can't be established.
RSA key fingerprint is 78:c6:41:47:3c:39:27:71:68:34:76:6e:86:d6:67:c2.
Are you sure you want to continue connecting (yes/no)? yes
Warning: Permanently added 'rac4,172.16.201.134' (RSA) to the list of known hosts.
Last login: Sun Jun 22 09:12:12 2008 from rac3.dbaexpert.com

ORACLE_BASE: /apps/oracle
BIN Directory: /apps/oracle/general/sh
[…]
$
```

You can see that we were able to connect directly to the rac4 server. You must repeat the connectivity to the host and also to the fully qualified hostname. In addition, you must also set up user equivalence to the local host by hostname and the local host with the fully qualified domain name. Here's a simple script that can be enhanced in your environment to check for proper user equivalence setup:

```
ssh rac3 date
ssh rac4 date
ssh rac3.dbaexpert.com date
ssh rac4.dbaexpert.com date
ssh rac3-priv date
ssh rac4-priv date
ssh rac3-priv.dbaexpert.com date
ssh rac4-priv.dbaexpert.com date
```

You should run this script on every RAC node. Notice that the ssh user equivalence connectivity test is even set up for the interconnect hostnames. Again, you will not be able to secure shell to the virtual hostnames yet. The VIPs will be enabled when root.sh is executed after Clusterware is installed on the last node.

How It Works

Setting up user equivalence is an important component to a successful RAC installation. During the installation, the Oracle Universal Installer (OUI) must copy files and execute programs on the RAC nodes. Setting up user equivalence allows the OUI to copy files and execute programs without being prompted for a password.

For some reason or another, user equivalence poses some problems for DBAs. One common issue DBAs run into is directory permissions for the oracle user account. Often, the home directory for oracle has write privileges granted to the world or even to the oinstall or dba group. ssh2 protocol considers this a security violation and will not allow a promptless login.

> **■Note** If you execute the ssh-keygen executable, you will destroy user equivalence. For this reason, you should consider making a copy of the id_rsa.pub file and the id_rsa file as id_rsa.HOSTNAME and id_rsa.pub.HOSTNAME. In the event that another DBA executes the ssh-keygen executable, you can revert to the original versions, instead of having to copy the id_rsa.pub entry to all the authorized_keys files.

13-6. Checking the OS and Hardware Configuration

Problem

The SAs, SAN engineers, and network administrators prepared the RAC environment. Before you install Oracle Clusterware, you want to perform preliminary validations to check whether the OS and hardware configuration are adequately configured.

Solution

Using the Cluster Verification Utility (cluvfy), you can check your Linux hardware configuration before actually starting to install Oracle Clusterware:

```
./runcluvfy.sh stage -post hwos -n rac3,rac4 -s /NFS -verbose
```

Executing cluvfy will yield output similar to the following. If the output from the hardware/OS cluster verify is acceptable, you can proceed with the next check, which is to perform the pre-Clusterware installation checks.

```
Performing post-checks for hardware and operating system setup

Checking node reachability...

Check: Node reachability from node "rac3"
  Destination Node                      Reachable?
  ------------------------------------  ------------------------
  rac3                                  yes
  rac4                                  yes
Result: Node reachability check passed from node "rac3".

Checking user equivalence...

Check: User equivalence for user "oracle"
  Node Name                             Comment
  ------------------------------------  ------------------------
  rac4                                  passed
  rac3                                  passed
Result: User equivalence check passed for user "oracle".

Checking node connectivity...
```

```
Interface information for node "rac4"
   Interface Name    IP Address     Subnet        Subnet Gateway  Default Gateway
Hardware Address
   ----------------  ------------  ------------  ------------  ------------
------------
   eth0              172.16.201.134  172.16.201.0  0.0.0.0       172.16.201.2
00:0C:29:E7:A6:A7
   eth1              192.168.2.4   192.168.2.0   0.0.0.0       172.16.201.2
00:0C:29:E7:A6:B1


Interface information for node "rac3"
   Interface Name    IP Address     Subnet        Subnet Gateway  Default Gateway
Hardware Address
   ----------------  ------------  ------------  ------------  ------------
------------
   eth0              172.16.201.132  172.16.201.0  0.0.0.0       172.16.201.2
00:0C:29:AB:66:8E
   eth1              192.168.2.3   192.168.2.0   0.0.0.0       172.16.201.2
00:0C:29:AB:66:98


Check: Node connectivity of subnet "172.16.201.0"
   Source                          Destination                     Connected?
   -----------------------------  -----------------------------  ----------------
   rac4:eth0                       rac3:eth0                       yes
Result: Node connectivity check passed for subnet "172.16.201.0" with node(s)
rac4,rac3.

Check: Node connectivity of subnet "192.168.2.0"
   Source                          Destination                     Connected?
   -----------------------------  -----------------------------  ----------------
   rac4:eth1                       rac3:eth1                       yes
Result: Node connectivity check passed for subnet "192.168.2.0" with node(s)
rac4,rac3.

Interfaces found on subnet "172.16.201.0" that are likely candidates for VIP:
rac4 eth0:172.16.201.134
rac3 eth0:172.16.201.132

Interfaces found on subnet "192.168.2.0" that are likely candidates for a private
interconnect:
rac4 eth1:192.168.2.4
rac3 eth1:192.168.2.3
```

Result: Node connectivity check passed.

Checking shared storage accessibility...

"/NFS" is shared.

Shared storage check was successful on nodes "rac4,rac3".

Post-check for hardware and operating system setup was successful.

How It Works

You can take advantage of the runcluvfy.sh shell script prior to installing Oracle Clusterware to check your hardware components. The runcluvfy.sh shell script resides in the installation media and is accessible once you unzip the downloaded Clusterware software from Oracle Technology Network (OTN) using the URL http://otn.oracle.com.

Oracle started to ship the cluvfy utility as part of the software stack as of Oracle Database 10*g* Release 2. DBAs should master the cluvfy utility. The cluvfy utility can be leveraged to check the successful completion of each stage of the RAC implementation and can save RAC implementers an enormous amount of time and headaches by diagnosing potential issues in the RAC topology. The cluvfy utility is designed to be executed at each stage of the RAC installation. The valid stages of RAC installations are as follows:

```
-post hwos    :  post-check for hardware and operating system
-pre  cfs     :  pre-check for CFS setup
-post cfs     :  post-check for CFS setup
-pre  crsinst :  pre-check for CRS installation
-post crsinst :  post-check for CRS installation
-pre  dbinst  :  pre-check for database installation
-pre  dbcfg   :  pre-check for database configuration
```

After the Oracle Clusterware installation, you can run the cluvfy command with the post crsinst option to verify a successful installation:

```
/apps/oracle/product/CRS/bin/cluvfy stage -post crsinst -n rac3,rac4
```

Another important stage to execute the cluvfy utility is before the database installation. You can execute the cluvfy utility with the -pre dbinst option, as shown here:

```
crs > cluvfy stage -pre dbinst -n rac3,rac4
```

In addition to checking the RAC environment at each stage of a RAC implementation, you can also check the components of the RAC environment such as clustered file system integrity, OCR integrity, cluster integrity, cluster manager integrity, node connectivity, reachability between nodes, space availability, minimum space requirements, and so on. You can execute the cluvfy comp -list command to review all the options.

13-7. Installing Oracle Clusterware

Problem

Your company decided to implement Oracle RAC. The DBA team is responsible for installing and setting up Oracle RAC. You want to start by installing Oracle Clusterware.

Solution

Let's install and configure Oracle Clusterware. First, you must download the Oracle Clusterware software from the OTN web site. Just like you invoke the runInstaller executable for database installations, you execute the same runInstaller executable from the unzipped clusterware directory. When you launch the OUI, you will be presented with the Welcome screen. You can click the Next button to be directed to the Specify Home Details screen. On this screen, specify a name for the Clusterware home directory and the destination directory where you want to install Oracle Clusterware.

■**Note** Please do not install Oracle Clusterware in the same subdirectory level as your Oracle Home for the database binaries. Oracle Clusterware is an in-place patch maintenance and upgrade. If your Oracle Clusterware directory happens to be /apps/oracle/product/10.2.0/CRS and you upgrade to Oracle Clusterware 11*g*, you will be running the 11.1 software release from a 10.2 directory name structure.

Click the Next button to be routed to the Product-Specific Prerequisite Checks screen. Make sure that all components pass the prerequisite checks and that you see the message "Check complete. The overall result of this check is: Passed" at the bottom of the screen.

After you confirm that all the prerequisites are met, click the Next button. You will be directed to the Specify Cluster Configuration screen, as displayed in Figure 13-2.

Check the public node name, the private node name, and the virtual hostname, and then confirm that the entry made by the OUI is correct. If the entry is inaccurate, click the Edit button, and correct the entry. If the entry is correct, proceed by clicking the Add button to be directed to the Add a New Node to the Existing Cluster pop-up window, as displayed in Figure 13-3.

On this screen, enter the public node, the private node, and the virtual hostname, and click the OK button. You will notice the standard implemented: the virtual hostname has -vip appended to the hostname, and the private hostname has -priv appended to the hostname. Your company should create a standard naming convention and be consistent across other RAC implementations.

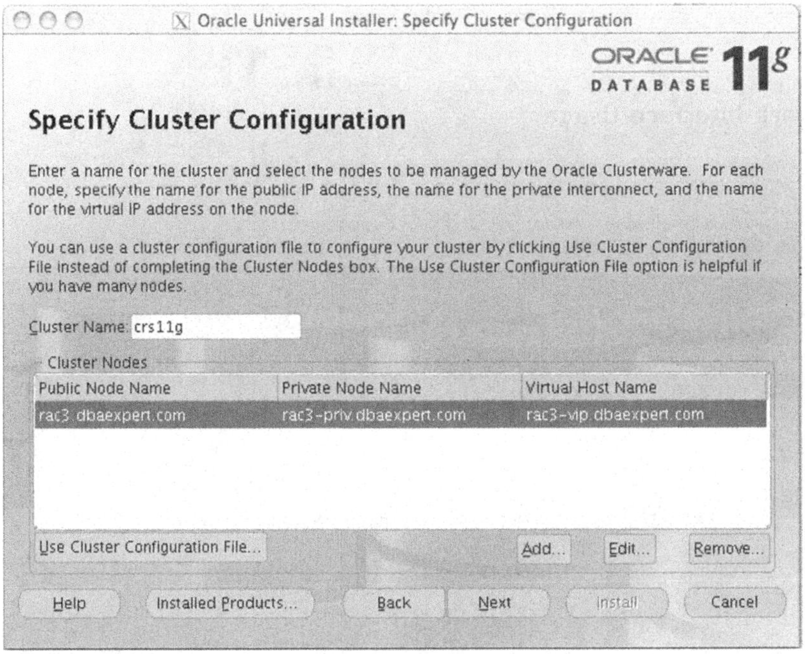

Figure 13-2. *Specify Cluster Configuration screen*

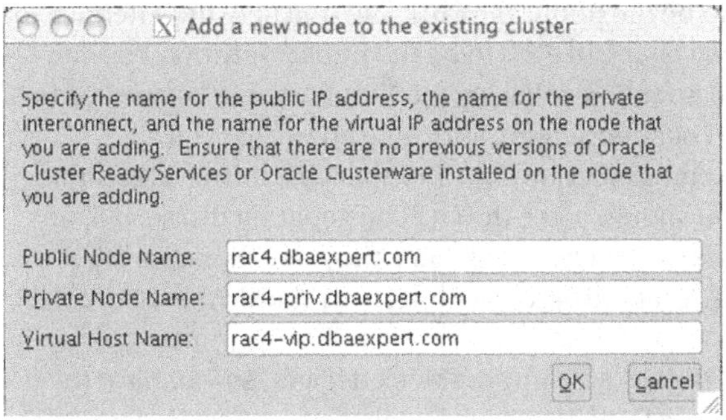

Figure 13-3. *Adding a new node to the existing cluster screen*

Now the Specify Cluster Configuration screen will reflect the new RAC node. Next, enter additional RAC nodes as necessary by clicking the Add button. Once you have added all the RAC nodes, you can proceed to the next screen by clicking the Next button; you'll be routed to the Specify Network Interface Usage screen, as displayed in Figure 13-4.

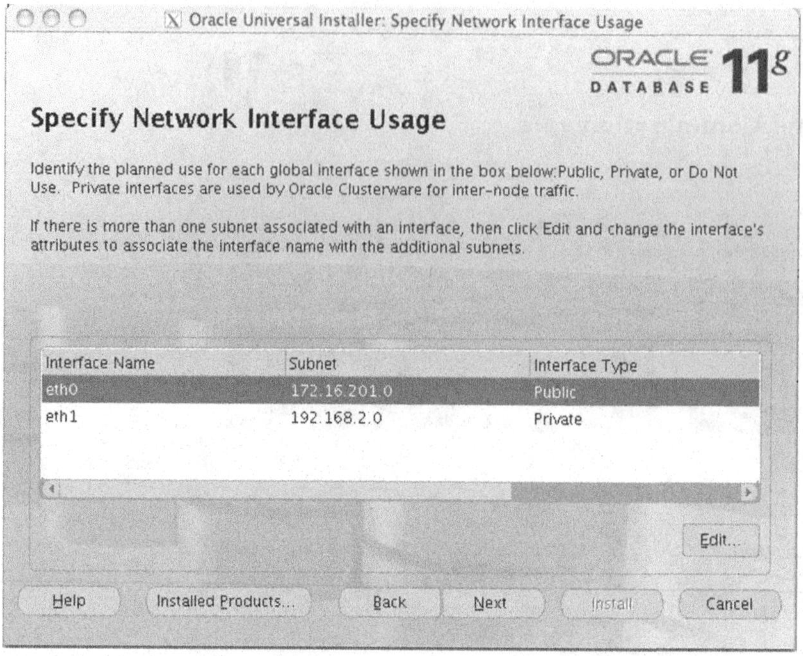

Figure 13-4. *Specify Network Interface Usage screen*

Please select one network interface to be the public network and one network interface to be the private network. In our example, we changed eth0 to be the public network. You can proceed with the Oracle Clusterware configuration by clicking the Next button to be directed to the Specify Oracle Cluster Registry (OCR) Location screen, as displayed in Figure 13-5.

On this screen, choose the Normal Redundancy option, and specify a mirrored location for the OCR disk. Unlike this example, you should place the OCR on separate disks, NFS, or clustered filesystems. As of Oracle Database 10g Release 2, Oracle provides the support for a mirrored OCR disk. Even if you are mirroring at the hardware level, you should mirror the OCR disk for additional redundancy.

In Oracle Database 10g Release 2, OUI does not support block devices, so you have to provide raw devices for both OCR and Voting Disk. In Oracle Database 11g, Oracle extends support for block devices in the OUI.

Note Please notice the disk space requirements for the OCR disk. In Oracle Database 10g Release 2, the amount of space required for the OCR disk was 100MB. As of Oracle Database 11g, the disk requirement for the OCR disk is 256MB of disk space.

For simplicity, we recommend that when sizing the OCR or voting disk, you ask for 512MB or 1GB to be consistent and ask the SAs to carve out five 512MB or 1GB LUNs for the OCR and voting disk.

After you specify the OCR disk, you can proceed to the next screen by clicking the Next button. You will be directed to the Specify Voting Disk Location screen, as displayed in Figure 13-6.

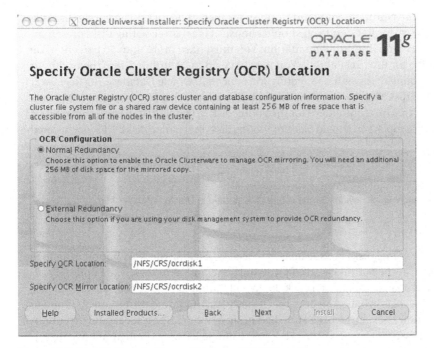

Figure 13-5. *Specify Oracle Cluster Registry (OCR) Location screen*

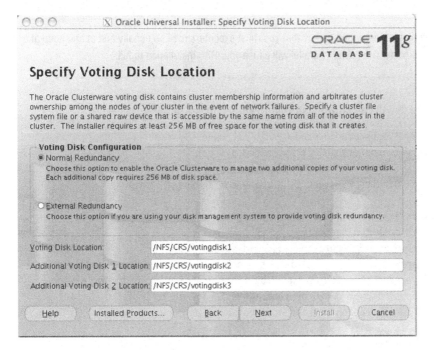

Figure 13-6. *Specify Voting Disk Location screen*

Again, select the Normal Redundancy option for the voting disks. The voting disk is a single point of failure for RAC, and you should choose at least three voting disks on separate disks or filesystems for a RAC implementation. You must have more than 50 percent of the voting disks online for RAC availability. You may have up to 32 voting disks. The option to specify multiple voting disk was a new feature introduced in Oracle Database 10*g* Release 2. Similar to the OCR disk, the size requirements for the voting disk is increased to 256MB as of Oracle Database 11*g*. The requirement for the voting disk in Oracle Database 10*g* was 20MB. Again, unlike this example, you should place the voting disk on separate disks, NFS, or clustered filesystems.

Note You can specify block devices for the voting disk starting in Oracle Database 11*g*.

Once multiple voting disks are specified, proceed by clicking the Next button to go to the Summary screen. On the Summary screen, you have the option to review the options you chose. Once you are satisfied, you can click the Install button to initiate the software install.

Once the software is installed on both the primary RAC node and the remote RAC node(s), several configuration assistants will be launched in silent mode. Upon successful execution of the configuration assistants, you will be presented with the Execute Configuration Scripts screen to run the root.sh script from the $ORA_CRS_HOME directory.

Caution: An important lesson to share is that you must execute root.sh serially and at one node at a time. Attempting to execute root.sh in parallel will cause your RAC installation to fail.

Running root.sh will yield output similar to what you see here:

```
WARNING: directory '/apps/oracle/product' is not owned by root
WARNING: directory '/apps/oracle' is not owned by root
WARNING: directory '/apps' is not owned by root
Checking to see if Oracle CRS stack is already configured

Setting the permissions on OCR backup directory
Setting up Network socket directories
Oracle Cluster Registry configuration upgraded successfully
The directory '/apps/oracle/product' is not owned by root. Changing owner to root
The directory '/apps/oracle' is not owned by root. Changing owner to root
The directory '/apps' is not owned by root. Changing owner to root
clscfg: EXISTING configuration version 4 detected.
clscfg: version 4 is 11 Release 1.
Successfully accumulated necessary OCR keys.
Using ports: CSS=49895 CRS=49896 EVMC=49898 and EVMR=49897.
node <nodenumber>: <nodename> <private interconnect name> <hostname>
node 1: rac3 rac3-priv rac3
```

```
node 2: rac4 rac4-priv rac4
clscfg: Arguments check out successfully.

NO KEYS WERE WRITTEN. Supply -force parameter to override.
-force is destructive and will destroy any previous cluster
configuration.
Oracle Cluster Registry for cluster has already been initialized
Startup will be queued to init within 30 seconds.
Adding daemons to inittab
Expecting the CRS daemons to be up within 600 seconds.
Cluster Synchronization Services is active on these nodes.
        rac3
        rac4
Cluster Synchronization Services is active on all the nodes.
Waiting for the Oracle CRSD and EVMD to start
Oracle CRS stack installed and running under init(1M)
```
Running vipca(silent) for configuring nodeapps

```
Creating VIP application resource on (2) nodes...
Creating GSD application resource on (2) nodes...
Creating ONS application resource on (2) nodes...
Starting VIP application resource on (2) nodes...
Starting GSD application resource on (2) nodes...
Starting ONS application resource on (2) nodes...


Done.
```

This particular output happens to be the root.sh output from the last node in the RAC environment. Notice the line in the output that is in bold and reads "Running vipca(silent) for configuring nodeapps." The VIPCA is invoked in silent mode to set up the VIP, GSD, and ONS services.

■**Note** If the VIPCA raises an error, you can correct the error by executing the vipca manually. To execute vipca, set your DISPLAY environment variable to a valid X server, and execute vipca from the CRS $ORACLE_ HOME. You will be directed to another GUI tool to set up the VIPs for the RAC instances. The VIPCA will add the virtual IP addresses and another network interface, something like bond1:1 or eth1:1 depending on the NIC associated with the public network.

How It Works

You just performed an Oracle Database 11*g* Release 1 Clusterware installation. If you are running Oracle Database 10*g* Release 2, you must install the base Oracle Database 10*g* Release 2 Clusterware software (10.2.0.1) and then install the patchset to upgrade to the 10.2.0.3 or 10.2.0.4 release.

Oracle introduced the CRS bundle patch for Oracle Clusterware for enhanced reliability of Oracle Clusterware 10.2.0.2 and newer releases. We strongly recommend you download the CRS bundle patch for your version of Clusterware and apply the patches using opatch. You can download the CRS bundle patch for your specific version of Oracle Clusterware. Each CRS bundle patch is inclusive and contains all the patches from the previous bundle patch. Please review MetaLink Note 405820.1 for additional details.

13-8. Removing Oracle Clusterware Software

Problem

You run into numerous errors during the Clusterware installation. You tried to debug the issues but realize that you have to restart from the beginning. You want to completely remove any remnants of the installation and start again.

Solution

The following script example is an excerpt from MetaLink Note 239998.1 and can be executed to completely remove the existence of Oracle Clusterware:

```
rm /etc/oracle/*
rm -f /etc/init.d/init.cssd
rm -f /etc/init.d/init.crs
rm -f /etc/init.d/init.crsd
rm -f /etc/init.d/init.evmd
rm -f /etc/rc2.d/K96init.crs
rm -f /etc/rc2.d/S96init.crs
rm -f /etc/rc3.d/K96init.crs
rm -f /etc/rc3.d/S96init.crs
rm -f /etc/rc5.d/K96init.crs
rm -f /etc/rc5.d/S96init.crs
rm -Rf /etc/oracle/scls_scr
rm -f /etc/inittab.crs
cp /etc/inittab.orig /etc/inittab
```

Once you remove all the remnants of Oracle Clusterware from the /etc directory, you want to make sure there are no traces of the executables in memory. You can check for background processes running with the following ps -ef command:

```
ps -ef |egrep -i "crs|css|evm|d.bin"
```

If the output results in any processes running, you should terminate all the processes with the kill -9 command. Next, you should clear out the OCR and voting disk(s) with the dd command, similar to what is provided here:

```
# dd if=/dev/zero of=/dev/raw/raw11 bs=8192 count=12000
```

Lastly, as root, remove the CRS install directory with the rm -rf command. An example of such a command is shown here:

```
rm -rf /apps/oracle/product/CRS
```

How It Works

When you install Oracle Clusterware, numerous scripts are scattered in the /etc directories. Not only do you have to remove the Clusterware HOME directory, but you also need to purge all the Clusterware scripts in the /etc directory. This solution is derived from Oracle MetaLink Note 239998.1 that explains all the files that need to be deleted to completely remove Oracle Clusterware for all operating systems.

In addition to removing all the installation files, you also need to delete the voting disk and OCR disk. If your voting and OCR disks happen to be on raw devices, you can use the dd command to clear out the contents of the files.

■**Note** Starting in Oracle Database 11*g*, voting and OCR disks can be on block devices. Raw device support continues to be phased out with each release.

13-9. Registering RAC Resources

Problem

You want to register RAC resources such as ASM, the database, and other RAC components with the OCR.

Solution

srvctl accepts an add argument to register a configuration information to the OCR. To register an ASM instance into the OCR, you can use the syntax provided here:

```
srvctl add asm -n rac3 -i +ASM1 -o /apps/oracle/product/10.2.0/ASM
```

The -n option specifies the node name. The -i option specifies the ASM instance name. Lastly, the -o option specifies the location of the Oracle ASM HOME directory. You must repeat the srvctl add asm command for each of the ASM instances. You can execute the srvctl command from one node.

The srvctl syntax to add the database is slightly different. You must first enter the configuration information for the database and then provide configuration information for each RAC instance. To add the configuration information for the database, you can use the add database option like you see here:

```
srvctl add database -d VISK -o /apps/oracle/product/10.2.0/RACDB
```

Next, you must add RAC instance configuration information using the add instance option:

```
srvctl add instance -d VISK -i VISK1 -n rac1
```

You need to repeat the add instance command for each RAC instance.

How It Works

The `srvctl` executable is the interface to interact with the CRS and the OCR. Oracle recommends the database and instance registration with the `srvctl` executable. You can add other resources including `service`, `nodeapps`, and `listener` with the add option.

Once you have successfully added a resource, you can check on the status of the resource with the `status` option of the `srvctl` command. An example to display the status of the RACQA database would look like this:

```
$ srvctl status database -d RACQA
Instance RACQA1 is running on node rac3
Instance RACQA2 is running on node rac4
```

13-10. Starting and Shutting Down RAC Resources

Problem

You want to start up/shut down a service across the entire RAC environment with a single command.

Solution

Once the ASM instance and the database information are captured within the OCR, you can use the `start`/`stop` command to shut down the database or ASM at the RAC level. To start a database, you can use the `start database` option like this:

```
srvctl start database -d VISK
```

To start an individual instance, you must specify the instance name with the `-i` option like this:

```
srvctl start instance -d VISK -i VISK1
```

To stop a database, you can use the `stop database` option similar to what you see here:

```
srvctl stop database -d VISK
```

Note You may not realize the significance of the `start` and `stop` commands at the database level if you are running a two- or three-node RAC. DBAs who run RAC environments that are four nodes or more will probably appreciate the `start database` and `stop database` options. If you happen to be running a ten-node RAC, you can shut down all ten RAC instances with a single command.

The `stop database` option also accepts an `-o` option to specify abort mode. The `stop database` option will stop all the services and instances associated with the database across all the nodes. If you want to abort the RAC instances, you can use the `-o` option like this:

```
srvctl stop database -d VISK -o abort
```

You can stop a single instance of the RAC environment using the -i option:

```
srvctl stop instance -d VISK -i VISK1
```

Just like you can shut down the database with the stop option, you can start up the database with the start option. Similarly, you can start up an instance with the start instance option. The stop instance option also accepts an -o option to specify abort mode.

How It Works

We recommend that DBAs exclusively use srvctl to set up a service for the database and to start/stop the database using the srvctl tool. Not only can you manage the database, but the database listener and services such as SERVICE_NAMES can also be managed. Table 13-1 lists additional start/stop srvctl commands that are frequently utilized to manage services.

Table 13-1. *Starting and Starting the Database Listener and nodeapps*

Resource Name to Start/Stop	Example
Nodeapps	srvctl start nodeapps -n RAC1
	srvctl stop nodeapps -n RAC2
Listener	srvctl stop listener -b rac1 -l VISK_RAC1
	srvctl stop listener -b rac1 -l VISK_RAC2

13-11. Obtaining Help for the srvctl Command

Problem

You want to see manual pages for certain srvctl commands.

Solution

Oracle provides syntax help for the srvctl executable. By simply typing srvctl -h without any arguments, detailed usage for all the argument options display on the screen. If you want to obtain detailed usage information for a specific option, you can pass arguments to srvctl with the -h option.

To get help about how to add a database service, you can type srvctl add service -h. Requesting help for this command yields this output:

```
$ srvctl add service -h
Usage: srvctl add service -d <name> -s <service_name> -r "<preferred_list>" [-a
"<available_list>"] [-P <TAF_policy>]
    -d <name>           Unique name for the database
    -s <service>        Service name
    -r "<pref_list>"    List of preferred instances
    -a "<avail_list>"   List of available instances
```

As another example, say you want to print the usage to remove a database from OCR since this command is rarely executed:

```
$ srvctl remove database -h
Usage: srvctl remove database -d <name> [-f]
    -d <name>          Unique name for the database
    -f                 Force remove
    -h                 Print usage
```

How It Works

You can get help for just about all the available options to srvctl. srvctl accepts the following arguments for the help parameter:

```
srvctl <command> <target> -h
```

Table 13-2 lists possible command and target options to receive help for.

Table 13-2. *Command and Target of the Command*

Command	Target of the Command
add	database
config	instance
disable	service
enable	nodeapps
getenv	asm
modify	listener
Relocate (service only)	
remove	
setenv	
start	
status	
stop	
unsetenv	

You can specify valid combinations from the command and target columns for help.

13-12. Viewing CRS Resources

Problem

You want to view CRS resources and obtain status information.

Solution

You can view CRS status information using the `crs_stat` executable. The `-t` option shows the output in tabular format, as shown here:

```
$ crs_stat -t
Name            Type         Target   State    Host
-------------------------------------------------------------
ora....A1.inst  application  ONLINE   ONLINE   rac3
ora....A2.inst  application  ONLINE   ONLINE   rac4
ora.RACQA.db    application  ONLINE   ONLINE   rac4
ora....C3.lsnr  application  ONLINE   ONLINE   rac3
ora.rac3.gsd    application  ONLINE   ONLINE   rac3
ora.rac3.ons    application  ONLINE   ONLINE   rac3
ora.rac3.vip    application  ONLINE   ONLINE   rac3
ora....C4.lsnr  application  ONLINE   ONLINE   rac4
ora.rac4.gsd    application  ONLINE   ONLINE   rac4
ora.rac4.ons    application  ONLINE   ONLINE   rac4
ora.rac4.vip    application  ONLINE   ONLINE   rac4
```

`crs_stat` also has a `-v` option for verbose output. Let's look at the `ora.RACQA.RACQA1.inst` resource with the `-v` option:

```
$ crs_stat -v ora.RACQA.RACQA1.inst
NAME=ora.RACQA.RACQA1.inst
TYPE=application
RESTART_ATTEMPTS=5
RESTART_COUNT=0
FAILURE_THRESHOLD=0
FAILURE_COUNT=0
TARGET=ONLINE
STATE=ONLINE on rac3
```

With the verbose output, additional information such as restart attempts, restart count, failure threshold, and failure count are exposed for each of the resources. You can also execute the `-v` option with the `-t` option. Executing the command yields this output:

```
$ crs_stat -t -v
Name            Type         R/RA   F/FT   Target   State    Host
----------------------------------------------------------------------------
ora....A1.inst  application  0/5    0/0    ONLINE   ONLINE   rac3
ora....A2.inst  application  0/5    0/0    ONLINE   ONLINE   rac4
ora.RACQA.db    application  0/0    0/1    ONLINE   ONLINE   rac4
ora....C3.lsnr  application  0/5    0/0    ONLINE   ONLINE   rac3
ora.rac3.gsd    application  0/5    0/0    ONLINE   ONLINE   rac3
ora.rac3.ons    application  0/3    0/0    ONLINE   ONLINE   rac3
ora.rac3.vip    application  0/0    0/0    ONLINE   ONLINE   rac3
ora....C4.lsnr  application  0/5    0/0    ONLINE   ONLINE   rac4
ora.rac4.gsd    application  0/5    0/0    ONLINE   ONLINE   rac4
ora.rac4.ons    application  0/3    0/0    ONLINE   ONLINE   rac4
ora.rac4.vip    application  0/0    0/0    ONLINE   ONLINE   rac4
```

You will notice the R/RA columns for restart count and restart attempts. Similarly, you will notice the F/FT columns for failure count and failure thresholds.

Executing the crs_stat command with the -p option will provide even more detailed information about the resource.

How It Works

The crs_stat command displays the status of the cluster services and reads directly from the OCR. Unfortunately, the output is not very readable. With the -t option, the output is significantly better except the resource column is abbreviated and often hard to read.

Oracle support provides an elaborate awk script in MetaLink Note 259301.1 that provides the crs_stat output in readable format to view the resource name column in entirety. Here we incorporated Oracle's awk script in a shell script called dba_crs. Executing dba_crs, you can see the complete resource name:

```
$ ./dba_crs
HA Resource                          Target       State
-----------                          ------       -----
ora.RACQA.RACQA1.inst                ONLINE       ONLINE on rac3
ora.RACQA.RACQA2.inst                ONLINE       ONLINE on rac4
ora.RACQA.db                         ONLINE       ONLINE on rac4
ora.rac3.RACQA_RAC3.lsnr             ONLINE       ONLINE on rac3
ora.rac3.gsd                         ONLINE       ONLINE on rac3
ora.rac3.ons                         ONLINE       ONLINE on rac3
ora.rac3.vip                         ONLINE       ONLINE on rac3
ora.rac4.RACQA_RAC4.lsnr             ONLINE       ONLINE on rac4
ora.rac4.gsd                         ONLINE       ONLINE on rac4
ora.rac4.ons                         ONLINE       ONLINE on rac4
ora.rac4.vip                         ONLINE       ONLINE on rac4
```

13-13. Debugging srvctl

Problem

You want to determine why a certain srvctl command is failing. You want to see srvctl in verbose mode.

Solution

The easiest way to enable debugging is to set the Unix environment variable called SRVM_TRACE to TRUE:

```
export SRVM_TRACE=true
```

Once you set the SRVM_TRACE environment variable, you can execute the srvctl command, and your output will be displayed in debug mode. Here's an example of an srvctl output with SRVM_TRACE set to TRUE:

```
[…]
m[ain] [19:51:59:385] [HAOperationResult.getOutputAll:115]  errLine is [CRS-0215:
Could not start resource 'ora.RACQA.RACQA2.inst'.]
[main] [19:51:59:385] [ParallelServerHA.startInstance:1419]  Failed to start RACQA2
 on rac4 error=CRS-0215: Could not start resource 'ora.RACQA.RACQA2.inst'.
[main] [19:51:59:386] [RemoteResponseEvent.<init>:62]  Creating Rmi Data Event
[main] [19:51:59:388] [HAOperationResult.getOutputAll:114]  outLine is []
[main] [19:51:59:388] [HAOperationResult.getOutputAll:115]  errLine is [CRS-0215:
Could not start resource 'ora.RACQA.RACQA2.inst'.]
PRKP-1001 : Error starting instance RACQA1 on node rac3
rac3:ora.RACQA.RACQA1.inst:
rac3:ora.RACQA.RACQA1.inst:SQL*Plus: Release 11.1.0.6.0 - Production on Tue Jun 24
19:51:33 2008
rac3:ora.RACQA.RACQA1.inst:
rac3:ora.RACQA.RACQA1.inst:Copyright (c) 1982, 2007, Oracle.  All rights reserved.
rac3:ora.RACQA.RACQA1.inst:
rac3:ora.RACQA.RACQA1.inst:Enter user-name: Connected to an idle instance.
rac3:ora.RACQA.RACQA1.inst:
rac3:ora.RACQA.RACQA1.inst:SQL> ORA-00119: invalid specification for system
parameter LOCAL_LISTENER
rac3:ora.RACQA.RACQA1.inst:ORA-00132: syntax error or unresolved network name
'LISTENER_RACQA1'
rac3:ora.RACQA.RACQA1.inst:ORA-01078: failure in processing system parameters
rac3:ora.RACQA.RACQA1.inst:SQL> Disconnected
rac3:ora.RACQA.RACQA1.inst:
CRS-0215: Could not start resource 'ora.RACQA.RACQA1.inst'.
PRKP-1001 : Error starting instance RACQA2 on node rac4
CRS-0215: Could not start resource 'ora.RACQA.RACQA2.inst'.
```

The output of the srvctl command in debug mode is quite lengthy; the output that is provided here is just a snippet of the entire output. In this particular example, the output provides some relevant information about the local listener as the starting point to diagnose the problem.

How It Works

The easiest way to enable the srvctl command in debug mode is to set the SRVM_TRACE environment variable to TRUE. If you want to disable debug mode, you can unset the SRVM_TRACE variable using the unset command:

```
unset SRVM_TRACE
```

13-14. Configuring the hangcheck-timer Kernel Module

Problem

You want to load the hangcheck-timer to ensure that the RAC node is evicted from the cluster under unstable conditions in order to prevent database corruptions.

Solution

To manually load the hangcheck-timer, you can execute the insmod command. First, locate the hangcheck-timer by executing the find command in the /lib/modules directory path:

```
# find /lib/modules -name 'hangcheck*'
/lib/modules/2.6.9-42.0.0.0.1.EL/kernel/drivers/char/hangcheck-timer.ko
/lib/modules/2.6.9-42.0.0.0.1.ELsmp/kernel/drivers/char/hangcheck-timer.ko
```

Change your directory to the location of the hangcheck-timer kernel module. As the root user, load the hangcheck-timer into the kernel using the insmod command, as you see here:

```
# cd  /lib/modules/2.6.9-42.0.0.0.1.ELsmp/kernel/drivers/char/
# insmod hangcheck-timer.ko hangcheck_tick=30 hangcheck_margin=180
```

Once the hangcheck-timer kernel module is loaded into the kernel, you can confirm the existence of the module in the kernel using the lsmod command, as you see here:

```
# lsmod |grep -i hangcheck
hangcheck_timer        7897  0
```

As the root user, you can view the log entries in the /var/log/messages file to confirm that the hangcheck-timer started successfully. Here's a snippet of the /var/log/messages file:

```
# tail /var/log/messages
[…]
Jun 21 17:10:30 rac3 kernel: Hangcheck: starting hangcheck timer 0.9.0 (tick is 30
seconds, margin is 180 seconds).
Jun 21 17:10:30 rac3 kernel: Hangcheck: Using monotonic_clock().
```

To survive node reboots, the /etc/modprobe.conf file must have the following line added:

```
options hangcheck-timer hangcheck_tick=30 hangcheck_margin=180
```

How It Works

Linux has a kernel module named hangcheck-timer to monitor the health of the RAC environment and to restart a RAC node in the event of availability and reliability problems. Starting in Oracle 9*i* Release 2 (9.2.0.2), Oracle supports the hangcheck-timer loaded into the Linux kernel to monitor and detect various system hangs and pauses. The hangcheck-timer module simply sets a timer and checks the timer after a configurable amount of time. If a delay is detected and if that delay exceeds a given margin of time, the server is rebooted.

The hangcheck-timer module leverages the Time Stamp Counter (TSC) CPU register of the CPU and is incremented with each clock signal. Utilizing the CPU, the kernel module provides precise and accurate time measurements under normal conditions. When a delay is detected, the delay can be an indication of a system hang. If the delay is longer than the specified threshold, the RAC node is evicted.

The hangcheck-timer module has two parameters: hangcheck-tick and hangcheck-margin. The hangcheck-tick specifies the time between system health checks. The hangcheck-tick parameter has a default value of 60 seconds. The recommended value for this parameter by Oracle is 30 seconds. The hangcheck-margin parameter specifies the allowable hang delay in seconds that will be tolerated before hangcheck-timer evicts the RAC node. The default value is 180 seconds and happens to be the recommended setting by Oracle.

A RAC node will be evicted when the system hang time is greater than the result of the following calculation:

```
hangcheck_tick + hangcheck_margin
```

Starting in Oracle Database 11g, the hangcheck-timer module is accompanied by the Process Monitor Daemon (oprocd), which monitors the system state of cluster nodes. The oprocd can detect hang conditions that the hangcheck-timer misses. hangcheck-timer is good for detecting driver failures (which would require reboots), whereas, oprocd is used to detect node stalls.

13-15. Starting and Stopping Oracle Clusterware

Problem

You want to start/stop Oracle Clusterware.

Solution

To start Oracle Clusterware, you can execute the crsctl command and pass the correct arguments, start crs, to initiate a startup of the CRS:

```
$ sudo -u root -s $ORACLE_HOME/bin/crsctl start crs
Attempting to start Oracle Clusterware stack
The CRS stack will be started shortly
```

To stop Oracle Clusterware, you can also execute the crsctl command with the argument stop crs to initiate the shutdown of CRS:

```
$ sudo -u root -s $ORACLE_HOME/bin/crsctl stop crs
Stopping resources. This could take several minutes.
Successfully stopped CRS resources.
Stopping CSSD.
Shutting down CSS daemon.
Shutdown request successfully issued.
```

How It Works

Root privileges are required to start or shut down Oracle Clusterware. In Oracle Database 10g Release 1, the /etc/init.d/init.crs script was the preferred script to start and shut down Clusterware. As of Oracle Database 10g Release 2, the $ORA_CRS_HOME/bin/crsctl script became the supported script to start and shut down Oracle Clusterware. Starting and stopping Oracle Clusterware involves starting/shutting down all the RAC-related background processes such as CRSD, OPROCD, OCSSD, EVMD, and ONS.

13-16. Enabling and Disabling CRS from Autostartup

Problem

You want to enable or disable the automatic startup of Oracle Clusterware when the server boots.

Solution

To disable Oracle Clusterware from automatically starting when the server reboots, you can specify the `disable crs` option to the `crsctl` command:

```
crs > sudo -u root -s $ORACLE_HOME/bin/crsctl disable crs
Oracle Clusterware is disabled for start-up after a reboot.
```

Likewise, to start Oracle Clusterware with a server reboot, you can execute the `crsctl` command with the argument `enable crs`:

```
sudo -u root -s $ORACLE_HOME/bin/crsctl enable crs
Oracle Clusterware is enabled for start-up after a reboot.
```

How It Works

You may have some issues with your hardware and want to stop CRS from automatically starting or stopping. One such reason can be because your device names do not survive reboots. For example, with each reboot, the device names for OCR and voting disks may change. You can then disable Oracle Clusterware from automatically starting. Upon a server boot, the SA can map the correct block or raw devices for the OCR and voting disk, and then you or the SA can manually start Clusterware. Once the SA has some available time, the SA can write scripts with udev and effectively implement device-naming persistency.

13-17. Checking the Viability of Oracle Clusterware

Problem

You want to check the condition of Oracle Clusterware.

Solution

You can check the state of Oracle Clusterware with the `crsctl` command and the `check crs` option, as shown here:

```
crs > crsctl check crs
Cluster Synchronization Services appears healthy
Cluster Ready Services appears healthy
Event Manager appears healthy
```

Alternatively, you can check each of the daemons including CSSD, CRSD, and EVMD:

```
crs > crsctl check cssd
Cluster Synchronization Services appears healthy
rac4.dbaexpert.com:/apps/oracle/general/sh
crs > crsctl check crsd
Cluster Ready Services appears healthy
rac4.dbaexpert.com:/apps/oracle/general/sh
crs > crsctl check evmd
Event Manager appears healthy
```

How It Works

To check the condition of Oracle Clusterware, you can execute the `crsctl` command with the check option. In Oracle Database 11*g*, another check option is provided for the `crsctl` command to check the cluster:

```
crs > crsctl check cluster
rac3     ONLINE
rac4     ONLINE
```

13-18. Converting a Stand-Alone Database to RAC

Problem

You want convert a non-RAC database into a RAC database.

Solution

Assuming that all the hardware requirements are satisfied and all the preliminary tasks are complete including a successful installation of Oracle Clusterware, the conversion from a stand-alone database to a RAC database is relatively straightforward. In this solution, we will provide the detailed steps required to convert a stand-alone database to a RAC database.

First, you must add a separate redo log thread for each instance. If the database has four redo log groups for thread 1, you must add four redo groups to thread 2 (your second RAC instance). Here's the syntax to add four redo groups for thread 2:

```
1  alter database add logfile thread 2 group 11
2  ('/u04/oradata/DBAPROD/DBAPROD2_redo_01a.rdo',
   '/u03/oradata/DBAPROD/DBAPROD2_redo_01b.rdo') size 200m
10:13:40 SQL> /
Database altered.

1  alter database add logfile thread 2 group 12
2* ('/u05/oradata/DBAPROD/DBAPROD2_redo_02a.rdo',
   '/u02/oradata/DBAPROD/DBAPROD2_redo_02b.rdo') size 200m
10:15:44 SQL> /
Database altered.
```

```
1  alter database add logfile thread 2 group 13
2* ('/u04/oradata/DBAPROD/DBAPROD2_redo_03a.rdo',
   '/u03/oradata/DBAPROD/DBAPROD2_redo_03b.rdo') size 200m
10:16:44 SQL> /
Database altered.

1  alter database add logfile thread 2 group 14
2* ('/u05/oradata/DBAPROD/DBAPROD2_redo_14a.rdo',
   '/u02/oradata/DBAPROD/DBAPROD2_redo_14b.rdo') size 200m
10:18:03 SQL> /
Database altered.
```

For RAC databases on ASM, the syntax would resemble the example here, assuming that the db_create_file_dest and db_create_online_log_dest_1 parameters have the value of '+data':

```
alter database add logfile thread 2 group 21 size 100m;
alter database add logfile thread 2 group 22 size 100m;
alter database add logfile thread 2 group 23 size 100m;
alter database add logfile thread 2 group 24 size 100m;
```

After you add the redo groups, you must enable the thread using the alter database enable command:

```
alter database enable thread 2;
```

Note You must add groups for each of the RAC instances. For example, if you have a four-node RAC, you will have to repeat the steps outlined previously two more times.

In addition to adding redo groups for each thread, you must also add an undo tablespace for each of the RAC instances. The syntax to create another undo tablespace looks like this:

```
1* create undo tablespace undo_rbs2
   datafile '/u02/oradata/DBATOOLS/undo_rbs2_01.dbf' size 4000m
SQL> /
```

Again, you must create an undo tablespace for each of your RAC instances. Next, you must create the RAC views by executing catclust.sql from $ORACLE_HOME/rdbms/admin as sysdba. RAC views enable you to obtain information about all the RAC nodes at once instead of having to log on to each of the RAC nodes. For example, if you want to view active sessions across all the RAC nodes, you can query the GV$SESSION view instead of the V$SESSION view. Likewise, if you are interested in blocking locks at the entire RAC level, you can query the GV$LOCK view instead of the V$LOCK view.

You are almost done. You must now modify the initialization parameters or spfile to recognize the database as a RAC database:

```
# ------- RAC Specifics ---
*.cluster_database_instances=2
*.cluster_database=true
DBAPROD1.thread=1
DBAPROD1.instance_number=1
DBAPROD1.undo_tablespace='UNDO_RBS1'
#
DBAPROD2.thread=2
DBAPROD2.instance_number=2
DBAPROD2.undo_tablespace='UNDO_RBS2'
*.remote_login_passwordfile='exclusive'

# 10g parameters
*.db_create_file_dest='+data'
*.db_create_online_log_dest_1='+data'
```

You can execute the srvctl command to register the database in the OCR. To register the database as a RAC database, you can execute these commands:

```
srvctl add database -d DBAPROD -o /apps/oracle/product/10.2.0/RACDB
srvctl add instance -d DBAPROD -i DBAPROD1 -n rac3
srvctl add instance -d DBAPROD -i DBAPROD2 -n rac4
```

As the final step, you must restart the database.

How It Works

We provided the steps to convert a stand-alone database to a RAC-enabled database to demonstrate that the conversion to a RAC database is not a black box—you can see from the solution that RAC conversion is not rocket science. The following are the steps to convert a stand-alone non-RAC database to a RAC database:

1. Create redo groups for each RAC instance.

2. Create an undo tablespace for each RAC instance.

3. Enable threads for each RAC instance.

4. Execute catclust.sql from $ORACLE_HOME/rdbms/admin.

5. Register the database and instance using the srvctl command.

6. Make appropriate changes to the spfile or initialization file.

7. Bounce the database.

■**Note** You can also migrate to RAC with the rconfig tool introduced in Oracle Database 10g Release 2. rconfig provides another method to convert a single-instance non-RAC database to RAC. For additional information, please review Oracle's MetaLink Note 387046.1.

13-19. Bonding Network Interface Cards

Problem

You want to pair network interface cards for performance and reliability.

Solution

Bonding a network card is relatively straightforward. First, you have to configure the Linux bond drivers. For example, in Red Hat 4, you must modify the /etc/modprobe.conf file to enable the bonding driver. You must add entries for each of the logical interfaces in the modprobe.conf file that resemble this:

```
alias bond0 bonding
alias bond1 bonding
options bonding miimon=100 mode=1
```

In this particular solution, you are adding two bonded interfaces, one for the private inter-connect and the other for the public network. You also have four network interfaces, eth0, eth1, eth2, and eth3.

If you have not bonded network interfaces before, most likely the bonding module is not loaded into the kernel. As root, execute the insmod bonding.ko command from the /lib/modules/`uname -r`/kernel/drivers/net/bonding directory to insert the module into the kernel. To confirm that the bonding module is loaded, you can leverage the lsmod command piped to the grep command, as shown here, to provide the status of the modules in the kernel:

```
# lsmod |grep -i bonding
bonding               65128  0
```

Once you confirmed that the bonding module is loaded into the kernel, you can proceed by configuring the logical interfaces by creating or modifying two configuration files in the /etc/sysconfig/network-scripts directory called ifcfg-bond0 and ifcfg-bond1. The entries for ifcfg-bond0 look like this for the private network:

```
DEVICE=bond0
IPADDR=192.168.1.20
NETWORK=192.168.1.0
NETMASK=255.255.255.0
USERCTL=no
BOOTPROTO=none
ONBOOT=yes
```

You must modify the ifcfg-eth0 and ifcfg-eth1 files, which are the interface cards for ifcfg-bond0. Let's start by modifying the ifcfg-eth0 file with the settings you see here:

```
DEVICE=eth0
USERCTL=no
ONBOOT=yes
MASTER=bond0
SLAVE=yes
BOOTPROTO=none
```

Similarly, let's modify the ifcfg-eth1 file so it looks like what is shown here:

```
DEVICE=eth1
USERCTL=no
ONBOOT=yes
MASTER=bond0
SLAVE=yes
BOOTPROTO=none
```

Now, you need to repeat the procedures described earlier to configure the ifcfg-bond1 interface for the public network interface. The ifcfg-bond1 interface file needs to resemble this:

```
DEVICE=bond1
IPADDR=72.99.67.100
NETWORK=72.99.67.0
NETMASK=255.255.255.0
USERCTL=no
BOOTPROTO=none
ONBOOT=yes
```

The key difference between ifcfg-bond0 and ifcfg-bond1 are the IPADDR, NETWORK, and NETMASK lines. After the ifcfg-bond1 file is created, you can proceed to modify the ifcfg-eth3 and ifcfg-eth4 files. You can create these two files to look like ifcfg-eth0 and ifcfg-eth1 and modify the DEVICE and MASTER names accordingly.

To enable the newly configured bonded network, you need to bounce the networking services. You can shut down all the interfaces with the service network stop command. As the final step, you need to start the bonded network interfaces by executing the service network start command.

How It Works

The Linux kernel comes with a bonding module that provides NIC teaming capabilities. The kernel bonding module teams multiple physical interfaces to a single logical interface.

Bonding or pairing a network is an important concept for RAC. Network interfaces that are not bonded are a single point of failure. Just as every other component of the RAC is built for redundancy, so must the network infrastructure be.

In the /etc/modprobe.conf file, we specified options bonding miimon=100 mode=1. The miimon parameter stands for Media Independent Interface Monitor and represents the frequency for link monitoring. The value for miimon is specified in milliseconds (ms), is set to zero by default, and is disabled. The mode parameter specifies the type of configuration to be deployed. A value of 0, which is the default, indicates that a round-robin policy will be implemented, and each of the interfaces will take turns servicing requests. You can use a round-robin policy for load balancing. A value of 1 indicates that an active backup policy will be deployed. In an active backup policy, only one slave in the bond is active. One and only one device will transmit at any given moment. A value of 6 indicates adaptive load balancing.

In the ifcfg-eth[x] files, the MASTER parameter indicates the logical interface to which the particular NIC belongs. The SLAVE parameter indicates that the participating NIC is a member of bond interface. A SLAVE can belong to only one master.

13-20. Implementing RAC on NFS

Problem

You want to implement RAC on NFS filesystems. You want to take advantage of Oracle Database 11g Direct NFS.

Solution

To implement Oracle Direct NFS, you must have an existing NFS mount point that is presented to all the RAC nodes. The mount options for NFS are irrelevant since Oracle Direct NFS will override and configure settings optimally. Oracle Direct NFS setup involves manipulating the oranfstab file. The oranfstab file can reside in several locations. Oracle will always check the $ORACLE_HOME/dbs directory first. If the oranfstab file does not exist, it will search in the /etc directory. If an oranfstab file does not exist, Oracle will utilize the operating system /etc/mtab file. Oracle's Direct NFS client looks for mount point settings in the following order:

1. $ORACLE_HOME/dbs/oranfstab

2. /etc/oranfstab

3. /etc/mtab

To enable Direct NFS, you must replace the standard Oracle Disk Manager (ODM) driver with the ODM NFS library. For the client to work, you need to shut down the database and create a symbolic link from the standard ODM library to point to the NFS ODM library. Before you create the symbolic link, you should rename the original file libodm11.so to libodm11.so.ORIG for backup purposes. Next, you will create the symbolic link libodm11.so to point to libnfsodm11.so. Here are the steps to set up the NFS ODM library file:

1. cd $ORACLE_HOME/lib

2. mv libodm11.so libodm11.so.ORIG

3. ln -s libnfsodm11.so libodm11.so

Next, create the oranfstab file in the $ORACLE_HOME/dbs directory. The oranfstab file is not a requirement to implement Direct NFS. The oranfstab file is a special file to list additional options specific for Oracle Database to Direct NFS. The oranfstab file has the following attributes for each NFS server to be accessed using Direct NFS:

Server: NFS server name

Path: IP or hostname of up to four network paths to the NFS server

Export: Exported path from the NFS server

Mount: Local mount point for the NFS server

For this simple demonstration, you will just have one entry in the oranfstab file. The contents of the oranfstab file look like this:

```
server: nas150
path: 192.168.1.150
export: /apps/oracle/share mount: /oradata
```

An example of an oranfstab with multiple paths looks like this:

```
server: nas150
path: 192.168.1.1
path: 192.168.1.2
path: 192.168.1.3
path: 192.168.1.4

export: /oradata/share1 mount: /oradata1
```

In this example, four paths are specified in the oranfstab file. You may specify up to four paths by IP address or name as displayed by the ifconfig command. The Direct NFS client will perform load balancing across all four paths to the NAS server. If an I/O request to a specific path fails, Direct NFS will reissue the I/O request over the remaining paths.

How It Works

Oracle Database 11*g* delivers the highly anticipated new feature called Direct NFS. RAC and non-RAC customers who leverage NFS today on filers can take advantage of Oracle's new Direct NFS. Direct NFS provides simplicity and performance for database implementations on network-attached storage (NAS). Customers have opted for NFS solutions over block devices for simplicity and lower cost, and Direct NFS makes NFS implementations even simpler and faster.

Oracle Direct NFS is an NFS client built directly into the database kernel. With Oracle Direct NFS, the database kernel performs all the tuning processes automatically. DBAs and system administrators are no longer responsible for being intimate with all the tuning parameters associated with NFS.

Note Implementation of RAC on NFS is common with customers who utilize NAS storage. If you are not on Oracle Database 11*g*, you must use the following NFS mount options for RAC:

```
netapp1:/nasvol/u03  /u03  nfs  rw,rsize=32768,wsize=32768,tcp,hard,nointr,
nfsvers=3,bg,actimeo=0,timeo=600,suid,async
```

13-21. Adding Voting Disks

Problem

You have only one voting disk, and you want to follow Oracle best practices and create two additional voting disks.

Solution

Oracle Clusterware should be shut down while adding voting disks. With Clusterware offline, you should also back up the voting disk. If your voting disks are on raw devices, as the oracle user, execute the dd command and back up the voting disk as you see here:

```
$ dd if=raw1 of=/apps/oracle/vote.bkup
103680+0 records in.
103680+0 records out.
```

Before you start adding raw devices for voting disk, you should clear out the contents of the raw devices using the dd command in conjunction with the /dev/zero device. Here we will clear out the contents of the /dev/raw/raw2 and /dev/raw/raw3 devices:

```
$ dd if=/dev/zero of=/dev/raw/raw2 bs=1024000 count=50
50+0 records in.
50+0 records out.
$ dd if=/dev/zero of=/dev/raw/raw3 bs=1024000 count=50
50+0 records in.
50+0 records out.
```

The crsctl command with the -force option must be used to add the voting disk since the CRS stack is down. Here we will add the /dev/raw/raw2 and /dev/raw/raw3 devices to the voting disk configuration with the CRS stack down:

```
$ crsctl add css votedisk /dev/raw/raw2 -force
Now formatting voting disk: /dev/raw/raw2.
Successful addition of voting disk /dev/raw/raw2.

$ crsctl add css votedisk /dev/raw/raw3 -force
Now formatting voting disk: /dev/raw/raw3.
Successful addition of voting disk /dev/raw/raw3.
```

Once the voting disks are successfully added, you can restart CRS by executing the crsctl start crs command from the $ORA_CRS_HOME/bin directory.

How It Works

The RAC configuration supports up to 32 voting disks. The voting disk is the heartbeat of RAC. The RAC environment must have at least 50 percent of the voting disk online to remain available. Once you have successfully added the voting disks, you can execute the crsctl command with the query option to view voting disk information, as shown here:

```
$ crsctl query css votedisk
  0.      0    /dev/raw/raw1
  1.      0    /dev/raw/raw2
  2.      0    /dev/raw/raw3
```

For additional information regarding how to add/remove/move/replace voting or OCR disks, please review Metalink Note 428681.1.

13-22. Removing/Moving a Voting Disk

Problem

You want to remove an existing voting disk or move a voting disk from one location to another.

Solution

You can simply remove a voting disk with the `crsctl` command as `root` since `root` owns the voting disk. To remove a voting disk, you would simply issue the `delete` option, as shown here:

```
# crsctl delete css votedisk /NFS/CRS/votingdisk3
Successful deletion of voting disk /NFS/CRS/votingdisk3.
```

To move a voting disk, you would proceed by adding a voting disk as shown in recipe 13-21.

How It Works

Moving a voting disk implies that you will delete the existing one and create a new voting disk on an alternate location. But if you have only one voting disk, you need to create a new one first before you can delete the original. If you have just one voting disk, this is a great opportunity you triple mirror your voting disks with Oracle. Once again, we recommend to triple mirror your voting disk to avoid a single point of failure.

13-23. Implementing RAC on OCFS2

Problem

You want to implement RAC on Oracle Cluster File Systems version 2 (OCFS2) filesystems.

Solution

You must first install the OCFS2 RPMs. If you are registered with Oracle's Unbreakable Linux Network (ULN), you can take advantage of the `up2date` command. In this solution, we will show how to execute the `up2date` command to install the `ocfs2-tools`, `ocfs2console`, and `ocfs2` RPMs. In the example here, we will install the `ocfs2` driver module using the `$(uname -r)` syntax to derive the kernel release:

```
# up2date --install ocfs2-$(uname -r)
```

Installing the `ocsf2` RPM will automatically download the `ocfs2-tools` RPM based on dependency requirements. The `ocfs2-tools` RPM provides the command-line interface to the OCFS2 tool. Although `ocfs2console` RPM is not required, we recommend that you install the `ocfs2console` RPM by executing the `up2date` command with the `ocfs2console` RPM as the argument, as displayed here:

```
# up2date --install  ocfs2console
```

The ocfs2console RPM provides the GUI front end for OCFS2. If you do not have a license for Oracle's ULN, you can download the RPMs from http://oss.oracle.com and install them with the rpm -ihv {RPM_NAME} syntax. You must install the OCFS2 RPMs on each of the RAC nodes.

You can confirm that OCFS2 RPMs are installed on the RAC nodes by executing an rpm query on the OCFS2 modules:

```
# rpm -qa |grep -i ocfs2
ocfs2-tools-1.2.2-2
ocfs2-2.6.9-42.0.0.0.1.ELsmp-1.2.3-2
ocfs2console-1.2.2-2
ocfs2-2.6.9-42.0.0.0.1.EL-1.2.3-2
```

Once you verified that OCFS2 RPMs are installed on each of the RAC nodes, you are ready to start configuring OCFS2. OCFS2 comes with a cluster stack called O2CB. The O2CB cluster stack handles the communication between the nodes and the cluster filesystem and includes services such as a node manager, a distributed lock manager, and a heartbeat service. You will need to start the O2CB cluster stack before you can proceed to format and mount the filesystem. The ocfs2console GUI tool provides the easiest and recommended method to configure the O2CB cluster stack. The ocfs2console provides the capability to manage OCFS2 volumes providing the mechanism to format, tune, mount, and unmount OCFS2 volumes.

To configure OCFS2 with the GUI tool, as root, launch the ocfs2console from the /usr/sbin directory. If your Linux server does not have X server software installed, set DISPLAY to another server, to a VNC server, or to your desktop that has Hummingbird or other third-party X server software installed.

Note For X server configuration information, please review Chapter 15.

Launching the ocfs2console tool displays the screen shown in Figure 13-7.

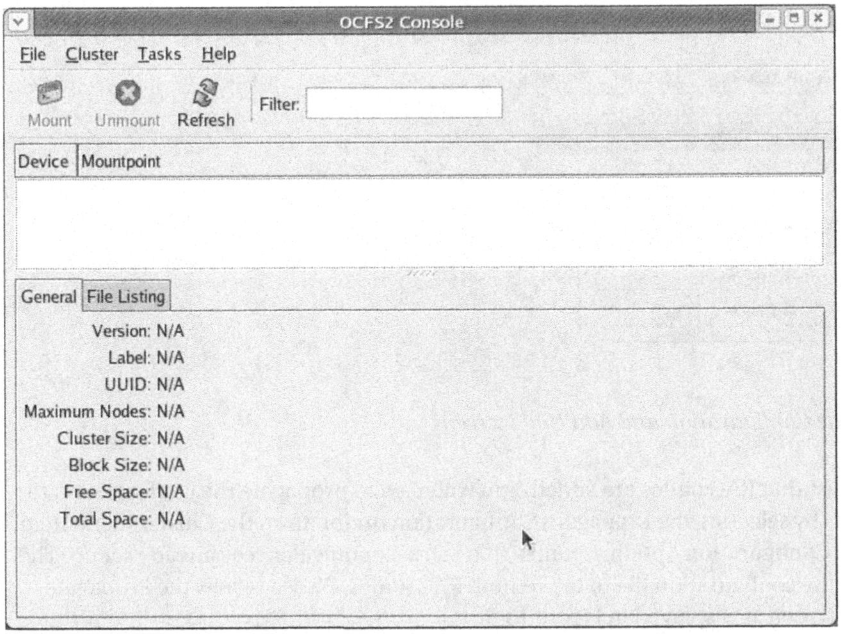

Figure 13-7. *OCFS2 Console screen*

On the OCFS2 Console screen, click the Cluster menu, and select the Configure Nodes option to start the cluster stack. An informational window will be displayed to show that the cluster stack has been started. The cluster.conf configuration file will be created in the /etc/ocfs2 directory if it does not already exist. The message on the window will indicate that the cluster stack needs to be running for any clustering functionality to work and that you will need to run the command /etc/init.d/o2cb enable to have the cluster stack started upon reboot. Click the Close button, and the Node Configuration screen will be displayed. On the Node Configuration screen, click the Add button to add a node to the OCFS2 cluster. Figure 13-8 shows both the Node Configuration and Add Node screens.

On the Add Node screen, enter the hostname, IP address, and IP port of the OCFS2 cluster. Click the OK button once the host information is entered. Repeat the steps outlined to add the remaining node that will participate in the OCFS2 cluster.

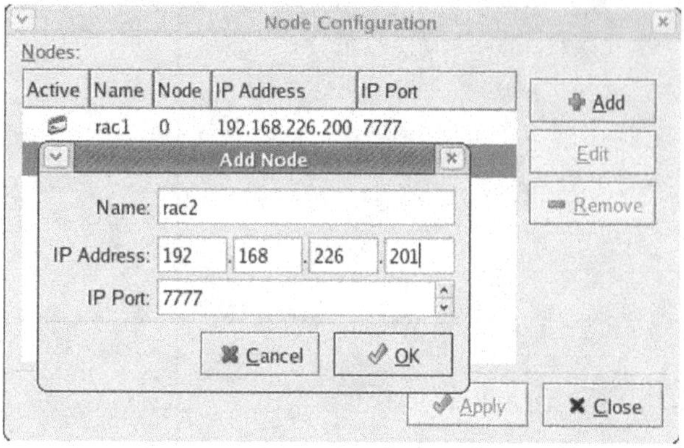

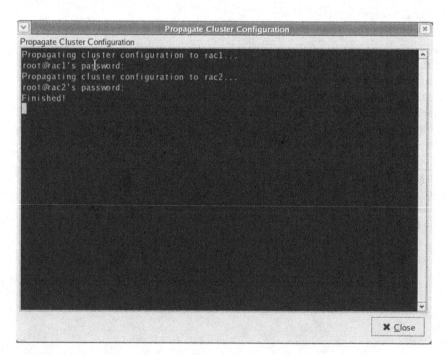

Figure 13-8. *Node Configuration and Add Node screens*

After all the other RAC nodes are added, you will need to propagate the configuration to the other nodes by selecting the Propagate Configuration option from the Cluster menu item. The Propagate Configuration option assumes that ssh user equivalence is already set up. This screen pushes the configuration file to the remote RAC nodes. Please review the Propagate Configuration screen as displayed in Figure 13-9.

Figure 13-9. *Propagate Cluster Configuration screen*

Once the propagate cluster configuration process is complete, you can quit the application from the File menu item. You can review the /etc/ocfs2/cluster.conf file to view the members of the OCFS2 cluster:

```
# cat cluster.conf
node:
    ip_port = 7777
    ip_address = 192.168.226.200
    number = 0
    name = rac1
    cluster = ocfs2

node:
    ip_port = 7777
    ip_address = 192.168.226.201
    number = 1
    name = rac2
    cluster = ocfs2

cluster:
    node_count = 2
    name = ocfs2
```

In addition to storing all the information that was entered from the ocfs2console tool, the cluster.conf file contains information about how many nodes are part of the cluster and the name of the cluster. ocfs2 is the default name of the cluster.

Now, let's configure the o2cb driver to automatically load after a reboot on each of the Linux servers. Before you can configure o2cb, you must unload the modules since ocfs2consolsole loaded the drivers earlier. In the next example, you will pass the configure argument to the /etc/init.d/o2cb command to load the drivers on reboot of the server.

```
Configuring the O2CB driver.

This will configure the on-boot properties of the O2CB driver.
The following questions will determine whether the driver is loaded on
boot.  The current values will be shown in brackets ('[]').  Hitting
<ENTER> without typing an answer will keep that current value.  Ctrl-C
will abort.

Load O2CB driver on boot (y/n) [y]:
Cluster to start on boot (Enter "none" to clear) [ocfs2]:
Specify heartbeat dead threshold (>=7) [7]: 61
Writing O2CB configuration: OK
Loading module "configfs": OK
Mounting configfs filesystem at /config: OK
Loading module "ocfs2_nodemanager": OK
Loading module "ocfs2_dlm": OK
Loading module "ocfs2_dlmfs": OK
Mounting ocfs2_dlmfs filesystem at /dlm: OK
Starting O2CB cluster ocfs2: OK
```

You can verify that the cluster stack is loaded by executing the o2cb status command on each RAC node, as shown in this example:

```
[root@rac2 ocfs2]# /etc/init.d/o2cb status
Module "configfs": Loaded
Filesystem "configfs": Mounted
Module "ocfs2_nodemanager": Loaded
Module "ocfs2_dlm": Loaded
Module "ocfs2_dlmfs": Loaded
Filesystem "ocfs2_dlmfs": Mounted
Checking O2CB cluster ocfs2: Online
Checking O2CB heartbeat: Not active
```

■**Note** For all o2cb command options, you can execute the o2cb command with a help argument from the /etc/init.d directory:

```
# ./o2cb help
Usage: ./o2cb {start|stop|restart|force-reload|enable|disable|configure|load|
unload|online|offline|force-offline|status}
```

When the disks are presented to each of the RAC nodes, you can proceed to the next step, which is to format the disks. There are two ways to format an OCFS2 disk, the ocfs2console GUI tool or interactively with the mkfs.ocfs2 command-line utility. The simplest and recommended way to format a disk is with the ocfs2console tool. Again, launch the ocfs2console tool, click the Tasks menu item, and select the Format option. Formatting a disk occurs on only one node. You should see a Format window similar to what is displayed in Figure 13-10.

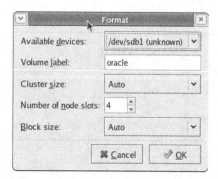

Figure 13-10. *Format device*

Select an option from the Available Devices drop-down menu, and select the cluster size. By default, the cluster size is set to Auto, but you can select 4K, 8K, 16K, 32K, 64K, 128K, 256K, 512K, or 1M. For database files, Oracle recommends cluster sizes of 128KB or larger. The block size can be from 512 bytes to 4KB. Oracle recommends 4KB block sizes for most disk sizes. Both the cluster size or block size are not modifiable after the disk is initialized.

Click the OK button once you've chosen all the options. You will be prompted to make sure you really want to format the device.

The volume label is changeable after the disk is formatted. The number of node slots can be increased after the disk is formatted but cannot be decreased.

Once you have the disk(s) formatted, you can proceed to mounting the filesystem. ocfs2console supports mounting the OCFS2 filesystem. To mount a filesystem, select the formatted device, and click the Mount button at the left-top corner of the screen. A small window will appear with the mount point and options fields, as displayed in Figure 13-11.

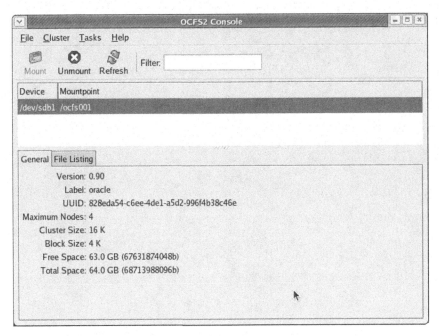

Figure 13-11. *Mount device*

One option that is worth noting is the _netdev option. This option specifies that network availability is required before mounting the filesystem after a reboot of the server.

Click the OK button after you enter the mount point and OCFS2 option(s). Your main ocfs2console window should look similar to Figure 13-12.

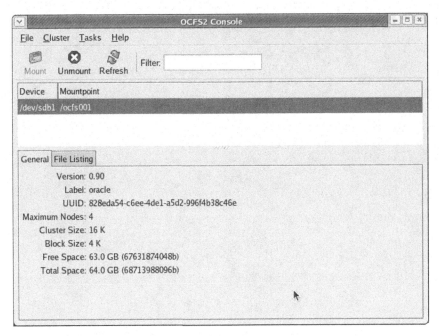

Figure 13-12. *Mounted filesystem*

Now your /ocfs001 filesystem is ready for RAC-related files. To mount the filesystem on reboot, you can add the following line in the /etc/fstab file of all the RAC nodes:

```
/dev/sdb1 /ocfs001 ocfs2 _netdev,datavolume,nointr 0 0
```

How It Works

Oracle Corporation introduced OCFS version 1.0 in December 2002 as open source software to the RAC community to support Linux 2.4 kernels. The design of the initial OCFS version was to provide an alternative solution for raw devices for database files.

For Linux 2.6 kernels, Oracle Corporation released OCFS version 2.0 (OCFS2) in September 2005 to support database files, Oracle binaries, and configuration files. OCFS2 is an extent-based, open source, POSIX-compliant shared disk filesystem. This recipe focuses only on OCFS2 since most Linux customers are running Linux 2.6 kernels.

Because the OCFS2 filesystem is a general-purpose clustered filesystem, Oracle customers also leverage this technology to provide highly available web servers, application servers, and file servers.

■**Note** Despite all the laborious efforts we went through to create the OCFS2 filesystem and present it to the RAC nodes, with the incredible advancement of ASM we do not recommend you use OCFS2 for RAC. You may consider storing the voting disk and OCR in the OCFS2 filesystem.

CHAPTER 14

■■■

Working Securely Across a Network

Secure communication is a concern, particularly when sharing confidential and vital information between people. Like in World War II, Winston Churchill, the prime minister of the United Kingdom, and Franklin D. Roosevelt, the president of the United States, shared critical military information, such as troop movements. To secure their voice conversations through the telephone, the SIGSALY (aka Green Hornet) was devised to encrypt and decrypt using cryptographic keys.

Nowadays, we cannot imagine anyone *not* worrying about network security. Even people who are not so technically savvy should be concerned. For instance, what if your bank's network is not secured and a hacker steals your bank account number and PIN? Likewise, a database administrator may want to connect to a Linux server situated in a remote geographical location or another room in the building while working at the office or at home. What if a co-worker is eavesdropping while that DBA is accessing sensitive data?

To address the network security concerns, version 1 of the Secure Shell (aka SSH) was hatched in 1995 but was replaced a year later by version 2 for security enhancements. SSH is a network protocol where the encrypted data traverses through the network using a secure channel between computers, as illustrated in Figure 14-1. The ssh protocol replaces the older network protocols, namely, telnet, rlogin, and rsh, as well as the scp command for the rcp command. The older protocols and commands were replaced since they lack the security feature; it just was not considered when they were initially designed.

Linux Server #1   Linux Server #2

Figure 14-1. *SSH connection*

In this chapter, we'll focus the discussion on how to log on securely to a remote Linux server through SSH, as well as how to generate the server's SSH host key, how to use the SSH public key for authentication in lieu of the username's password, how to securely copy files between Linux servers, and how to secure an unsecured connection.

14-1. Setting Up SSH

Problem

You want to configure SSH so you can have a secured and encrypted connection to your remote Linux server.

Solution

Before you configure SSH, ensure that you have the required packages, namely, openssh, openssh-server, openssh-clients, and openssh-askpass. You can verify the SSH packages installed on your server by running the rpm command as follows:

```
# rpm -qa | grep -i ssh
openssh-3.9p1-8.RHEL4.24
openssh-askpass-gnome-3.9p1-8.RHEL4.24
openssh-askpass-3.9p1-8.RHEL4.24
openssh-server-3.9p1-8.RHEL4.24
openssh-clients-3.9p1-8.RHEL4.24
```

Note Run the command ssh -V to check the type and version of SSH installed on your server.

Before you can connect to your remote Linux server, the SSH daemon server (sshd) must be running. You can run sshd as follows:

```
# service sshd start
Starting sshd:                                          [  OK  ]
```

You can also run sshd by calling the following script, which is the same script called by the previous command:

```
# /etc/rc.d/init.d/sshd start
Starting sshd:                                          [  OK  ]
```

However, if sshd is already started, then you can restart it, as shown here. Another way is to issue the command /etc/rc.d/init.d/sshd restart:

```
# service sshd restart
Stopping sshd:                                          [  OK  ]
Starting sshd:                                          [  OK  ]
```

For sshd to start automatically when the Linux server is rebooted, you need to have sshd activated. You can activate sshd using either chkconfig, ntsysv, or system-config-services.

For the chkconfig command, use the --level option, and provide the runlevel in which you want sshd to start. The following command indicates that sshd is configured to start in runlevels 2, 3, 4, and 5:

```
# chkconfig --level 2345 sshd on
```

■**Note** For a discussion of the Linux system V init runlevels, please review Chapter 11.

For the ntsysv command, also use the --level option, and specify the runlevels for sshd to start. If no runlevels are specified, then sshd will be activated only on the current runlevel. The following command will run ntsysv and will affect only runlevels 3 and 5:

```
# ntsysv --level 35
```

■**Note** You can also launch ntsysv through the text mode setup utility by running the operating system setup command and selecting System Services from the menu.

After you launch the ntsysv command, the screen of the text console service configuration tool will appear, as shown in Figure 14-2. Navigate by scrolling down using the arrow keys until the cursor is on sshd. The asterisk (*) inside the square brackets indicates that the status of the service is active, while empty square brackets means that it is not active. You can press the spacebar to toggle the status to become active or not active. To save the changes, click the Tab key to highlight the Ok button, and press the Enter key.

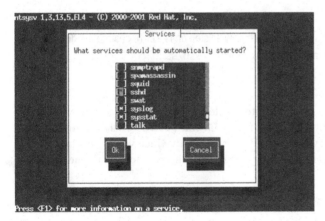

Figure 14-2. ntsysv

Another option to activate sshd is to run the system-config-services command; you can launch this tool as follows:

```
# /usr/sbin/system-config-services
```

After you launch system-config-services, the GUI-based service configuration tool will appear, as shown in Figure 14-3. Navigate by scrolling down to the sshd service, and check the adjacent box to activate it. In this dialog box, you also have the option to start, stop, and restart the sshd service, as well as check the status and process ID.

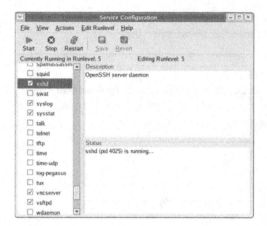

Figure 14-3. *system-config-services*

How It Works

By default, the required SSH packages are included in major Linux distributions. Otherwise, you can download them from any Linux package download site, such as http://www.openssh.com.

Once the SSH packages are installed on your remote Linux server, you can activate and run the sshd daemon, and it should be ready to accept SSH connections. You can, however, make some changes, such as modifying the default port number on which sshd should be listening.

Note The default SSH port number that the Linux server will listen on is 22. To change the default SSH port number, modify the value of the parameter Port in the /etc/ssh/sshd_config file.

The file /etc/ssh/sshd_config is the SSH systemwide configuration file at the Linux server, which is the computer that you want to connect via SSH, while /etc/ssh/ssh_config is the configuration file for the SSH client, which is the computer from which you are initiating SSH. If you make some changes to the /etc/ssh/sshd_config file, then you need to reload sshd by running service sshd reload as follows:

```
[root@BLLNX2 stage]# service sshd reload
Reloading sshd:                                         [  OK  ]
```

You can also run the command service sshd restart, or another method is to stop and start the sshd service, which will give the same results, as follows:

```
# service sshd stop
Stopping sshd:                                          [  OK  ]
# service sshd start
Starting sshd:                                          [  OK  ]
```

To verify the runlevel that sshd is configured to start, run the chkconfig command with the --list option. As shown here, sshd is set to start on runlevels 2, 3, 4, and 5:

```
# chkconfig --list sshd
sshd            0:off   1:off   2:on   3:on   4:on   5:on   6:off
```

Once sshd is running, issue the following operating system command to verify whether the corresponding sshd process is running. If there are no results, then this means sshd is not running yet. So, you need to run the service sshd start command to manually start sshd:

```
# ps -ef | grep -v grep | grep ssh
root      4025      1  0 16:32 ?        00:00:00 /usr/sbin/sshd
```

■**Note** To disallow the root user to log on via SSH, set the parameter PermitRootLogin to no in the /etc/ssh/sshd_config file. Once the non-root users have successfully logged on to the Linux server via SSH, they can then then run the su - root command or run the sudo command instead.

14-2. Generating Host Keys

Problem

The SSH host key of your remote Linux server is lost, is corrupted, or was not generated when the SSH packages were installed or during the first run. You want to generate a new SSH host key.

Solution

To generate a new SSH host key of the Linux server, log on as root, and run the ssh-keygen command with the -t option, which indicates the type of key to be generated. You must provide the -f option followed by the file name of the key file. If you omit the -f option, then it will create the public key for the operating system account root instead of the SSH host key on the Linux server.

The following example will generate the SSH host key for the RSA type. If the files of the SSH host keys already exist, then you are asked whether you want to overwrite them. Next, you are asked to provide the passphrase.

```
[root@BLLNX2 ~]# ssh-keygen -t rsa -f /etc/ssh/ssh_host_rsa_key
Generating public/private rsa key pair.
/etc/ssh/ssh_host_rsa_key already exists.
Overwrite (y/n)? y
Enter passphrase (empty for no passphrase):
Enter same passphrase again:
Your identification has been saved in /etc/ssh/ssh_host_rsa_key.
Your public key has been saved in /etc/ssh/ssh_host_rsa_key.pub.
The key fingerprint is:
43:1a:78:99:d0:d1:5b:3a:4b:a3:f9:0f:4b:d7:cd:63 root@BLLNX2
```

■**Note** For security reasons, we recommend you supply a passphrase when creating the SSH host key. This prevents non-root users from peeking on the SSH host key by running ssh-keygen with the -y option, which is discussed in detail in the next section.

How It Works

The SSH host key is like a master key that is used to encrypt and decrypt the data that traverses between the remote Linux server and the client computer, where you want to initiate the SSH connection. This secures your connection to the remote Linux server and eliminates vulnerability to man-in-the-middle attacks.

When creating a new SSH host key, you need to provide the type of key that corresponds to the version of SSH and the kind of encryption algorithm, which is either RSA or DSA. The valid values for the type of key are rsa1, rsa, and dsa. rsa1 refers to RSA of SSH version 1 (SSHv1), while rsa and dsa are for SSH version 2 (SSHv2).

■**Note** If your Linux server supports only SSH version2, set the value of the parameter Protocol to 2 in /etc/ssh/sshd_config.

To create the RSA host key, run ssh-keygen with the -t rsa option; this will create two files, namely, /etc/ssh/ssh_host_rsa_key and /etc/ssh/ssh_host_rsa_key.pub. For the DSA host key, run -keygen with the -t dsa option; this will create /etc/ssh/ssh_host_dsa_key and /etc/ssh/ssh_host_dsa_key.pub. Both ssh_host_rsa_key and ssh_host_dsa_key contain the private and public key, while ssh_host_rsa_key.pub and ssh_host_dsa_key.pub contain only the public key. The public key is used to encrypt the data, while the private key is used to decrypt the data.

The first time you log on to the remote Linux server, which is the computer you are connecting to via SSH, you are prompted to confirm the server's SSH host key fingerprint, as shown here. If you accept it, the file $HOME/.ssh/known_hosts will be created on the local Linux server, which is the computer from where you initiated the SSH connection. $HOME/.ssh/known_hosts contains the server's SSH host key.

```
[bslopuz@BLLNX1 ~]$ ssh bllnx2
The authenticity of host 'bllnx2 (192.168.0.12)' can't be established.
RSA key fingerprint is 5b:0f:a0:df:e0:9a:90:db:c7:bb:82:5c:15:d5:da:78.
Are you sure you want to continue connecting (yes/no)? yes
Warning: Permanently added 'bllnx2,192.168.0.12' (RSA) to the list of known hosts.
bslopuz@bllnx2's password:
Last login: Fri Jul 18 14:51:13 2008 from bllnx1
[bslopuz@BLLNX2 ~]$
```

To determine the SSH key fingerprint on the remote Linux server, run the ssh-keygen command with the -l option, as shown here. This is to verify whether you have the correct SSH host key fingerprint of the remote Linux server that you want to connect via SSH.

```
[root@BLLNX2 ~]# ssh-keygen -l -f /etc/ssh/ssh_host_rsa_key.pub
2048 4f:14:67:02:ba:6b:f0:84:65:d4:e2:31:c7:ee:a9:10 /etc/ssh/ssh_host_rsa_key.pub
```

Meanwhile, to determine the SSH host key on the remote Linux server, run the `ssh-keygen` command with the `-y` option, as shown here. For security reasons, you can be asked to provide the passphrase that you supplied when creating the SSH host key.

```
[root@BLLNX2 ssh]# ssh-keygen -y -f /etc/ssh/ssh_host_rsa_key
Enter passphrase:
ssh-rsa AAAAB3NzaC1yc2EAAAABIwAAAQEAvTP3/fa21nnbpkaXUsPLtCViVaQrK5Dejh3jHcoYggwiDKWZ
5H7DebomI5WGrjFnTRtlMw6w/R7NTKWN9qJ5kEQBG4zM+AV9Bmm+8jHKL3i/YuR6w7qDROCUYMuVnfk+5C4H
TArCSv8v6XbzbrgSDT/jI8QCKuaOlvqrgDGCAaPt6qKhR8qluOFACLyrGIZbmygwwCImollzNjkKO8OSYFFp
aJfw+OpuEDjkKlRN21K9rUJrbx38uRUd/ANy1bWJH4WehdMvjvZkOIh3a2+VLmzpLtkqXCJ7L2+/wIVyoZ5U
8SO+15SkOtzKH9OjatwvsV3eqDe6ivD/lYYTOaewXQ==
```

On your local client computer, run the `tail` command, as shown in the following example. Check the SSH host key, which are the characters after `ssh-rsa`, and compare them against the results of the `ssh-keygen -y` option.

```
[oracle@BLLNX1 ~]$ tail -1 $HOME/.ssh/known_hosts
bllnx2,192.168.0.12 ssh-rsa AAAAB3NzaC1yc2EAAAABIwAAAQEAvTP3/fa21nnbpkaXUsPLtCViVaQr
K5Dejh3jHcoYggwiDKWZ5H7DebomI5WGrjFnTRtlMw6w/R7NTKWN9qJ5kEQBG4zM+AV9Bmm+8jHKL3i/YuR6
w7qDROCUYMuVnfk+5C4HTArCSv8v6XbzbrgSDT/jI8QCKuaOlvqrgDGCAaPt6qKhR8qluOFACLyrGIZbmygw
wCImollzNjkKO8OSYFFpaJfw+OpuEDjkKlRN21K9rUJrbx38uRUd/ANy1bWJH4WehdMvjvZkOIh3a2+VLmzp
LtkqXCJ7L2+/wIVyoZ5U8SO+15SkOtzKH9OjatwvsV3eqDe6ivD/lYYTOaewXQ==
```

However, when a new SSH host key is generated on the remote Linux server, you will experience the following error messages the next time you log on. You can also encounter a similar problem if you reinstalled Linux on the server with the same hostname and IP address, because a new SSH host key is also generated.

```
[oracle@BLLNX1 ~]$ ssh BLLNX2
@@@@@@@@@@@@@@@@@@@@@@@@@@@@@@@@@@@@@@@@@@@@@@@@@@@@@@@@@@@@@@@
@    WARNING: REMOTE HOST IDENTIFICATION HAS CHANGED!     @
@@@@@@@@@@@@@@@@@@@@@@@@@@@@@@@@@@@@@@@@@@@@@@@@@@@@@@@@@@@@@@@
IT IS POSSIBLE THAT SOMEONE IS DOING SOMETHING NASTY!
Someone could be eavesdropping on you right now (man-in-the-middle attack)!
It is also possible that the RSA host key has just been changed.
The fingerprint for the RSA key sent by the remote host is
5b:0f:a0:df:e0:9a:90:db:c7:bb:82:5c:15:d5:da:78.
Please contact your system administrator.
Add correct host key in /home/oracle/.ssh/known_hosts to get rid of this message.
Offending key in /home/oracle/.ssh/known_hosts:2
RSA host key for bllnx2 has changed and you have requested strict checking.
Host key verification failed.
```

To resolve this problem, you can rename `$HOME/.ssh/known_hosts`, but this is not advisable since you will lose the reference of the SSH host keys of the other servers. Another workaround is to edit `$HOME/.ssh/known_hosts` and remove the entry that corresponds to the hostname or IP address and type of SSH host key of the remote Linux server that you want to connect via SSH.

However, before you edit $HOME/.ssh/known_hosts, we recommend you make another copy of the said file.

14-3. Logging On Securely

Problem

You want to log on to a remote Linux server through a secured and encrypted connection.

Solution

On the local server, run the ssh command followed by the hostname or IP address of the remote Linux server that you want to connect. Afterward, supply the password of the corresponding operating system user on the remote Linux server.

In the first line of the following example, the operating system prompt [oracle@BLLNX1 ~]$ indicates that the operating system username is oracle logged on to the local Linux server BLLNX1. The following ssh command will connect to the remote Linux server BLLNX2 and will log on to the same operating system username oracle. You will then be prompted to provide the password of the operating system user on the remote Linux server.

```
[oracle@BLLNX1 ~]$ ssh BLLNX2
oracle@bllnx2's password:
Last login: Wed Jul 16 20:48:19 2008 from bllnx1
[oracle@BLLNX2 ~]$
```

Once you have successfully logged on, you can verify whether you are already in the remote Linux server. In the following example, the operating system prompt is obvious that you are now logged on as oracle on server BLLNX2. However, you can run the operating system commands echo $HOSTNAME and echo $USER, as shown here, to display the hostname of the Linux server and operating system username, respectively:

```
[oracle@BLLNX2 ~]$ echo $HOSTNAME
BLLNX2
[oracle@BLLNX2 ~]$ echo $USER
oracle
```

How It Works

Before you can run ssh on your local server, ensure that the packages open-ssh and openssh-clients are already installed. Otherwise, you can download them from any Linux package download site, such as http://www.openssh.com.

To connect to the remote Linux server from another Unix/Linux computer or Mac OS, run the ssh command. If you are initiating the SSH connection from Windows, we recommend you use the PuTTY software, as illustrated in recipe 1-1. Another option is to download and install OpenSSH for Windows.

The first time you log on to the remote Linux server via SSH, you will be prompted to confirm the SSH host key fingerprint of the remote Linux server, as shown here. Once you accept the SSH host key fingerprint, then a row will be added in $HOME/.ssh/known_hosts of the local Linux server, which contains the hostname, the IP address, and the SSH host key of the remote Linux server.

```
[oracle@BLLNX1 ~]$ ssh BLLNX2
The authenticity of host 'bllnx2 (192.168.0.12)' can't be established.
RSA key fingerprint is 5b:0f:a0:df:e0:9a:90:db:c7:bb:82:5c:15:d5:da:78.
Are you sure you want to continue connecting (yes/no)? yes
Warning: Permanently added 'bllnx2,192.168.0.12' (RSA) to the list of known hosts.
oracle@bllnx2's password:
Last login: Wed Jul 16 20:49:43 2008 from bllnx1
[oracle@BLLNX2 ~]$
```

Note You can run the command ssh-keygen -l -f /etc/ssh/ssh_host_rsa_key and
ssh-keygen -y -f /etc/ssh/ssh_host_rsa_key to verify the SSH host key fingerprint and SSH
host key of the server.

To log on to a different operating system user when connecting to the remote Linux server,
you need to add the -l option followed by the username, as shown here. Notice in the first line of
the following example, the prompt is [oracle@BLLNX1 ~]$. This means the current operating system
username is oracle and the hostname is BLLNX1. In the last line, the prompt is [bslopuz@BLLNX2 ~]$.
This means you are now logged in as the username bslopuz of the remote server BLLNX2.

```
[oracle@BLLNX1 ~]$ ssh  -l bslopuz  BLLNX2
bslopuz@bllnx2's password:
Last login: Wed Jul 16 20:34:08 2008 from bllnx1
[bslopuz@BLLNX2 ~]$
```

Another way to connect using a different username than you are currently logged on with
is to run the command ssh bslopuz@bllnx2, where the username and hostname are concatenated
with the @ character, as follows:

```
[oracle@BLLNX1 ~]$ ssh bslopuz@BLLNX2
bslopuz@bllnx2's password:
Last login: Wed Jul 16 21:45:23 2008 from bllnx1
```

By default, the SSH daemon server (sshd) is listening on port number 22. If the parameter
Port in /etc/ssh/sshd_config on the remote Linux server is pointing to a number other than 22,
then you need to add the -p option when running the ssh command followed by the correct
SSH port number, as shown here:

```
[oracle@BLLNX1 ~]$ ssh -p 72 BLLNX2
oracle@bllnx2's password:
Last login: Wed Jul 16 20:52:10 2008 from bllnx1
[oracle@BLLNX2 ~]$
```

Note If you want to run an X Window application on the remote Linux server, then run the ssh command with
the -X option. For additional information about running an X Window application via SSH, please review recipe 15-5.

If you cannot connect to your remote Linux server via SSH, run the ping command, as shown here. This is to verify whether you have a direct connection to the Linux server. The -c3 option of the ping command means it will send requests to the remote Linux server only three times.

```
[oracle@BLLNX1 ~]$ ping -c3 BLLNX2
PING BLLNX2 (192.168.0.12) 56(84) bytes of data.
64 bytes from BLLNX2 (192.168.0.12): icmp_seq=1 ttl=64 time=0.221 ms
64 bytes from BLLNX2 (192.168.0.12): icmp_seq=2 ttl=64 time=0.229 ms
64 bytes from BLLNX2 (192.168.0.12): icmp_seq=3 ttl=64 time=0.226 ms

--- BLLNX2 ping statistics ---
3 packets transmitted, 3 received, 0% packet loss, time 2000ms
rtt min/avg/max/mdev = 0.221/0.225/0.229/0.012 ms
```

However, if you are passing through a proxy server before you can connect to the remote Linux server, then we recommend you use the PuTTY software, because it is easy to configure the proxy server settings, as illustrated in recipe 1-1. If the remote Linux server is behind a firewall, then check with your system administrator (SA) to see whether the corresponding SSH port number is open.

To monitor the OS users connecting to the remote Linux server via SSH, check the /var/log/secure file, as shown here. This log file provides important information, such as the date and time that a particular operating system user is logged on, the hostname or IP address from where the SSH connection is initiated, and the relevant messages why you are perhaps unable to log on.

```
[root@BLLNX2 ~]# tail -f /var/log/secure
Jul 15 00:57:26 BLLNX2 sshd[25321]: pam_unix(sshd:auth): authentication failure;
logname= uid=0 euid=0 tty=ssh ruser= rhost=bllnx1  user=oracle
Jul 15 00:57:28 BLLNX2 sshd[25321]: Failed password for oracle from 192.168.0.11
port 12674 ssh2
Jul 15 00:57:41 BLLNX2 sshd[25321]: Accepted password for oracle from 192.168.0.11
port 12674 ssh2
Jul 15 00:57:41 BLLNX2 sshd[25321]: pam_unix(sshd:session): session opened for user
oracle by (uid=0)
```

Note To troubleshoot SSH connections, run the ssh command with the -v option to display debugging messages. For more debugging messages, run with the -vvv option instead. We also recommend you review the /var/log/secure and /var/log/messages files.

14-4. Copying Files Securely

Problem

You want to copy the files between Linux servers through a secured and encrypted connection.

Solution

Run the scp command to copy files between Linux servers through SSH. To run the scp command, provide the source files and target files. These files can be in the local and/or remote Linux servers. In the following example, the file /rmanbkup/DB11G/uajllfa5_1_1.tar is copied from server BLLNX1 to the /stage directory on server BLLNX2. You will be prompted for a password of the username on the remote Linux server.

```
[oracle@BLLNX1 ~]$ scp /rmanbkup/DB11G/uajllfa5_1_1.tar BLLNX2:/stage
oracle@bllnx2's password:
uajllfa5_1_1.tar                              100% 1934MB   7.3MB/s   04:25
```

■**Note** The sftp command is another protocol to securely transfer files between Linux servers. However, we excluded examples of the sftp command, since the sftp protocol is not yet an Internet standard.

How It Works

Like the ssh command, the first time you run the scp command to securely copy files to the remote Linux server via SSH, you will be prompted to confirm the SSH host key fingerprint of the remote Linux server, as shown here. Once you accept the SSH host key fingerprint, a row will be added in $HOME/.ssh/known_hosts of the local Linux server, which contains the hostname, IP address, key type, and SSH host key of the remote Linux server.

```
[oracle@BLLNX1 ~]$ scp $HOME/temp/exp_scott.dmp BLLNX2:/stage
The authenticity of host 'bllnx2 (192.168.0.12)' can't be established.
RSA key fingerprint is 5b:0f:a0:df:e0:9a:90:db:c7:bb:82:5c:15:d5:da:78.
Are you sure you want to continue connecting (yes/no)? yes
Warning: Permanently added 'bllnx2,192.168.0.12' (RSA) to the list of known hosts.
oracle@bllnx2's password:
exp_scott.dmp                                 100%   72KB  72.0KB/s   00:00
```

■**Note** The scp command replaces the rcp command, because the latter is not a secure way of copying files between Linux servers, particularly when the data is traversing the Internet. So, we recommend you use the scp command to safeguard your critical data.

The following is the syntax of the scp command. The hostnames can be different Linux servers. If no hostnames are defined, then the files will be copied to the same local Linux server. The usernames may be different between the local and remote Linux servers.

```
scp [<option>] [source_user@]source_host:]source_file
    [[target_user@]target_host:]target_file
```

■**Note** PuTTY also provides a `pscp.exe` client to securely copy files from the Microsoft Windows environment to a Unix/Linux environment. You can download `pscp.exe` from PuTTY's download page.

To copy recursively all the files and directories, use the -r option. The following command will copy all the files and subdirectories of $HOME/temp of the local server BLLNX1 to a remote Linux server BLLNX2 under the directory $HOME/temp1:

```
[oracle@BLLNX1 ~]$ scp -r $HOME/temp bllnx2:$HOME/temp1
```

Like the `cp` command, use a wildcard, such as the asterisk (*), to copy selected files. The following command will copy all the files with an extension of log in the directory /stage on the remote Linux server BLLNX2 to the directory $HOME/temp on the local Linux server BLLNX1.

```
[oracle@BLLNX1 ~]$ scp BLLNX2:/stage/*.log $HOME/temp
oracle@bllnx2's password:
adrci_output01.log                       100%  638      0.6KB/s   00:00
rmanbkup.log                             100% 1289KB    1.3MB/s   00:00
rman_debug01.log                         100%  42KB    42.0KB/s   00:00
```

Table 14-1 shows the common options of the `scp` command. You can run `man scp` to determine other options.

Table 14-1. *Common Options of scp Command*

Option	Meaning
p	Preserve the permission and date timestamp of the source file.
P	Get the SSH port number of the remote Linux server.
q	Hide the progress meter.
r	Copy recursively all subdirectories and their files.
v	Display debugging messages.

14-5. Authenticating Through Public Keys

Problem

You want to log on to a remote Linux server when connecting via SSH. You want to authenticate using a public key instead of typing the operating system (OS) password.

Solution

In the following example, the OS username oracle is currently logged on to the local Linux server BLLNX1 and will log on to the remote Linux server BLLNX2. Perform the following steps to use a public key for authentication in lieu of a password prompt:

1. On the local Linux server BLLNX1, run the ssh-keygen command with the -t rsa option to generate the RSA public key or the -t dsa for the DSA public key. If the files of the RSA and DSA keys already exist, then you will be asked whether you want to overwrite them. If no, then you can skip this step, but ensure that you remember their passphrases, because you will need them later. If yes, you are prompted to provide the passphrase, which is used to access the newly created private key. Afterward, the names of the private and public key files and key fingerprints are displayed.

   ```
   [oracle@BLLNX1 ~]$ /usr/bin/ssh-keygen -t rsa
   Generating public/private rsa key pair.
   Enter file in which to save the key (/home/oracle/.ssh/id_rsa):
   /home/oracle/.ssh/id_rsa already exists.
   Overwrite (y/n)? y
   Enter passphrase (empty for no passphrase):
   Enter same passphrase again:
   Your identification has been saved in /home/oracle/.ssh/id_rsa.
   Your public key has been saved in /home/oracle/.ssh/id_rsa.pub.
   The key fingerprint is:
   c9:31:c8:df:a3:80:ef:38:d2:be:20:a7:12:e8:bd:68 oracle@BLLNX1
   ```

2. On the local Linux server BLLNX1, provide the read, write, and execute permission only to the owner for security reasons so the private and public keys are not accessible to others.

   ```
   [oracle@BLLNX1 ~]$ chmod 700 $HOME/.ssh
   [oracle@BLLNX1 ~]$ chmod 600 $HOME/.ssh/*
   ```

3. Copy the public key from the local Linux server BLLNX1 to the remote Linux server BLLNX2. You may need to supply the password of the OS user on the remote Linux server BLLNX2. This public key must be from the OS username on the local Linux server, which is the computer where you want to initiate the logon to the remote Linux server and connect via SSH.

   ```
   [oracle@BLLNX1 ~]$ scp $HOME/.ssh/id_rsa.pub BLLNX2:$HOME
   oracle@bllnx2's password:
   id_rsa.pub                                100%  395     0.4KB/s   00:00
   ```

■**Note** We recommend you make local copies of the key files, such as id_rsa and id_rsa.pub. So, just in case someone mistakenly executes ssh-keygen -t rsa, at least you can always restore the original copies.

---

4. Create the directory $HOME/.ssh if not yet available on the remote Linux server BLLNX2:

```
[oracle@BLLNX2 ~]$ mkdir $HOME/.ssh
```

5. On the remote Linux server BLLNX2, append the public key from the local Linux server BLLNX2 to $HOME/.ssh/authorized_keys. Afterward, delete the key file $HOME/id_rsa.pub on the remote Linux server BLLNX2, which you copied from the local Linux server BLLNX1.

```
[oracle@BLLNX2 ~]$ cat $HOME/id_rsa.pub >> $HOME/.ssh/authorized_keys
[oracle@BLLNX2 ~]$ rm $HOME/id_rsa.pub
```

6. On the remote Linux server BLLNX2, provide the read, write, and execute permission only to the owner for security reasons. So, other users cannot access and modify $HOME/.ssh/authorized_keys.

```
[oracle@BLLNX2 ~]$ chmod 700 $HOME/.ssh
[oracle@BLLNX2 ~]$ chmod 600 $HOME/.ssh/authorized_keys
```

7. After the public key is successfully appended to $HOME/.ssh/authorized_keys on the remote Linux server BLLNX2, you can now log on without supplying the password of the OS user when connecting via SSH to the remote Linux server BLLNX2, as shown here. Instead, you will be prompted for the passphrase, which is actually the passphrase you supplied when creating the public key on the local Linux server BLLNX1.

```
[oracle@BLLNX1 ~]$ ssh BLLNX2
Enter passphrase for key '/home/oracle/.ssh/id_rsa':
Last login: Wed Jul 16 20:55:23 2008 from bllnx1
```

Note If you immediately press the Enter or Return key when asked to provide the passphrase, or if you provide the passphrase incorrectly three times, then you will be prompted instead for the actual password of the OS username that you want to log on to the remote Linux server.

How It Works

To authenticate using the public key, run the ssh-keygen command to generate the public key at the local Linux server, which is the computer from where you are going to initiate the SSH connection. Afterward, copy the newly generated public key, and append it to the $HOME/.ssh/authorized_keys on the remote Linux server, which is the computer where you are going to connect via SSH.

The ssh-keygen will create the RSA and DSA key files, which are used to encrypt and decrypt the data. For RSA, use the -t rsa option command, which will create two files, namely, $HOME/.ssh/id_rsa and $HOME/.ssh/id_rsa.pub. For DSA, use the -t dsa option, which will create $HOME/.ssh/id_dsa and $HOME/.ssh/id_dsa.pub.

$HOME/.ssh/id_rsa and $HOME/.ssh/id_dsa contain both the private key and the public key, while $HOME/.ssh/id_rsa.pub and $HOME/.ssh/id_dsa.pub contain just the public key. The public key is used to encrypt the data, while the private key is used to decrypt the data. So, for security reasons, ensure that both the private key and the public key files are writable and readable only by the owner.

When creating the public key, you are prompted to provide the passphrase, which can be a string of arbitrary length. The passphrase is your password to decrypt the data. Even if the private and public keys are stolen, they are useless without the passphrase, because the data cannot be decrypted. So, it is important that you keep the passphrase to yourself and don't share it with others.

To change the passphrase, run the ssh-keygen command with the -p option, as shown here. However, you have to supply the old passphrase before you can change it. This is to prevent unauthorized users from changing your passphrase.

```
[oracle@BLLNX1 ~]$ ssh-keygen -p
Enter file in which the key is (/home/oracle/.ssh/id_rsa):
Enter old passphrase:
Key has comment '/home/oracle/.ssh/id_rsa'
Enter new passphrase (empty for no passphrase):
Enter same passphrase again:
Your identification has been saved with the new passphrase.
```

Using the public key as a way to authenticate when connecting to the remote Linux server via SSH can be a security risk. For example, if other OS users can modify your $HOME/.ssh/authorized_keys, then they can append their own public key to the said file. As a result, they can log on to your account on the remote Linux server even without knowing your password.

As a security measure, we recommend you provide a passphrase when creating the public key and don't share the passphrase with anyone. Also, run the chmod 700 $HOME command. This is to ensure that the directories and files underneath the $HOME directory are writable, readable, and executable only by the owner. This prevents other OS users to peek and alter any files starting from your $HOME directory.

After you have successfully logged in, run the following OS commands to verify the OS username and hostname of the remote Linux server BLLNX2, as shown here. Even though that information is sometimes obvious in the OS prompt, but it's a good exercise to verify it.

```
[oracle@BLLNX2 ~]$ echo $HOSTNAME
BLLNX2
[oracle@BLLNX2 ~]$ echo $USER
oracle
```

14-6. Configuring a Promptless Logon

Problem

You want to log on without providing the remote OS user's password and public key's passphrase when connecting through SSH to a remote Linux server.

Solution

In the following example, the OS username oracle is currently logged to the local Linux server BLLNX1 and will log on to the remote Linux server BLLNX2. Perform the following steps to set up a promptless logon when connecting to the remote Linux server via SSH:

1. Create the public key on the local Linux server BLLNX1 and OS username where you are going to initiate the SSH connection. For additional details, please refer to recipe 14-5, since you need to perform the same steps as in that recipe.

2. Run the SSH agent, and capture the output to $HOME/ssh-agent.sh:

```
[oracle@BLLNX1 ~]$ /usr/bin/ssh-agent > $HOME/ssh-agent.sh
```

3. Run $HOME/ssh-agent.sh to set the environment variables SSH_AUTH_SOCK and SSH_AGENT_PID:

```
[oracle@BLLNX1 ~]$ source $HOME/ssh-agent.sh
Agent pid 3948
```

4. Run the ssh-add command, and provide the passphrase you supplied when the public key was created on the local Linux server:

```
[oracle@BLLNX1 ~]$ /usr/bin/ssh-add
Enter passphrase for /home/oracle/.ssh/id_rsa:
Identity added: /home/oracle/.ssh/id_rsa (/home/oracle/.ssh/id_rsa)
```

5. As shown here, the OS username oracle on the local Linux server BLLNX1 can now log on to the remote Linux server BLLNX2 without providing the OS user password and the public key passphrase:

```
[oracle@BLLNX1 ~]$ ssh BLLNX2
Last login: Wed Jul 16 21:38:44 2008 from bllnx1
[oracle@BLLNX2 ~]$
```

How It Works

In recipe 14-5, you used a public key for authentication in lieu of the OS username's password on the remote Linux server. However, you are asked to provide the passphrase, which is generated when the public key was created on the local Linux server. So, you are still prompted to enter something.

For a complete promptless logon to the remote Linux server when connecting via SSH, run the ssh-agent and ssh-add commands. The ssh-agent command will create a socket and cache the passphrase of the private key. This will also create a new directory under /tmp, as defined in the environment variable SSH_AUTH_SOCK. The ssh-add command will add the RSA and DSA identities and present them to the SSH agent. Afterward, you can now log on to the remote Linux server without any prompt for a password or passphrase.

To verify the key fingerprints, run the ssh-add command with the -l option to check what's presented to the SSH agent. Next, run the ssh-keygen command with the -l option followed by the path name of the private key file. As shown here, notice that both outputs have a similar key fingerprint, which is c9:31:c8:df:a3:80:ef:38:d2:be:20:a7:12:e8:bd:68.

```
[oracle@BLLNX1 ~]$ /usr/bin/ssh-add -l
2048 c9:31:c8:df:a3:80:ef:38:d2:be:20:a7:12:e8:bd:68 /home/oracle/.ssh/id_rsa (RSA)
```

```
[oracle@BLLNX1 ~]$ /usr/bin/ssh-keygen -l -f $HOME/.ssh/id_rsa
2048 c9:31:c8:df:a3:80:ef:38:d2:be:20:a7:12:e8:bd:68 /home/oracle/.ssh/id_rsa.pub
```

To delete the identities presented to the SSH agent, run ssh-add with the -d option. To delete everything, use the -D option instead:

```
[oracle@BLLNX1 ~]$ /usr/bin/ssh-add -d
Identity removed: /home/oracle/.ssh/id_rsa (/home/oracle/.ssh/id_rsa.pub)
```

For a promptless logon, the critical key is to ensure that the environment variable SSH_AUTH_SOCK is pointing to the correct path name before connecting through SSH. Otherwise, you will be prompted again for the passphrase once you exit from your shell or log out of system. A workaround is to run the ssh-agent command and capture the output to $HOME/ssh-agent.sh. Before you connect to the remote Linux server via SSH, you must run $HOME/ssh-agent.sh in order to set the same value to the environment variable SSH_AUTH_SOCK. This setting should be the same when the ssh-agent command was first executed.

To schedule the ssh or scp command in the cron job, ensure that the environment variable SSH_AUTH_SOCK is set correctly each time you log on to the OS username on the local Linux server. To do this, we recommend you add the following lines in $HOME/.bashrc, as shown here. Notice that you send the output to /dev/null when you run $HOME/ssh-agent.sh. This is to avoid displaying the SSH agent process ID every time you log on to that OS username.

```
if [ -f $HOME/ssh-agent.sh ]; then
  source $HOME/ssh-agent.sh > /dev/null
fi
```

If you think you have configured everything correctly but still get prompted for the passphrase, you'll need to troubleshoot. Begin by verifying that the OS process of the SSH agent is still active and the environment variables are set correctly. Issue the ps -ef | grep ssh-agent command to determine the process ID of the SSH agent, as follows:

```
[oracle@BLLNX1 ~]$ ps -ef | grep ssh-agent
root      2378  2298  0 Jul17 ?        00:00:00 /usr/bin/ssh-agent
/usr/bin/dbus-launch --exit-with-session /etc/X11/xinit/Xclients
oracle    3948     1  0 00:49 ?        00:00:03 ssh-agent
oracle   12092  4295  0 11:02 pts/5    00:00:00 grep ssh-agent
```

Afterward, run the env | grep SSH command to display the environment variables, as shown here. The value of the SSH_AGENT_PID and the process ID of the SSH agent should be the same. In the example, the process ID is 3948:

```
[oracle@BLLNX1 ~]$ env | grep SSH
SSH_AGENT_PID=3948
SSH_AUTH_SOCK=/tmp/ssh-Obtikk3947/agent.3947
SSH_ASKPASS=/usr/libexec/openssh/gnome-ssh-askpass
```

Also, the value of the environment variable SSH_AUTH_SOCK should be pointing to an existing path name. To verify, run the ls command as follows:

```
[oracle@BLLNX1 ~]$ ls -l /tmp/ssh-Obtikk3947/agent.3947
srw------- 1 oracle oinstall 0 Jul 18 00:49 /tmp/ssh-Obtikk3947/agent.3947
```

After you have successfully logged on, run the following OS commands to verify the OS username and hostname of the remote Linux server BLLNX2, as shown here. Even though those information are sometimes obvious in the OS prompt, it's a good exercise to verify them.

```
[oracle@BLLNX2 ~]$ echo $HOSTNAME
BLLNX2
[oracle@BLLNX2 ~]$ echo $USER
oracle
```

14-7. Securing an Unsecured Connection

Problem

You want to secure a telnet connection to a remote Linux server.

Solution

As illustrated in Figure 14-4, you have only telnet access from servers BLLNX1 and BLLNX2 to server BLLNX4, but you have ssh access from BLLNX1 to BLLNX2. In this scenario, the server BLLNX1 is the local or client server, where the ssh and telnet commands are initiated, while the target server is BLLNX4, which is the computer you want to connect to using the telnet command.

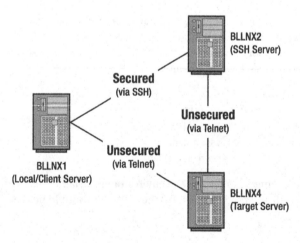

Figure 14-4. *SSH tunneling*

Furthermore, the SSH daemon server (sshd) is running on server BLLNX2 but is not running on server BLLNX4, which is the computer you want to log on to from server BLLNX1. However, telnet is configured on server BLLNX4. In this situation, you cannot connect from server BLLNX1 directly to server BLLNX4 through SSH.

To secure your connection from the client server BLLNX1 to target server BLLNX4, the Internet Protocol traffic is passed through the SSH server BLLNX2, where the data is encrypted and forwarded to server BLLNX4 via SSH tunneling. To implement SSH tunneling, issue the following ssh command with the -L option on server BLLNX1. You will be prompted for the password of the username on the SSH server BLLNX2.

```
[bslopuz@BLLNX1 ~]$ ssh bslopuz@BLLNX2 -L 2300:BLLNX4:23 -f -N
bslopuz@bllnx2's password:
```

Afterward, you can issue the telnet command on the client server BLLNX1, as shown here, and you will be asked to provide the username's password on the target server BLLNX4:

```
[bslopuz@BLLNX1 ~]$ telnet localhost 2300
Trying 127.0.0.1...
Connected to localhost (127.0.0.1).
Escape character is '^]'.
Red Hat Enterprise Linux AS release 4 (Nahant Update 6)
Kernel 2.6.9-67.EL on an i686
login: oracle
Password:
Last login: Sun Jul 20 01:21:31 from BLLNX4
[oracle@BLLNX4 ~]$
```

How It Works

telnet is a client-server protocol that is unsecured unlike the ssh protocol, because the data is not encrypted when it traversed through the network between computers. So, hackers can easily trace and read the usernames and passwords, which they can use to access the servers. This exposes the data and makes the server vulnerable to unauthorized access.

Note The default port number for the telnet protocol is 23.

For servers where the SSH daemon service (sshd) is not enabled or running, a workaround is to implement SSH tunneling, which secures the network access, such as the telnet protocol. In fact, you can even deploy SSH tunneling to secure the unsecured connection to your mail server or when using the VNC free edition (refer to recipe 16-7 for additional information).

In the following example, run the ssh command to log on to bslopuz on the server BLLNX2, where sshd is running. To implement SSH tunneling, use the -L option, which forwards the IP traffic from the local port number 2300 on server BLLNX1 to port number 23 on the target server BLLNX4. Add the -f option for SSH to wait in the background before commands are executed on the local server BLLNX2. Meanwhile, the -N option prevents a particular user from executing commands on the server BLLNX2.

```
[bslopuz@BLLNX1 ~]$ ssh bslopuz@BLLNX2 -L 2300:BLLNX4:23 -f -N
```

To run the telnet command, connect to the localhost or 127.0.0.1 to loop back to the local server, which is BLLNX1. This is followed by 2300, which is the local port number assigned in -L 2300:BLLNX4:23 when running the ssh command.

```
[bslopuz@BLLNX1 ~]$ telnet localhost 2300
```

For troubleshooting, run the ssh command with the -v option to display debugging messages. For more debugging messages, run with the -vvv option instead. The following is a snippet of the debugging message, which shows the local port number 2300 is being forwarded to server BLLNX4 on port 23. So, make sure those port numbers are not blocked by the firewall of those servers. You can get assistance with your system administrator to resolve the firewall issue.

```
debug1: Connection to port 2300 forwarding to BLLNX4 port 23 requested.
debug1: channel 2: new [direct-tcpip]
debug1: channel 2: free: direct-tcpip: listening port 2300 for BLLNX4 port 23,
connect from 127.0.0.1 port 63216, nchannels 3
```

On the server BLLNX4, where sshd is running, issue the tail -f /var/log/secure command to display the messages of the logon and logout to the SSH server. You can use this to monitor the SSH connections to server BLLNX4.

```
[root@BLLNX2 ~]# tail -f /var/log/secure
Jul 21 01:38:21 BLLNX2 sshd[26793]: Accepted password for bslopuz from 192.168.0.11
port 28686 ssh2
Jul 21 01:38:21 BLLNX2 sshd[26793]: pam_unix(sshd:session): session opened for user
bslopuz by (uid=0)
```

After you have successfully logged on, run the following OS commands to verify the OS username and hostname of the remote Linux server BLLNX4, as shown here. Even though that information is sometimes obvious in the OS prompt, it's a good exercise to verify them.

```
[oracle@BLLNX4 ~]$ echo $HOSTNAME
BLLNX4
[oracle@BLLNX4 ~]$ echo $USER
oracle
```

Note You can take advantage of SSH tunneling to bypass security protocols. For example, if the default SSH port number 22 is blocked in your company's firewall, then a workaround is to use a dummy port number that is not blocked and forward the IP traffic to the SSH port number of the target server, which is the computer you want to connect outside your company's network, passing through a designated SSH server

---

CHAPTER 15

■ ■ ■

Managing X Window

Many database administrators will argue that most Linux servers do not need X Window even when hosting an Oracle database. In fact, as you read the previous chapters of this book, you will realize that you can manage your Oracle database on a Linux server using a text console; you really don't need a graphical console. In recipes 10-11 and 10-12, you will learn how to install the Oracle RDBMS software, as well as how to create an Oracle Database without running the Oracle Universal Installer (OUI) that requires a graphical display.

However, for database administrators planning to migrate from a Windows environment and wanting to explore Oracle Database on a Linux environment, typing (and remembering exactly) the operating system (OS), SQL, and RMAN commands via a command line can be intimidating. If you prefer to run GUI-based programs, such as using the Database Configuration Assistant to create an Oracle database, then this chapter is definitely for you.

To understand the concept of X Window System in a Linux environment, you need to review the analogy of a client and a server in a networked environment. However, an X client and an X server both can be hosted on a single computer (which is an uncommon feature in a typical client/server environment) or two disparate computers on a network, as illustrated in Figure 15-1. But the terminology is backward from what many expect. An X server, for example, is what you run on your client PC to interact with your application. So, the application you run on some remote machine is actually the client. The application you run locally (X Window) is actually the server.

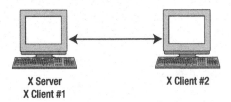

Figure 15-1. *X clients on local or remote Linux servers*

In this chapter, you will learn how to configure, start, and stop an X server, as well as how to redirect and secure an X display to a remote computer. You will also learn how to switch between desktop environments, as well as how to change the look and feel when running an X terminal. If using Windows as your client computer, you can explore OpenSSH for Windows or perhaps use Virtual Network Computing (VNC), which is discussed in detail in Chapter 16.

15-1. Configuring an X Server

Problem

You want to configure an X Window server on a Linux server so you can run GUI-based applications, such as the Database Configuration Assistant to create an Oracle database.

Solution

To set up an X Window server (often called just an *X server*) on your Linux server, you need to edit the X Window configuration file, called xorg.conf. That file is usually found in the /etc/X11 directory. The following are three ways to edit the /etc/X11/xorg.conf file:

- Directly modifying the /etc/X11/xorg.conf file

- Running the system-config-display application

- Running the Xorg application

■**Note** The /etc/X11/xorg.conf file is analogous to the /etc/X11/XF86Config file on older Linux distributions.

Running system-config-display

You need to log on as root or have sudo access to allow you to run system-config-display. Otherwise, you will be prompted for the root password, as illustrated in the results here:

```
$ system-config-display
You are attempting to run "system-config-display" which requires administrative
privileges, but more information is needed in order to do so.
Password for root:
```

A screen of Linux display settings will appear, similar to that shown in Figure 15-2. On the Settings tab, you can change the screen resolution and color depth, which are dependent on the capability of your hardware.

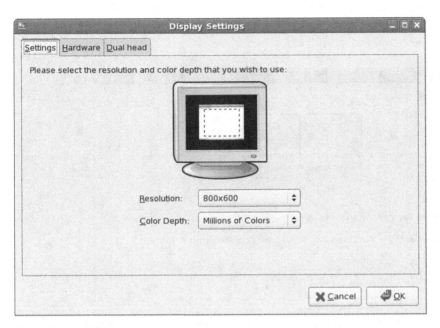

Figure 15-2. *Display settings*

On the Hardware tab, as shown in Figure 15-3, you can configure the monitor type and video card, which you can select from a list.

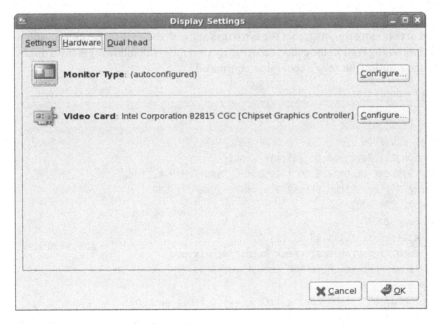

Figure 15-3. *Hardware display settings*

You can also add and configure a second monitor display on the Dual Head tab, as shown in Figure 15-4.

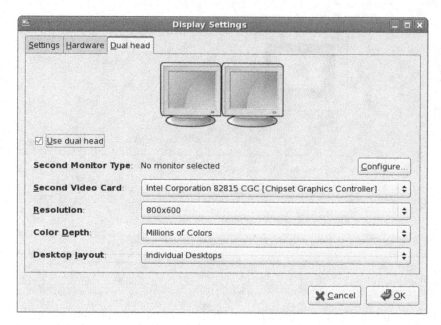

Figure 15-4. *Dual-head display settings*

Running Xorg

Another method to configure the xorg.conf file is to run Xorg with the configure option, which creates a temporary configuration file called /root/xorg.conf.new. The following is the snippet of the results when running the Xorg -configure command:

```
# /usr/bin/Xorg -configure

X Window System Version 7.1.1
Release Date: 12 May 2006
X Protocol Version 11, Revision 0, Release 7.1.1
Build Operating System: Linux 2.6.20-1.2952.fc6 i686 Red Hat, Inc.
Current Operating System: Linux BLLNX2 2.6.18-8.el5xen #1 SMP
Wed Jun 6 00:05:22 EDT 2007 i686
Build Date: 07 June 2007
Build ID: xorg-x11-server 1.1.1-48.13.el5.0.1
        Before reporting problems, check http://wiki.x.org
        to make sure that you have the latest version.
Module Loader present
Markers: (--) probed, (**) from config file, (==) default setting,
        (++) from command line, (!!) notice, (II) informational,
        (WW) warning, (EE) error, (NI) not implemented, (??) unknown.
(==) Log file: "/var/log/Xorg.0.log", Time: Wed Aug 27 23:53:17 2008
```

Note When running `Xorg -configure`, you can experience the error message "Fatal server error: Server is already active for display 0. If this server is no longer running, remove /tmp/.X0-lock and start again." To avoid this error, you need to delete the said file described in the error message.

Afterward, you need to test the `/root/xorg.conf.new` configuration by executing the command `X-config /root/xorg.conf.new`. If the X server runs fine using the newly created configuration file, `/root/xorg.conf.new`, then copy that file to `/etc/X11/xorg.conf`.

How It Works

When you start the X server, it reads the `xorg.conf` file that is located by default in the `/etc/X11` directory. The `/etc/X11/xorg.conf` file contains configurations of the system resources, video card, keyboard, mouse, and monitor for a Linux server running the X Window System.

In the "Solution" section, we described three methods to create and update the `/etc/X11/xorg.conf` file. One of the methods is to manually modify the file, which we don't recommend, except if you are sure of the changes. However, regardless of the method you want to pursue, make sure to back up or create another copy of the `/etc/X11/xorg.conf` file before you attempt to modify it. That way, you can always revert to the original settings in case the new changes do not work.

The GUI-based Linux display settings tool, or `system-config-display`, probes your video card and selects the appropriate drivers. If the video card cannot be detected, then you can select from the list of supported video cards. The `system-config-display` utility will write the changes directly to the `/etc/X11/xorg.conf` file.

If you are having problems running `system-config-display`, then an alternative option is to use `Xorg` as described in the solution. You can also run `Xorg` with the `probeonly` option to diagnose an X server problem.

Note When troubleshooting X server, always check the log files `/var/log/messages` and `/var/log/Xorg.0.log`.

15-2. Starting an X Server

Problem

You want to start an X server on the Linux server so you can run GUI-based software applications.

Solution

The following are three ways to start X server on your Linux server:

- *Method #1*: Manually run the `X` command.

- *Method #2*: Run `init 5` or `telinit 5`.

- *Method #3*: Modify `/etc/inittab`, and reboot the server.

The first method happens to be the most involved and requires manually starting the X server on the console of your Linux server. Follow these steps:

1. If you are prompted to log on, then log on as the OS user from which you want to run the X server.

2. Run the X server by typing the X command followed by ampersand (&), as shown in the following line of code. Make sure you add & at the end so the X server will run in the background. That way, you can still type other OS commands in the same console session.

   ```
   $ X &
   ```

3. Press Ctrl+Alt+F7 to change to the graphical console. An *x* will appear in the center of a blank screen, which represents the cursor of your mouse.

4. Press Ctrl+Alt+F1 to return to the text console session.

The second method for starting an X server is to run the init 5 or telinit 5 command as root on the OS prompt. Afterward, a GUI-based logon screen may appear. The third method is to change the value of the initdefault variable to 5 in the /etc/inittab file, as shown here. But you must reboot the Linux server to effect the changes made in the /etc/inittab file.

```
id:5:initdefault:
```

Note To show the details of the X server, run the OS command xdpyinfo.

How It Works

If the runlevel of your Linux server is set to 5, the X server is automatically started when the Linux server is rebooted. However, if the Linux server starts with a runlevel 3, where the default screen display is a text console and you want to run some GUI-based applications such as dbca to create an Oracle Database, then you need to manually start the X server on your Linux server.

You can start the X server in three ways. First, you can manually start the X server by running the X command, as demonstrated in the "Solution" section. Another method is to run either the init or telinit command and pass 5 as a parameter, but you must be root or have sudo access to run those commands. Finally, if you want X server to automatically run every time a Linux server is rebooted, then you need to change the id directive in /etc/inittab to runlevel 5.

Nowadays, the majority of DBAs do not work in front of the console of the server. So, when the Linux server is booted, starting the X server is not necessary. But if you have enough physical memory on your Linux server, then we recommend you use the third method. If the current level is 3, then use either the first or second method to start the X server. However, we recommend the second method, because it is simpler and requires fewer steps than the X command.

Note Running an X server on your Linux database server can pose security issues, because another client can access and observe your keystrokes. For security measures, we recommend you employ access control using xhost or tunnel X over SSH, as discussed in recipes 15-4 and 15-5.

The X command actually calls Xorg, as illustrated in the results here:

```
# which X
/usr/X11R6/bin/X
# ls -l /usr/X11R6/bin/X
lrwxrwxrwx  1 root root 4 May 19 17:39 /usr/X11R6/bin/X -> Xorg
# which Xorg
/usr/X11R6/bin/Xorg
# ls -l /usr/X11R6/bin/Xorg
-rws--x--x  1 root root 2002691 Oct  9  2007 /usr/X11R6/bin/Xorg
```

Note The X command may be in a different directory from other Linux distributions, so run the command which X to determine the exact directory.

Instead of running the X command to start the X server, you can optionally run the startx command. The startx command then invokes the X command on your behalf and also launches a graphical display manager. The default display manager of most Linux distributions is GNOME. If you prefer another graphical display manager, refer to recipe 15-6 on how to switch from GNOME to KDE, and vice versa.

Once an X server is already running, then you can press Ctrl+Alt+F1 to change to a text console or press Alt+F7 at the same time to change to the graphical console. You can repeat these steps to go back and forth between the text and graphical consoles.

Note When running the X server, make sure that the X Font server is running. To verify, run the service xfs status command.

15-3. Stopping the X Server

Problem

You want to stop the X server running on your Linux server. You may want to do that, for example, to save on resources such as the memory consumed by GUI-based software applications.

Solution

There are three ways to stop an X server:

- *Method #1*: Run init 3 or telinit 3.

- *Method #2*: Press Ctrl+Alt+Backspace.

- *Method #3*: Modify /etc/inittab, and reboot the server.

For the first method, perform the following steps to manually stop the X server on your Linux server:

1. If the X Window system is already running, then press Ctrl+Alt+F1 to change to a text console.

2. If you are prompted to log on, then log on as root.

3. Issue either init 3 or telinit 3 to stop the X server.

   ```
   # init 3
   ```

For the second method, perform the following steps:

1. Press Alt+F7 to change to the graphical console. If you are already on the graphical console, then you can skip this step.

2. Press Ctrl+Alt+Backspace to stop the X server.

For the third method, change the value of the initdefault variable to 3 in the /etc/inittab file, as shown here:

```
id:3:initdefault:
```

However, you must then reboot the Linux server to effect the changes.

How It Works

You can stop an X server in three ways. You can manually stop the X server by running either init 3 or telinit 3 on the text console to change the current runlevel to 3. But you must be root or have sudo access to run these commands. If the current runlevel is already 3, then you can press Ctrl+Alt+Backspace when you are on the graphical console. However, if you don't want the X server to automatically run every time the Linux server is rebooted, then change the id directive to runlevel 3 in the /etc/inittab.

The first and second methods are dependent on the current runlevel. If the current runlevel is 5 and you perform the second method, then it will always return to graphical login screen. So, perform the first method if the current level is 5. Otherwise, you can perform the second method.

Issue the `runlevel` command to display the previous and current runlevels. In the following example, the first character is N, which means that the runlevel is not changed yet, while the second character indicates that the current runlevel is 5.

```
# runlevel
N 5
```

15-4. Displaying an X Client on a Remote Server

Problem

You want to run an X client or a GUI-based software application on your local Linux server, but X server is not running. Instead, you want to redirect the graphical display to a remote Linux server, where an X server is running.

Solution

In the following example, the operating system (OS) user `oracle` is currently logged in on the local Linux server BLLNX1, where you want to run an X client or a GUI-based software application, but an X server is not running. Meanwhile, server BLLNX2 is a remote Linux server, where an X server is running.

Perform the following steps to redirect the graphical display to server BLLNX2 when running an X client or a GUI-based software application such as `dbca` to create an Oracle Database on server BLLNX1:

1. On server BLLNX1, set the OS environment variable `DISPLAY` to point to server BLLNX2.

   ```
   [oracle@BLLNX1 ~]$ export DISPLAY=BLLNX2:2.0
   ```

2. Run `dbca` on server BLLNX1.

   ```
   [oracle@BLLNX1 ~]$ dbca
   ```

▪Note If the OS environment variable `DISPLAY` is not set, then you may experience the error message "DISPLAY not set. Set DISPLAY environment variable, then re-run." To resolve this error, make sure you set the OS environment variable `DISPLAY` to point to a server where the X server is running.

---

3. Next, the Database Configuration Assistant (DBCA) screen will appear, as shown in Figure 15-5. Behind the DBCA screen, notice that the output of the OS command `uname -a` that is executed on the terminal window confirms that the server is BLLNX2.

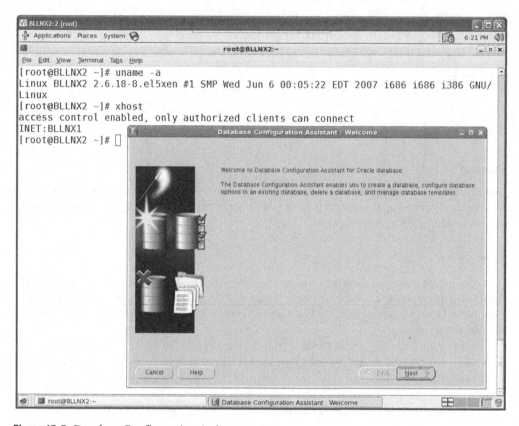

Figure 15-5. *Database Configuration Assistant screen*

How It Works

Usually you run an X client or GUI-based software application and have the graphical display on the local Linux server, where you are currently logged in. But what if the X server is not running on the local Linux server? Your option is to redirect the graphical display to another remote Linux server where an X server is running.

However, you may experience the following error, as shown here, because most likely the local Linux server, which is server BLLNX1 in the example illustrated in the "Solution" section, is not granted access control on the remote Linux server, which is server BLLNX2.

```
[oracle@BLLNX1 ~]$ dbca
Xlib: connection to "BLLNX2:2.0" refused by server
Xlib: No protocol specified
```

To confirm whether access has been granted, run the OS command xhost without any parameter on server BLLNX2. If the message says access control enabled, only authorized clients can connect and server BLLNX1 is not in the list, then that explains why you are getting the earlier error message when running the dbca. For example:

```
[root@BLLNX2 ~]# xhost
access control enabled, only authorized clients can connect
```

You can resolve this problem in two ways: one is to run the command xhost +BLLNX1 from server BLLNX2. The other is to run the command xhost + on server BLLNX2. Using the first approach allows only clients from the host BLLNX1 to connect. For example:

```
[root@BLLNX2 ~]# xhost +BLLNX1
BLLNX1 being added to access control list
[root@BLLNX2 ~]# xhost
access control enabled, only authorized clients can connect
INET:BLLNX1
```

On the other hand, the OS command xhost + will grant access control to all servers that have direct access to BLLNX2. We don't recommend, though, that you grant that much access, because you are basically allowing access from any server. For example:

```
[root@BLLNX2 ~]# xhost +
access control disabled, clients can connect from any host
[root@BLLNX2 ~]# xhost
access control disabled, clients can connect from any host
INET:BLLNX1
```

To revoke access control, run the OS command xhost -BLLNX1 to revoke the privilege from the specific server BLLNX1, as shown in the following example. Notice in the results of the first OS command xhost without any parameters, server BLLNX1 is on the list. Meanwhile, after you run the OS command xhost -BLLNX1, server BLLNX1 is no longer on the list during the second time that you run the OS command xhost without any parameters.

```
[root@BLLNX2 ~]# xhost
access control disabled, clients can connect from any host
INET:BLLNX1
[root@BLLNX2 ~]# xhost -BLLNX1
BLLNX1 being removed from access control list
[root@BLLNX2 ~]# xhost
access control disabled, clients can connect from any host
```

However, if you issued the OS command xhost + earlier and the message says access control disabled, clients can connect from any host when you issue the OS command xhost without any parameter, then any server, such as server BLLNX1, can still access server BLLNX2 even though you have already revoked the privilege from the specific server BLLNX1. To revoke access control from all servers, you can issue xhost -, as shown here:

```
[root@BLLNX2 ~]# xhost -
access control enabled, only authorized clients can connect
[root@BLLNX2 ~]# xhost
access control enabled, only authorized clients can connect
```

After you have issued the OS command xhost -, you may experience the following error messages when logging in as non-root on the local Linux server:

```
[oracle@BLLNX2 ~]$ xterm
Xlib: connection to ":2.0" refused by server
Xlib: No protocol specified
xterm Xt error: Can't open display: :2.0
```

To resolve this issue, you need to run the command xhost +localhost or xhost +BLLNX2 as root, as shown here:

```
[root@BLLNX2 ~]# xhost +localhost
localhost being added to access control list
[root@BLLNX2 ~]# xhost
access control enabled, only authorized clients can connect
INET:localhost.localdomain
```

15-5. Tunneling X Over SSH

Problem

You want to run an X client or a GUI-based software application on a remote Linux server. However, you want to log on to that remote Linux server through a secured connection and have the data encrypted that is traversing between servers.

Solution

In the following example, the operating system (OS) user oracle is currently logged in on the local Linux server BLLNX1, while server BLLNX2 is the remote Linux server. Perform the following steps to connect to server BLLNX2 from server BLLNX1 through SSH, and execute an X software application on server BLLNX2.

1. On the local Linux server BLLNX1, run ssh with the -X (uppercase X) option, as shown here. You may be prompted to provide a password of the OS user on BLLNX2.

   ```
   [oracle@BLLNX1 ~]$ ssh -X BLLNX2
   oracle@bllnx2's password:
   Warning: No xauth data; using fake authentication data for X11 forwarding.
   Last login: Sat Aug 30 04:46:18 2008 from bllnx1
   ```

2. If X11Forwarding is properly set up, the DISPLAY variable is automatically set up once you are successfully connected to the remote Linux server, as shown here:

   ```
   [oracle@BLLNX2 ~]$ echo $DISPLAY
   localhost:11.0
   ```

3. Once you are successfully connected to server BLLNX2, you can now run an X client or GUI-based software application on server BLLNX2. To test this, we recommend you run a simple X client, such as xclock, as shown in Figure 15-6.

Figure 15-6. *xclock display*

■**Note** The default port for X server is 6000. If this port is blocked, a workaround is to run ssh with the -X option to display the X Window application, such as xclock or Oracle's dbca.

How It Works

Recipe 15-4 allows you to redirect a graphical display to a remote Linux server. However, the data traversing between the servers is not secured, since it is not encrypted. For security reasons, we recommend you forward or tunnel the graphical display through SSH, as shown in this recipe.

■**Note** To learn how to configure SSH tunneling using PuTTY, refer to recipe 1-1.

To forward the display of an X client or GUI-based software application on a remote Linux server, run ssh with the -X (uppercase X) option. The -x (lowercase X) option disables X forwarding. However, before you can start to connect using ssh, make sure that the Secure Shell daemon, or sshd, is already running on the remote Linux server. Otherwise, you need to review Chapter 14, particularly recipe 14-1, which discusses in detail how to set up ssh.

When running an X client or GUI-based software application on a remote Linux server, you may receive message Warning: Remote host denied X11 forwarding. Also, if you run an X client or GUI-based software, you will receive the message Error: Can't open display. To resolve these errors, make sure X11Forwarding is set to yes in the /etc/ssh/sshd_config file on the remote Linux server.

■**Note** To troubleshoot your SSH connection, run the `ssh` command with the `-v` option to display debugging messages. For more debugging messages, run with the `-vvv` option instead. We also recommend you review the `/var/log/secure` and `/var/log/messages` files.

15-6. Changing Desktop Environment

Problem

You want to change your Linux desktop environment from GNU Network Object Model Environment (GNOME) to K Desktop Environment (KDE), and vice versa.

Solution

In the following example, perform these steps to switch between the desktop environments GNOME and KDE:

1. Log on as `root`, and edit the `/etc/sysconfig/desktop` file. For help on editing a file, please refer to Chapter 4.

2. Change the value of the `DESKTOP` variable to either `GNOME` or `KDE`. In the following example, we run the `cat` command to display the contents of the `/etc/sysconfig/desktop` file, and as you can see, the `DESKTOP` variable is set to `KDE`.

   ```
   # cat /etc/sysconfig/desktop
   #DESKTOP="GNOME"
   DESKTOP="KDE"
   #DESKTOP="XDM"
   ```

■**Note** We excluded X Display Manager, or XDM, in the discussion, since it is not available on some Linux distributions such as RHEL5.

3. Finally, you need to restart the X server. To start and stop the X server, please refer to recipes 15-2 and 15-3.

How It Works

On most Linux distributions, the default desktop environment is GNOME. However, if you prefer another one, such as KDE, then you need to modify the DESKTOP variable in the /etc/sysconfig/desktop file. When the X server is started, the /etc/X11/prefdm file is called and reads the /etc/sysconfig/desktop file.

For Microsoft Windows, you have only the Windows desktop environment. With Linux you have several choices, but the most popular desktop environments are GNOME and KDE. The individual desktop environments have their own tools, but their functionalities are almost similar. Like in KDE, the default file manager is Konqueror, and in GNOME it's Nautilus. Even though some Linux users will argue that perhaps GNOME is better than KDE, or vice versa, the preferred Linux desktop environment is really dependent on the tools, as well as the look and feel you are comfortable with.

Figure 15-7 shows a sample screen of the GNOME desktop environment.

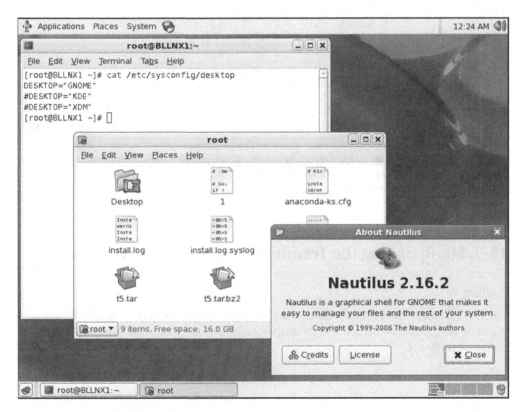

Figure 15-7. *GNOME desktop environment*

Figure 15-8 shows Nautilus as the default file manager for the KDE desktop environment.

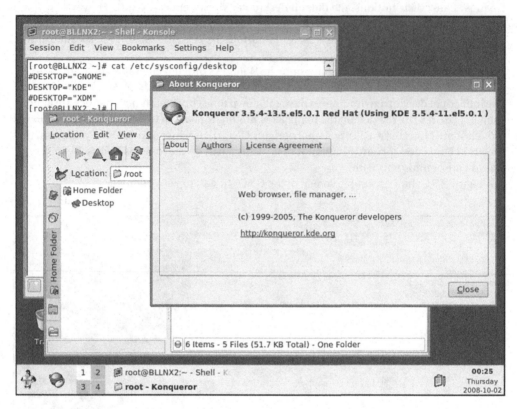

Figure 15-8. *KDE desktop environment*

15-7. Manipulating the Terminal Emulator for X Windows

Problem

You want to launch the default X terminal and change the look and feel to support different database environments, namely, the development, quality assurance, and production database environments.

Solution

To launch an X Window terminal, you can execute the xterm command. If your operating system environment variable DISPLAY is set up correctly to a Hummingbird X Server, Reflection X Server, or Cygwin X Server (or if you are running X Server locally), a small white terminal will appear. This small window will probably not be adequate to support the day-to-day activities of today's DBA who supports many database environments. More than likely, you will need a larger window, a title to specify the name of the window, different colors to easily identify the environment, and a larger scroll buffer area. Here's several xterm examples you can execute in your environment to support multiple database environments:

```
xterm -sl 32000 -sb -title "Production" -geometry 128x40 -bg red -fg white &
xterm -sl 32000 -sb -title "QA" -geometry 128x40 -bg yellow -fg black &
xterm -sl 32000 -sb -title "Development" -geometry 128x40 -bg blue -fg white &
```

Each of the xterm windows is designed with different background colors with the -bg parameter to differentiate database environments. In our example, the blue window represents the
development environment, the yellow window represents the QA environment, and, of course,
the red window represents the production environment. DBAs should be cognitive of the color
scheme and exercise extra caution by remembering that while in the red background, they are
logged in the production database server.

In addition to the background colors, we defined the scroll length buffer as 32,000 lines.
The default scroll buffer is 64 lines above the top of the window. The scroll buffer of 32,000 lines,
designated by the -sl parameter, will consume more memory on the server but will prove to be
well worth it, especially when diagnosing problems.

The title of the windows can also be defined with the -title parameter. The -title parameter
should be enclosed with double quotes so that you can customize titles to suit your requirements.

The dimensions of the xterm window can be managed with the -geometry parameter. The
-geometry parameter defines the window size and position. You can define a specific font, font
size, and other attributes with the -font parameter. The simplest way to designate the font and
size attributes is by executing the xfontsel command. Executing the xfontsel command will
open another X window similar to what is displayed in Figure 15-9.

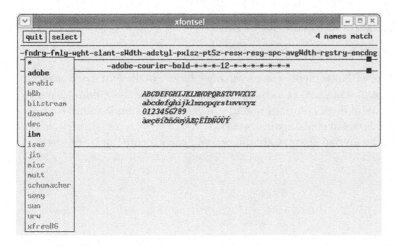

Figure 15-9. *xfontsel window*

When you decide on the font type and size attributes, you can click the select button and
paste in another terminal with the xterm command. The xterm command will look like the
following command:

```
xterm -font -adobe-courier-bold-*-*-*-12-*-*-*-*-*-*-*
```

Once you are satisfied with the font look and feel, you can go back to the xfontsel window
and click the quit button.

Another popular parameter for xterm is the -e parameter. With the -e option, you can specify the program and arguments to run in the xterm window. Here's an example of how the -e option can be manipulated:

```
xterm -e "ssh rac3 -l root"
```

How It Works

xterm is the standard terminal emulator that runs in X Windows. Other terminal emulators in Linux include Konsole (the default KDE terminal), GNOME Terminal (the default GNOME terminal), rxvt (a slimmed-down replacement for xterm), and Eterm. xterm is the standard de facto for terminals in all the Unix operating systems. No matter whether you are running Linux, Sun Solaris, IBM AIX, or HP/UX, xterm will look and behave the same. One behavior includes the ability to copy and paste. Within an xterm window, if you highlight a word or a sentence, the highlighted portion will automatically be copied to the memory buffer. To copy the memory buffer, you simply press the middle mouse button; for a two-button mouse, the middle button is most often the trackball. You can press on the track ball to paste the contents of the memory buffer. If you have the old traditional two-button mouse, pressing both the left and right buttons at the same time will paste the memory buffer.

Similarly, if you hold the Ctrl key and simultaneously press the left, middle, or right button, you will see the following menu options:

- Press Ctrl and the left mouse button for Main Options.

- Press Ctrl and the right mouse button for VT Fonts.

- Press Ctrl and the middle mouse button for VT Options.

For example, with the VT Fonts menu, you can change the size of the font to unreadable, tiny, small, medium, large, and huge. As you change the size of the font, the window diameter will change respectively. With the VT Options menu, you can modify simple things such as enabling or disabling scrollbars or enabling reverse video.

For assistance with the myriad of xterm arguments, you can execute the xterm -help command.

CHAPTER 16

■■■

Managing Remote Servers with VNC

Fewer and fewer database administrators are working in front of the console of the servers hosting their Oracle databases. It is common now to see the database servers or data centers located in separate geographical areas from DBAs. For example, a database server might be hosted somewhere in New York City, while the DBA is in the city of Orlando enjoying the sunny weather.

DBAs can now easily access database servers remotely using their preferred protocols, such as `telnet`, `rsh`, `rlogin`, or `ssh`, and using the various tools on the market today. Some of those tools are freely available for download, particularly those such as PuTTY and VNC.

Software such as PuTTY, described earlier in Chapter 1, allows you to remotely access a server via `telnet` or `ssh` from a Windows client. PuTTY allows you to configure proxy settings and `ssh` port tunneling, as well as to save configurations so that you don't have to type everything each time you need to connect to the same database server.

In most cases, accessing a database server in a command-line mode via PuTTY is all you need. However, you may sometimes need to access a database server in a way that lets you run GUI-based software. For example, you may need to run Oracle's Database Configuration Assistant (DBCA) to create an Oracle database or run some other X Window System–based software. In this situation, Virtual Network Computing (VNC) comes in handy.

VNC is a thin-client product of RealVNC, which is based in Cambridge, United Kingdom. VNC allows you to access the database server in a graphical way. This feature is useful to DBAs, because Oracle requires an X server to display its Java-based screens for Oracle database installation, creation, and configuration, as well as Oracle listener setup. In other words, you can run the same GUI-based applications on your local VNC-client computer that you can actually run on the console of the database server.

To run VNC, you need two components: the server and viewer, as shown in Figure 16-1. The VNC server component runs on the computer you want to monitor. The VNC viewer component runs on the computer from which you want to monitor the remote server. Both components need to be installed before you can initiate a VNC session. VNC runs on most operating systems, including Unix, Linux, Windows, and Mac OS.

VNC Viewer
(Client)
    VNC Server
(Database Server)

Figure 16-1. *VNC connection*

Aside from routing the output to the VNC server, you can also route the display to other X servers that are available on the market today, such as Cygwin/X, Reflections X, and Hummingbird. However, we recommend VNC, because it is freely available and is usually included by default in most Linux distributions, such as Red Hat Enterprise Linux, Novell SUSE Linux Enterprise, and Oracle Enterprise Linux (OEL). Also, VNC has rich features, such as 2048-bit RSA server authentication, 128-bit AES session encryption, HTTP proxy, file transfer, desktop scaling, and screen sharing.

In this chapter, you will learn where to download the VNC software, how to install and configure the VNC server on your remote Linux database server and the VNC viewer on your client computer, how to share and secure your VNC connection, how to configure proxy server, and how to troubleshoot VNC issues.

As you put into practice what you have read in this chapter, such as using the VNC software to access and manage your remote Linux database server from anywhere and anytime, you will learn to appreciate the benefits provided to you as the DBA, such as flexibility, convenience, better collaboration with your team members, data security, and potential cost savings to your company.

16-1. Downloading the VNC Software

Problem

You want to download the VNC software to allow you to manage and display the console of your remote Linux database server from your client computer. You want to work in an X Window System environment instead of a command-line prompt.

Solution

You need two components to run VNC: the VNC server running on your remote Linux database server and the VNC viewer on your client computer. Perform the following steps to download the VNC software for the two computers:

1. Go to http://www.realvnc.com/products/download.html, and click the Download & Try button that corresponds to the type of VNC you want to download.

2. On the next screen, you are asked to provide your name, your e-mail address, the organization that you belong to, and so on. You can also skip these settings and immediately click the Proceed to Downloads button.

3. Click the Download button that corresponds to the operating system and processor type of your system, as well as the type of compressed file you want to download.

Note To determine the processor type of your Linux system to see whether you have x86, x64, or ia64, issue the Linux command `uname -a` or `uname -m`.

   4. Select I Accept These Terms and Conditions after you review the VNC end user license agreement. Finally, click the Download button, and save the file to a specific directory.

How It Works

For VNC to work, you need to download and install the VNC server on your remote Linux database server and the VNC viewer on your client computer. You have three different VNC editions to choose from, namely, the Free Edition, Personal Edition, and Enterprise Edition.

For Linux, you can download either the Enterprise Edition or the Free Edition, because the Personal Edition is not available for Unix/Linux. By default, the Free Edition is included in most Linux distributions, such as Red Hat, SUSE, and OEL. However, the Personal Edition and Enterprise Edition have some advantages over the Free Edition, such as encryption, authentication, and proxy server features. If you want to take advantage of these features, download the Enterprise Edition, and replace the Free Edition, which is usually included as a package on your Linux distribution. The Enterprise Edition and Personal Edition, however, require a license key before you can start the VNC server.

16-2. Installing the VNC Software

Problem

You want to install the VNC server on your remote Linux database server and the VNC viewer on your Windows client computer, where you want to manage and access your remote Linux database server.

Solution

For VNC to work, you need to install the VNC server on your remote Linux database server and the VNC viewer on your client computer. On your server, you can choose to install the VNC server's Enterprise Edition or Free Edition. To install, you must log on as root and then run the `rpm --upgrade` command:

```
# rpm --upgrade /home/bslopuz/download/vnc/vnc-E4_4_1-x86_linux.rpm
Checking for xauth... [OK]
Updating /etc/pam.d/vncserver
Looking for font path... unix/:7100 (from /etc/X11/xorg.conf).
Looking for RGB database... /usr/X11R6/lib/X11/rgb from /etc/X11/xorg.conf
Checking for single sign-on support... Not found
areConfigKeysValid: exception Private key not found
Generating primes:
   p: .........................................
   q: ....................................................................
filename=/root/.vnc/private.key
A new secure key has been generated and stored.
```

To install the VNC viewer on your Windows client computer, you must log on as the administrator and double-click the file vnc-E4_3_2-x86_x64_win32.exe. Just accept the default installation directory, C:\Program Files\RealVNC\VNC4, and ensure that you select at least the VNC viewer as one of the components to install.

How It Works

To manage and access your remote Linux database server from your Windows client computer using the VNC software, you must install the VNC server on your remote Linux database server and install the VNC viewer on your Windows client computer. However, you can install the VNC server and VNC viewer on both computers. So, you can also manage and access other servers from your Linux database server.

On Linux, you can install VNC server's Enterprise Edition or Free Edition, because the Personal Edition is not available for Linux. On your Windows machine, you can install the VNC viewer's Free Edition, Personal Edition, or Enterprise Edition.

Before you install the VNC software on your remote Linux database server, you can run the Linux command rpm -qa to verify the current version of the VNC software installed. The results shown here indicate that the VNC software installed is Enterprise Edition version 4.3.2-1:

```
# rpm -qa | grep vnc
vnc-E-4.3.2-1
```

If you want to remove the currently installed VNC software, then run the rpm --erase command:

```
# rpm --erase vnc-E-4.3.2-1
```

If you have a subscription to the Red Hat Network or Oracle's Unbreakable Linux Network, then run the up2date command to download and install the VNC packages. For example:

```
# up2date vnc
Fetching Obsoletes list for channel: el4_i386_latest...
Fetching rpm headers...
########################################
Name                            Version        Rel
----------------------------------------------------------
vnc                             4.0            11.el4          i386
Testing package set / solving RPM inter-dependencies...
########################################
vnc-4.0-11.el4.i386.rpm:   ######################### Done.
Preparing               ########################################### [100%]
Installing...
  1:vnc                  ########################################### [100%]
```

16-3. Manually Starting and Stopping the VNC Server

Problem

You want to manually start and stop the VNC server on your remote Linux database server.

Solution

To manually start the VNC server on your Linux database server, log on or su to the OS user where you want to run the VNC server. The example shown here will make vncuser the current OS user:

```
# su - vncuser
```

Then, type vncserver and a port number where you want the VNC server to be listening. The port number is optional, and the default value is 1. The following example shows the VNC server being started in its default configuration:

```
$ vncserver
VNC Server Enterprise Edition E4.4.1 (r12183) - built May 12 2008 12:08:54
Copyright (C) 2002-2008 RealVNC Ltd.
See http://www.realvnc.com for information on VNC.
You will require a password to access your desktops.

Password:
Verify:
Generating primes:
  p: ...........................................
  q: ....................................................................
filename=/home/vncuser/.vnc/private.key
A new secure key has been generated and stored.
Running applications in /home/vncuser/.vnc/xstartup
Log file is /home/vncuser/.vnc/BLLNX3:1.log
New desktop is BLLNX3:1
```

This next example shows how to specify a port number. It starts the VNC server to listen at port number 9:

```
$ vncserver  :9
VNC Server Enterprise Edition E4.4.1 (r12183) - built May 12 2008 12:08:54
Copyright (C) 2002-2008 RealVNC Ltd.
See http://www.realvnc.com for information on VNC.
You will require a password to access your desktops.

Password:
Verify:
Generating primes:
  p: .........................................................................
  q: ....................................................................
filename=/home/vncuser/.vnc/private.key
A new secure key has been generated and stored.
Running applications in /home/vncuser/.vnc/xstartup
Log file is /home/vncuser/.vnc/BLLNX3:9.log
New desktop is BLLNX3:9
```

Note To have a similar look and feel of your desktop as when you log on to the console of the Linux server, uncomment or add `unset SESSION_MANAGER` and `/etc/X11/xinit/xinitrc` to the `$HOME/.vnc/xstartup` file.

To manually stop the VNC server on your Linux database server, run the Linux command `vncserver -kill`, and provide the same port number you used when starting the VNC server. For example:

```
# /usr/bin/vncserver -kill :9
Killing Xvnc process ID 13836
```

How It Works

You start the VNC server on your remote Linux database server by running `vncserver` and a port number. Like the other Linux daemons—such as `httpd`, which usually listens on port number 80, and `sshd`, which usually listens on 22—the VNC server listens on port number 5901 by default. If you include a port number when running `vncserver`, the actual port number is plus 5900. For example, if you run `vncserver :9`, then the VNC server listens on port number 5909.

The first time you run VNC Server Enterprise Edition on your Linux server, you must issue the command `vnclicense -add <license key>` to install the license key. However, the license key is not required if you are using the VNC Free Edition. For example, to add the license key, use this:

```
# /usr/bin/vnclicense -add FR46B-N43LQ-4YUD2-A27B6-4N2YA
```

Note You can purchase a VNC license at `http://www.realvnc.com/cgi-bin/purchase.cgi?product=enterprise4/Xvnc&productTypes=LICENSE`.

For security reasons, we recommend you don't run the VNC server under a privileged user, such as `root` or `oracle` (in other words, the Oracle RDBMS software owner). If you run the VNC server as `root`, then any remote VNC user will have `root` privileges once they are connected to your Linux server, and that is a security risk. Instead, we recommend you create a new Linux user and launch the VNC server from that account. Once a remote user is connected to the server, then they can `su` to `root` or `oracle` to perform any needed administrative tasks.

In the following example, the `groupadd` command creates a new group called `vncuser`; the `useradd` command creates a new user called `vncuser`, and the `-g` option will associate this user to the group `vncuser`. The `passwd` command prompts you to assign a new password for OS user `vncuser`. For additional details about creating OS groups and users, check recipes 3-12 and 3-14.

```
# groupadd vncuser
# useradd vncuser -g vncuser
# passwd vncuser
```

The first time you launch vncserver for a particular OS user, you will be prompted for a password, and the relevant VNC files, such as the security key or the private.key file, will be created in the .vnc directory under the home directory of that OS user. In the example shown here, the su command makes vncuser the current OS user, and the ls -al $HOME/.vnc command displays the files in the .vnc directory under the home directory of OS username vncuser:

```
# su - vncuser

$ ls -al $HOME/.vnc
total 28
drwxr-xr-x 2 vncuser vncuser 4096 May  3 08:52 .
drwx------ 4 vncuser vncuser 4096 May  3 08:52 ..
-rwxrwxr-x 1 vncuser vncuser  799 May  3 08:52 BLLNX3:9.log
-rw-rw-r-- 1 vncuser vncuser    5 May  3 08:52 BLLNX3:9.pid
-rw------- 1 vncuser vncuser    8 May  3 08:52 passwd
-rw------- 1 vncuser vncuser 2824 May  3 08:52 private.key
-rwxr-xr-x 1 vncuser vncuser  171 May  3 08:52 xstartup
```

Subsequent restarts of the VNC server will not ask you to set the password, and they won't regenerate the secure key. However, you can run the Linux command vncpasswd to change the VNC server password for an OS user, as shown here:

```
# /usr/bin/vncpasswd
Password:
Verify:
```

To generate a new secure key or private.key under the $HOME/.vnc directory, run the Linux command vnckeygen. For example:

```
# /usr/bin/vnckeygen -f
Generating primes:
  p: .....................
  q: ..........
filename=/home/vncuser/.vnc/private.key
A new secure key has been generated and stored.
```

The next time you run the VNC viewer on your client computer when a new security key is generated, you will be prompted with a screen similar to Figure 16-2.

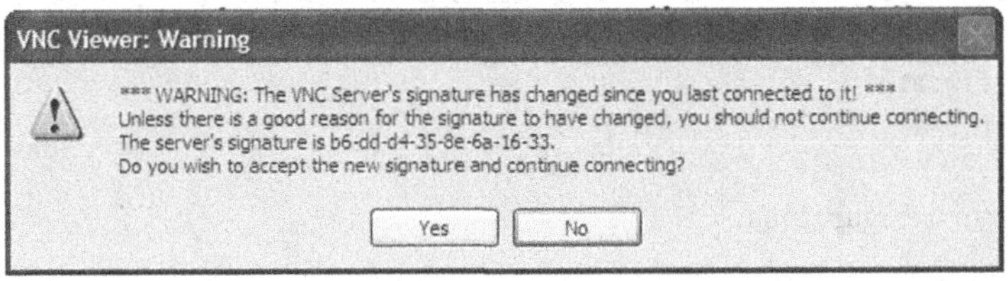

Figure 16-2. *VNC server signature*

In case you forget the port number on which the VNC server is listening, you can run the Linux command ps -ef. The following example illustrates this. In the results, Xvnc :9 indicates that the VNC server is listening on port number 5909.

```
# ps -ef | grep Xvnc
vncuser   8443    1 0 08:52 ?        00:00:00 Xvnc :9 -PasswordFile
/home/vncuser/.vnc/passwd -auth /home/vncuser/.Xauthority -desktop BLLNX3:9
(vncuser) -pn -httpd <inline> -fp unix/:7100 -co /usr/share/X11/rgb
root      8444 8443 0 08:52 ?        00:00:00 Xvnc :9 -PasswordFile
/home/vncuser/.vnc/passwd -auth /home/vncuser/.Xauthority -desktop BLLNX3:9
(vncuser) -pn -httpd <inline> -fp unix/:7100 -co /usr/share/X11/rgb
root      8777 7233 0 08:58 pts/0    00:00:00 grep Xvnc
```

16-4. Automatically Starting the VNC Server

Problem

You want the VNC server to automatically start when your Linux database server is rebooted.

Solution

Perform the following steps to ensure that the VNC server will automatically start when your Linux database server is rebooted:

1. Modify the /etc/sysconfig/vncservers file, and insert the line VNCSERVERS="<port#>: <OS_user>". In the example, the VNC server is owned by vncuser to listen on port number 5909.

    ```
    # cat /etc/sysconfig/vncservers
    VNCSERVERS="9:vncuser"
    ```

2. Check the existence of the file /etc/init.d/vncserver. If it is not available, then create the file, and insert the following lines:

    ```
    #!/bin/bash
    #
    # chkconfig: - 91 35
    # description: Starts and stops vncserver. \
    #              used to provide remote X administration services.

    # Source function library.
    . /etc/init.d/functions

    # Source networking configuration.
    . /etc/sysconfig/network

    # Check that networking is up.
    [ ${NETWORKING} = "no" ] && exit 0
    ```

```
unset VNCSERVERARGS
VNCSERVERS=""
[ -f /etc/sysconfig/vncservers ] && . /etc/sysconfig/vncservers

prog=$"VNC server"

start() {
    echo -n $"Starting $prog: "
    ulimit -S -c 0 >/dev/null 2>&1
    RETVAL=0
    if [ ! -d /tmp/.X11-unix ]
    then
        mkdir -m 1777 /tmp/.X11-unix || :
        restorecon /tmp/.X11-unix 2>/dev/null || :
    fi
    NOSERV=1
    for display in ${VNCSERVERS}
    do
        NOSERV=
        echo -n "${display} "
        unset BASH_ENV ENV
        DISP="${display%%:*}"
        export USER="${display##*:}"
        export VNCUSERARGS="${VNCSERVERARGS[${DISP}]}"
        runuser -l ${USER} -c "cd ~${USER} && [ -f .vnc/passwd ] && " || \
                                "vncserver :${DISP} ${VNCUSERARGS}"
        RETVAL=$?
        [ "$RETVAL" -ne 0 ] && break
    done
    if test -n "$NOSERV"; then echo -n "no displays configured "; fi
    [ "$RETVAL" -eq 0 ] && success $"vncserver startup" || \
        failure $"vncserver start"
    echo
    [ "$RETVAL" -eq 0 ] && touch /var/lock/subsys/vncserver
}

stop() {
    echo -n $"Shutting down $prog: "
    for display in ${VNCSERVERS}
    do
        echo -n "${display} "
        unset BASH_ENV ENV
        export USER="${display##*:}"
        runuser ${USER} -c "vncserver -kill :${display%%:*}" >/dev/null 2>&1
    done
```

```
        RETVAL=$?
        [ "$RETVAL" -eq 0 ] && success $"vncserver shutdown" || \
            failure $"vncserver shutdown"
        echo
        [ "$RETVAL" -eq 0 ] && rm -f /var/lock/subsys/vncserver
}


# See how we were called.
case "$1" in
  start)
        start
        ;;
  stop)
        stop
        ;;
  restart|reload)
        stop
        sleep 3
        start
        ;;
  condrestart)
        if [ -f /var/lock/subsys/vncserver ]; then
            stop
            sleep 3
            start
        fi
        ;;
  status)
        status Xvnc
        ;;
  *)
        echo $"Usage: $0 {start|stop|restart|condrestart|status}"
        exit 1
esac
```

3. Ensure that /etc/init.d/vncserver has an execute permission:

```
# ls -l /etc/init.d/vncserver
-rw-r--r-- 1 root root 488 Apr 28 23:37 /etc/init.d/vncserver
# chmod a+x /etc/init.d/vncserver
# ls -l /etc/init.d/vncserver
-rwxr-xr-x 1 root root 488 Apr 28 23:37 /etc/init.d/vncserver
```

4. Create a softlink in /etc/rc.d/rc3.d and /etc/rc.d/rc5.d:

```
# ln -s /etc/init.d/vncserver /etc/rc.d/rc5.d/S91vncserver
# ls -l /etc/rc.d/rc5.d/S91vncserver
lrwxrwxrwx 1 root root 21 Apr 28 23:48 /etc/rc.d/rc5.d/S91vncserver ->
/etc/init.d/vncserver
# ln -s /etc/init.d/vncserver /etc/rc.d/rc3.d/S91vncserver
# ls -l /etc/rc.d/rc3.d/S91vncserver
lrwxrwxrwx 1 root root 21 Apr 28 23:49 /etc/rc.d/rc3.d/S91vncserver ->
/etc/init.d/vncserver
```

5. Enable the VNC service using the chkconfig command:

```
# chkconfig --level 35 vncserver on
# chkconfig --list | grep vnc
vncserver       0:off   1:off   2:off   3:on    4:off   5:on    6:off
```

6. If possible, log on as root, and issue the Linux command reboot to manually restart your Linux database server. Otherwise, you can manually restart the VNC service by executing the Linux command /sbin/service vncserver restart.

7. Issue the Linux command ps -ef | grep Xvnc to verify whether the VNC server started automatically after the reboot. The following is an example. In the results, the VNC server is listening on port number 9 running under Linux user vncuser.

```
# ps -ef | grep Xvnc
vncuser 11585     1 0 04:43 pts/4    00:00:00 Xvnc :9 -PasswordFile
/home/vncuser/.vnc/passwd -auth /home/vncuser/.Xauthority -desktop BLLNX3:9
(vncuser) -pn -httpd <inline> -fp unix/:7100 -co /usr/share/X11/rgb
root      11586 11585  0 04:43 pts/4    00:00:00 Xvnc :9 -PasswordFile
/home/vncuser/.vnc/passwd -auth /home/vncuser/.Xauthority -desktop BLLNX3:9
(vncuser) -pn -httpd <inline> -fp unix/:7100 -co /usr/share/X11/rgb
root      11689 12895  0 04:44 pts/4    00:00:00 grep Xvnc
```

How It Works

In some environments in which you heavily use VNC, you may want to automate the restart of the VNC server. If the VNC service is enabled at the OS level, one of the files that will be executed during the system startup is /etc/init.d/vncserver. That script in turn reads the file /etc/sysconfig/vncservers. The /etc/sysconfig/vncservers file contains the OS user under which the VNC server will run and the port number on which the VNC server will listen.

■**Note** Once the VNC server is automatically started, you can still manually stop and start the VNC server, as discussed in recipe 16-3. You may, for example, want to manually stop the VNC server because you lack memory resources on the machine where it is running.

16-5. Starting the VNC Viewer

Problem

You want to start the VNC viewer on your client machine, which is either your Windows computer or another Linux server. From that client, you want to manage and access your remote Linux database server.

Solution

To start the VNC viewer on your Windows computer, run the program `C:\Program Files\RealVNC\VNC4\vncviewer.exe`, or you can navigate to that program by selecting Start ➤ All Programs ➤ RealVNC ➤ VNC viewer 4 ➤ Run VNC viewer. You will be presented with a Connection Details dialog box, as shown in Figure 16-3.

Figure 16-3. *VNC viewer connection details*

In the Connection Details dialog box, provide the hostname or IP address of your remote Linux database server, as well as the port number on which the VNC server is listening. Click the OK button to confirm.

To start the VNC viewer on your Linux server, run the Linux command `/usr/bin/vncviewer` as follows (assuming port number 9):

```
# /usr/bin/vncviewer BLLNX3:9
```

You will be prompted for a username and password, as shown in Figure 16-4. Depending upon the security settings in the VNC server, you may be prompted only for a password.

Figure 16-4. *VNC viewer password prompt*

Once your username and password are successfully verified, the screen of your remote Linux database server is displayed, as shown in Figure 16-5. You can now start to access and manage your remote Linux database server just as if you were in front of the console.

If you don't have the VNC viewer installed on your client computer and your Internet browser supports Java applets, then you can open the URL `http://<host>:<port>`, where `<host>` is the hostname or IP address of the VNC server and `<port>` is the port number on which the VNC server is listening minus 100. For instance, if the VNC server's IP address is 192.168.0.13 and the server is listening on port number 5909, the URL will be `http://192.168.0.13:5809`.

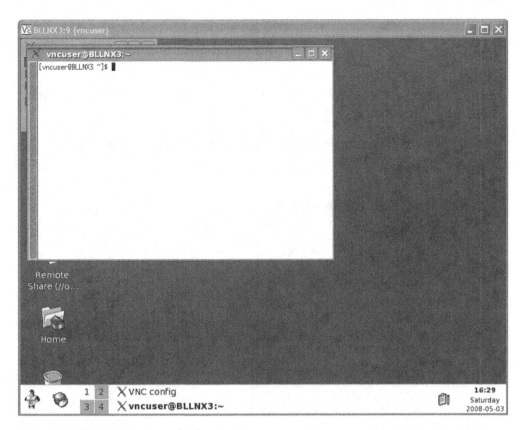

Figure 16-5. *VNC viewer screen display*

How It Works

Before you can run the VNC viewer on your client computer, you need to ensure that the VNC server is running on your remote Linux database server and listening on a specific port number. For details on how to install and start the VNC server, review the first four recipes in this chapter.

However, if the VNC viewer is not installed on your client computer, such as a computer in an Internet café or perhaps in an airport, you can still access the VNC viewer using a Java-capable Internet browser. This provides great flexibility, since you are no longer confined to working in your office to perform DBA tasks. (Work from your local café instead!) But ensure that your VNC connection is secured, which you will learn more about in recipe 16-7.

If you have the VNC server's Enterprise Edition running on your remote Linux database server, you cannot use the VNC viewer's Free Edition because of its security limitations. Instead, you must use the VNC viewer's Personal Edition or Enterprise Edition version 4.

16-6. Sharing a VNC Connection

Problem

You want to share your VNC connection with another team member who is located in another area in your building or on the other side of the globe. You want to share so that you and the other team member can collaborate and access the same display together in real time when managing a remote Linux database server.

Solution

Before you launch the VNC viewer on your client computer, perform the following steps to configure the shared connection option:

1. Start the VNC viewer (for details on starting the VNC viewer, check recipe 16-5).

2. Click the Options button, as shown in Figure 16-6.

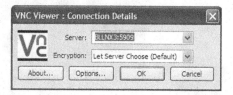

Figure 16-6. *VNC viewer connection details*

3. In the VNC viewer Options dialog box, as shown in Figure 16-7, click the Misc tab.

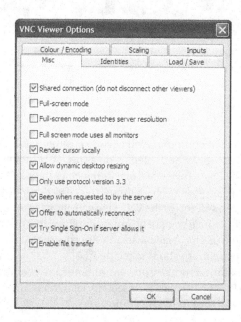

Figure 16-7. *VNC viewer miscellaneous options*

4. Select the Shared Connection (Do Not Disconnect Other Viewers) box. If you leave this unchecked, then other previously connected VNC viewers will be terminated.

5. Finally, click the OK button.

However, if you want to share VNC connections with a server all the time regardless of your VNC viewer settings, then add the AlwaysShared parameter when starting the VNC server on your remote Linux database server:

```
# /usr/bin/vncserver :9 -AlwaysShared
```

If the VNC server is already running, then execute the vncconfig command to dynamically change the value of the AlwaysShared parameter. To enable the AlwaysShared parameter, set it to 1, or set it to 0 to disable it. For example:

```
# /usr/bin/vncconfig -set AlwaysShared=1
```

Note To determine the current values of VNC server parameters, such as AlwaysShared, issue the Linux command /usr/bin/vncconfig -get AlwaysShared.

If you don't want to share VNC connections with a particular server, then set the NeverShared parameter to 1, or set it to 0 to disable it. For example:

```
# /usr/bin/vncconfig -set NeverShared=1
```

With this setting, remote users cannot share their connections even when selecting the Shared Connection (Do Not Disconnect Other Viewers) checkbox shown in Figure 16-7.

How It Works

You can configure the sharing of VNC connections either on the remote Linux database server, where the VNC server is running, or on your client computer, where you want to run the VNC viewer. The VNC's screen-sharing feature allows a team of DBAs to collaborate from anywhere anytime, which saves a lot of time and dollars since they don't have to be at the site where the database server is hosted.

Configuring the VNC viewer to share a VNC connection works only if the VNC server parameters AlwaysShared and NeverShared are disabled, which are the default settings. If you enable the AlwaysShared parameter in the VNC server, then the VNC connection will always be shared regardless of the configuration you set in the VNC viewer.

However, if you enable the NeverShared parameter in the VNC server, then the VNC connection is not shared, even if you enable the AlwaysShared parameter. In this case, if you open a second VNC connection to access the same VNC server and port number, the first VNC connection will be automatically disconnected. In other words, there can be only one VNC connection at a time to the said VNC server and port number. But if the DisconnectClients parameter is disabled (the default is enabled) in the VNC server, then the second VNC connection will be refused, and the first one will remain connected.

When the VNC server is already running, you can change its parameters, such as AlwaysShared, on the fly using vncconfig. However, this works starting in VNC server version 4 only.

16-7. Securing a VNC Connection

Problem

You want to secure your VNC connection. Also, you want to have a good authentication method when users access the remote Linux database server from your client computer using the VNC viewer.

Solution

To enhance a user's authentication and the security of your VNC connection, we recommend you add the following parameters when starting the VNC server:

- SecurityTypes: Sets the security method to employ. Valid values are None, VncAuth, RA2, and RA2ne.

- UserPasswdVerifier: Sets the method to authenticate the users. Valid values are None, VncAuth, and UnixAuth.

- AllowedUsers or AllowedGroups: Sets the Linux users or groups that are allowed to access.

- QueryConnect: Sets whether the user has to wait for confirmation before they can connect. Set it to 1 to enable this feature, or set it to 0 to disable it.

You can pass these parameters when manually starting your VNC server. For example:

```
# su - vncuser -c "/usr/bin/vncserver :9 -SecurityTypes="RA2" \
        -UserPasswdVerifier="UnixAuth" -AllowedGroups=vncadmin:f,vncuser:v \
        -QueryConnect=1"
```

You can also configure the parameters to take effect when the VNC server is automatically started during the reboot of your remote Linux database server, as discussed in recipe 16-4. To that end, add the following lines to your /etc/sysconfig/vncservers file:

```
VNCSERVERS="9:vncuser"
VNCSERVERARGS[9]=" -SecurityTypes=RA2 -UserPasswdVerifier=UnixAuth " \
                "-AllowedGroups=vncadmin:f,vncuser:v -QueryConnect=1"
```

The first argument you are passing in VNCSERVERARGS corresponds to the port number on which the VNC server is listening. In this example, the port number is 9.

Note If the VNC server is already running, you can dynamically set parameters by running the Linux command /user/bin/vnconfig. For example, to dynamically set the SecurityTypes parameter, run the command as follows: /usr/bin/vncconfig -set SecurityTypes=RA2.

The syntax for the parameters `AllowedUsers` and `AllowedGroups` is `name[:permission]`. The `name` is a Linux user when setting `AllowedUsers` and a Linux group when specifying a value for the `AllowedGroups` parameter. The following are the valid `permission` values and their meanings:

- v: The user can see the VNC display.

- p: The user has mouse access.

- k: The user has keyboard access.

- c: The user is allowed to copy/paste to and from the clipboard.

- q: This is similar to `QueryConnect=0`.

- d: This is like having the permissions v, p, k, and c.

- f: The user has a full-access privilege, which is similar to v, p, k, c, and q.

How It Works

We recommend you use the latest version of the VNC Server Enterprise Edition, since it employs 2048-bit RSA server authentication and 128-bit AES session encryption. If you use the VNC Server Free Edition, be aware that no security feature is available. However, you need to purchase a license key for the VNC Server Enterprise Edition.

■**Note** To secure the connection to the server when using the VNC Server Free Edition, forward the VNC connection through SSH, which is discussed in recipe 14-7.

As a security measure, we recommend you do not run the VNC server as `root`, because you don't want to allow users to have `root` access privilege once they are connected to the server. We recommend you create another Linux user with minimal privileges and run the VNC server under that new Linux user (see recipe 16-3 for details). Once a remote user is connected to the server, then they can `su` to `oracle` to perform any needed DBA tasks.

To encrypt a VNC connection, set the `SecurityTypes` parameter to `RA2`. For password encryption, set `SecurityTypes` to `RA2ne`. In that case, however, the VNC connection will not be encrypted. Thus, we recommend you set `SecurityTypes` to `RA2` and not worry about the password, since the VNC connection is encrypted. In other words, all data traversing between the VNC server and the VNC viewer are encrypted, including the password.

Also, set `UserPasswdVerifier` to `UnixAuth`, instead of `VncAuth`. That way, the OS user's password is managed at the OS level, which requires less maintenance, because you don't have to maintain two passwords: one in the VNC and the other at the OS level.

We recommend you do not set `SecurityTypes` or `UserPasswdVerifier` to `None`, because you are basically then allowing any users to access the VNC server without providing a password. This is like having your main door at your home with no locks at all.

If the QueryConnect parameter is enabled and you don't have the q privilege, as assigned in the parameter AllowedUsers or AllowedGroups, then you have to wait for a confirmation whether you are accepted, rejected, or granted "view-only" privilege when accessing the VNC server, as shown in Figure 16-8. This is to avoid unauthorized access initiated from a specific host or user.

Figure 16-8. *QueryConnect prompt*

If you have several users who will be sharing access to the same VNC server and port number, we recommend you create at least two Linux groups. The first Linux group (you can call it vncadmin) has a full-access privilege when accessing the VNC server, while the other one (you can name it vncuser) has the viewing-only option and no access to the keyboard and mouse. So if you want to add users to access the VNC server later, then you just add the user to the corresponding Linux group, that is, vncadmin or vncuser, and you don't have to modify the VNC server configuration, such as AllowedUsers or AllowedGroups.

You can also dynamically change the permission of the user using vncconfig. If you run vncconfig without any parameters, the VNC Config dialog box appears, as shown in Figure 16-9. When you click the Connections button, the Active Connections dialog box appears. To change the permission of a particular connection, highlight the corresponding connection, and then click the Change button.

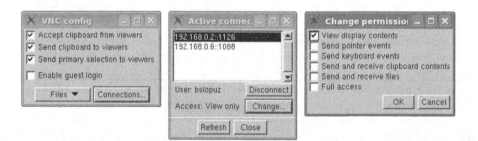

Figure 16-9. *VNC configuration*

16-8 Accessing VNC via a Proxy Server

Problem

You want to use VNC to access a remote Linux database server that is outside your company's network, and all your Internet connections pass through a proxy server.

Solution

Perform the following steps to configure the proxy settings in your VNC viewer:

1. Start the VNC viewer (for details on starting the VNC viewer, check recipe 16-5).

2. Provide the appropriate hostname or IP address of the remote Linux database server, as well as the corresponding port number where the VNC server is listening, as shown in Figure 16-10.

Figure 16-10. *VNC viewer connection details*

3. Click the Options button, and the VNC viewer Properties dialog box will appear, as shown in Figure 16-11.

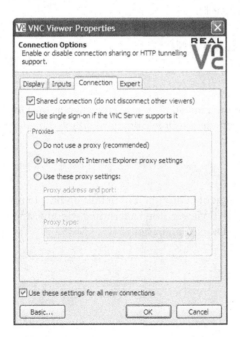

Figure 16-11. *VNC proxy server configuration*

4. Click the Connection tab.

5. In the Proxies section, select the Use These Proxy Settings radio button, and provide the appropriate hostname or IP address of the corresponding proxy server and its port number where the proxy server is listening, as well as the proxy type. If you have already configured a proxy setting in Microsoft Internet Explorer, then select Use Microsoft Internet Explorer Proxy Settings instead.

6. Click the OK button.

7. Finally, click Connect button.

How It Works

Nowadays, the Internet connections of most companies that are going outside their network pass through a proxy server for security and performance reasons. These are usually common for IT shops where the DBAs are accessing the servers of their clients or at their home while working from their office. For details about the hostname or IP address of your proxy server, its port number, and the proxy type, you need to contact your company's system or network administrators.

To configure the proxy server setting using the VNC viewer, you must download and use the Personal Edition or Enterprise Edition, because the proxy server feature is not available in the Free Edition. The proxy server is a new feature included in the VNC viewer's version 4.4, which was released in May 2008. Prior to version 4.4, you can configure SSH tunneling and proxy server using PuTTY, as explained in recipe 1-1.

16-9. Running X Applications with VNC

Problem

You want to run an X application at your remote Linux database server, such as the Oracle Database Configuration Assistant (DBCA) to create the Oracle database from your client computer.

Solution

First, you need to run the VNC viewer at your client computer. For details on how to run the VNC viewer, review recipe 16-5. Then, in the VNC viewer, open a terminal window, and log on to the Linux user who will be the owner of the Oracle database:

```
$ xhost localhost
localhost being added to access control list
$ su - oracle
Password:
$ dbca
```

You will see a screen similar to Figure 16-12.

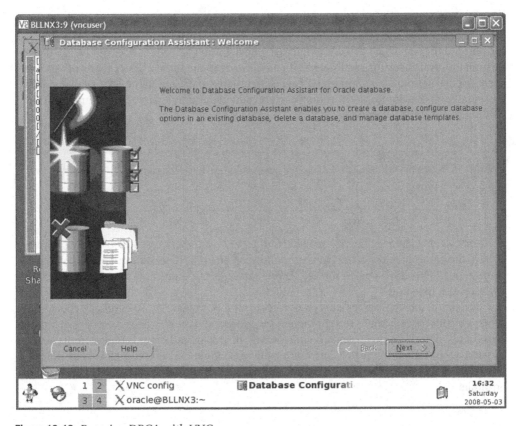

Figure 16-12. *Running DBCA with VNC*

How It Works

Once the VNC viewer display is available on your client machine and you have access to the mouse and keyboard, as granted by the VNC parameters AllowedUsers and AllowedGroups, you can then run any X application, such as Oracle's DBCA. Any X application that you run will look and feel just as if you were running it on the console of your remote Linux database server.

16-10. Troubleshooting VNC

Problem

You cannot access the remote Linux database server. You are having problems running the VNC server or the VNC viewer.

Solution

When troubleshooting VNC, you may need to check the following areas to narrow down the cause of the problem.

VNC Server

Check that the VNC server is running on your remote Linux database server and is listening at the port number on which you are trying to connect. If the VNC server does not run at all, we recommend you check the parameters you are passing to the server. Check for errors such as spelling mistakes or invalid parameter values. If possible, try running the VNC server without any parameters except for the port number, and add your parameters one at a time until you determine the culprit parameter.

Note To display the VNC server's options and parameters, run the Linux command /usr/bin/vncserver -list.

You can check the log file. That log file is at $HOME/.vnc/<hostname>:<port#>.log, where $HOME is the home directory of the Linux user under which the VNC server is running, <hostname> corresponds to the hostname of the VNC server, and <port#> represents the port on which the VNC server is listening.

By default, the VNC server's log parameter is set to *:stderr:30. To configure the VNC server's log file, specify the VNC parameter -log <logname>:<dest>:<level>, where <logname> is the name of the log writer, <dest> is either stderr or stdout, and <level> ranges from 0 to 100. To gather extra details in the VNC server's log file, you may set <level> to 100. For example, the following command starts the VNC server to listen on port 9 and logs extra details in the standard error file:

```
vncserver :9 -log *:stderr:100
```

We recommend you display the VNC server's log file while you monitor incoming VNC connections. Use the tail command with the -f option for that purpose, as shown in the following example:

```
[vncuser@BLLNX3 .vnc] $ tail -f $HOME/.vnc/BLLNX3:9.log
Mon May  5 17:19:27 2008
 TcpSocket:    connected to 127.0.0.1::21053
Warning: Tried to connect to session manager, networkIdsList argument is NULL
X Error of failed request:  86
  Major opcode of failed request:  51 (X_SetFontPath)
  Serial number of failed request:  8
  Current serial number in output stream:   10
startkde: Starting up...
kbuildsycoca running...
Klipper is already running!
```

VNC Viewer

To avoid any compatibility issues, ensure that the version of the VNC viewer you are using on your client computer matches the version of your VNC server on your remote Linux database server. For example, if the VNC server is Enterprise Edition version 4, then use VNC Viewer Enterprise Edition version 4 on your client computer.

If you still have issues with your VNC viewer on your client computer, we recommend you connect to the VNC server using your Internet browser. Most Internet browsers nowadays support Java applets, enabling you to connect. For additional information on how to start the VNC viewer, review recipe 16-5.

Connectivity

Verify that you can connect from your client computer to your remote Linux database server, and vice versa. Run the ping command from the OS command prompt of your client computer. In the following example, the IP address of the remote Linux database server is 192.168.0.13, while the client computer's IP address is 192.168.0.6:

```
C:\>ipconfig

Windows IP Configuration
Ethernet adapter Local Area Connection:

        Connection-specific DNS Suffix  . :
        IP Address. . . . . . . . . . . : 192.168.0.6
        Subnet Mask . . . . . . . . . . : 255.255.255.0
        Default Gateway . . . . . . . . : 192.168.0.1

C:\>ping BLLNX3

Pinging BLLnx3 [192.168.0.13] with 32 bytes of data:

Reply from 192.168.0.13: bytes=32 time=15ms TTL=64
Reply from 192.168.0.13: bytes=32 time<1ms TTL=64
Reply from 192.168.0.13: bytes=32 time<1ms TTL=64
Reply from 192.168.0.13: bytes=32 time<1ms TTL=64

Ping statistics for 192.168.0.13:
    Packets: Sent = 4, Received = 4, Lost = 0 (0% loss),
Approximate round trip times in milli-seconds:
    Minimum = 0ms, Maximum = 15ms, Average = 3ms
```

Also, perform your tests the other way around. Try to ping the client computer from your remote Linux database server. For example:

```
[vncuser@BLLNX3 ~]$ hostname
BLLNX3
[vncuser@BLLNX3 ~]$ ping -c 3 192.168.0.6
PING 192.168.0.6 (192.168.0.6) 56(84) bytes of data.
64 bytes from 192.168.0.6: icmp_seq=1 ttl=128 time=0.625 ms
64 bytes from 192.168.0.6: icmp_seq=2 ttl=128 time=0.650 ms
64 bytes from 192.168.0.6: icmp_seq=3 ttl=128 time=0.676 ms

--- 192.168.0.6 ping statistics ---
3 packets transmitted, 3 received, 0% packet loss, time 2004ms
rtt min/avg/max/mdev = 0.625/0.650/0.676/0.029 ms
```

If you fail to make a connection using the `ping` command, then verify that you are using the correct hostname or IP address for the VNC server, and verify the correct port number on which the VNC server is supposed to listen. Also, check for a firewall that may be blocking your connections to the remote Linux database server from your client computer, and vice versa. If you need to connect to the remote Linux database server through a proxy server, then you need to set up your proxy server configuration. Configuring for a proxy server is discussed in recipe 16-8.

How It Works

For the VNC software to work, you need the three components to function properly: the VNC server listening at the remote Linux database server, the VNC viewer running at the client computer, and connectivity between the two computers. First, you need to identify the problematic area and start troubleshooting from there.

For the VNC server, you need to review the first four recipes in this chapter to ensure that it is installed correctly and is listening on the designated port number on your remote Linux database server. You can also monitor the messages generated in the VNC server's log file while connections are coming to the VNC server.

On the client computer, you need to check that the VNC viewer is running. If the VNC viewer is not available or not running correctly, then we recommend you connect using your Java-capable Internet browser. This is to ensure that you are using the same versions between the VNC server and the VNC viewer.

Last but not least, you can use the `ping` command to verify connectivity between the remote Linux database server and the client computer. If you still cannot connect at this point, we recommend you contact your system or network administrators to help you troubleshoot the connectivity issue between the remote Linux database server and your client computer.

APPENDIX A

RAID Concepts

In the not too distant past, a 100GB database was considered to be pretty big. Currently, 1–2TB defines the lower boundary for a large database. In the not too distant future, a petabyte (how to make a byte purr?), exabyte, and zettabyte will become commonly bandied terms near the DBA water cooler.

As companies store more and more data, the need for disk space continues to grow. Managing database storage is a key responsibility of every database administrator. DBAs are tasked with estimating the initial size of databases, recognizing growth patterns, and monitoring disk usage. Overseeing these operations is critical to ensuring the availability of company data. Here are some common tasks of DBAs associated with storage management:

- Determining disk architecture for database applications

- Planning database capacity

- Monitoring and managing growth of database files

Before more storage is added to a database server, the system administrators and database administrators typically (should) sit down and figure out what disk architecture offers the best availability and performance for a given budget. When working with system administrators, an effective DBA needs to be somewhat fluent in the language of disk technologies. Specifically, DBAs must have a basic understanding of RAID disk technology and its implications for database performance and availability.

Even if your opinion isn't solicited in regard to disk technology, you still need to be familiar with the basic RAID configurations that will allow you to make informed decisions about database tuning and troubleshooting. This appendix discusses the fundamental information a DBA needs to know about RAID.

Understanding RAID

As a DBA, you need to be knowledgeable about RAID designs to ensure that you use an appropriate disk architecture for your database application. RAID is an acronym for a Redundant Array of Inexpensive (or Independent) Disks. RAID technology allows you to configure several independent disks to logically appear as one disk to the application. There are two important reasons you would want to use RAID:

- To spread I/O across several disks, thus improving bandwidth

- To eliminate a lone physical disk as a single point of failure

If the database process that is reading and writing updates to disk can parallelize I/O across many disks (instead of a single disk), the bandwidth can be dramatically improved. RAID also allows you to configure several disks in such a way that you never have one disk as a single point of failure. For most database systems, it's critical to have redundant hardware to ensure database availability.

The purpose of this section is not to espouse one RAID technology over another. You'll find bazillions of blogs and white papers on the subject of RAID. Each source of information has its own guru that evangelizes one form of RAID over another. All of these sources have valid arguments on why their favorite flavor of RAID is the best for a particular situation.

Be wary of blanket statements regarding the performance and availability of RAID technology. For example, you might hear somebody state that RAID 5 is always better than RAID 1 for database applications. You might also hear somebody state that RAID 1 has superior fault tolerance over RAID 5. In most cases, the superiority of one RAID technology over another depends on several factors such as the I/O behavior of the database application and the various components of the underlying stack of hardware and software. You may discover that what performs well in one scenario is not true in another. It really depends on the entire suite of technology in use.

The goal here is to describe the performance and fault tolerance characteristics of the most commonly used RAID technologies. We explain in simple terms and with clear examples how the basic forms of RAID technology work. This base knowledge will allow you to make an informed disk technology decision dependent on the business requirements of your current environment. You should also be able to take the information contained in this section and apply that to the more sophisticated and emerging RAID architectures.

Defining Array, Stripe Width, Stripe Size, Chunk Size

Before we dive into the technical details of RAID, you first need to be familiar with a few terms, namely, array, stripe width, stripe size, and chunk size. An *array* is simply a collection of disks grouped together to appear as a single device to the application. Disk arrays allow for increased performance and fault tolerance.

The *stripe width* is the number of parallel pieces of data that can be written or read simultaneously to an array. The stripe width is usually equal to the number of disks in the array. In general (with all other factors being equal), the larger the stripe width size, the greater the throughput performance of the array. For example, you will generally see greater read/write performance from an array of twelve 32GB drives than from an array of four 96GB drives.

The *stripe size* is the amount of data you want written in parallel to an array of disks. Determining the optimal stripe size can be a highly debatable topic. Decreasing the stripe size usually increases the number of drives a file will utilize to store its data. Increasing the stripe size usually decreases the number of drives a file will employ to write and read to an array. The optimal stripe size depends on your database application I/O characteristics along with the hardware and software of the system.

Note The stripe size is usually a configurable parameter that can be dynamically configured by the storage administrator. Contrast that to the stripe width, which can be changed only by increasing or decreasing the physical number of disks.

The *chunk size* is the subset of the stripe size. The chunk size (also called *striping unit*) is the amount of data written to each disk in the array as part of a stripe size. Figure A-1 shows a 4KB stripe size that is being written to an array of four disks (a stripe width of 4). Each disk gets a 1KB chunk written to it.

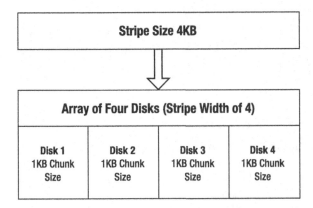

Figure A-1. *A 4KB stripe of data is written to four disks as 1KB chunks.*

The chunk size can have significant performance effects. An inappropriate chunk size can result in I/O being concentrated on single disks within the array. If this happens, you may end up with an expensive array of disks that performs no better than a single disk.

What's the correct chunk size to use for database applications? It depends somewhat on the average size of I/O your databases generates. Typically, database I/O consists of several simultaneous and small I/O requests. Ideally, each small I/O request should be serviced by one disk, with the multiple I/O requests spread out across all disks in the array. So, in this scenario you would want your chunk size to be a little larger than the average database I/O size.

■**Tip** You'll have to test your particular database and disk configuration to determine which chunk size results in the best I/O distribution for a given application and its average I/O size.

RAID 0

RAID 0 is commonly known as *striping*. Striping is a technique that writes chunks of data across an array of disks in a parallel fashion. Data is also read from disks in the same way. This allows several disks to participate in the read/write operations. The idea behind striping is that simultaneous access to multiple disks will have greater bandwidth than I/O to a single disk.

■**Note** One disk can be larger than the other disks in a RAID 0 device (and the additional space is still used). However, this is not recommended because I/O will be concentrated on the large disk where more space is available.

Figure A-2 demonstrates how RAID 0 works. This RAID 0 disk array physically comprises four disks. Logically, it looks like one disk (/mount01) to the application. The stripe of data written to the RAID 0 device consists of 16 bits: 0001001000110100. Each disk receives a 4-bit chunk of the stripe.

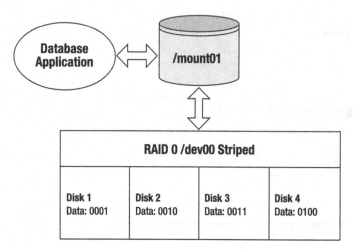

Figure A-2. *A four-disk RAID 0 striped device*

With RAID 0, your realized disk capacity is the number of disks times the size of the disk. For example, if you had four 100GB drives, then the overall realized disk capacity available to the application would be 400GB. In this sense, RAID 0 is a very cost-effective solution.

RAID 0 also provides excellent I/O performance. It allows for simultaneous reading and writing on all disks in the array. This spreads out the I/O, which reduces disk contention, alleviates bottlenecks, and provides excellent I/O performance.

The huge downside to RAID 0 is that it does not provide any redundancy. If one disk fails, the entire array fails. Therefore, you should never use RAID 0 for data you consider to be critical. You should use RAID 0 only for files that you can easily recover and only when you don't require a high degree of availability.

Tip One way to remember what RAID 0 means is that it provides "0" redundancy. You get zero fault tolerance with RAID 0. If one disk fails, the whole array of disks fails.

RAID 1

RAID 1 is commonly known as *mirroring*. Mirroring means that each time data is written to the storage device, it is physically written to two (or more) disks. In this configuration, if you lose one disk of the array, you still have another disk that contains a byte-for-byte copy of the data.

Figure A-3 shows how RAID 1 works. The mirrored disk array is composed of two disks. Disk 1b is a copy (mirror) of Disk 1a. As the data bits 0001 are written to Disk 1a, a copy of the data is also written to Disk 1b. Logically, the RAID 1 array of two disks looks like one disk (/mount01) to the application.

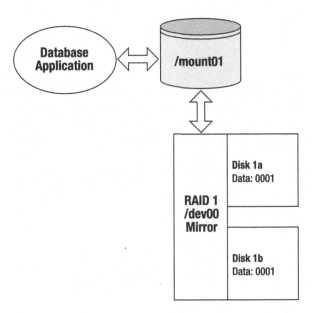

Figure A-3. *A RAID 1 two-disk mirror*

Write performance with RAID 1 takes a little longer (than a single disk) because data must be written to each participating mirrored disk. However, read bandwidth is increased because of parallel access to data contained in the mirrored array.

RAID 1 is popular because it's simple to implement and provides fault tolerance. You can lose one mirrored disk and still continue operations as long as there is one surviving member. One downside to RAID 1 is that it reduces the amount of realized disk space available to the application. Typically you will have only two disks in a mirrored array; however, keep in mind that you can have more than two disks in a mirror. The realized disk space in a mirrored array is the size of the disk. Here is the formula for calculating realized disk space for RAID 1:

```
Number of mirrored arrays * Disk Capacity
```

For example, say you have four 500GB disks and you want to create two mirrored arrays with two disks in each array. The realized available disk space is calculated as shown here:

```
2 arrays * 500 gigabytes = 1 terabyte
```

Another way of formulating this would be as follows:

```
(Number of disks available / number of disks in the array) * Disk Capacity
```

This formula also shows that the amount of disk space available to the application is 1TB:

```
(4 / 2) * 500 gigabytes = 1 terabyte
```

> **Tip** One way to remember the meaning of RAID 1 is that it provides 100 percent redundancy. You can lose one member of the RAID 1 array and still continue operations.

Generating Parity

Before discussing the next levels of RAID, it's important to understand the concept of parity and how it is generated. RAID 4 and RAID 5 configurations use parity information to provide redundancy against a single disk failure. For a three-disk RAID 4 or RAID 5 configuration, each write results in two disks being written to in a striped fashion, with the third disk storing the parity information.

Parity data contains the information needed to reconstruct data in the event one disk fails. Parity information is generated from an XOR (exclusive OR) operation. Table A-1 describes the inputs and outputs of an XOR operation. Table A-1 reads as follows: if one and only one of the inputs is a 1, then the output will be a 1; otherwise, the output is a 0.

Table A-1. *Behavior of an XOR Operation*

Input A	Input B	Output
1	1	0
1	0	1
0	1	1
0	0	0

For example, from the first row in Table A-1, if both bits are a 1, then the output of an XOR operation is a 0. From the second and third rows, if one bit is a 1 and if the other bit is a zero, then the output of an XOR operation is a 1. The last row shows that if both bits are a 0, then the output is a 0.

A slightly more complicated example will help clarify this concept. In this example there are three disks. As shown in Figure A-4, Disk 1 is written 0110, and Disk 2 is written 1110. Disk 3 contains the parity information generated by the output of an XOR operation on data written to Disk 1 and Disk 2.

Disk 1	Disk 2	Disk 3 (Parity)
Data: 0110	Data: 1110	Data: 1000

Figure A-4. *Disk 1 XOR Disk 2 = Disk 3 (parity)*

How was the 1000 parity information calculated? The first two bits of the data written to Disk 1 and Disk 2 are a 0 and a 1; therefore, the XOR output is a 1. The second two bits are both 1, so the XOR output is a 0. The third sets of bits are both 1, and the output is a 0. The fourth bits are both zeros, so the output is a 0. This discussion is summarized here in equation form:

```
Disk1 XOR Disk2 = Disk3 (parity disk)
----- --- ----- -----
0110  XOR 1110  = 1000
```

How does parity allow for the recalculation of data in the event of a failure? For this example, say we lose Disk 2. The information on Disk 2 can be regenerated by taking an XOR operation on the parity information (Disk 3) with the data written to Disk 1. An XOR operation of 0110 and 1000 yields 1110 (which was what was originally written to Disk 2). This is summarized in equation form:

```
Disk1 XOR Disk3 = Disk2
----- --- ----- -----
0110  XOR 1000  = 1110
```

You can perform an XOR operation with any number of disks. Say you have a four-disk configuration. Disk 1 is written 0101, Disk 2 is written 1110, and Disk 3 is written 0001. Disk 4 contains the parity information, which is the result of Disk 1 XOR Disk 2 XOR Disk 3:

```
Disk1 XOR Disk2 XOR Disk3 = Disk4 (parity disk)
----- --- ---- --- ----- -----
0101  XOR 1110 XOR 0001  = 1010
```

Say you lose Disk 2. To regenerate the information on Disk 2, you perform an XOR operation on Disk 1, Disk 3, and the parity information (Disk 4), which results in 1110:

```
Disk1 XOR Disk3 XOR Disk4 = Disk2
----- --- ----- --- ----- -----
0101  XOR 0001 XOR 1010  = 1110
```

You can always regenerate the data on the drive that becomes damaged by performing an XOR operation on the remaining disks with the parity information. RAID 4 and RAID 5 technologies use parity as a key component for providing fault tolerance. These parity-centric technologies are described in the next two sections.

RAID 4

RAID 4 is sometimes referred to as *dedicated parity*. RAID 4 writes a stripe (in chunks) across a disk array. One drive is always dedicated for parity information. A RAID 4 configuration minimally requires three disks: two disks for data and one for parity. The term *RAID 4* does not mean there are four disks in the array; there could be three or more disks in a RAID 4 configuration.

Figure A-5 shows a four-disk RAID 4 configuration. Disk 4 is the dedicated parity disk. The first stripe consists of the data 000100100011. Chunks of data 0001, 0010, and 0011 are written to Disks 1, 2, and 3, respectively. The parity value of 0000 is calculated and written to Disk 4.

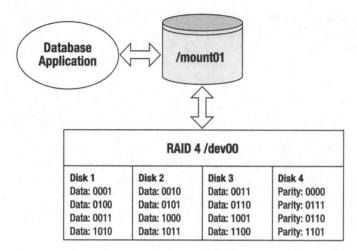

Figure A-5. *A four-disk RAID 4 dedicated parity device*

RAID 4 uses an XOR operation to generate the parity information. For each stripe in Figure A-5, the parity information is generated as follows:

```
Disk1 XOR Disk2 XOR Disk3 = Parity
----- --- ----- --- ----- ------
0001  XOR 0010  XOR 0011  = 0000
0100  XOR 0101  XOR 0110  = 0111
0111  XOR 1000  XOR 1001  = 0110
1010  XOR 1011  XOR 1100  = 1101
```

■**Tip** See the earlier "Generating Parity" section for details on how an XOR operation works.

RAID 4 requires that parity information be generated and updated for each write. Therefore, writes take longer in a RAID 4 configuration than a RAID 0 write. Reading from a RAID 4 configuration is fast because the data is spread across multiple drives (and potentially multiple controllers).

With RAID 4 you get more realized disk space than you do with RAID 1. The RAID 4 amount of disk space available to the application is calculated with this formula:

```
(Number of disks - 1) * Disk Capacity
```

For example, if you have four 100GB disks, then the realized disk capacity available to the application is calculated as shown here:

```
(4 -1) * 100 gigabytes = 300 gigabytes
```

In the event of a single disk failure, the remaining disks of the array can continue to function. For example, say Disk 1 fails. The Disk 1 information can be regenerated with the parity information, as shown here:

```
Disk2 XOR Disk3 XOR Parity = Disk1
----- --- ----- --- ------   -----
0010  XOR 0011  XOR 0000    = 0001
0101  XOR 0110  XOR 0111    = 0100
1000  XOR 1001  XOR 0110    = 0111
1011  XOR 1100  XOR 1101    = 1010
```

During a single disk failure, RAID 4 performance will be degraded because the parity information is required for generating the data on the failed drive. Performance will return to normal
levels after the failed disk has been replaced and its information regenerated. In practice, RAID
4 is seldom used because of the inherent bottleneck with the dedicated parity disk.

RAID 5

RAID 5 is sometimes referred to as *distributed parity*. RAID 5 is similar to RAID 4 except
that RAID 5 interleaves the parity information among all the drives available in the disk array.
A RAID 5 configuration minimally requires three disks: two for data and one for parity. The
term *RAID 5* does not mean there are five disks in the array; there can be three or more disks
in a RAID 5 configuration.

Figure A-6 shows a four-disk RAID 5 array. The first stripe of data consists of 000100100011.
Three chunks of 0001, 0010, and 0011 are written to Disks 1, 2, and 3 with the parity of 0000
written to Disk 4. The second stripe writes its parity information to Disk 1, the third stripe
writes its parity to Disk 2, and so on.

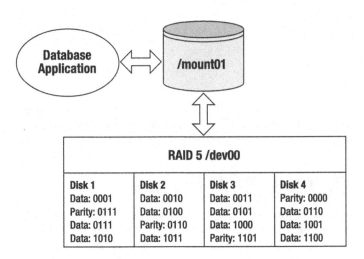

Figure A-6. *A four-disk RAID 5 distributed parity device*

RAID 5 uses an XOR operation to generate the parity information. For each stripe in
Figure A-6, the parity information is generated as follows:

```
0001  XOR 0010  XOR 0011  = 0000
0100  XOR 0101  XOR 0110  = 0111
0111  XOR 1000  XOR 1001  = 0110
1010  XOR 1011  XOR 1100  = 1101
```

■**Tip** See the earlier "Generating Parity" section for details on how an XOR operation works.

Like RAID 4, RAID 5 writes suffer a slight write performance hit because of the additional update required for the parity information. RAID 5 performs better than RAID 4 because it spreads the load of generating and updating parity information to all disks in the array. For this reason, RAID 5 is almost always preferred over RAID 4.

RAID 5 is popular because it combines good I/O performance with fault tolerance and cost effectiveness. With RAID 5 you get more realized disk space than you do with RAID 1. The RAID 5 amount of disk space available to the application is calculated with this formula:

```
(Number of disks - 1) * Disk Capacity
```

Using the previous formula, if you have four 100GB disks, then the realized disk capacity available to the application is calculated as follows:

```
(4 -1) * 100 gigabytes = 300 gigabytes
```

RAID 5 provides protection against a single disk failure through the parity information. If one disk fails, the information from the failed disk can always be recalculated from the remaining drives in the RAID 5 array. For example, say Disk 3 fails; the remaining data on Disk1, Disk 2, and Disk 4 can regenerate the required Disk 3 information as follows:

```
DISK1 XOR DISK2 XOR DISK4 = DISK3
----- --- ----- --- ----- 	-----
0001  XOR 0010  XOR 0000  = 0011
0111  XOR 0100  XOR 0110  = 0101
0111  XOR 0110  XOR 1001  = 1000
1010  XOR 1011  XOR 1100  = 1101
```

During a single disk failure, RAID 5 performance will be degraded because the parity information is required for generating the data on the failed drive. Performance will return to normal levels after the failed disk has been replaced and its information regenerated.

Building Hybrid (Nested) RAID Devices

The RAID 0, RAID 1, and RAID 5 architectures are the building blocks for more sophisticated storage architectures. Companies that need better availability can combine these base RAID technologies to build disk arrays with better fault tolerance. Some common hybrid RAID architectures are as follows:

- RAID 0+1 (striping, then mirroring)

- RAID 1+0 (mirroring, then striping)

- RAID 5+0 (RAID 5, then striping)

These configurations are sometimes referred to as *hybrid* or *nested* RAID levels. Much like Lego blocks, you can take the underlying RAID architectures and snap them together for some interesting configurations that have performance, fault tolerance, and cost advantages and disadvantages. These technologies are described in detail in the following sections.

Note Be aware that there exists some degree of confusion on the naming standards for various RAID levels. The most common industry standard for nested RAID levels is that RAID A+B means that first RAID level A is built and then RAID level B is layered on top of RAID level A. This standard is not consistently applied by all storage vendors. You'll have to carefully read the specifications for a given storage device to ensure that you understand which level of RAID is in use.

RAID 0+1

RAID 0+1 is a disk array that is first striped and then mirrored (a mirror of stripes). Figure A-7 shows an eight-disk RAID 0+1 configuration. Disks 1 through 4 are written to in a striped fashion. Disks 5 through 8 are a mirror of Disks 1 through 4.

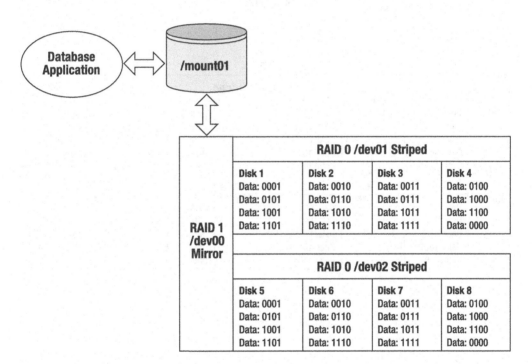

Figure A-7. *A RAID 0+1 striped and then mirrored device*

RAID 0+1 provides the I/O benefits of striping while providing the sturdy fault tolerance of a mirrored device. This is a relatively expensive solution because only half the disks in the array comprise your usable disk space. The RAID 0+1 amount of disk space available to the application is calculated with this formula:

```
(Number of disks in stripe) * Disk Capacity
```

Using the previous formula, if you have eight 100GB drives, with four drives in each stripe, then the realized disk capacity available to the application is calculated as shown here:

```
4 * 100 gigabytes = 400 gigabytes
```

The RAID 0+1 configuration can survive multiple disk failures only if the failures occur within one stripe. RAID 0+1 cannot survive two disk failures if one failure is in one stripe (/dev01) and the other disk failure is in the second stripe (/dev02).

RAID 1+0

RAID 1+0 is a disk array that is first mirrored and then striped (a stripe of mirrors). Figure A-8 displays an eight-disk RAID 1+0 configuration. This configuration is also commonly referred to as RAID 10.

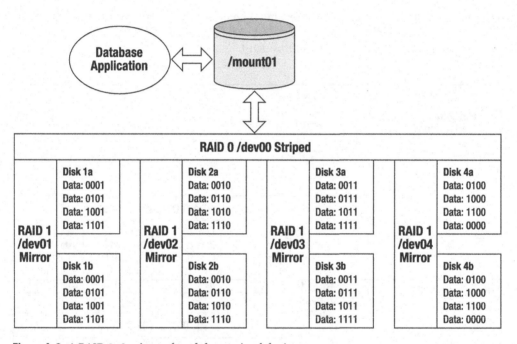

Figure A-8. *A RAID 1+0 mirrored and then striped device*

RAID 1+0 combines the fault tolerance of mirroring with the performance benefits of striping. This is a relatively expensive solution because only half the disks in the array comprise your usable disk space. The RAID 1+0 amount of disk space available to the application is calculated with this formula:

```
(Number of mirrored devices) * Disk Capacity
```

For example, if you start with eight 100GB drives and you build four mirrored devices of two disks each, then the overall realized capacity to the application is calculated as follows:

```
4 * 100 gigabytes = 400 gigabytes
```

Interestingly, the RAID 1+0 arrangement provides much better fault tolerance than RAID 0+1. Analyze Figure A-8 carefully. The RAID 1+0 hybrid configuration can survive a disk failure in each stripe, and it can also survive one disk failure within each mirror. For example, in this configuration, Disk 1a, Disk 2b, Disk 3a, and Disk 4b could fail, but the overall device would continue to function because of the mirrors in Disk 1b, Disk 2a, Disk 3b, and Disk 4a.

Likewise, an entire RAID 1+0 stripe could fail, and the overall device would continue to function because of the surviving mirrored members. For example, Disk 1b, Disk 2b, Disk 3b, and Disk 4b could fail, but the overall device would continue to function because of the mirrors in Disk 1a, Disk 2a, Disk 3a, and Disk 4a.

Many articles, books, and storage vendor documentation confuse the RAID 0+1 and RAID 1+0 configurations (refer to one when really meaning the other). It's important to understand the differences in fault tolerance between the two architectures. If you're architecting a disk array, ensure that you use the one that meets your business needs.

Both RAID 0+1 and RAID 1+0 architectures possess the excellent performance attributes of striped storage devices without the overhead of generating parity. Does RAID 1+0 perform better than RAID 0+1 (and vice versa)? Unfortunately, we're going to have to waffle a bit (no pun intended) on the answer to this question—it depends. Performance characteristics would be dependent on items such as the configuration of the underlying RAID devices, amount of cache, number of controllers, I/O distribution of the database application, and so on. We recommend you perform an I/O load test to determine which RAID architecture works best for your environment.

RAID 5+0

RAID 5+0 is a set of disk arrays that is first placed in a RAID 5 configuration and then striped. Figure A-9 displays the architecture of an eight-disk RAID 5+0 configuration.

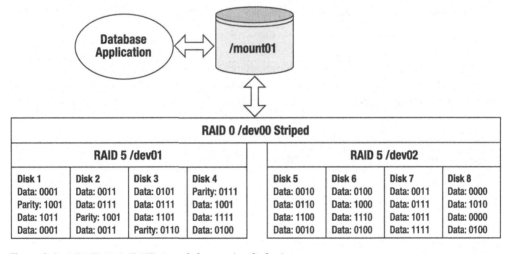

Figure A-9. *A RAID 5+0 (RAID 5 and then striped) device*

RAID 5+0 is sometimes referred to as *striping parity*. The read performance is slightly less than the other hybrid (nested) approaches. The write performance is good, though, because each stripe consists of a RAID 5 device. Because this hybrid is underpinned by RAID 5 devices, it is more cost effective than the RAID 0+1 and RAID 1+0 configurations. The RAID 5+0 amount of disk space available to the application is calculated with this formula:

```
(Number of disks - number of disks used for parity) * Disk Capacity
```

For example, if you start with eight 100GB disks, with four disks in each RAID 5 device, then the total realized capacity would be calculated as shown here:

```
(8 - 2) * 100 gigabytes = 600 gigabytes
```

RAID 5+0 can survive a single disk failure in either RAID 5 device. However, if there are two disk failures in one RAID 5 device, this will result in a failure of the entire RAID 5+0 device.

Determining Disk Requirements

Which RAID technology is best for your environment? It depends on your business requirements. Some storage gurus say use RAID 5 for databases, and others argue never to use RAID 5. There are valid arguments on both sides of fence. You may find yourself in a shop that already has a group of storage experts that predetermine the underlying disk technology without input from the DBA team. Ideally, you would like to be involved with architecture decisions that affect the database, but realistically that does not always happen.

Or you may find yourself in a shop that is constrained by cost and might reach the conclusion that a RAID 5 configuration is the only viable architecture. For your database application, you'll have to determine the cost-effective RAID solution that performs well while also providing the required fault tolerance. This will most likely require you to work with your storage experts to monitor disk performance and I/O characteristics.

■**Tip** See Chapter 8 for details on how to use tools like `iostat` and `sar` for monitoring disk I/O behavior.

Table A-2 summarizes the various characteristics of each RAID technology. These are general guidelines. Before you implement a production system, test the underlying architecture to ensure it meets your business requirements.

Table A-2. *Comparison of RAID Technologies*

Disk Technology	Read	Write	Fault Tolerance	Cost
RAID 0	Excellent	Excellent	Bad	Low
RAID 1	Good	Slow	Very Good	High
RAID 4	Good	Good	Good	Low
RAID 5	Good	Good	Good	Low
RAID 0+1	Good	Good	Very Good	High
RAID 1+0	Good	Good	Excellent	High
RAID 5+0	Good	Good	Good	Medium

Table A-2 is intended only to provide you with general heuristics for determining the appropriate RAID technology for your environment. There will be some technologists who might disagree with some of these general guidelines. From our experience, there are often two very opposing RAID opinions that both have valid points of view.

There are also variables that are unique to a particular environment that also influence what the best solution is. For this reason, it can be difficult to determine exactly which combination of chunk, stripe size, stripe width, underlying RAID technology, and storage vendor will work best over a wide variety of database applications. If you have the resources to test every permutation under every type of I/O load, then you probably can determine the perfect combination of the previously mentioned variables.

Realistically, few shops have the time and money to exercise every possible storage architecture for each database application. You'll have to work with your system administrator and storage vendor to architect a cost-effective solution for your business that performs well over a variety of database applications.

Caution Using RAID technology *does not* eliminate the need for a backup and recovery strategy. You should always have a strategy in place to ensure that you can restore and recover your database. You should periodically test your backup and recovery strategy to make sure it protects you in the event all disks fail (because of a fire, earthquake, tornado, avalanche, grenade, hurricane, and so on).

Capacity Planning

DBAs are often involved with disk storage capacity planning. DBAs need to ensure that adequate disk space will be available (both initially and for future growth) when the database server disk requirements are first spec'ed out (specified). When using RAID technologies, you need to be able to calculate the actual amount of disk space that will be available given the available disks.

DOES SIZE REALLY MATTER?

Humans have long been debating whether size really matters. The answer is "yes" when you're dealing with databases. Large databases (in terms of disk space, transactions/second, objects, number of users, and so on) present many challenges that never manifest themselves with small databases.

With large databases, performance, availability, and backup/recovery all become increasingly more difficult to manage as the database grows. DBAs need to understand how the underlying disk architectures affect performance and availability as the size of the database increases.

For example, when the system administrator says that there are X number of type Y disks configured with a given RAID level, you need to calculate whether there will be enough disk space for your database requirements. Table A-3 details the formulas used to calculate the amount of available disk space for each RAID level.

Table A-3. *Calculating the Amount of RAID Disk Space Realized*

Disk Technology	Realized Disk Capacity
RAID 0 (striped)	Num Disks in Stripe * Disk Size
RAID 1 (mirrored)	Num Mirrored Arrays * Disk Size
RAID 4 (dedicated parity)	(Num Disks – 1) * Disk Size
RAID 5 (distributed parity)	(Num Disks – 1) * Disk Size
RAID 0+1 (striped, then mirrored)	Num Disks in Stripe * Disk Size
RAID 1+0 (mirrored, then striped)	Num Mirrored Arrays * Disk Size
RAID 5+0 (RAID 5, then striped)	(Num Disks – Num Parity Disks) * Disk Size

Be sure to include in your disk space calculations the future database growth requirements. Also consider the amount of disk space needed for files such as database transaction logs and database binaries, as well as the space required for database backups (keep in mind you may want to keep multiple days worth of backups on disk).

■**Tip** A good rule of thumb is to keep one database backup on disk at all times and then back up the database backup files to tape (and then move the backup tapes offsite). This provides you with good performance that is required for routine backup and recovery tasks and also provides protection against complete disasters.

Summary

RAID is a cost-effective technology that underpins highly scalable and efficient storage systems. This technology provides you with a way to distribute the database I/O load over several disks and controllers. RAID also gives you a high degree of fault tolerance for disk devices. This allows you to build heavily used databases that perform well and are highly available.

As a DBA you should be somewhat knowledgeable of basic RAID concepts. This will enable you to clearly communicate your database performance and availability requirements with system administrators and storage experts. You don't have to be a RAID expert, but it helps to know what terms mean and how they can impact your database.

When planning for capacity requirements, it's helpful to understand the difference between the number of physical disks in a RAID device and the actual realized space made available to the application. An understanding of the costs vs. the benefits of each RAID technology will allow you to make better storage decisions in regard to database performance and availability.

APPENDIX B

■ ■ ■

Server Log Files

Server log files contain informational messages about the kernel, applications, and services running on the system. These files can be very useful for troubleshooting and debugging system-level issues. DBAs often look in the system log files as a first step in diagnosing server issues. Even if you're working with competent system administrators, you can still save yourself time (and gain valuable insights to the root cause of a problem) by inspecting the log files yourself.

Most of the system log files are located in the /var/log directory. Typically there is a log file for a specific application or service. For example, the cron utility has a log file named cron (no surprise) in the /var/log directory. Depending on your system, you may need root privileges to view certain log files.

The log files will vary somewhat by the version of Linux and the applications running on your system. Table B-1 contains the names of some of the more common log files and their descriptions.

Table B-1. *Typical Linux Log Files and Descriptions*

Log File Name	Purpose
/var/log/boot.log	System boot messages
/var/log/cron	cron utility log file
/var/log/maillog	Mail server log file
/var/log/messages	General system messages
/var/log/secure	Authentication log file
/var/log/wtmp	Login records
/var/log/yum.log	yum utility log file

Note Some utilities may have their own subdirectory under the /var/log directory.

Rotating Log Files

The system log files will continue to grow unless they are somehow moved or removed. Moving and removing log files is known as *rotating* the log files. Rotating means that the current log file is renamed and a new log file is created.

Most Linux systems use the logrotate utility to rotate the log files. This tool automates the rotation, compression, removal, and mailing of log files. Typically, you will want to rotate your log files so that they don't become too large and cluttered with old data. You'll also want to delete log files that are older than a certain number of days.

By default, on most Linux systems, the logrotate utility is automatically run from the cron scheduling tool. Here is a typical listing of the contents of the /etc/crontab file:

```
SHELL=/bin/bash
PATH=/sbin:/bin:/usr/sbin:/usr/bin
MAILTO=root
HOME=/
# run-parts
01 * * * * root run-parts /etc/cron.hourly
02 4 * * * root run-parts /etc/cron.daily
22 4 * * 0 root run-parts /etc/cron.weekly
42 4 1 * * root run-parts /etc/cron.monthly
```

Notice that the /etc/crontab uses the run-parts utility to run all scripts located within a specified directory. For example, when run-parts inspects /etc/cron.daily, it finds a file named logrotate that calls the logrotate utility. Listed next are the contents of a typical logrotate script:

```
#!/bin/sh
/usr/sbin/logrotate /etc/logrotate.conf
EXITVALUE=$?
if [ $EXITVALUE != 0 ]; then
    /usr/bin/logger -t logrotate "ALERT exited abnormally with [$EXITVALUE]"
fi
exit 0
```

The behavior of the logrotate utility is governed by the /etc/logrotate.conf file. Here's a listing of a typical /etc/logrotate.conf file:

```
# see "man logrotate" for details
# rotate log files weekly
weekly
# keep 4 weeks worth of backlogs
rotate 4
# create new (empty) log files after rotating old ones
create
# uncomment this if you want your log files compressed
#compress
```

```
# RPM packages drop log rotation information into this directory
include /etc/logrotate.d
# no packages own wtmp -- we'll rotate them here
/var/log/wtmp {
    monthly
    create 0664 root utmp
    rotate 1
}
# system-specific logs may be also be configured here.
```

By default, on most Linux systems, the logs are rotated weekly, and four weeks' worth of logs are preserved. These are designated by the lines `weekly` and `rotate 4` in the `/etc/logrotate.conf` file. You can change the values within the `/etc/logrotate.conf` file to suit the rotating requirements of your environment.

If you list the files in the /var/log directory, you may notice some log files ending with an extension of `.1` or `.gz`. This indicates that the `logrotate` utility is running on your system.

You can manually run the `logrotate` utility to rotate the log files. Use the `-f` option to force a rotation even if `logrotate` doesn't think it's necessary:

```
# logrotate -f /etc/logrotate.conf
```

Application-specific `logrotate` configurations are stored in the `/etc/logrotate.d` directory. Here we change directories to the `/etc/logrotate.d` directory and list some typical application logs on a Linux server:

```
# cd /etc/logrotate.d
# ls
acpid  cups  mgetty  ppp  psacct  rpm  samba  syslog  up2date  yum
```

Setting Up a Custom Log Rotation

The `logrotate` utility is sometimes perceived as a utility only for system administrators. However, any user on the system can utilize `logrotate` to rotate log files for applications that they have read/write permissions on the log files. For example, as the `oracle` user, you can use `logrotate` to rotate your database `alert.log` file. Here are the steps for setting up a job to rotate the alert log file of an Oracle database:

1. Create a configuration file named `alert.conf` in the directory /home/oracle/config (create the directory if it doesn't already exist):

   ```
   /oracle/RMDB1/admin/bdump/*.log {
   daily
   missingok
   rotate 7
   compress
   mail oracle@localhost
   }
   ```

In the previous configuration file, the first line specifies the location of the log file. The asterisk (wildcard) tells logrotate to look for any file with the extension of .log in that directory. The daily keyword specifies that the log file should be rotated on a daily basis. The missingok keyword specifies that logrotate should not throw an error if it doesn't find any log files. The rotate 7 keyword specifies that the log files should be kept for seven days. The compress keyword compresses the rotated log file. Lastly, a status e-mail is sent to the local oracle user on the server.

2. Create a cron job to automatically run the job on a daily basis:

```
0 9 * * * /usr/sbin/logrotate -s /home/oracle/config/alrotate.status
/home/oracle/config/alert.conf
```

The previous two lines of code should be one line in your cron table (it didn't fit nicely on this page on one line). The cron job runs the logrotate utility every day at 9 a.m. The -s (status) option directs the status file to the specified directory and file. The configuration file used is /home/oracle/config/alert.conf.

3. Manually test the job to see whether it rotates the alert log correctly. Use the -f switch to force logrotate to do a rotation:

```
$ /usr/sbin/logrotate -f -s /home/oracle/config/alrotate.status \
/home/oracle/config/alert.conf
```

As shown in the previous steps, you can use the logrotate utility to set up log rotation jobs. Similar examples of using the logrotate utility are shown in recipe 11-9. Juxtapose using logrotate instead of writing a custom shell script such as the one described in recipe 11-8.

Monitoring Log Files

Many Linux systems have graphical interfaces for monitoring and managing the log files. As a DBA, oftentimes you need to look only at a specific log file when trying to troubleshoot a problem. In these scenarios, it's usually sufficient to manually inspect the log files with a text editor such as vi or a paging utility such as more or less.

You also can monitor the logs with the logwatch utility. You can modify the default behavior of logwatch by modifying the logwatch.conf file. Depending on your Linux system, the logwatch.conf file is usually located in a directory named /etc/log.d. To print the default log message details, use the --print option:

```
# logwatch --print
```

Many system administrators set up a daily job to be run that automatically e-mails the logwatch report to a specified user. Usually this functionality is implemented as a script located in the /etc/cron.daily directory. The name of the script will vary by Linux system. Typically these scripts are named something like 0logwatch or 00-logwatch.

Index

Get the eBook for only $10!

Now you can take the weightless companion with you anywhere, anytime. Your purchase of this book entitles you to 3 electronic versions for only $10.

This Apress title will prove so indispensible that you'll want to carry it with you everywhere, which is why we are offering the eBook in 3 formats for only $10 if you have already purchased the print book.

Convenient and fully searchable, the PDF version enables you to easily find and copy code—or perform examples by quickly toggling between instructions and applications. The MOBI format is ideal for your Kindle, while the ePUB can be utilized on a variety of mobile devices.

Go to www.apress.com/promo/tendollars to purchase your companion eBook.

Apress®
THE EXPERT'S VOICE™

 *For the Complete Technology & Database Professional*

IOUG represents the **voice of Oracle technology and database professionals** - empowering you to be **more productive in your business** and career by **delivering education,** sharing **best practices** and providing technology direction and **networking opportunities.**

Context, Not Just Content

IOUG is dedicated to helping our members become an #IOUGenius by staying on the cutting-edge of Oracle technologies and industry issues through practical content, user-focused education, and invaluable networking and leadership opportunities:

- *SELECT Journal* is our quarterly publication that provides in-depth, peer-reviewed articles on industry news and best practices in Oracle technology

- Our #IOUGenius blog highlights a featured weekly topic and provides **content driven by Oracle professionals and the IOUG community**

- Special Interest Groups provide you the chance to collaborate with peers on the specific issues that matter to you and even take on leadership roles outside of your organization

- COLLABORATE is our once-a-year opportunity to connect with the members of not one, but three, Oracle users groups (IOUG, OAUG and Quest) as well as with the top names and faces in the Oracle community.

Who we are...

... **more than 20,000** database professionals, developers, application and infrastructure architects, business intelligence specialists and IT managers

... **a community of users** that share experiences and knowledge on issues and technologies that matter to you and your organization

Interested? Join IOUG's community of Oracle technology and database professionals at **www.ioug.org/Join.**

Independent Oracle Users Group | phone: (312) 245-1579 | email: membership@ioug.org
330 N. Wabash Ave., Suite 2000, Chicago, IL 60611